PHANTOM

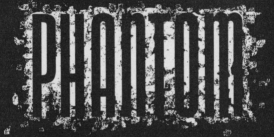

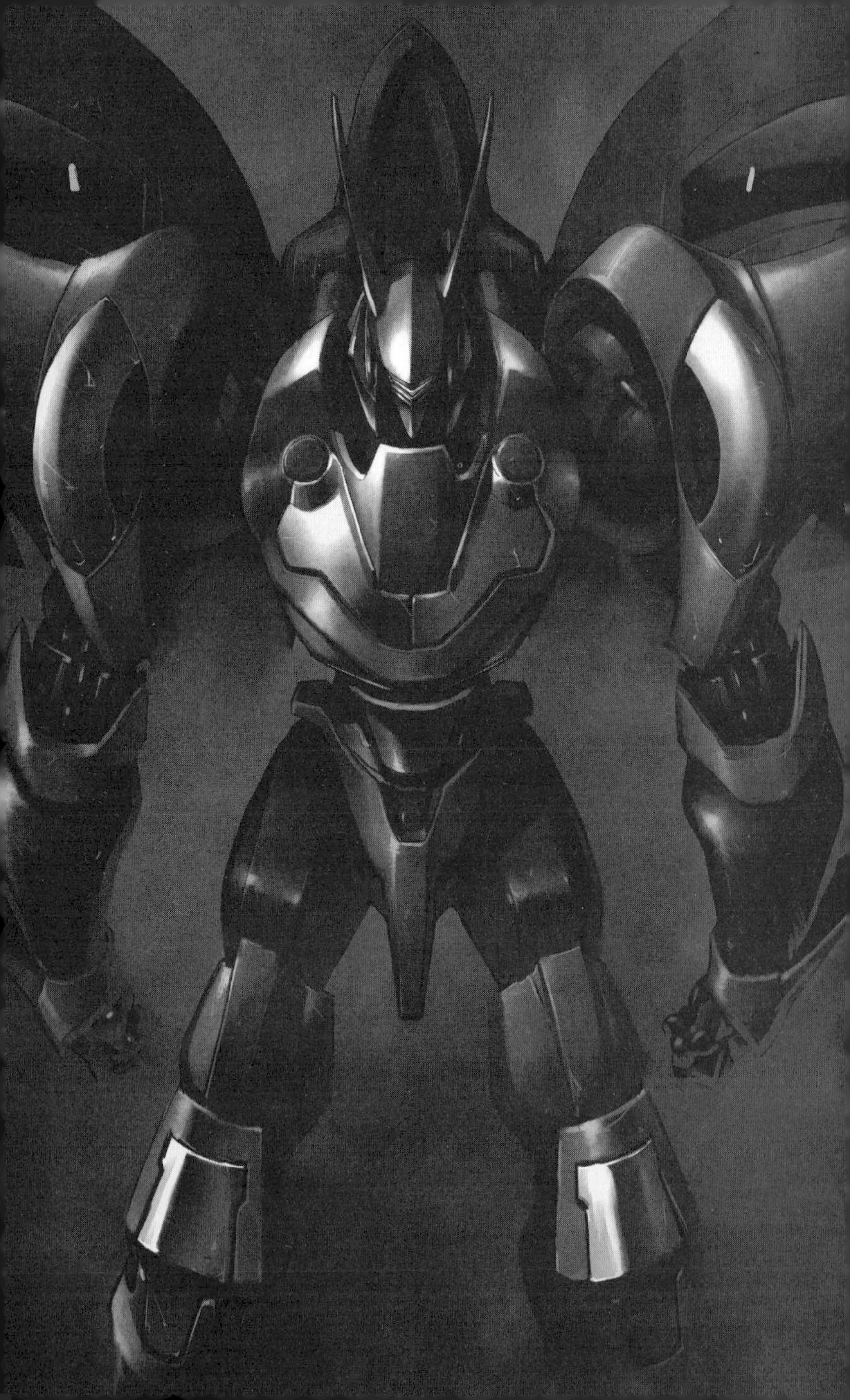

Volume 1

Story by Ki-Hoon Lee
Art by Seung-Yup Cho

HAMBURG // LONDON // LOS ANGELES // TOKYO

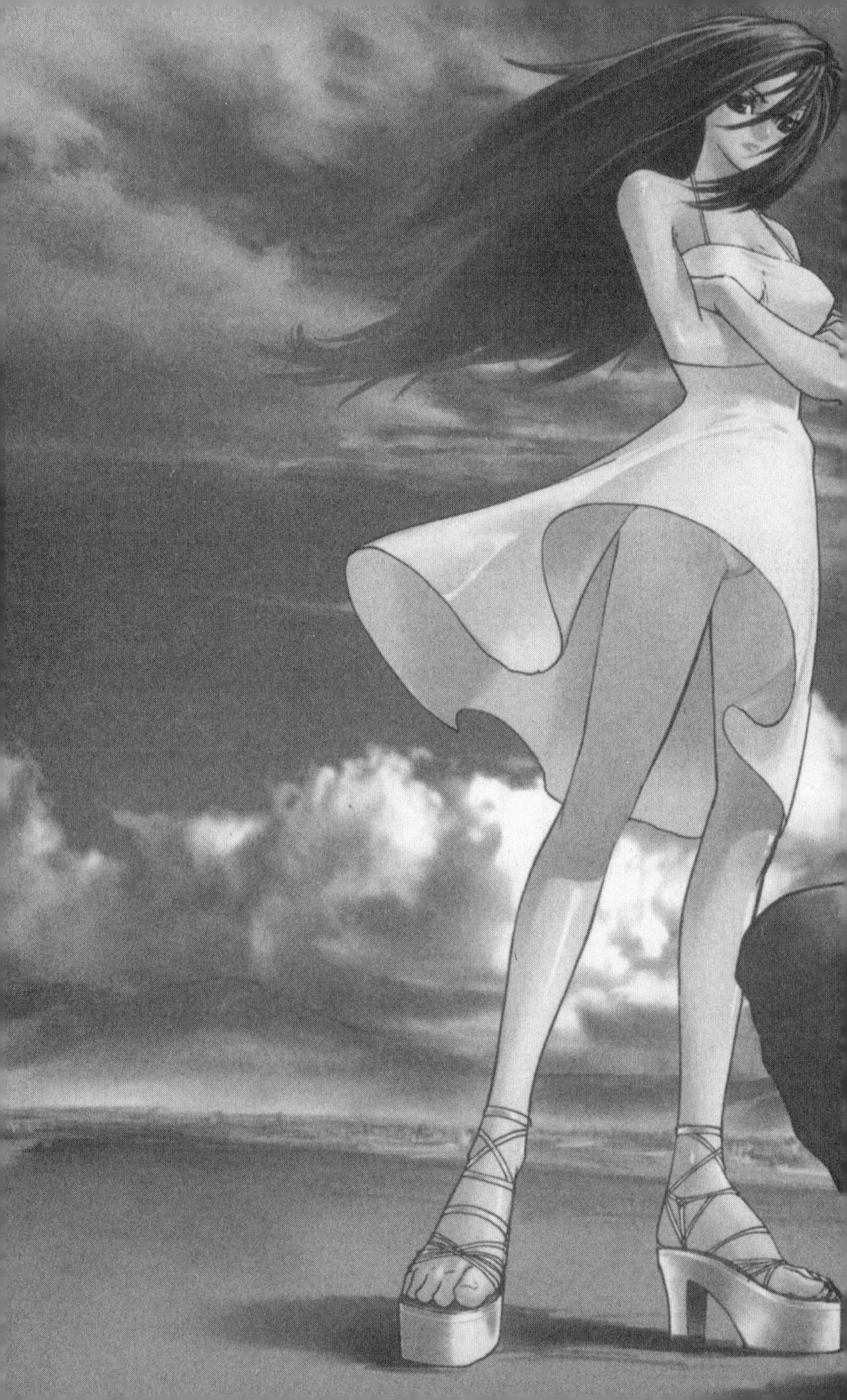

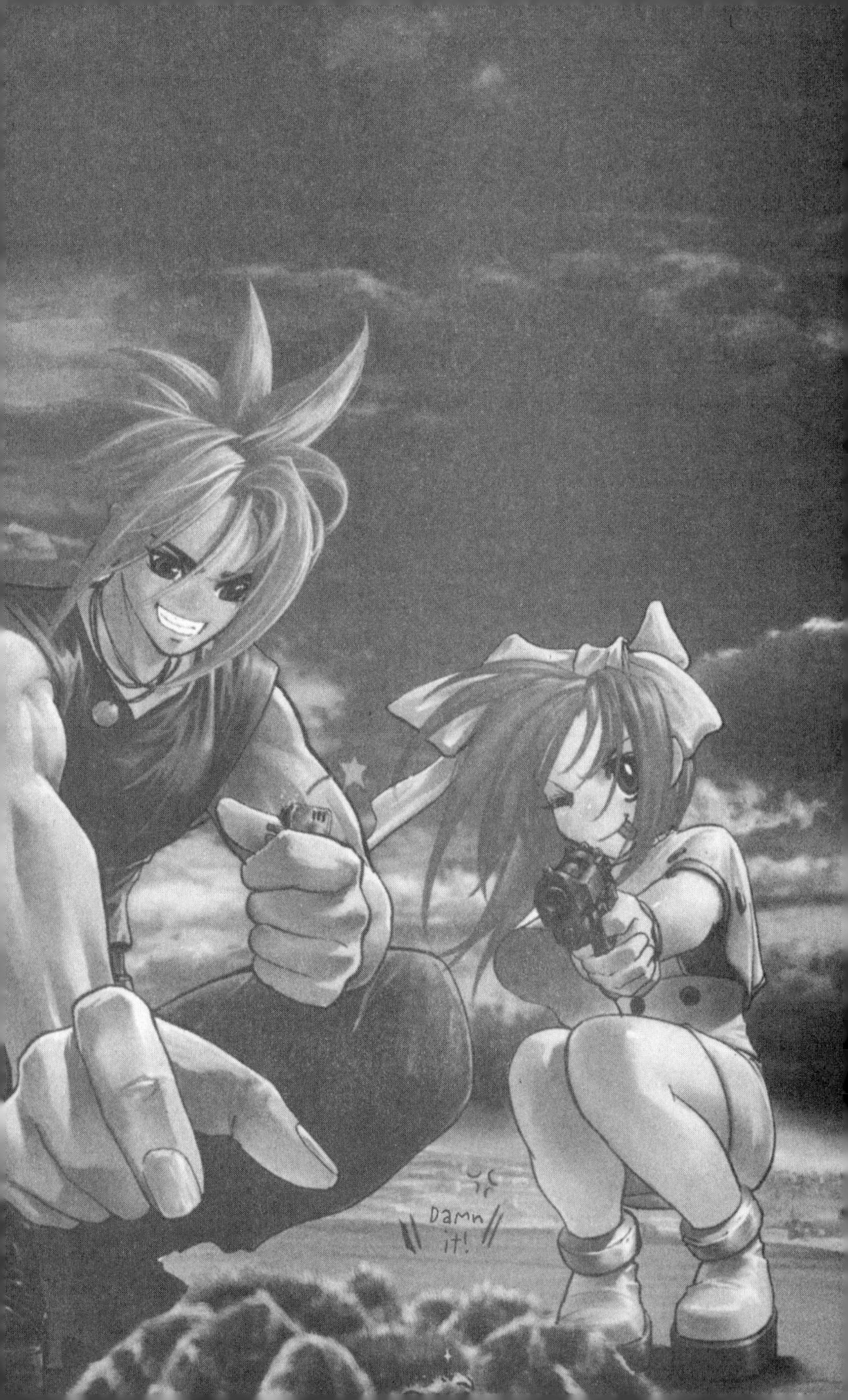
Damn it!

Phantom Vol. 1
Written by Ki-Hoon Lee
Illustrated by Seung-Yup Cho

Translation - Woo Sok Park
English Adaptation - Troy Lewter
Copy Editor - Stephanie Duchin
Retouch and Lettering - Samantha Yamanaka
Production Artist - Mike Estacio
Cover Design - Tomas Montalvo-Lagos

Editor - Hope Donovan
Digital Imaging Manager - Chris Buford
Pre-Production Supervisor - Erika Terriquez
Art Director - Anne Marie Horne
Production Manager - Elisabeth Brizzi
Managing Editor - Vy Nguyen
VP of Production - Ron Klamert
Editor-in-Chief - Rob Tokar
Publisher - Mike Kiley
President and C.O.O. - John Parker
C.E.O. and Chief Creative Officer - Stuart Levy

A **TOKYOPOP**® Manga

TOKYOPOP and are trademarks or registered trademarks of TOKYOPOP Inc.

TOKYOPOP Inc.
5900 Wilshire Blvd. Suite 2000
Los Angeles, CA 90036

E-mail: info@TOKYOPOP.com
Come visit us online at www.TOKYOPOP.com

ISBN: 978-1-59816-770-2

First TOKYOPOP printing: January 2007
10 9 8 7 6 5 4 3 2 1
Printed in the USA

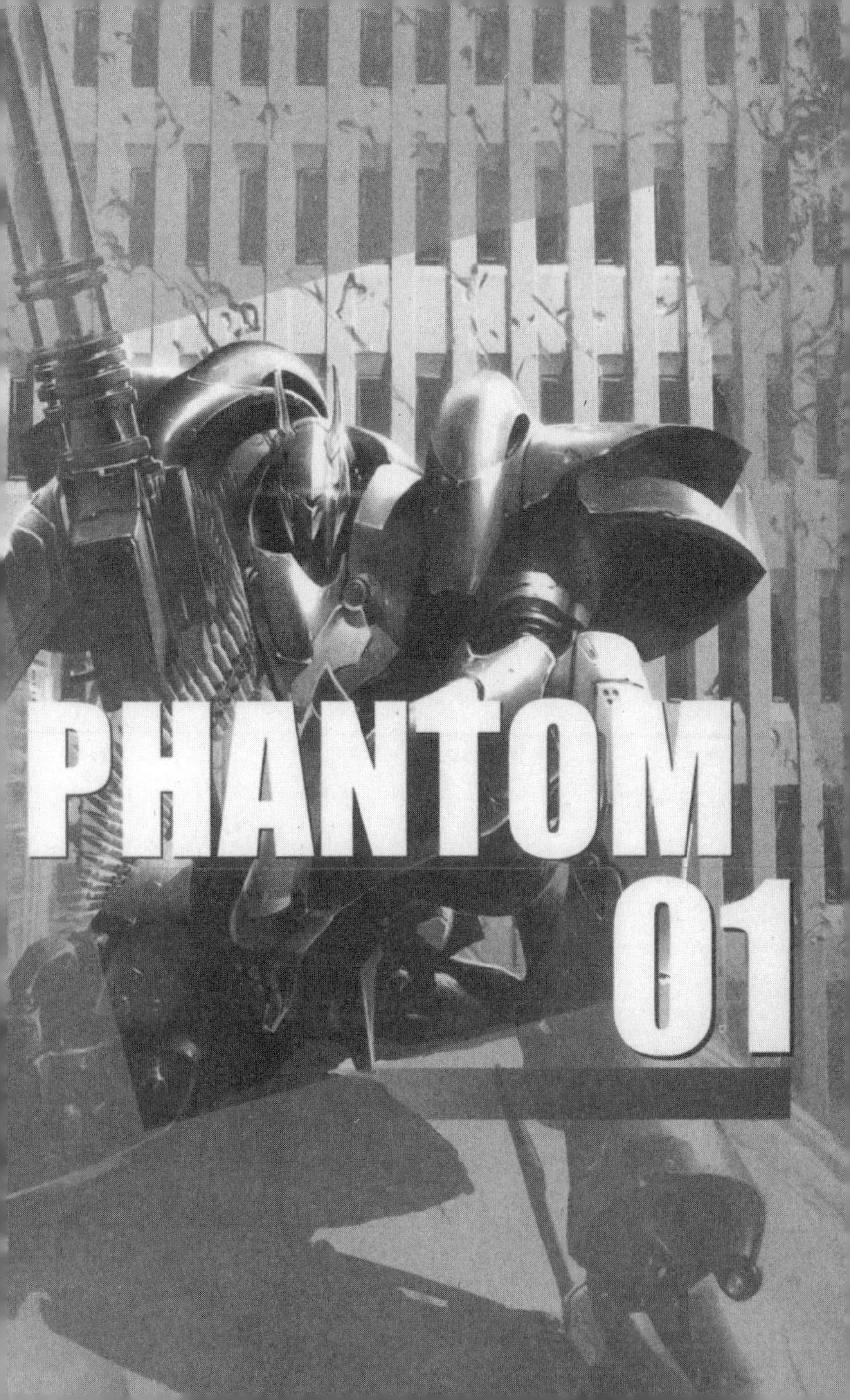
PHANTOM
01

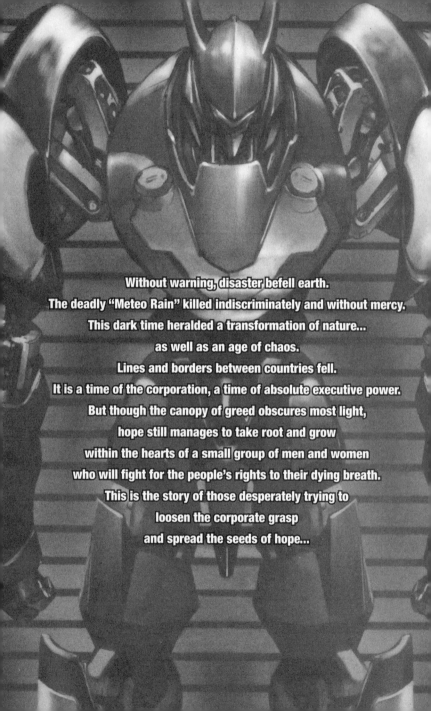

Without warning, disaster befell earth.
The deadly "Meteo Rain" killed indiscriminately and without mercy.
This dark time heralded a transformation of nature...
as well as an age of chaos.
Lines and borders between countries fell.
It is a time of the corporation, a time of absolute executive power.
But though the canopy of greed obscures most light,
hope still manages to take root and grow
within the hearts of a small group of men and women
who will fight for the people's rights to their dying breath.
This is the story of those desperately trying to
loosen the corporate grasp
and spread the seeds of hope...

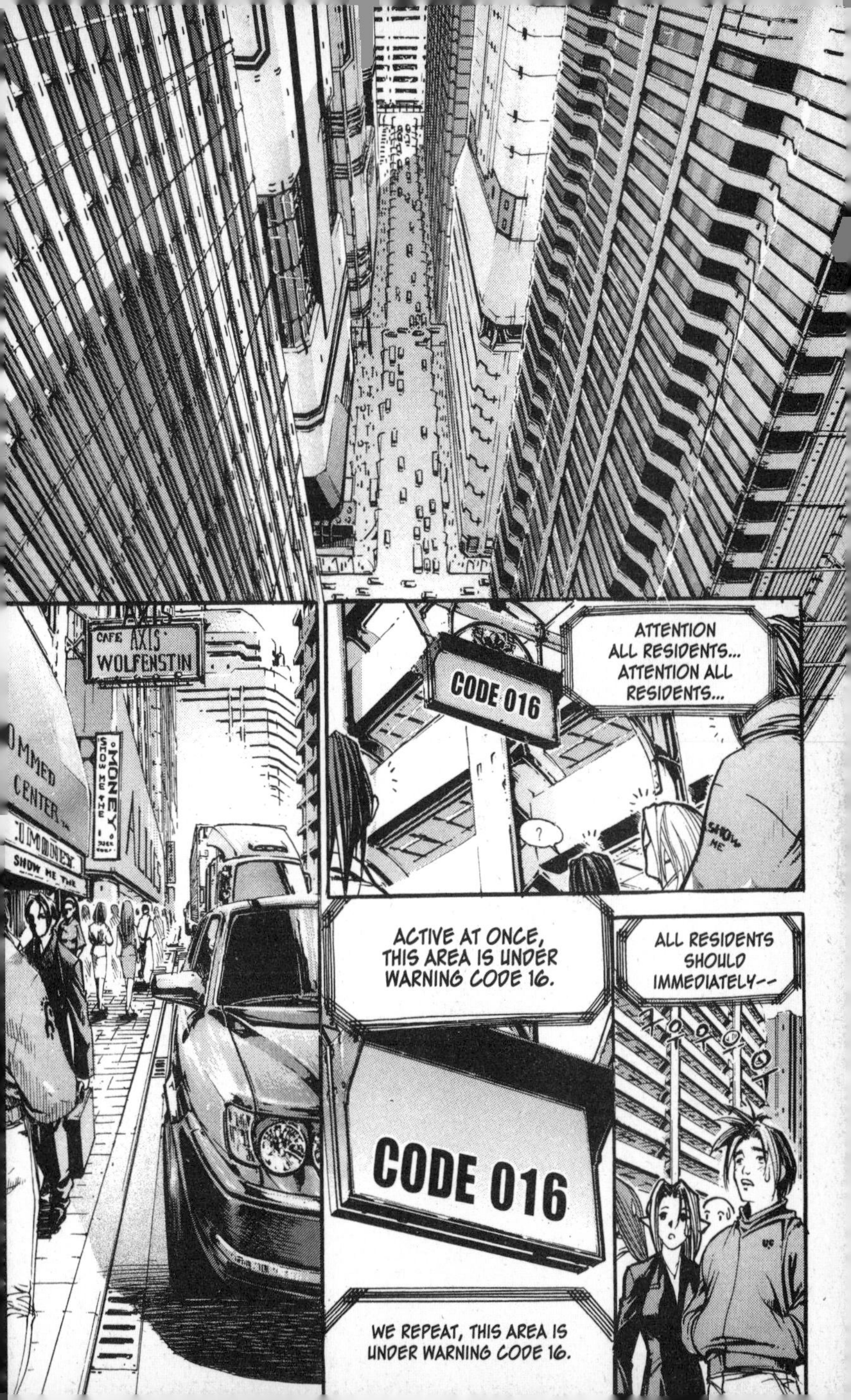
CAFE AXIS WOLFENSTIN
SHOW ME THE MONEY
CODE 016
ATTENTION ALL RESIDENTS... ATTENTION ALL RESIDENTS...
?
ACTIVE AT ONCE, THIS AREA IS UNDER WARNING CODE 16.
ALL RESIDENTS SHOULD IMMEDIATELY--
CODE 016
WE REPEAT, THIS AREA IS UNDER WARNING CODE 16.

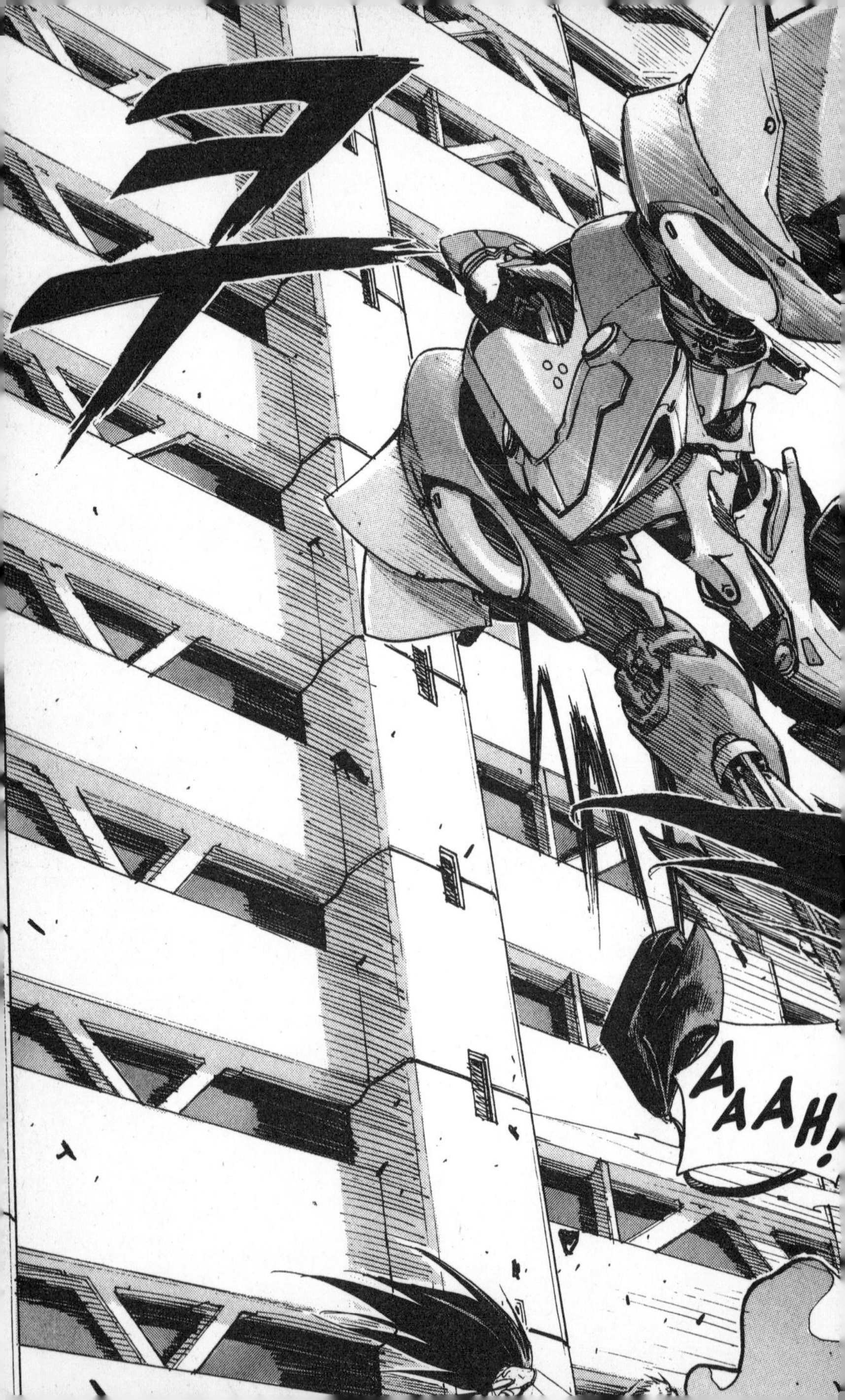

AAAH!

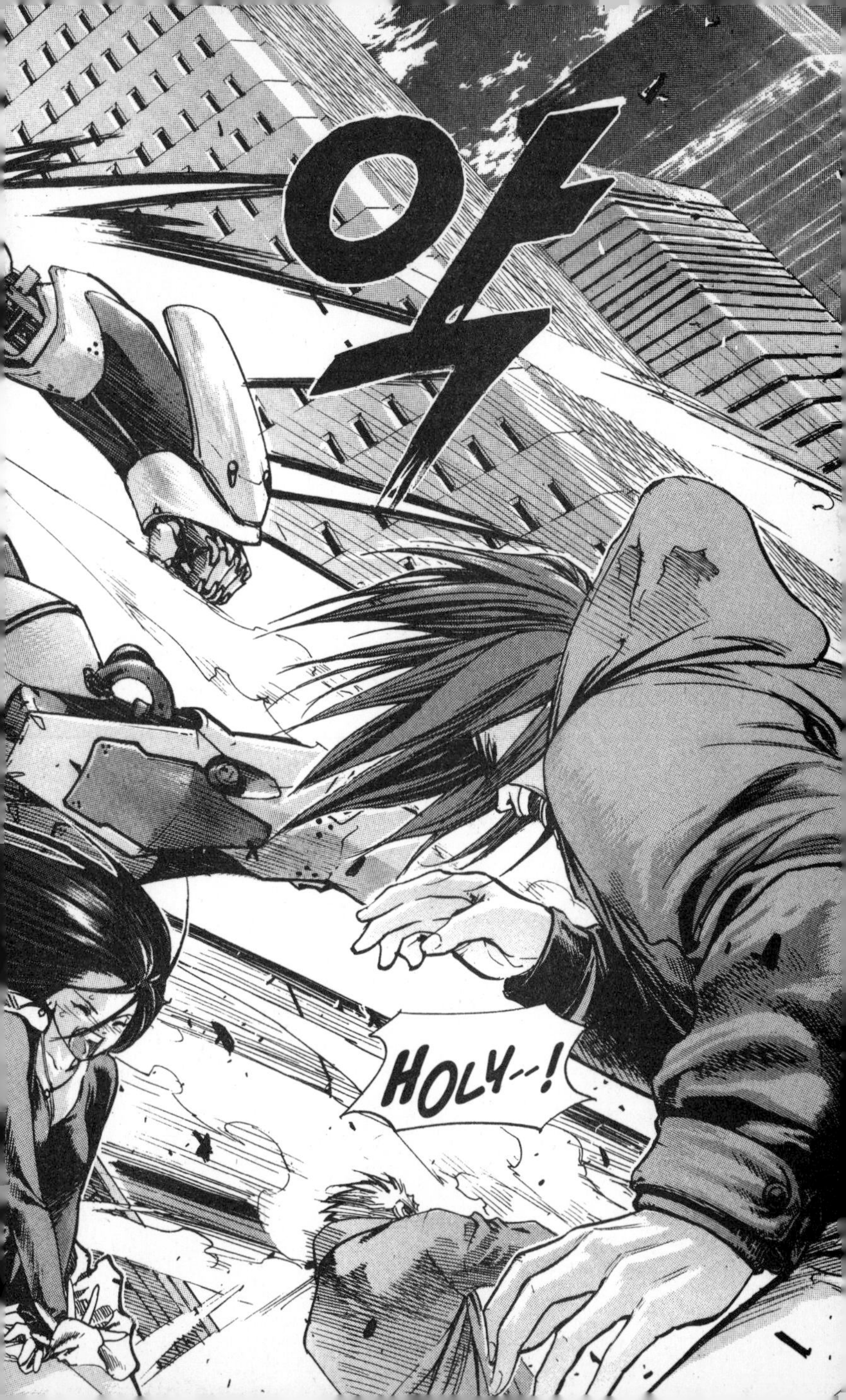
HOLY--!

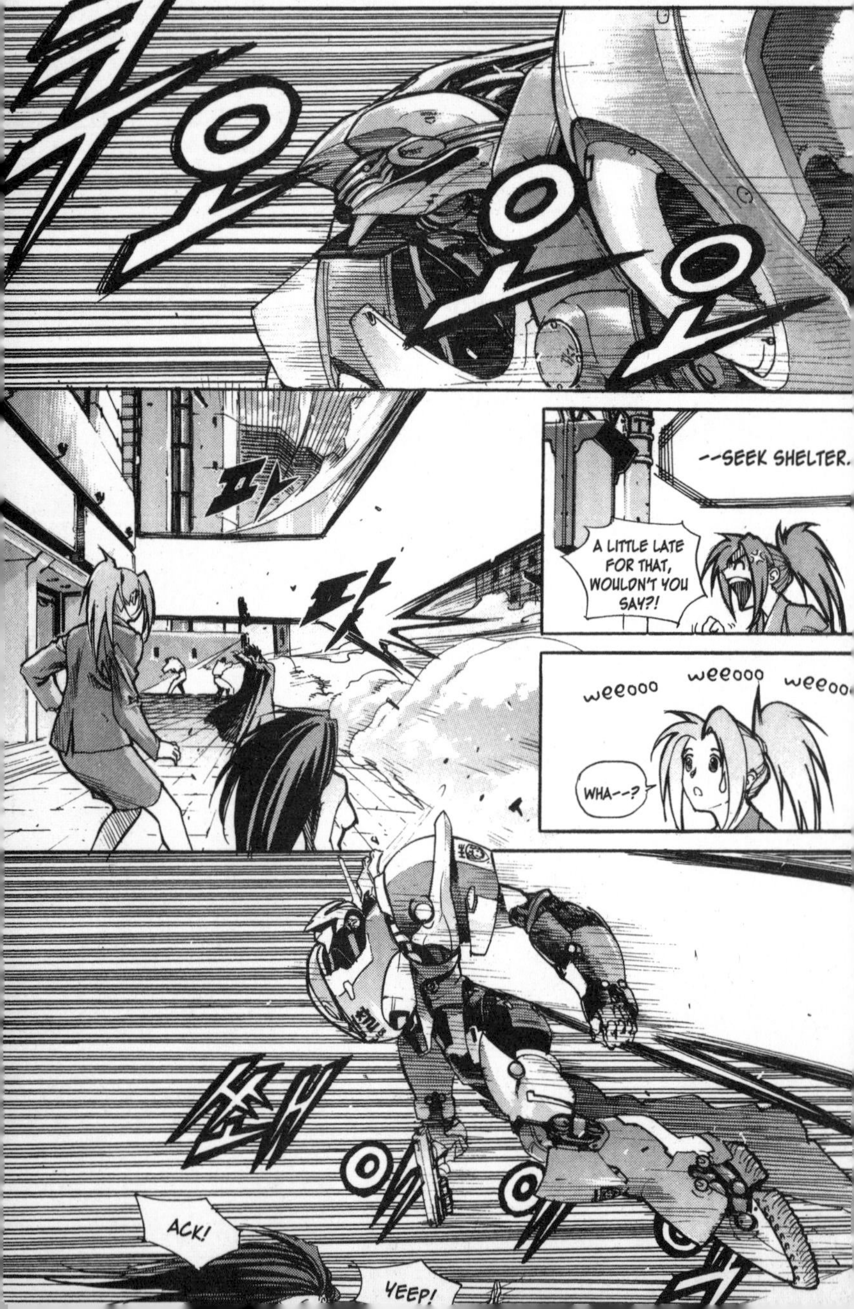
--SEEK SHELTER.
A LITTLE LATE FOR THAT, WOULDN'T YOU SAY?!
weeooo weeooo
WHA--?
ACK!
YEEP!

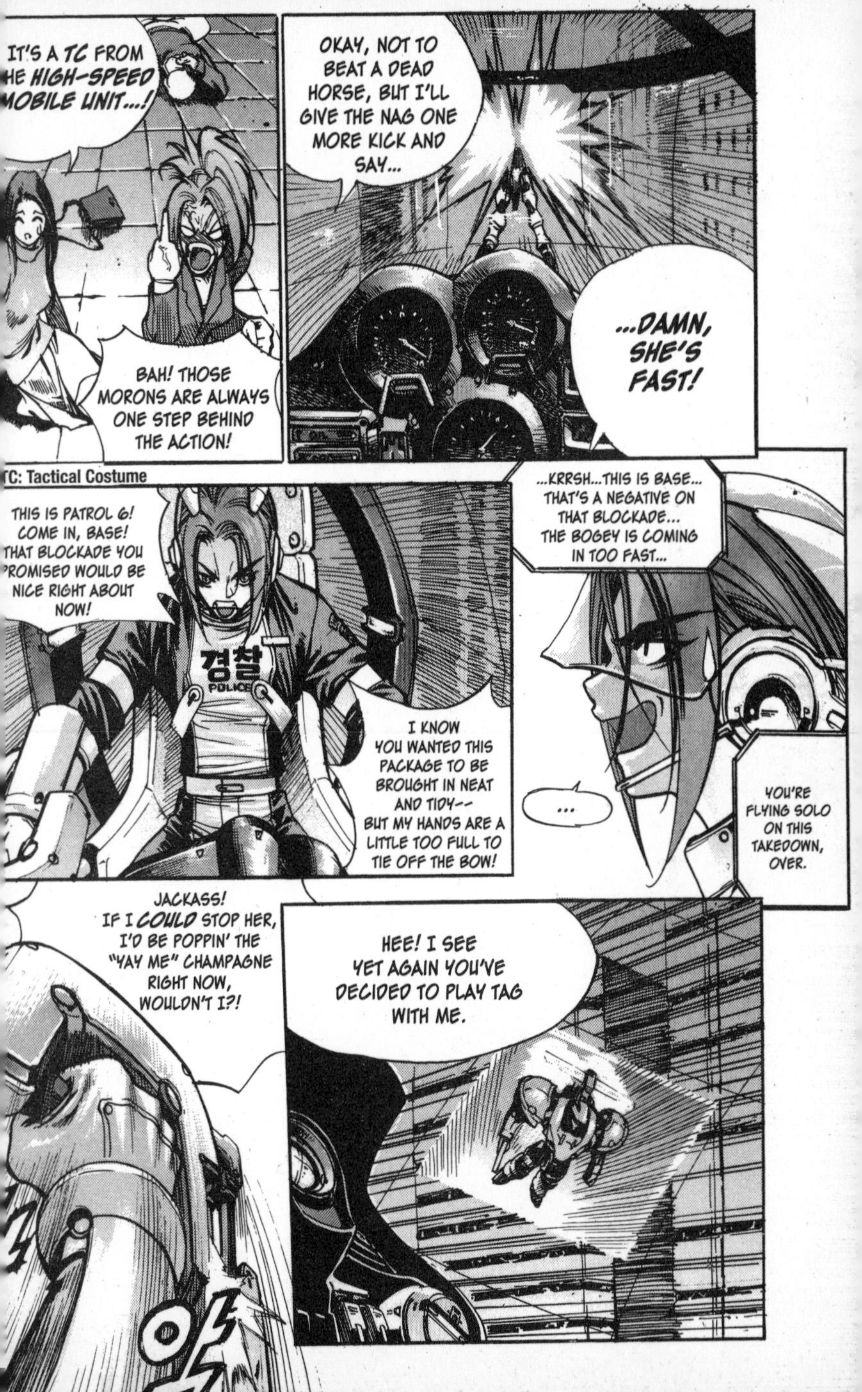
IT'S A *TC* FROM HE *HIGH-SPEED* MOBILE UNIT...!
BAH! THOSE MORONS ARE ALWAYS ONE STEP BEHIND THE ACTION!
OKAY, NOT TO BEAT A DEAD HORSE, BUT I'LL GIVE THE NAG ONE MORE KICK AND SAY...
...DAMN, SHE'S FAST!
THIS IS PATROL 6! COME IN, BASE! THAT BLOCKADE YOU PROMISED WOULD BE NICE RIGHT ABOUT NOW!
경찰
POLICE
I KNOW YOU WANTED THIS PACKAGE TO BE BROUGHT IN NEAT AND TIDY-- BUT MY HANDS ARE A LITTLE TOO FULL TO TIE OFF THE BOW!
...KRRSH...THIS IS BASE... THAT'S A NEGATIVE ON THAT BLOCKADE... THE BOGEY IS COMING IN TOO FAST...
...
YOU'RE FLYING SOLO ON THIS TAKEDOWN, OVER.
JACKASS! IF I *COULD* STOP HER, I'D BE POPPIN' THE "YAY ME" CHAMPAGNE RIGHT NOW, WOULDN'T I?!
HEE! I SEE YET AGAIN YOU'VE DECIDED TO PLAY TAG WITH ME.

TC: Tactical Costume

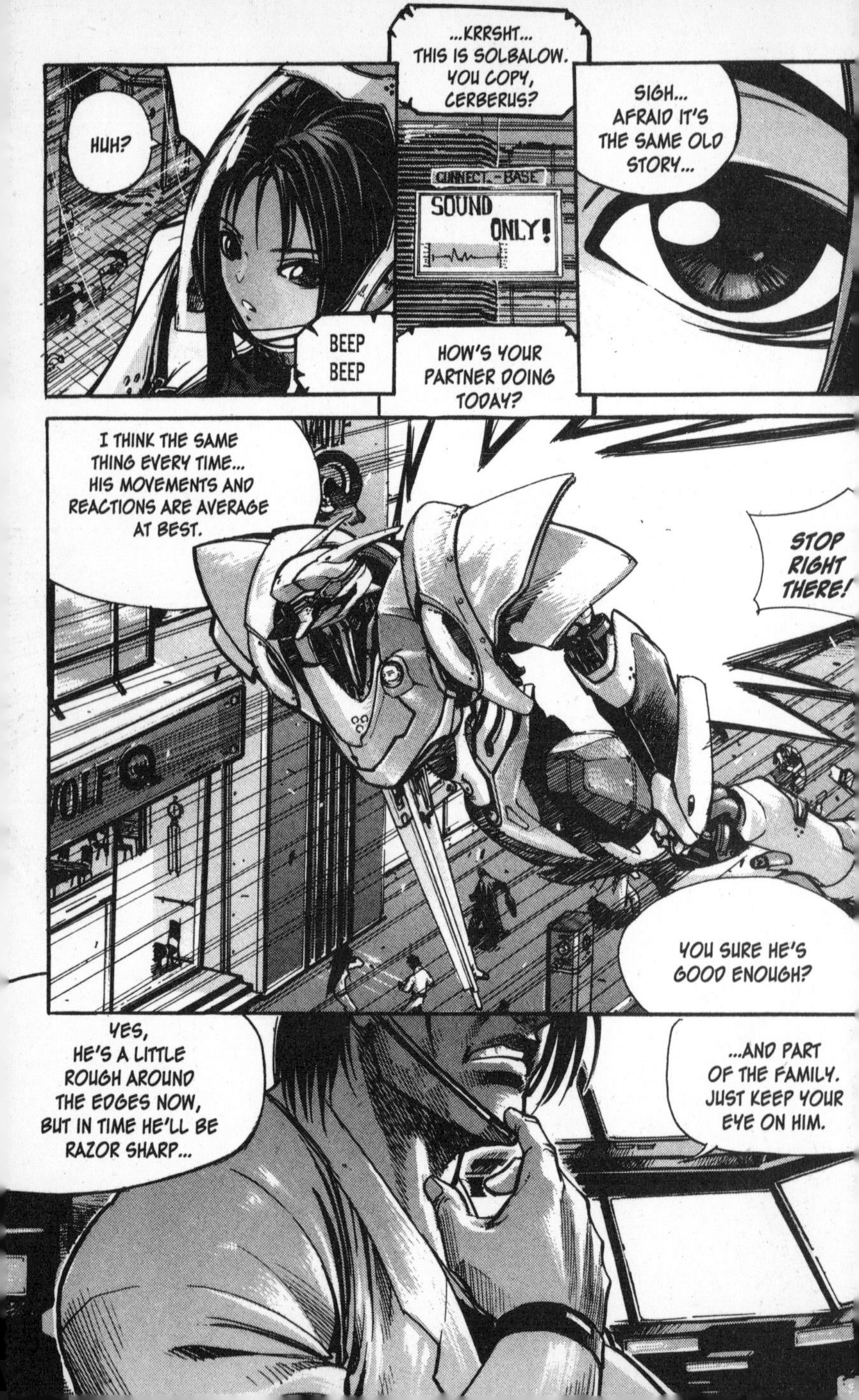
HUH?
BEEP BEEP
...KRRSHT... THIS IS SOLBALOW. YOU COPY, CERBERUS?
CONNECT. - BASE
SOUND ONLY!
HOW'S YOUR PARTNER DOING TODAY?
SIGH... AFRAID IT'S THE SAME OLD STORY...
I THINK THE SAME THING EVERY TIME... HIS MOVEMENTS AND REACTIONS ARE AVERAGE AT BEST.
WOLF
STOP RIGHT THERE!
YOU SURE HE'S GOOD ENOUGH?
YES, HE'S A LITTLE ROUGH AROUND THE EDGES NOW, BUT IN TIME HE'LL BE RAZOR SHARP...
...AND PART OF THE FAMILY. JUST KEEP YOUR EYE ON HIM.

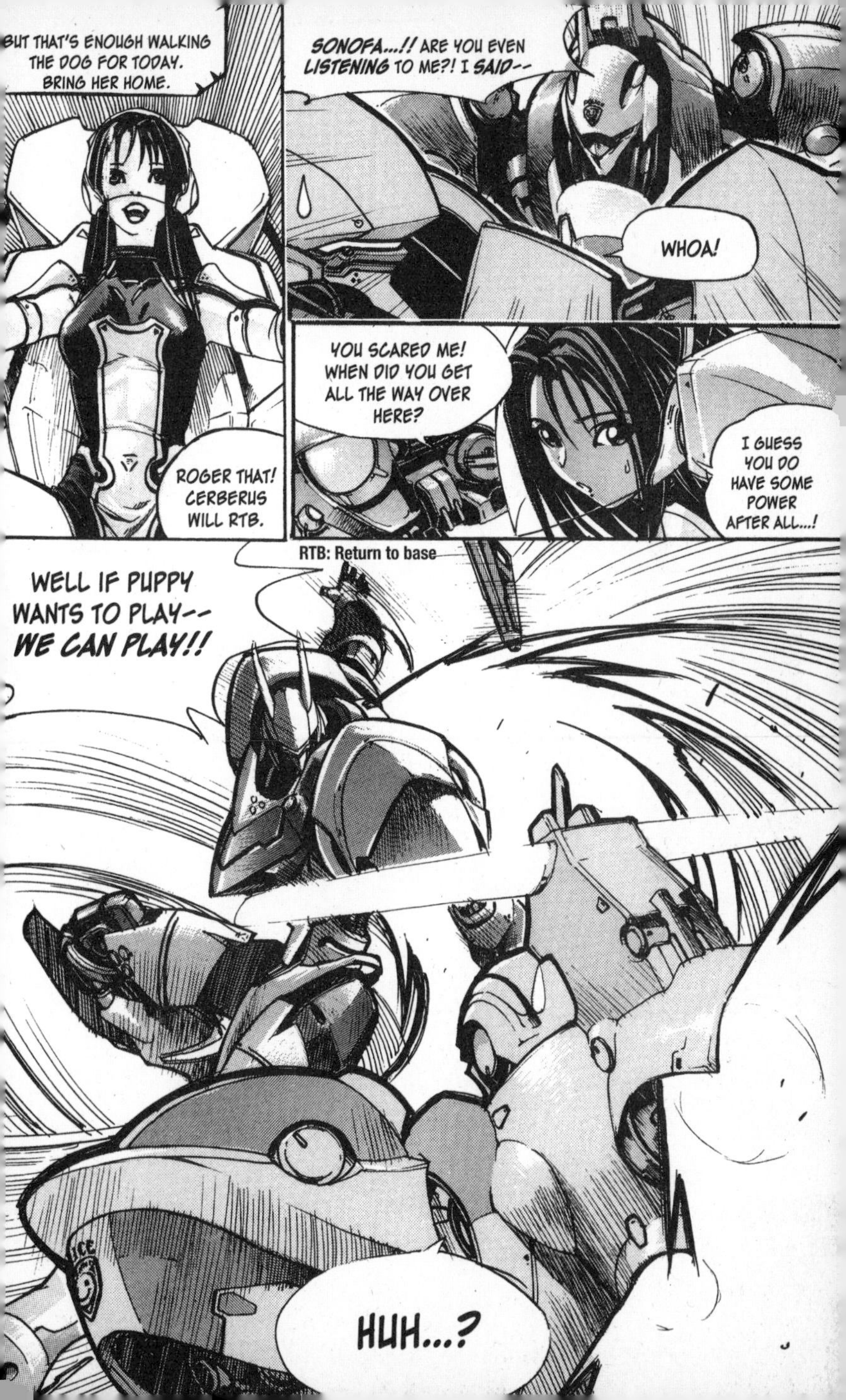
BUT THAT'S ENOUGH WALKING THE DOG FOR TODAY. BRING HER HOME.
ROGER THAT! CERBERUS WILL RTB.
SONOFA...!! ARE YOU EVEN LISTENING TO ME?! I SAID--
WHOA!
YOU SCARED ME! WHEN DID YOU GET ALL THE WAY OVER HERE?
I GUESS YOU DO HAVE SOME POWER AFTER ALL...!
RTB: Return to base
WELL IF PUPPY WANTS TO PLAY-- WE CAN PLAY!!
HUH...?

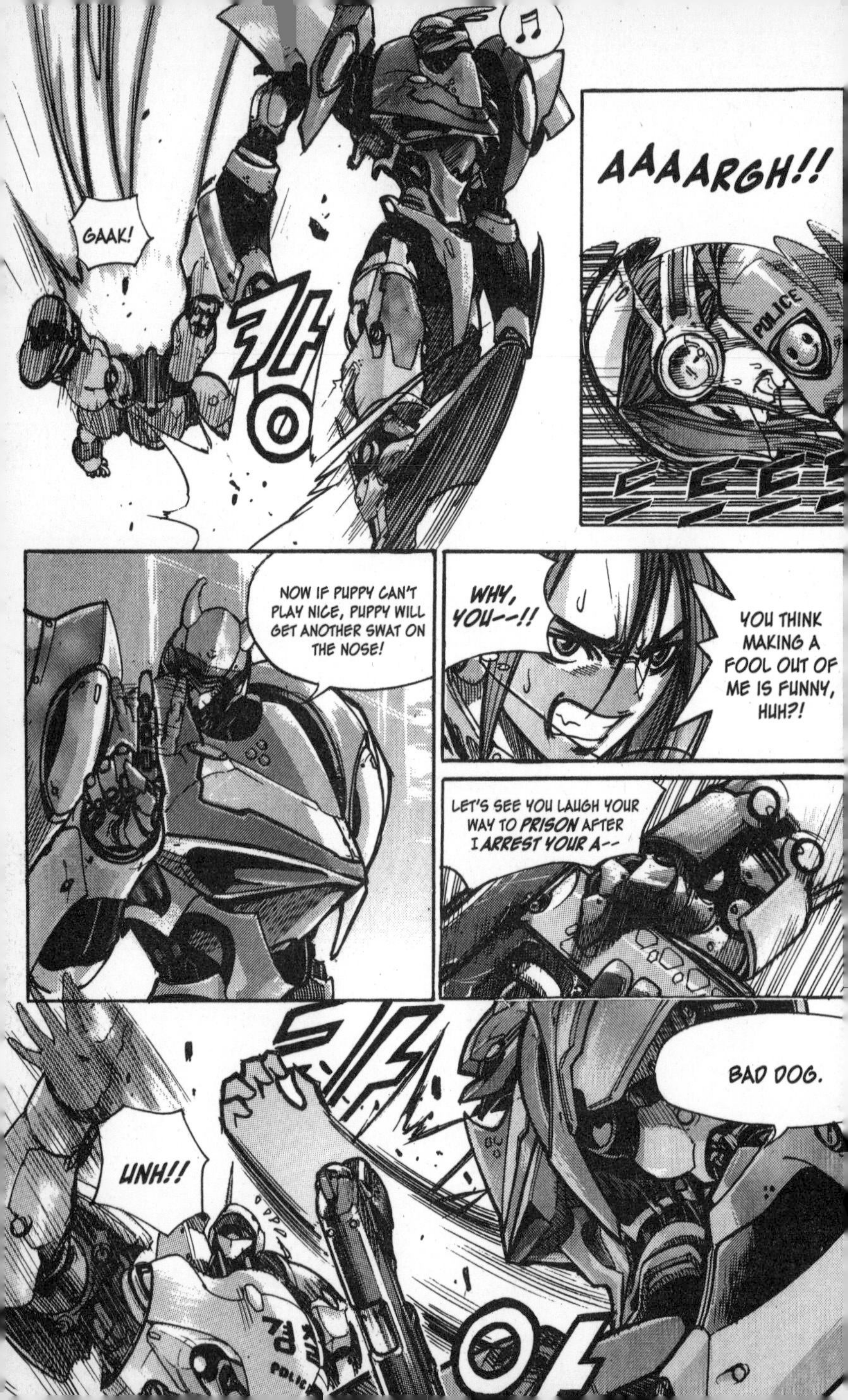
GAAK!
AAAARGH!!
NOW IF PUPPY CAN'T PLAY NICE, PUPPY WILL GET ANOTHER SWAT ON THE NOSE!
WHY, YOU--!!
YOU THINK MAKING A FOOL OUT OF ME IS FUNNY, HUH?!
LET'S SEE YOU LAUGH YOUR WAY TO PRISON AFTER I ARREST YOUR A--
UNH!!
BAD DOG.

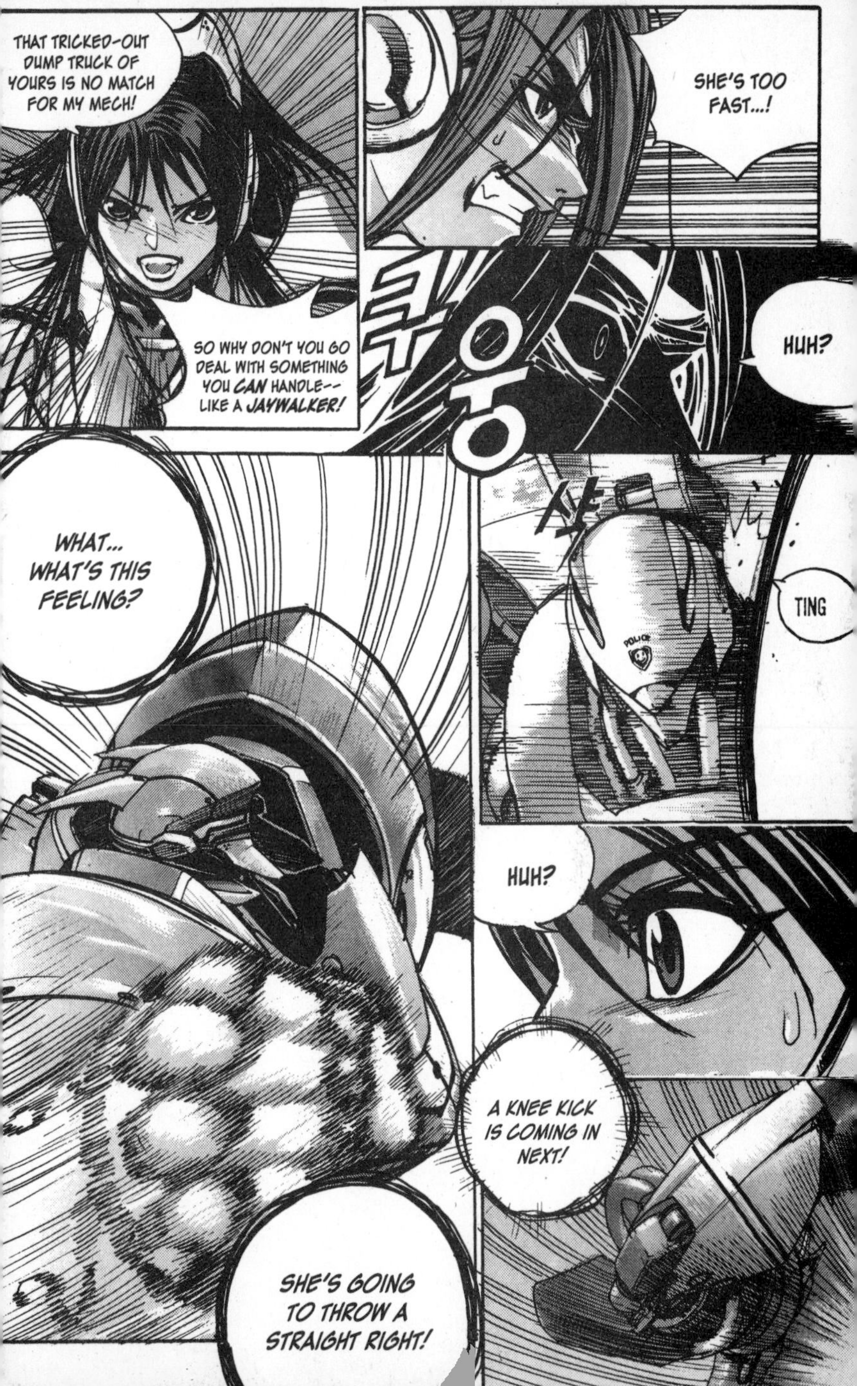
THAT TRICKED-OUT DUMP TRUCK OF YOURS IS NO MATCH FOR MY MECH!
SO WHY DON'T YOU GO DEAL WITH SOMETHING YOU CAN HANDLE-- LIKE A JAYWALKER!
SHE'S TOO FAST...!
HUH?
WHAT... WHAT'S THIS FEELING?
SHE'S GOING TO THROW A STRAIGHT RIGHT!
TING
HUH?
A KNEE KICK IS COMING IN NEXT!

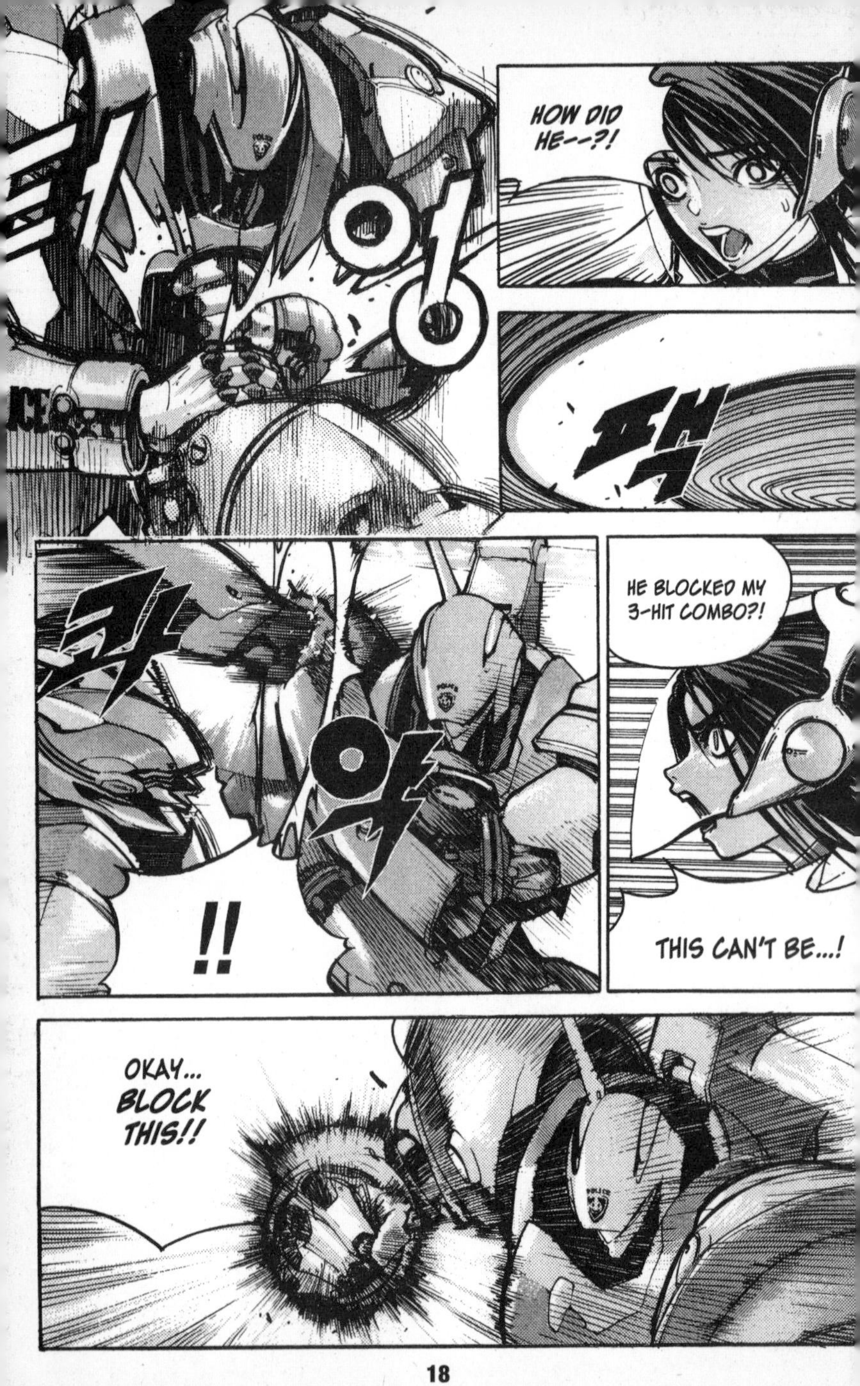
HOW DID HE--?!
!!
HE BLOCKED MY 3-HIT COMBO?!
THIS CAN'T BE...!
OKAY... BLOCK THIS!!

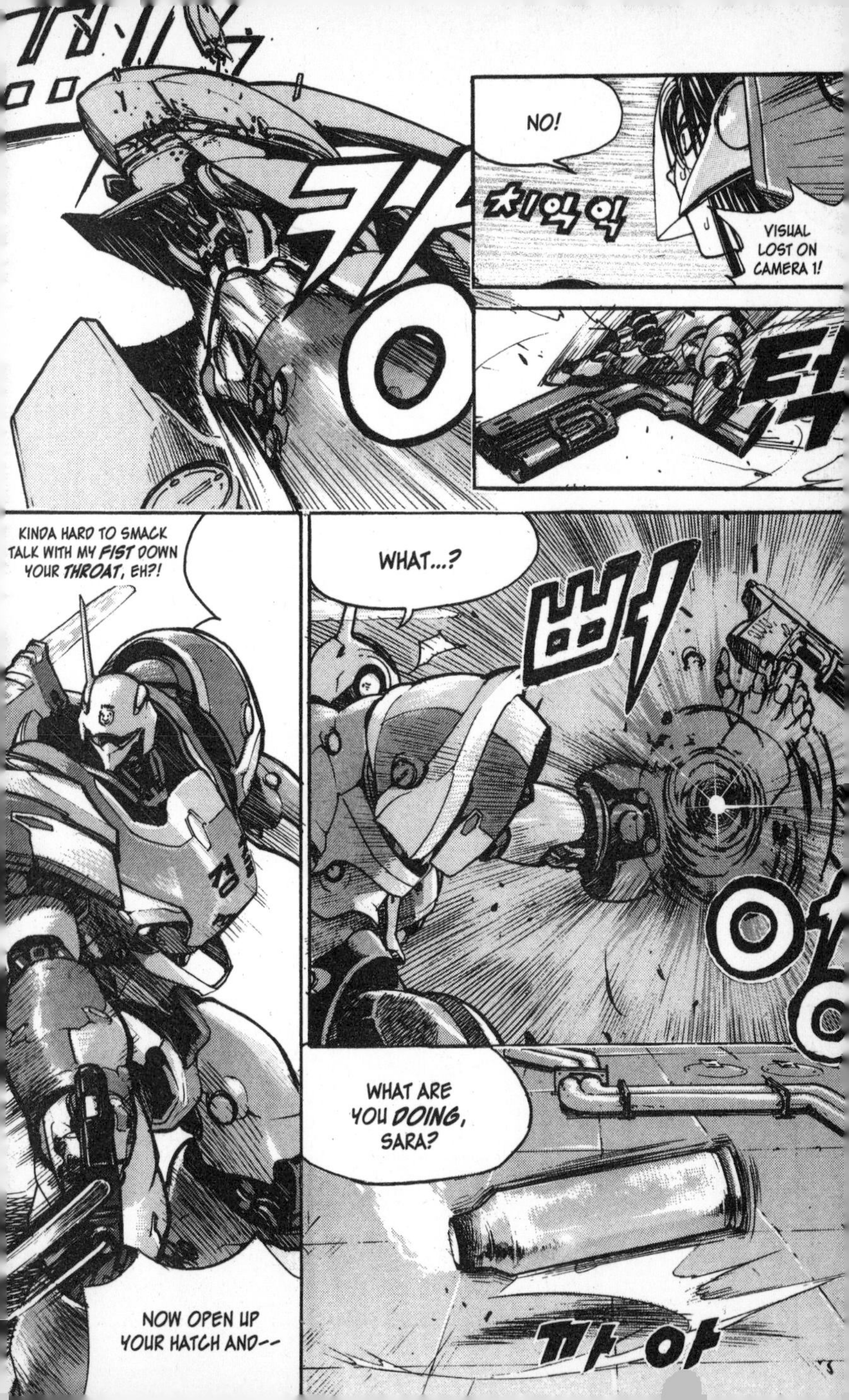
NO!
VISUAL LOST ON CAMERA 1!
KINDA HARD TO SMACK TALK WITH MY *FIST* DOWN YOUR *THROAT*, EH?!
NOW OPEN UP YOUR HATCH AND--
WHAT...?
WHAT ARE YOU *DOING*, SARA?

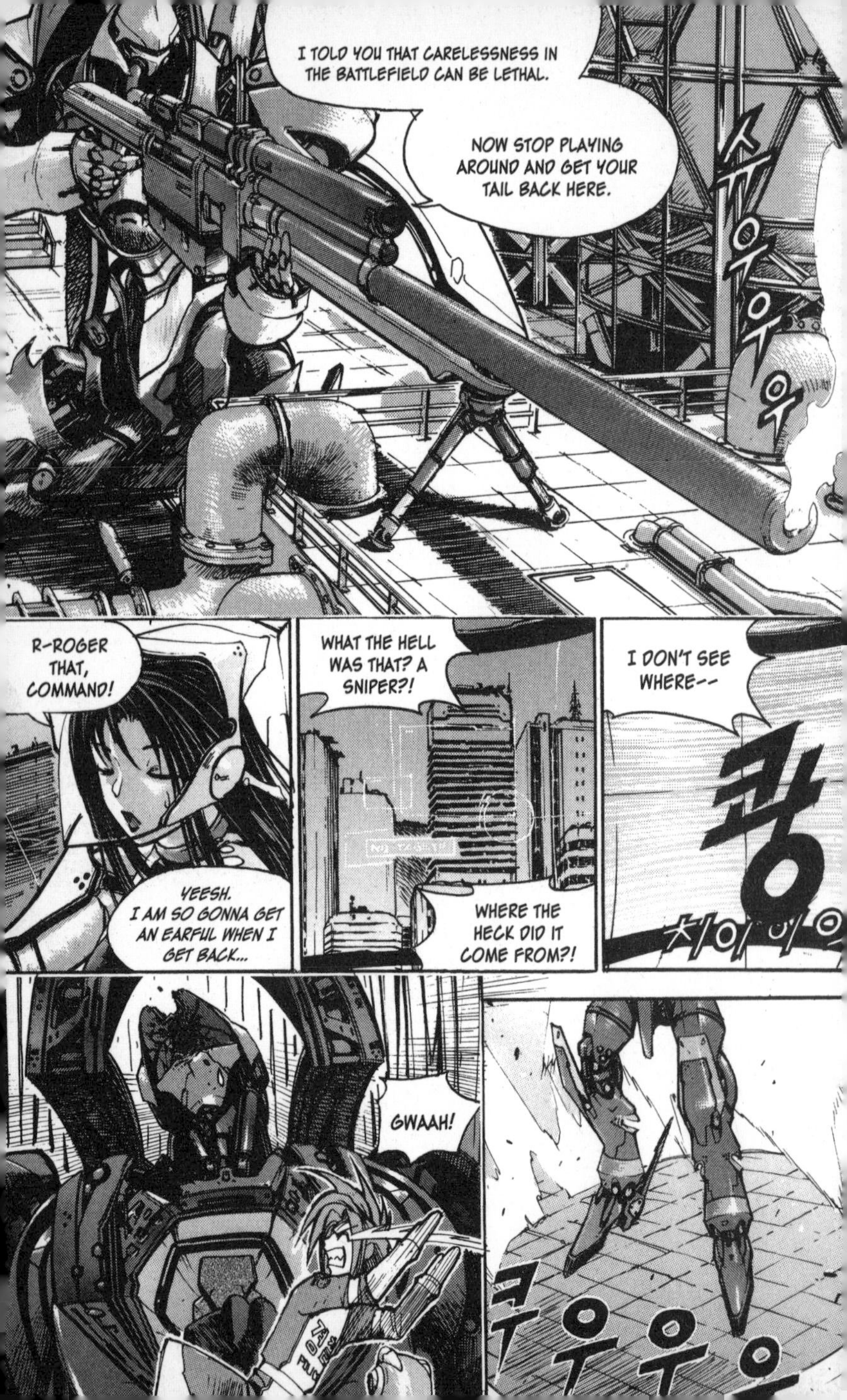
I TOLD YOU THAT CARELESSNESS IN THE BATTLEFIELD CAN BE LETHAL.
NOW STOP PLAYING AROUND AND GET YOUR TAIL BACK HERE.
R-ROGER THAT, COMMAND!
YEESH. I AM SO GONNA GET AN EARFUL WHEN I GET BACK...
WHAT THE HELL WAS THAT? A SNIPER?!
WHERE THE HECK DID IT COME FROM?!
I DON'T SEE WHERE--
쾅
GWAAH!

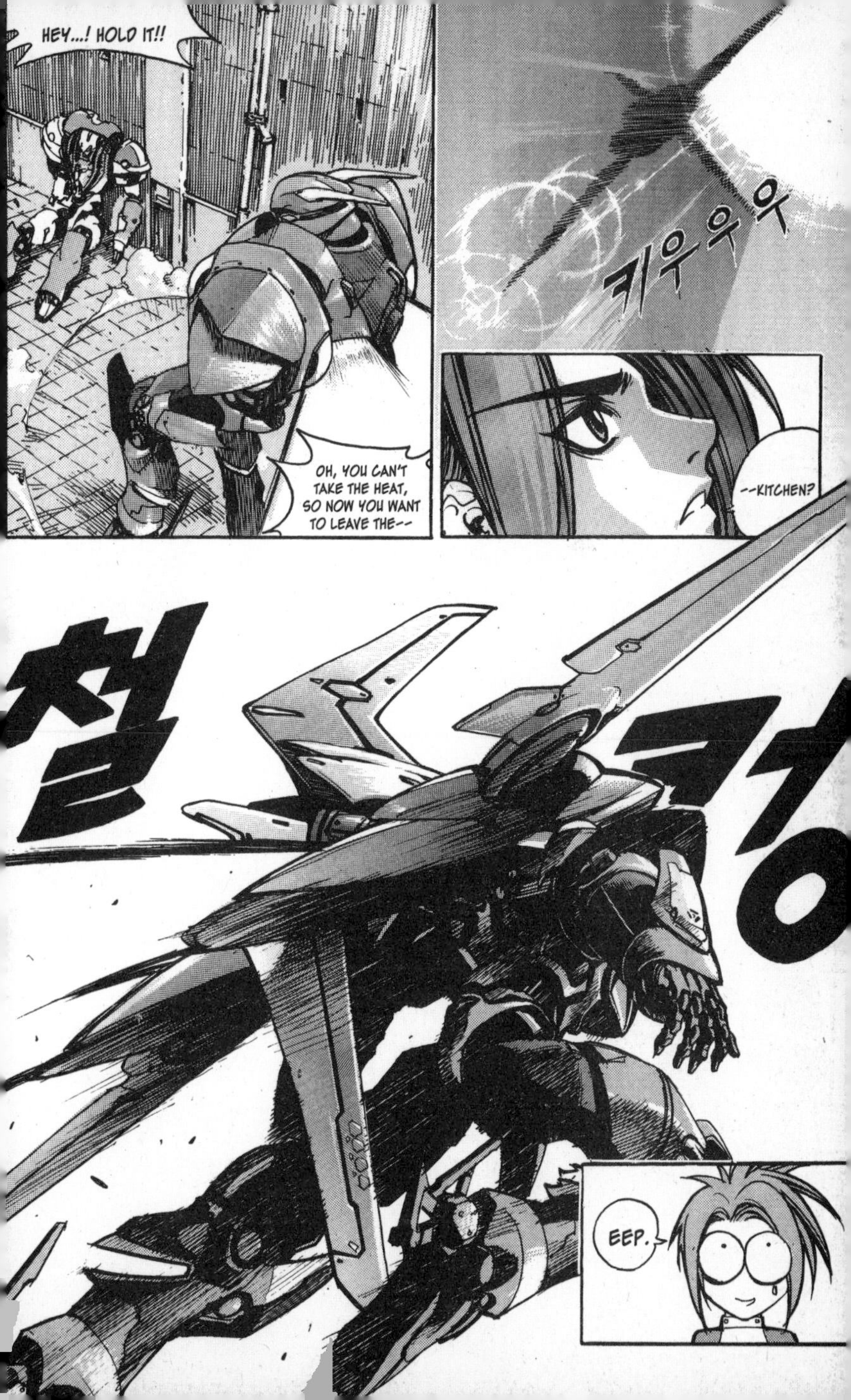
HEY...! HOLD IT!!
OH, YOU CAN'T TAKE THE HEAT, SO NOW YOU WANT TO LEAVE THE--
키우우우
--KITCHEN?
철컹
EEP.

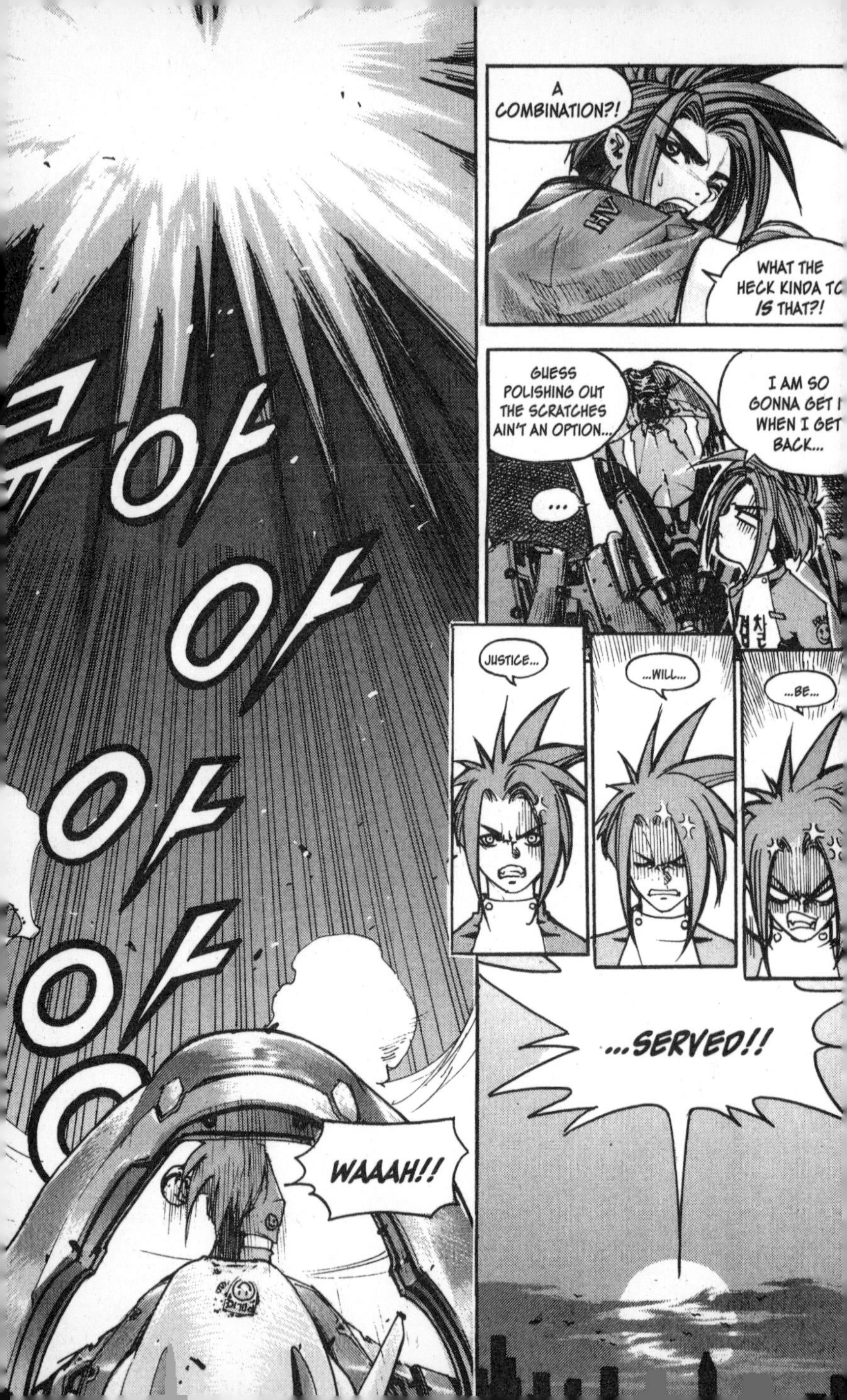
WAAAH!!
A COMBINATION?!
WHAT THE HECK KINDA TO IS THAT?!
GUESS POLISHING OUT THE SCRATCHES AIN'T AN OPTION...
I AM SO GONNA GET I WHEN I GET BACK...
...
JUSTICE...
...WILL...
...BE...
...SERVED!!

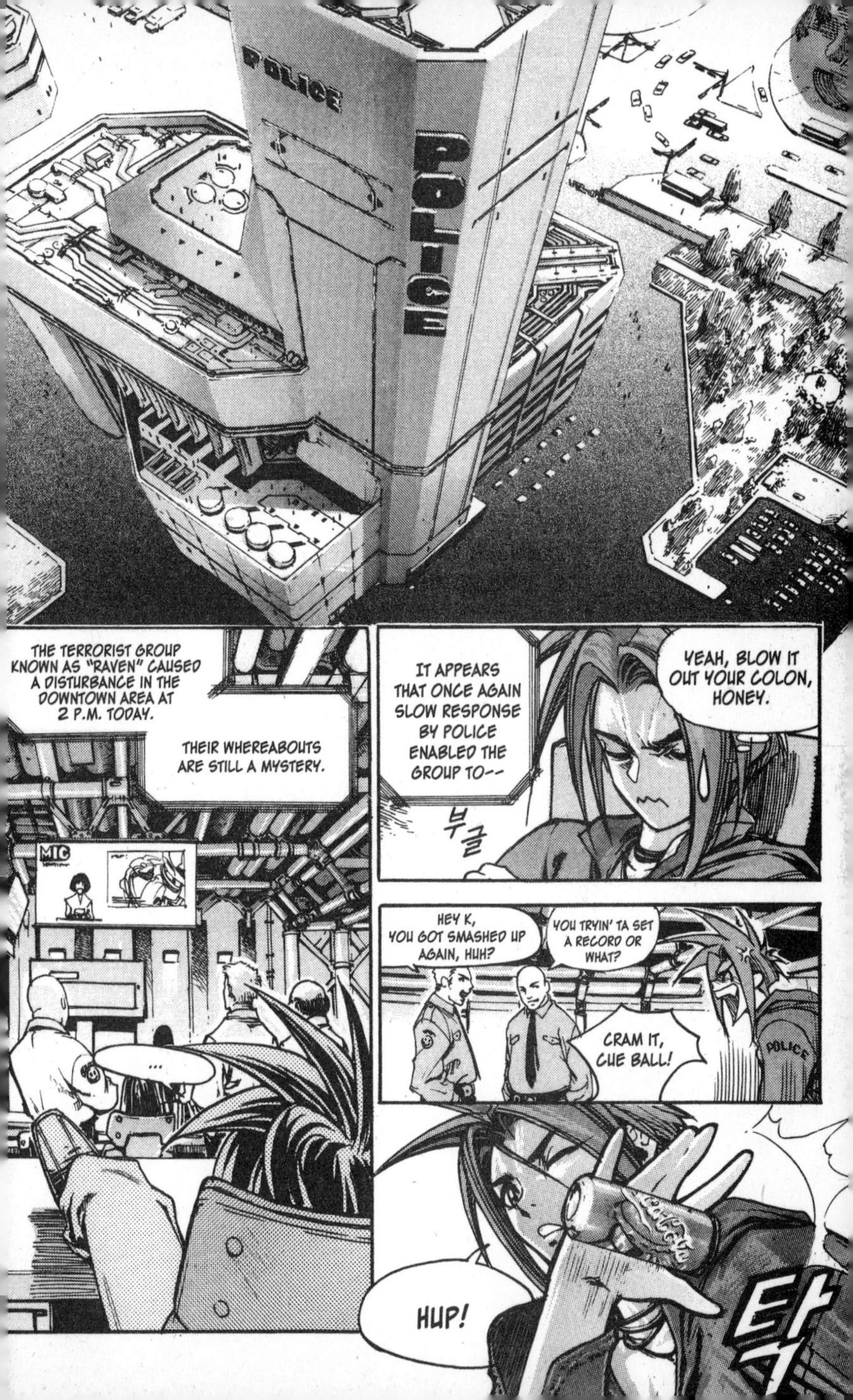
POLICE
POLICE
THE TERRORIST GROUP KNOWN AS "RAVEN" CAUSED A DISTURBANCE IN THE DOWNTOWN AREA AT 2 P.M. TODAY.
THEIR WHEREABOUTS ARE STILL A MYSTERY.
MTC
...
IT APPEARS THAT ONCE AGAIN SLOW RESPONSE BY POLICE ENABLED THE GROUP TO--
YEAH, BLOW IT OUT YOUR COLON, HONEY.
부글
HEY K, YOU GOT SMASHED UP AGAIN, HUH?
YOU TRYIN' TA SET A RECORD OR WHAT?
CRAM IT, CUE BALL!
POLICE
HUP!
탁

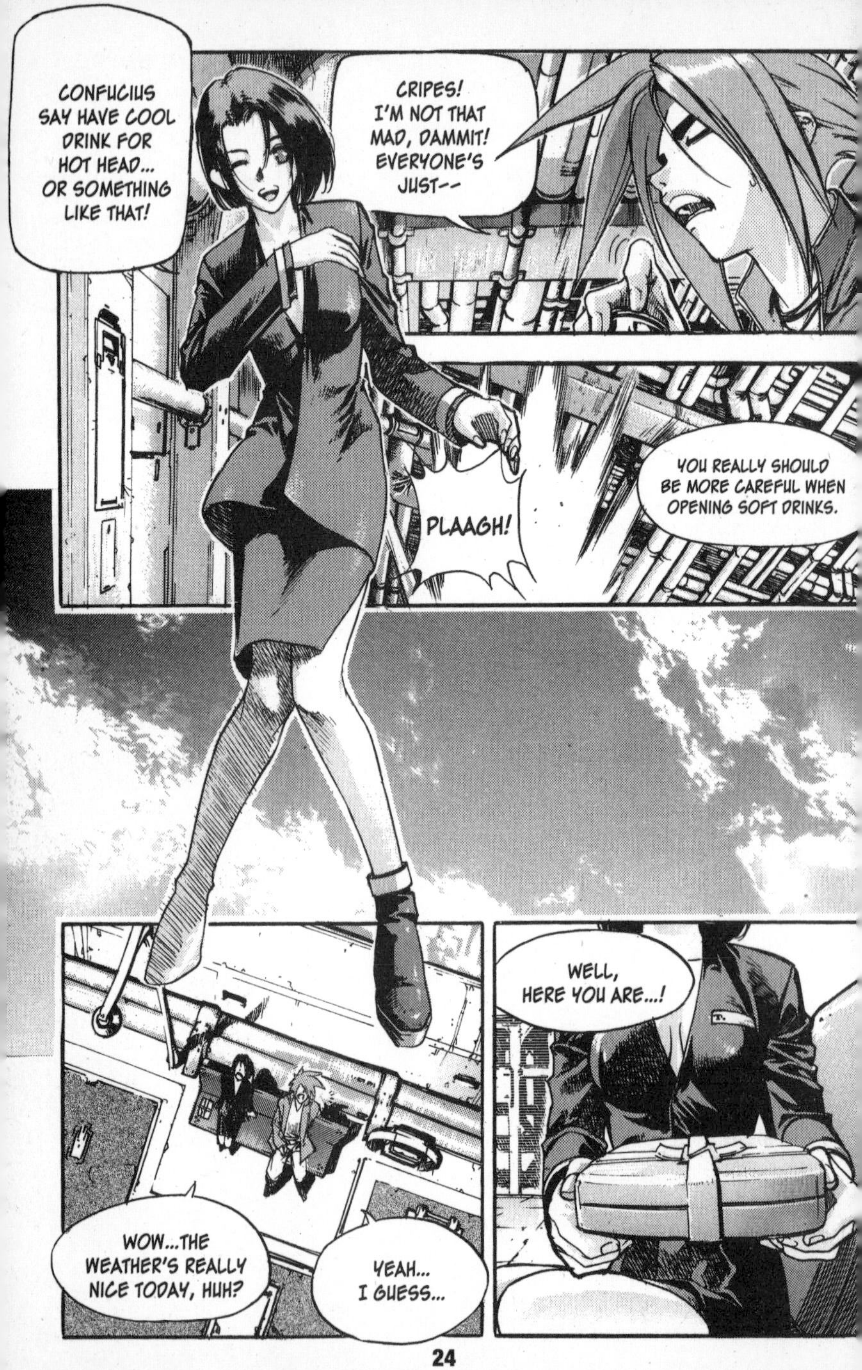
CONFUCIUS SAY HAVE COOL DRINK FOR HOT HEAD... OR SOMETHING LIKE THAT!
CRIPES! I'M NOT THAT MAD, DAMMIT! EVERYONE'S JUST--
PLAAGH!
YOU REALLY SHOULD BE MORE CAREFUL WHEN OPENING SOFT DRINKS.
WOW...THE WEATHER'S REALLY NICE TODAY, HUH?
YEAH... I GUESS...
WELL, HERE YOU ARE...!

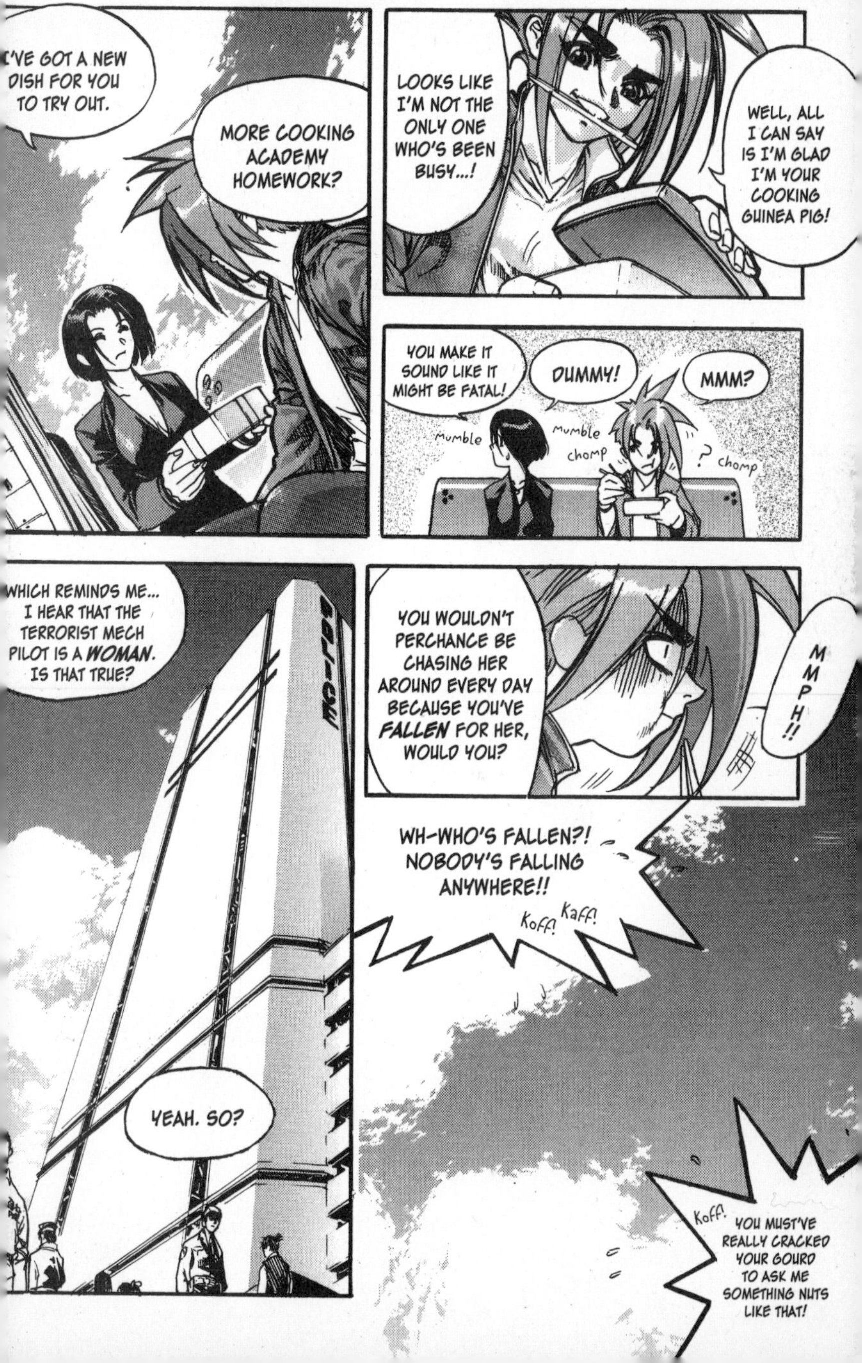
I'VE GOT A NEW DISH FOR YOU TO TRY OUT.
MORE COOKING ACADEMY HOMEWORK?
LOOKS LIKE I'M NOT THE ONLY ONE WHO'S BEEN BUSY...!
WELL, ALL I CAN SAY IS I'M GLAD I'M YOUR COOKING GUINEA PIG!
YOU MAKE IT SOUND LIKE IT MIGHT BE FATAL!
DUMMY!
MMM?
mumble
mumble
chomp
chomp
WHICH REMINDS ME... I HEAR THAT THE TERRORIST MECH PILOT IS A WOMAN. IS THAT TRUE?
YEAH. SO?
YOU WOULDN'T PERCHANCE BE CHASING HER AROUND EVERY DAY BECAUSE YOU'VE FALLEN FOR HER, WOULD YOU?
MMPH!!
WH-WHO'S FALLEN?! NOBODY'S FALLING ANYWHERE!!
Koff!
Kaff!
Koff!
YOU MUST'VE REALLY CRACKED YOUR GOURD TO ASK ME SOMETHING NUTS LIKE THAT!

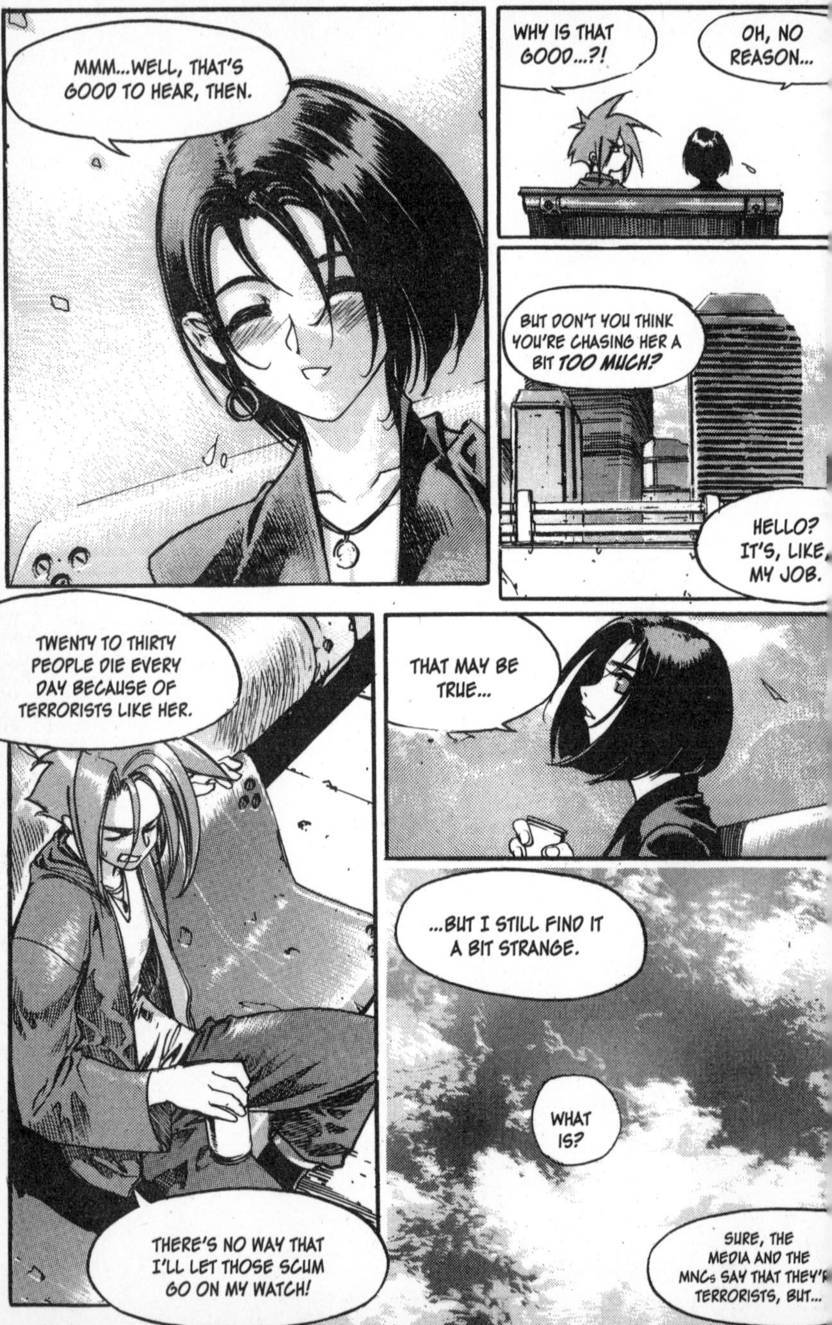
MMM...WELL, THAT'S GOOD TO HEAR, THEN.
WHY IS THAT GOOD...?!
OH, NO REASON...
BUT DON'T YOU THINK YOU'RE CHASING HER A BIT TOO MUCH?
HELLO? IT'S, LIKE, MY JOB.
TWENTY TO THIRTY PEOPLE DIE EVERY DAY BECAUSE OF TERRORISTS LIKE HER.
THERE'S NO WAY THAT I'LL LET THOSE SCUM GO ON MY WATCH!
THAT MAY BE TRUE...
...BUT I STILL FIND IT A BIT STRANGE.
WHAT IS?
SURE, THE MEDIA AND THE MNCs SAY THAT THEY'

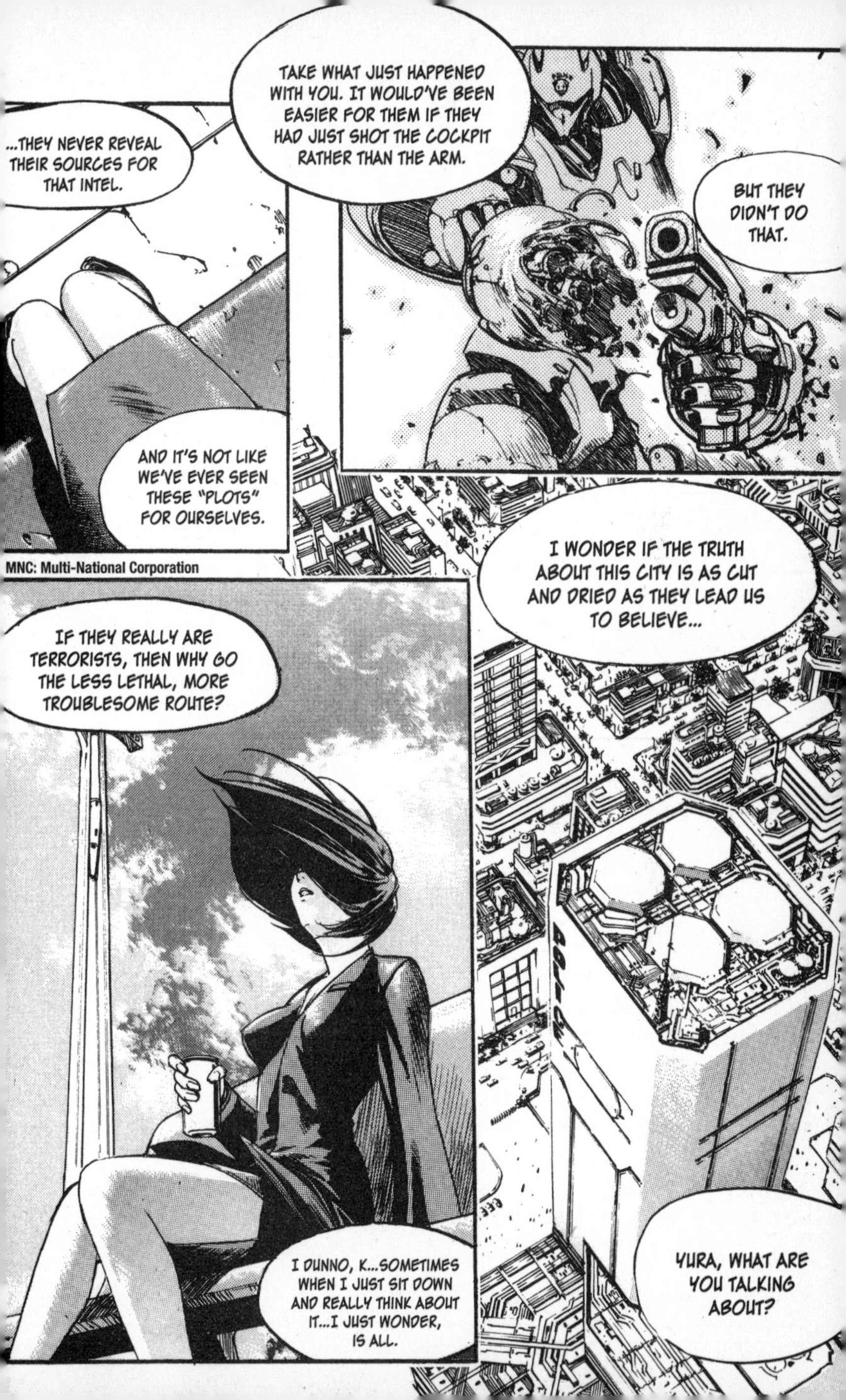
...THEY NEVER REVEAL THEIR SOURCES FOR THAT INTEL.
AND IT'S NOT LIKE WE'VE EVER SEEN THESE "PLOTS" FOR OURSELVES.
TAKE WHAT JUST HAPPENED WITH YOU. IT WOULD'VE BEEN EASIER FOR THEM IF THEY HAD JUST SHOT THE COCKPIT RATHER THAN THE ARM.
BUT THEY DIDN'T DO THAT.
IF THEY REALLY ARE TERRORISTS, THEN WHY GO THE LESS LETHAL, MORE TROUBLESOME ROUTE?
I WONDER IF THE TRUTH ABOUT THIS CITY IS AS CUT AND DRIED AS THEY LEAD US TO BELIEVE...
YURA, WHAT ARE YOU TALKING ABOUT?
I DUNNO, K...SOMETIMES WHEN I JUST SIT DOWN AND REALLY THINK ABOUT IT...I JUST WONDER, IS ALL.

MNC: Multi-National Corporation

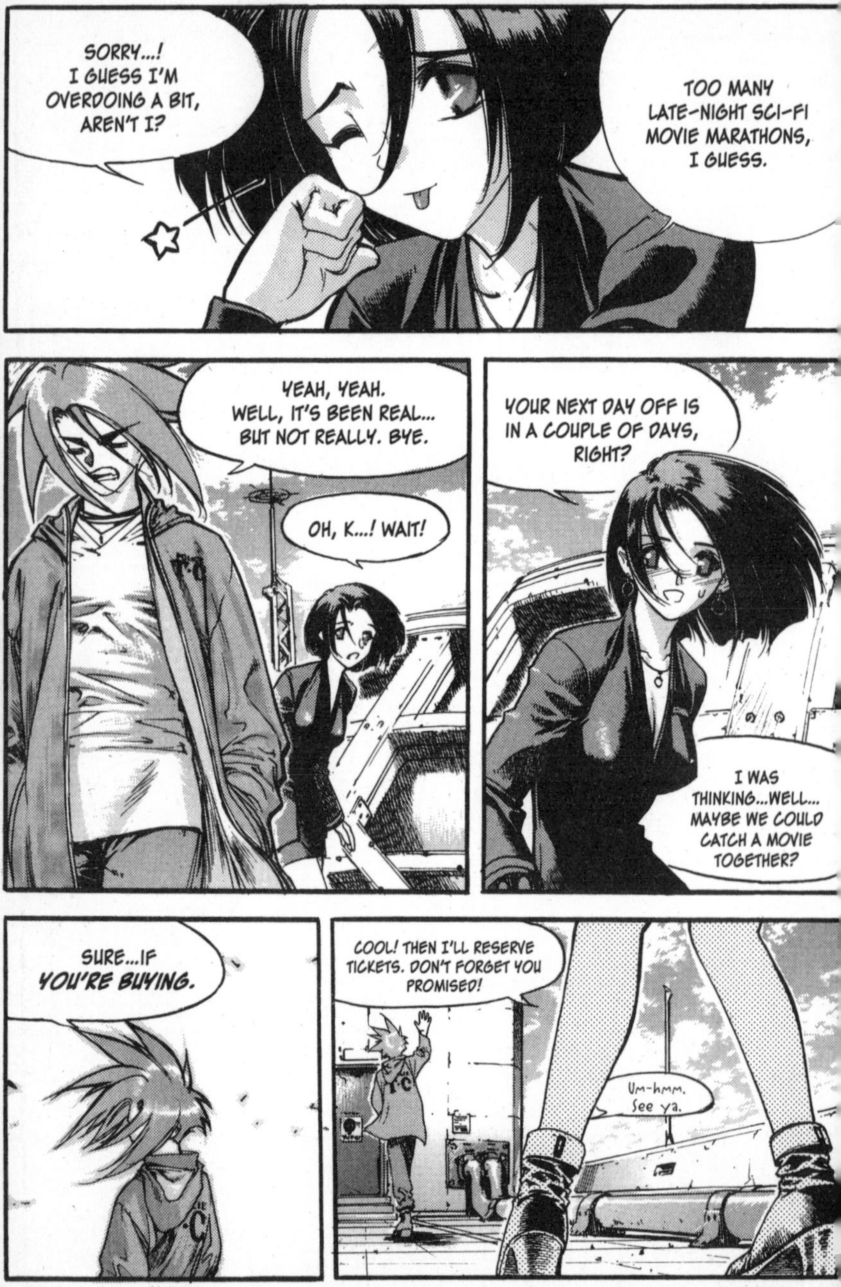
SORRY...! I GUESS I'M OVERDOING A BIT, AREN'T I?
TOO MANY LATE-NIGHT SCI-FI MOVIE MARATHONS, I GUESS.
YEAH, YEAH. WELL, IT'S BEEN REAL... BUT NOT REALLY. BYE.
OH, K...! WAIT!
YOUR NEXT DAY OFF IS IN A COUPLE OF DAYS, RIGHT?
I WAS THINKING...WELL... MAYBE WE COULD CATCH A MOVIE TOGETHER?
SURE...IF ***YOU'RE BUYING.***
COOL! THEN I'LL RESERVE TICKETS. DON'T FORGET YOU PROMISED!
Um-hmm. See ya.

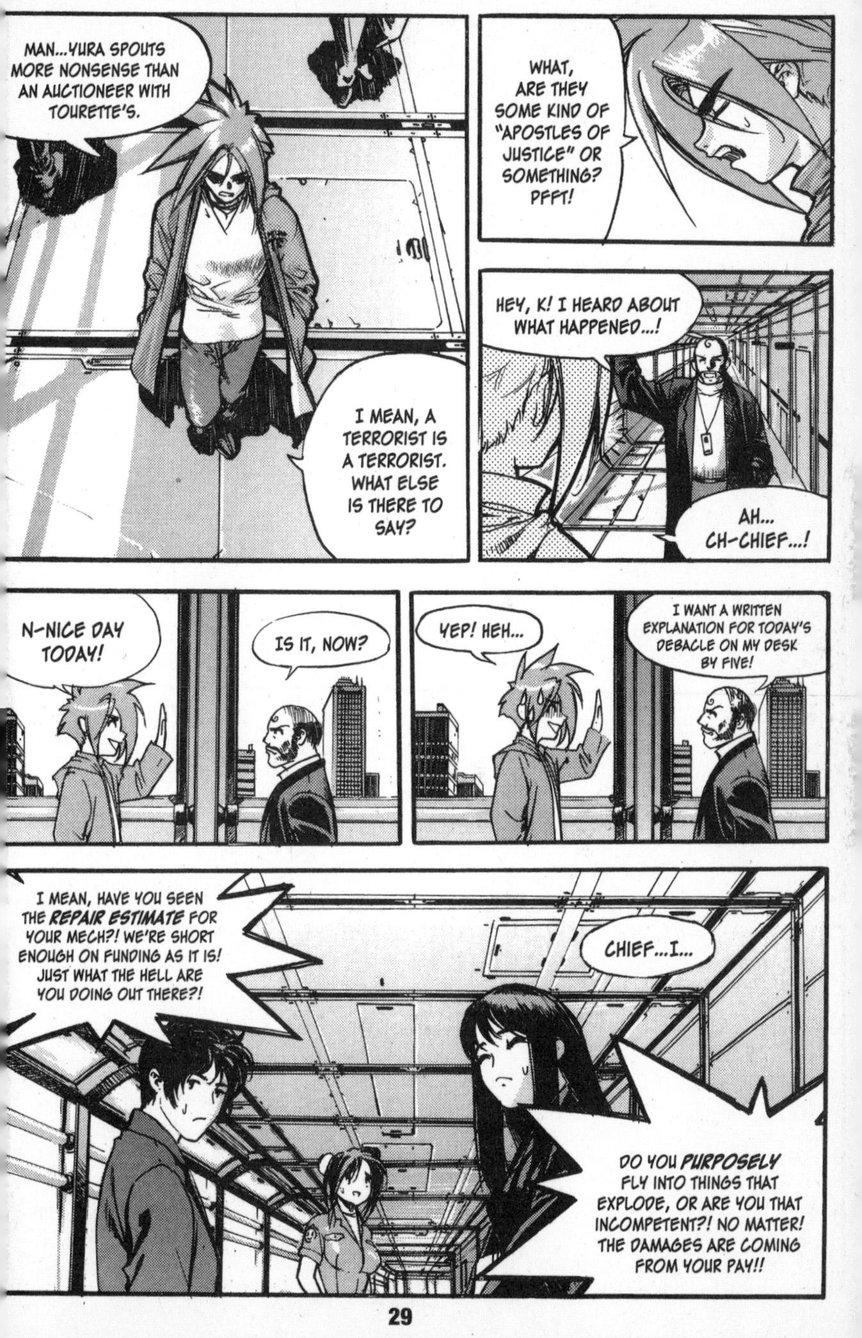

MAN...YURA SPOUTS MORE NONSENSE THAN AN AUCTIONEER WITH TOURETTE'S.
I MEAN, A TERRORIST IS A TERRORIST. WHAT ELSE IS THERE TO SAY?
WHAT, ARE THEY SOME KIND OF "APOSTLES OF JUSTICE" OR SOMETHING? PFFT!
HEY, K! I HEARD ABOUT WHAT HAPPENED...!
AH... CH-CHIEF...!
N-NICE DAY TODAY!
IS IT, NOW?
YEP! HEH...
I WANT A WRITTEN EXPLANATION FOR TODAY'S DEBACLE ON MY DESK BY FIVE!
I MEAN, HAVE YOU SEEN THE ***REPAIR ESTIMATE*** FOR YOUR MECH?! WE'RE SHORT ENOUGH ON FUNDING AS IT IS! JUST WHAT THE HELL ARE YOU DOING OUT THERE?!
CHIEF...I...
DO YOU ***PURPOSELY*** FLY INTO THINGS THAT EXPLODE, OR ARE YOU THAT INCOMPETENT?! NO MATTER! THE DAMAGES ARE COMING FROM YOUR PAY!!

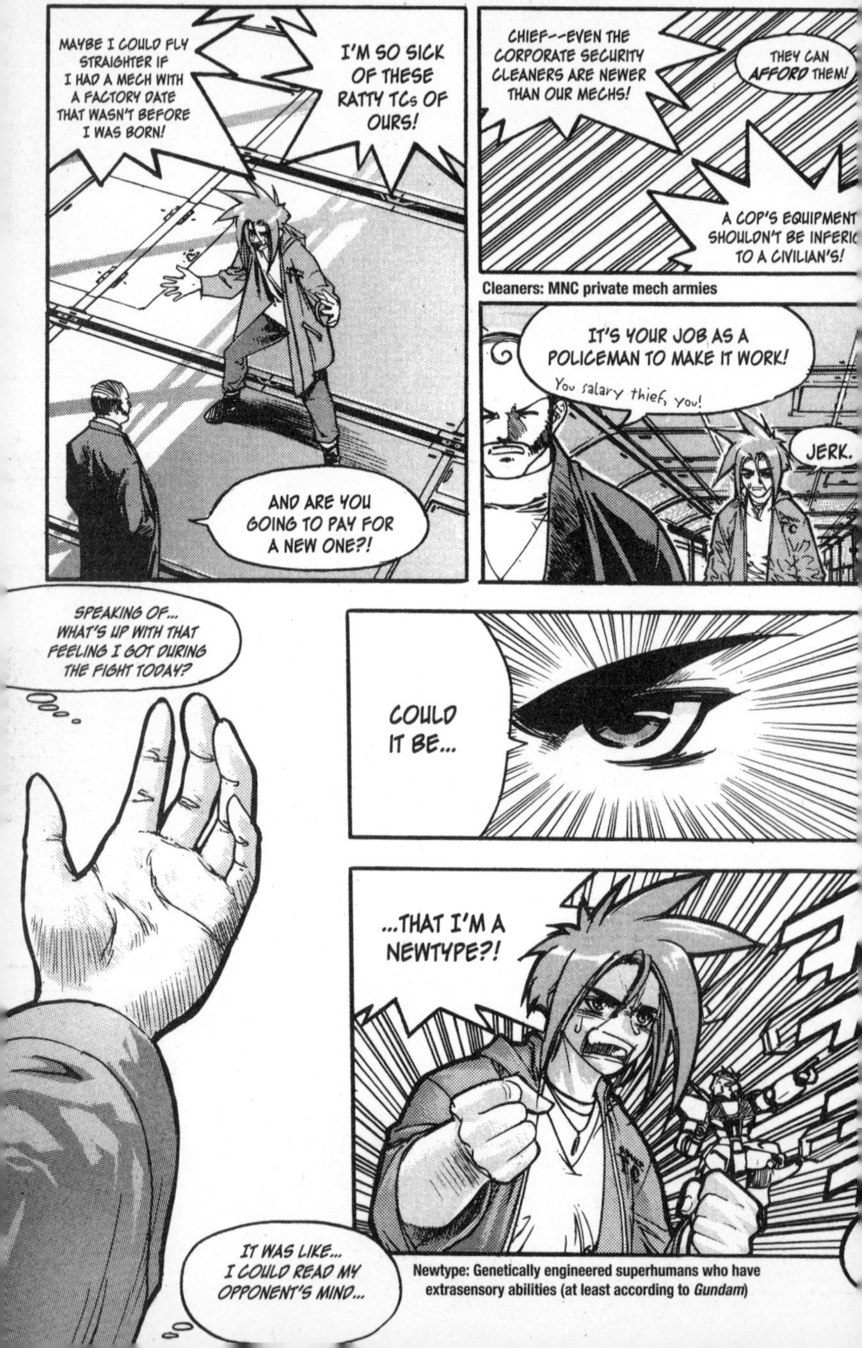
MAYBE I COULD FLY STRAIGHTER IF I HAD A MECH WITH A FACTORY DATE THAT WASN'T BEFORE I WAS BORN!
I'M SO SICK OF THESE RATTY TCs OF OURS!
AND ARE YOU GOING TO PAY FOR A NEW ONE?!
CHIEF--EVEN THE CORPORATE SECURITY CLEANERS ARE NEWER THAN OUR MECHS!
THEY CAN AFFORD THEM!
A COP'S EQUIPMENT SHOULDN'T BE INFERIC TO A CIVILIAN'S!
Cleaners: MNC private mech armies
IT'S YOUR JOB AS A POLICEMAN TO MAKE IT WORK!
You salary thief, you!
JERK.
SPEAKING OF... WHAT'S UP WITH THAT FEELING I GOT DURING THE FIGHT TODAY?
IT WAS LIKE... I COULD READ MY OPPONENT'S MIND...
COULD IT BE...
...THAT I'M A NEWTYPE?!
Newtype: Genetically engineered superhumans who have extrasensory abilities (at least according to Gundam)

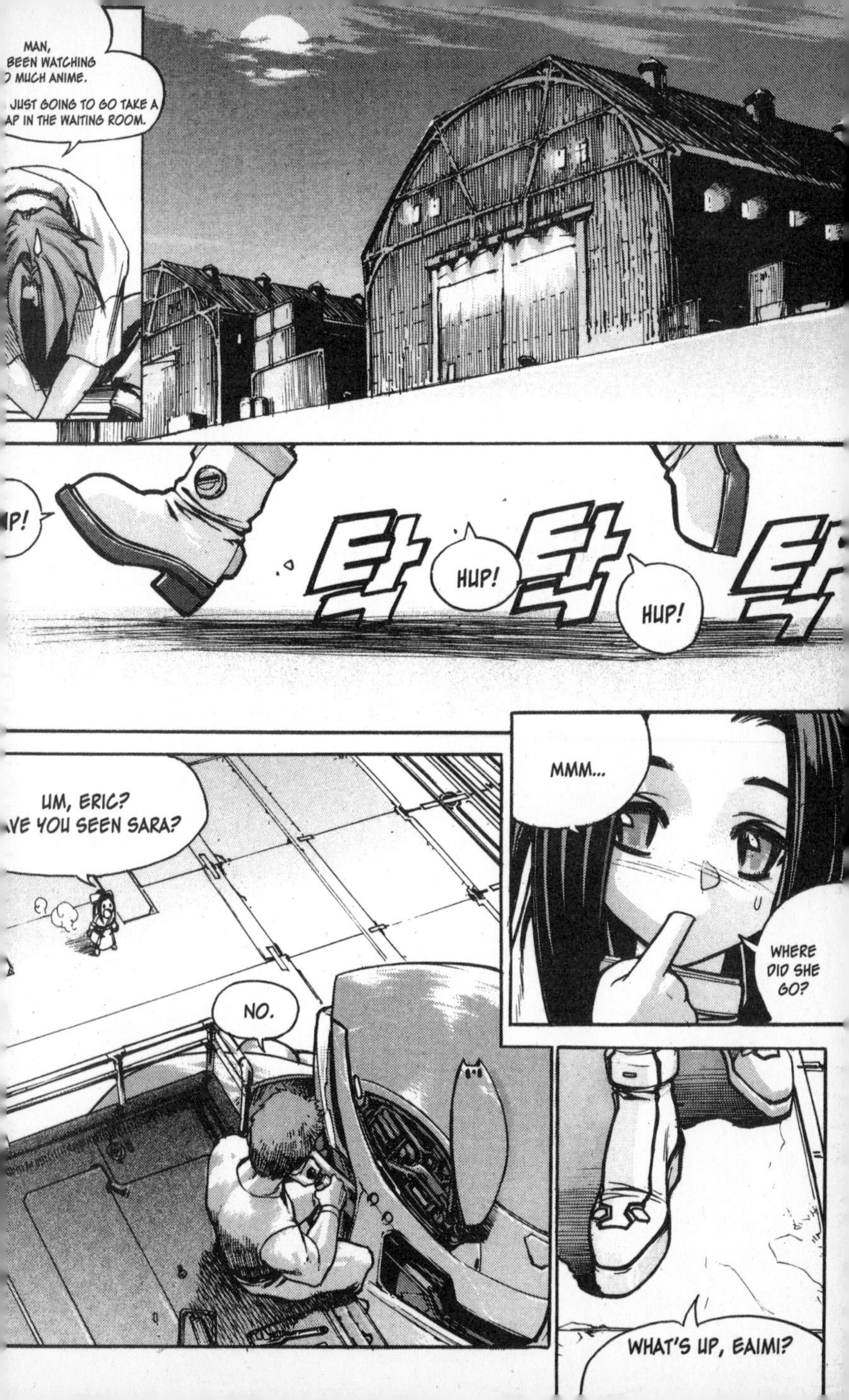
MAN, BEEN WATCHING O MUCH ANIME.
JUST GOING TO GO TAKE A AP IN THE WAITING ROOM.
P!
탁
HUP!
탁
HUP!
탁
UM, ERIC? VE YOU SEEN SARA?
NO.
MMM...
WHERE DID SHE GO?
WHAT'S UP, EAIMI?

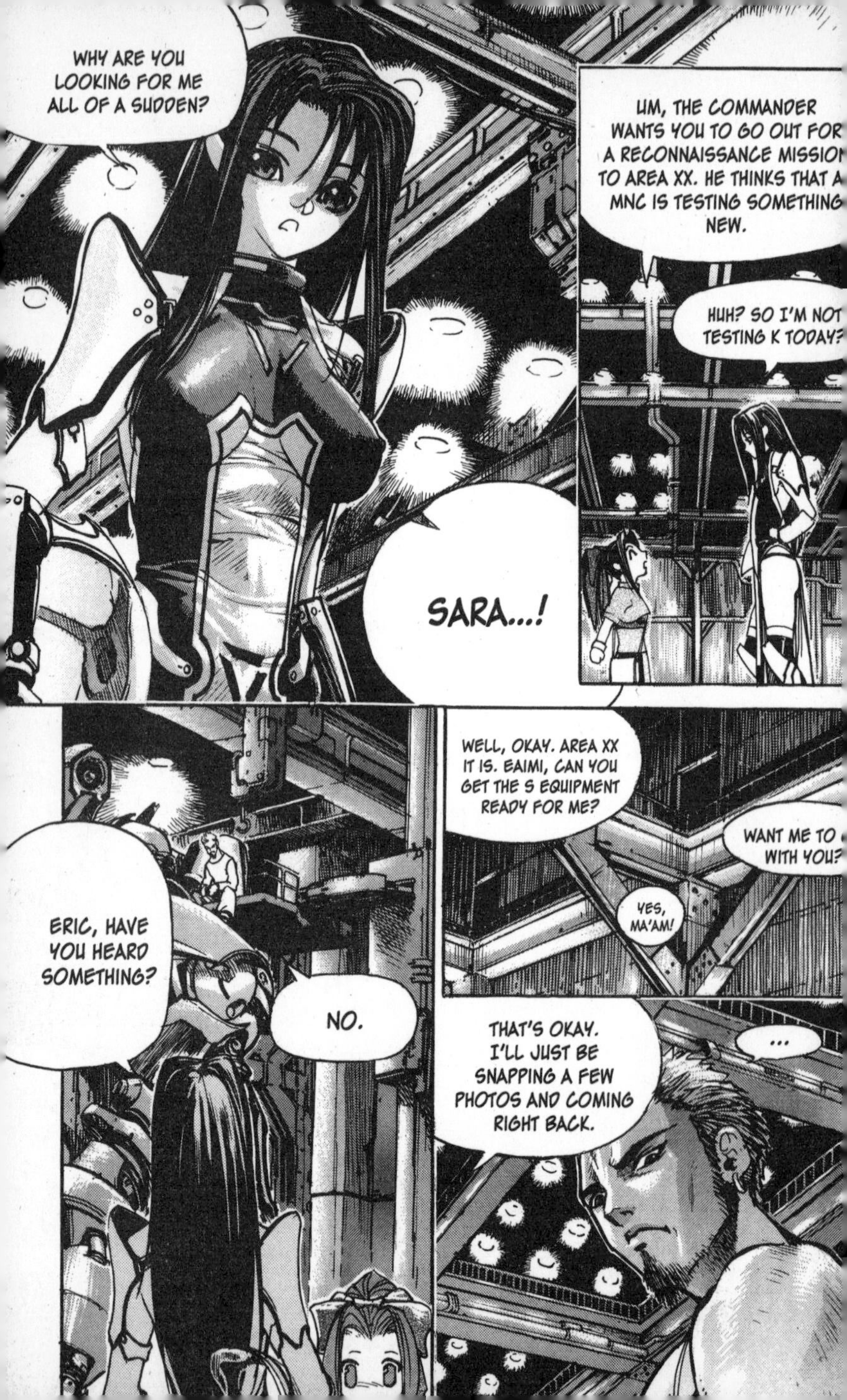

WHY ARE YOU LOOKING FOR ME ALL OF A SUDDEN?
SARA...!
UM, THE COMMANDER WANTS YOU TO GO OUT FOR A RECONNAISSANCE MISSIO TO AREA XX. HE THINKS THAT A MNC IS TESTING SOMETHING NEW.
HUH? SO I'M NOT TESTING K TODAY?
ERIC, HAVE YOU HEARD SOMETHING?
NO.
WELL, OKAY. AREA XX IT IS. EAIMI, CAN YOU GET THE S EQUIPMENT READY FOR ME?
WANT ME TO WITH YOU?
YES, MA'AM!
THAT'S OKAY. I'LL JUST BE SNAPPING A FEW PHOTOS AND COMING RIGHT BACK.
...

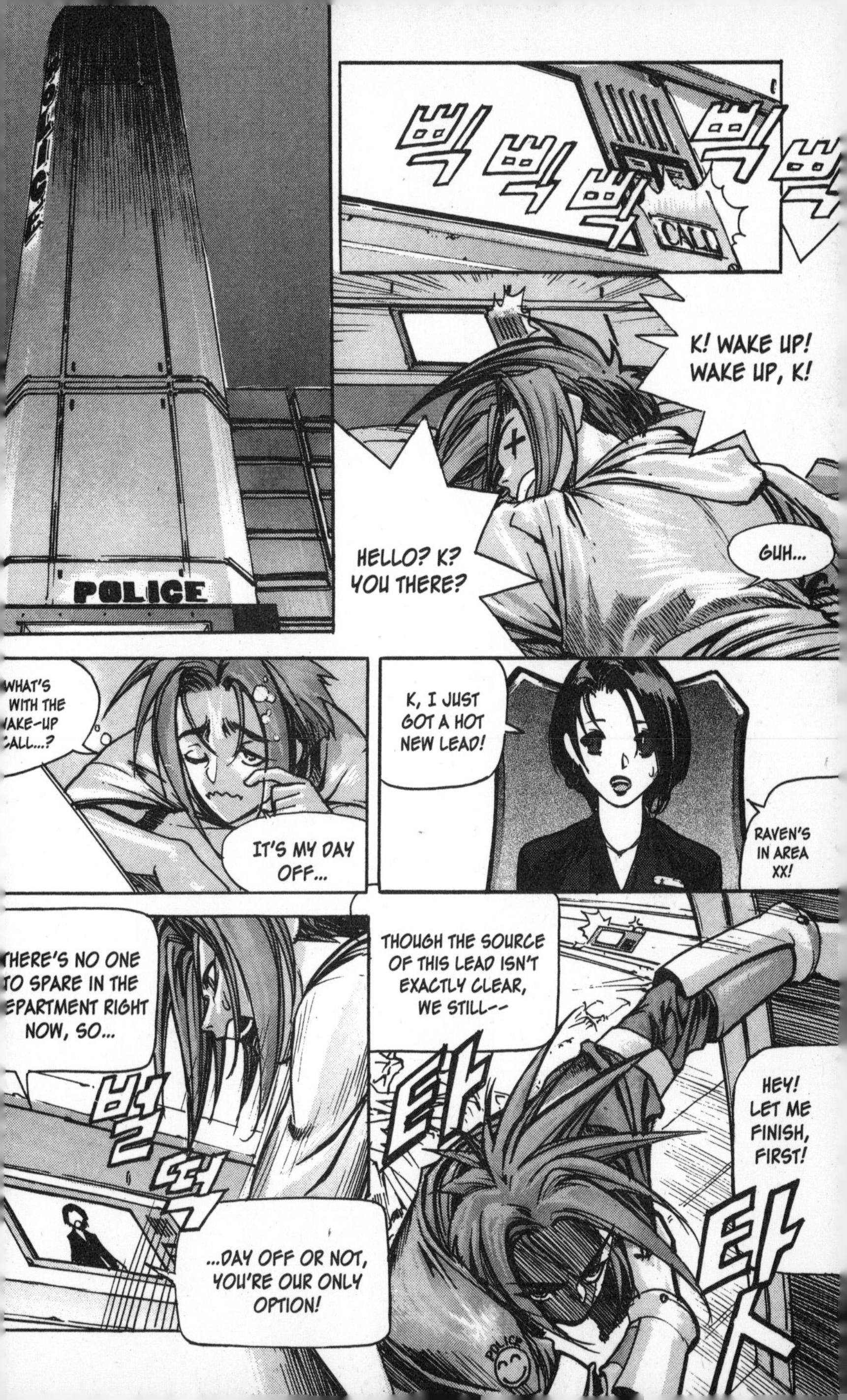
POLICE
삑 삑 삑
삑 삑
CALL
K! WAKE UP! WAKE UP, K!
HELLO? K? YOU THERE?
GUH...
WHAT'S WITH THE AKE-UP ALL...?
IT'S MY DAY OFF...
K, I JUST GOT A HOT NEW LEAD!
RAVEN'S IN AREA XX!
HERE'S NO ONE TO SPARE IN THE EPARTMENT RIGHT NOW, SO...
벌떡
...DAY OFF OR NOT, YOU'RE OUR ONLY OPTION!
THOUGH THE SOURCE OF THIS LEAD ISN'T EXACTLY CLEAR, WE STILL--
탁
HEY! LET ME FINISH, FIRST!
탁

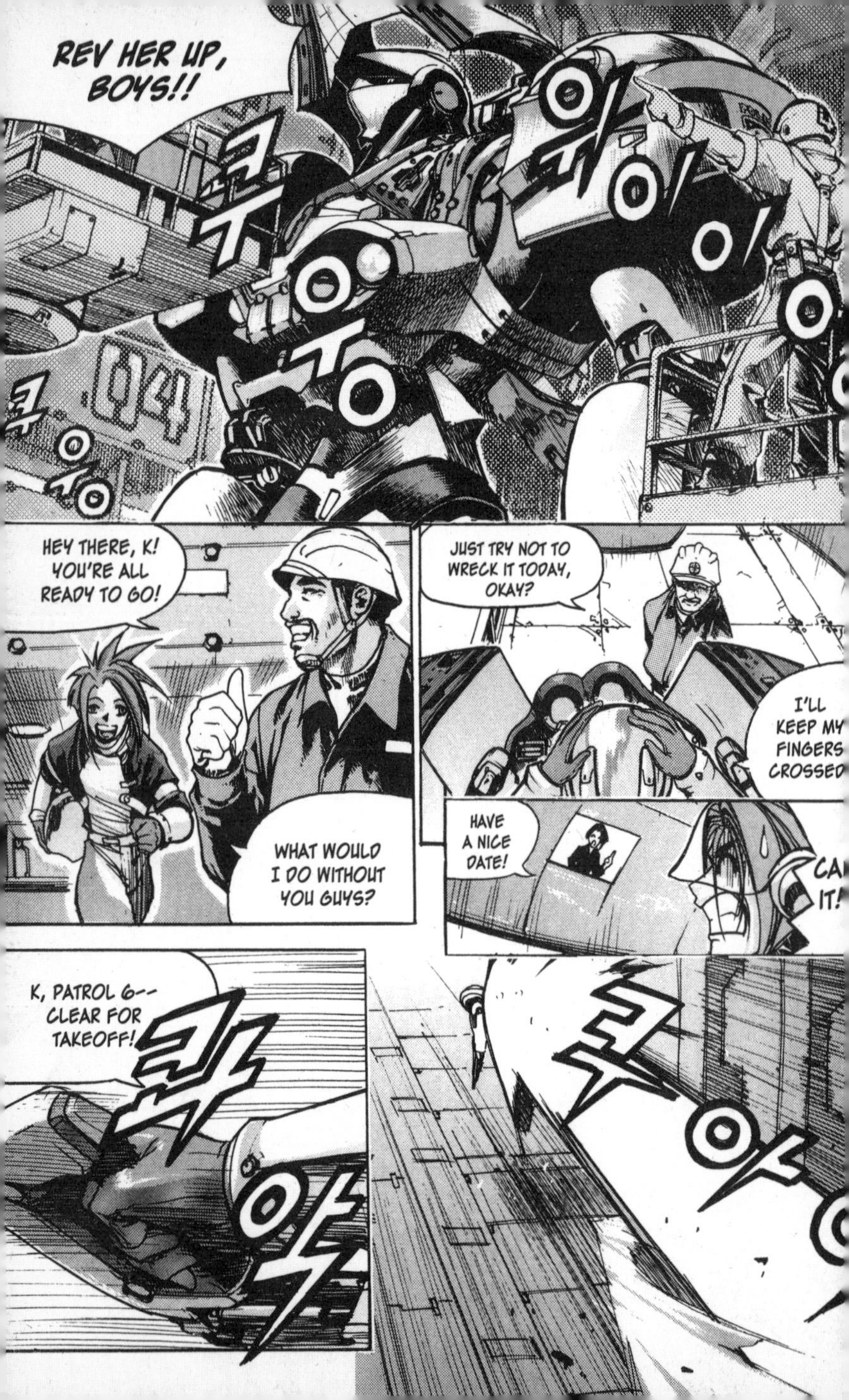

REV HER UP, BOYS!!
HEY THERE, K! YOU'RE ALL READY TO GO!
WHAT WOULD I DO WITHOUT YOU GUYS?
JUST TRY NOT TO WRECK IT TODAY, OKAY?
I'LL KEEP MY FINGERS CROSSED
HAVE A NICE DATE!
CA IT!
K, PATROL 6-- CLEAR FOR TAKEOFF!

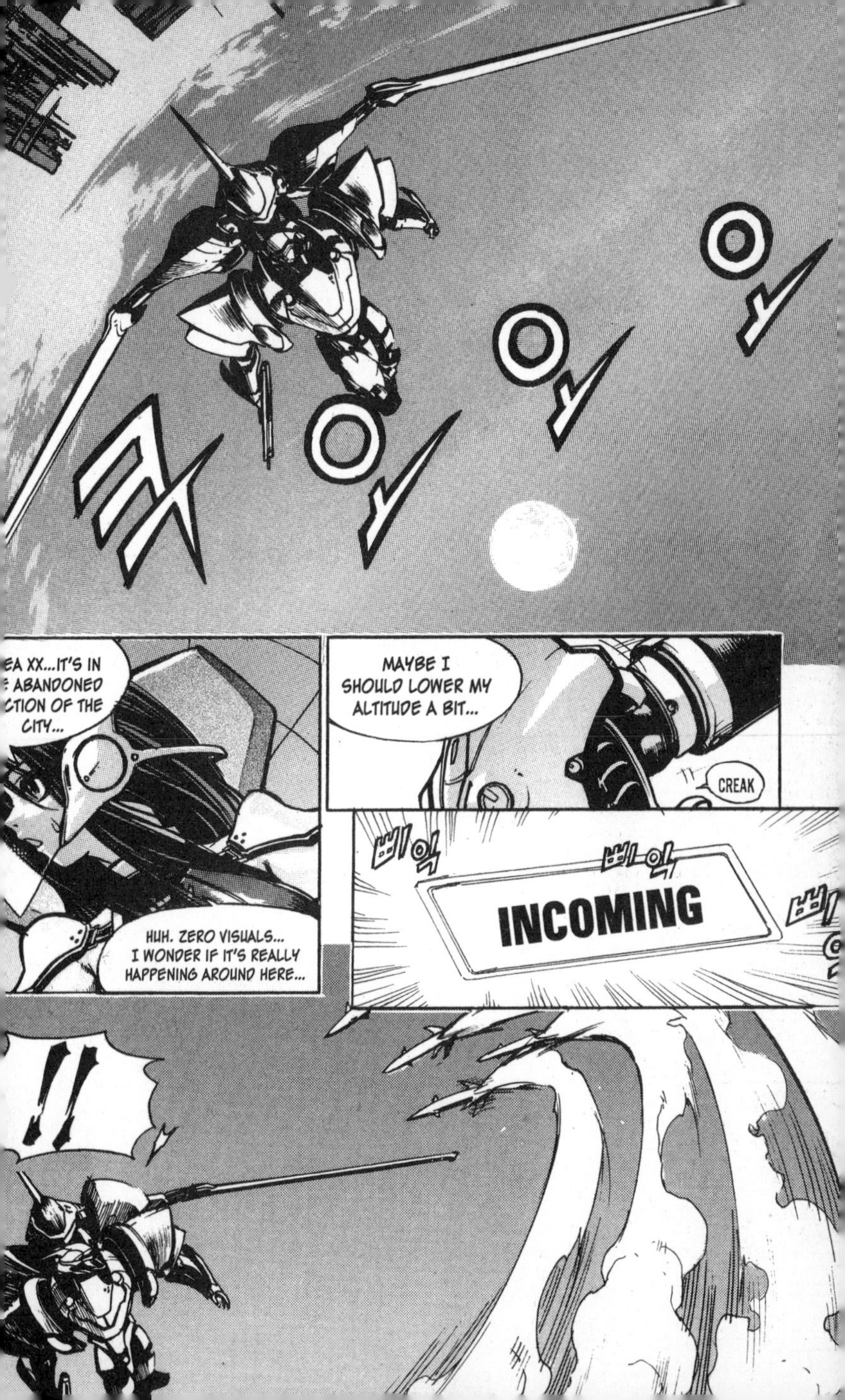
EA XX...IT'S IN
E ABANDONED
CTION OF THE
CITY...
HUH. ZERO VISUALS... I WONDER IF IT'S REALLY HAPPENING AROUND HERE...
MAYBE I SHOULD LOWER MY ALTITUDE A BIT...
CREAK
삐익
삐익
INCOMING
!!

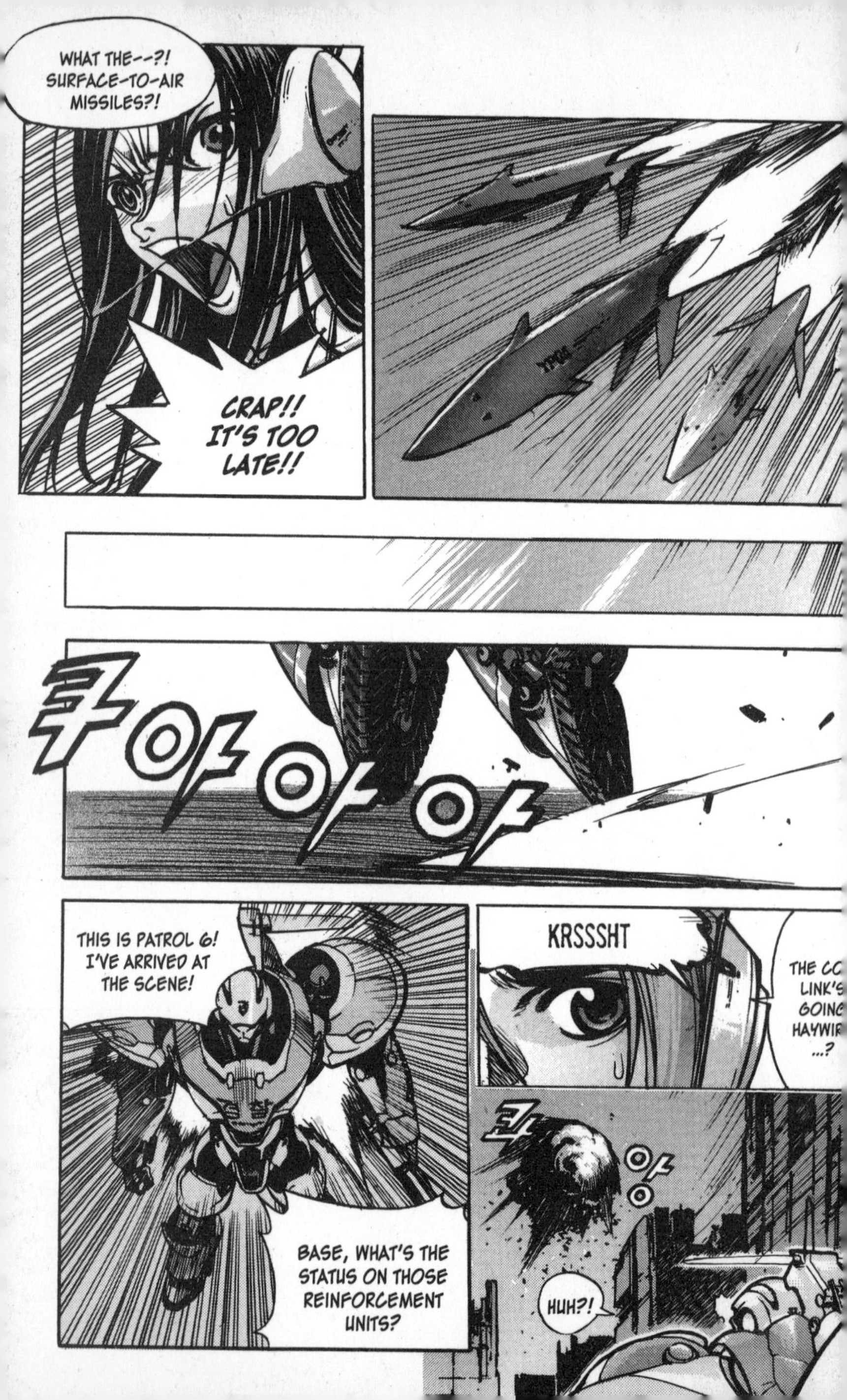
WHAT THE--?! SURFACE-TO-AIR MISSILES?!
CRAP!! IT'S TOO LATE!!
THIS IS PATROL 6! I'VE ARRIVED AT THE SCENE!
BASE, WHAT'S THE STATUS ON THOSE REINFORCEMENT UNITS?
KRSSSHT
THE CO LINK'S GOING HAYWIR ...?
HUH?!

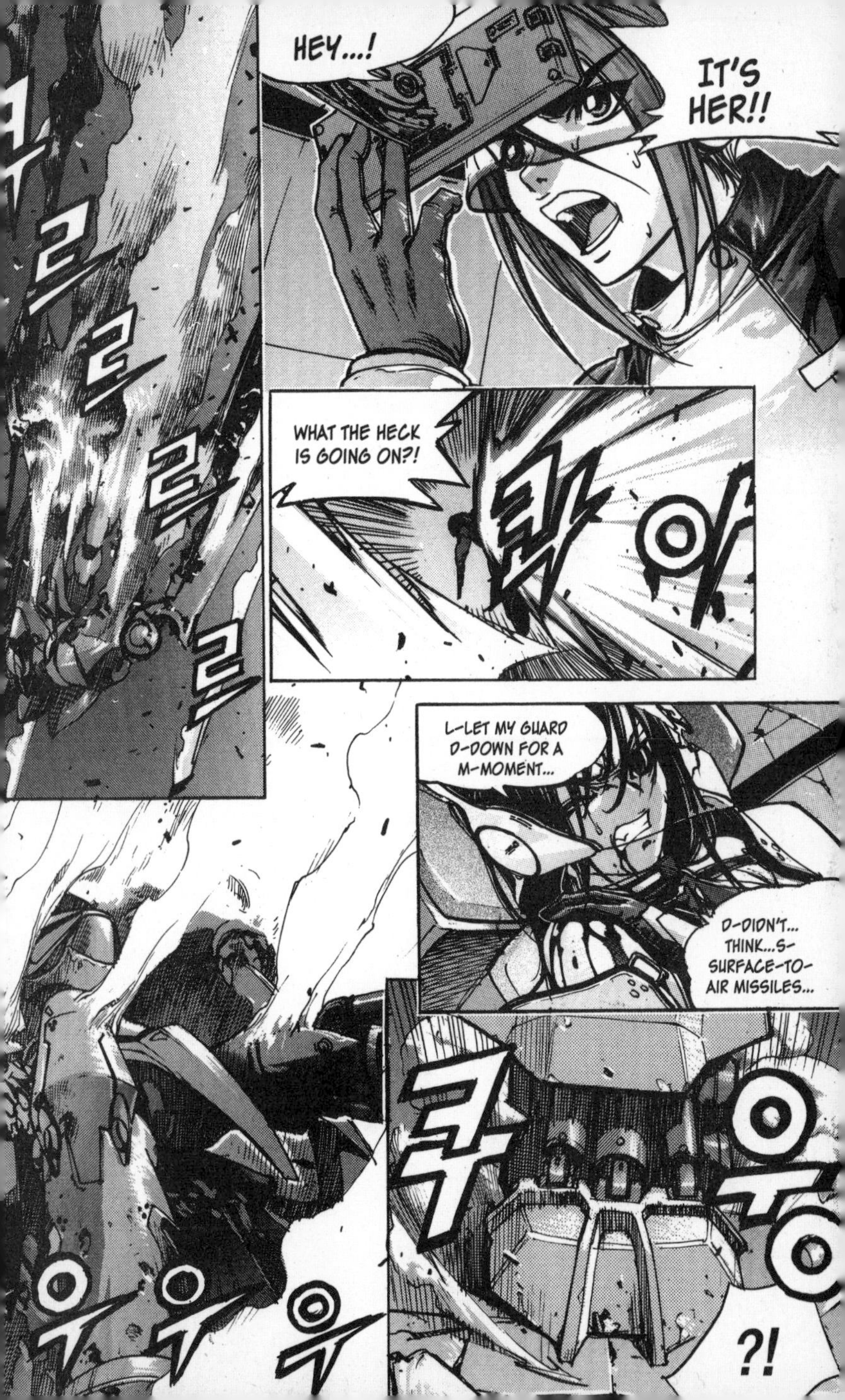
HEY...!
IT'S HER!!
WHAT THE HECK IS GOING ON?!
L-LET MY GUARD D-DOWN FOR A M-MOMENT...
D-DIDN'T... THINK...S-SURFACE-TO-AIR MISSILES...
?!

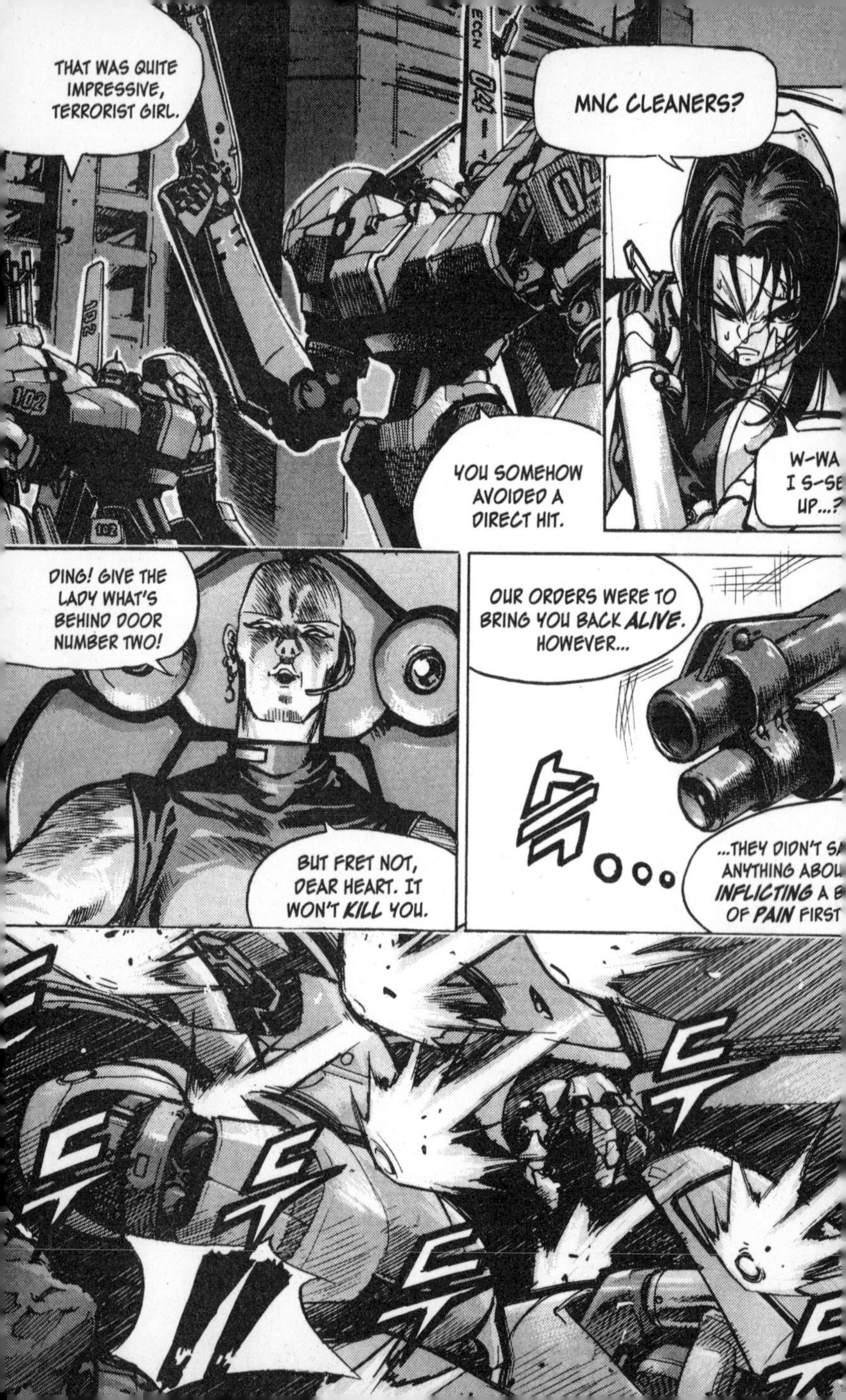
THAT WAS QUITE IMPRESSIVE, TERRORIST GIRL.
YOU SOMEHOW AVOIDED A DIRECT HIT.
MNC CLEANERS?
W-WA I S-SE UP...?
DING! GIVE THE LADY WHAT'S BEHIND DOOR NUMBER TWO!
BUT FRET NOT, DEAR HEART. IT WON'T KILL YOU.
OUR ORDERS WERE TO BRING YOU BACK ALIVE. HOWEVER...
...THEY DIDN'T SA ANYTHING ABOU INFLICTING A B OF PAIN FIRST

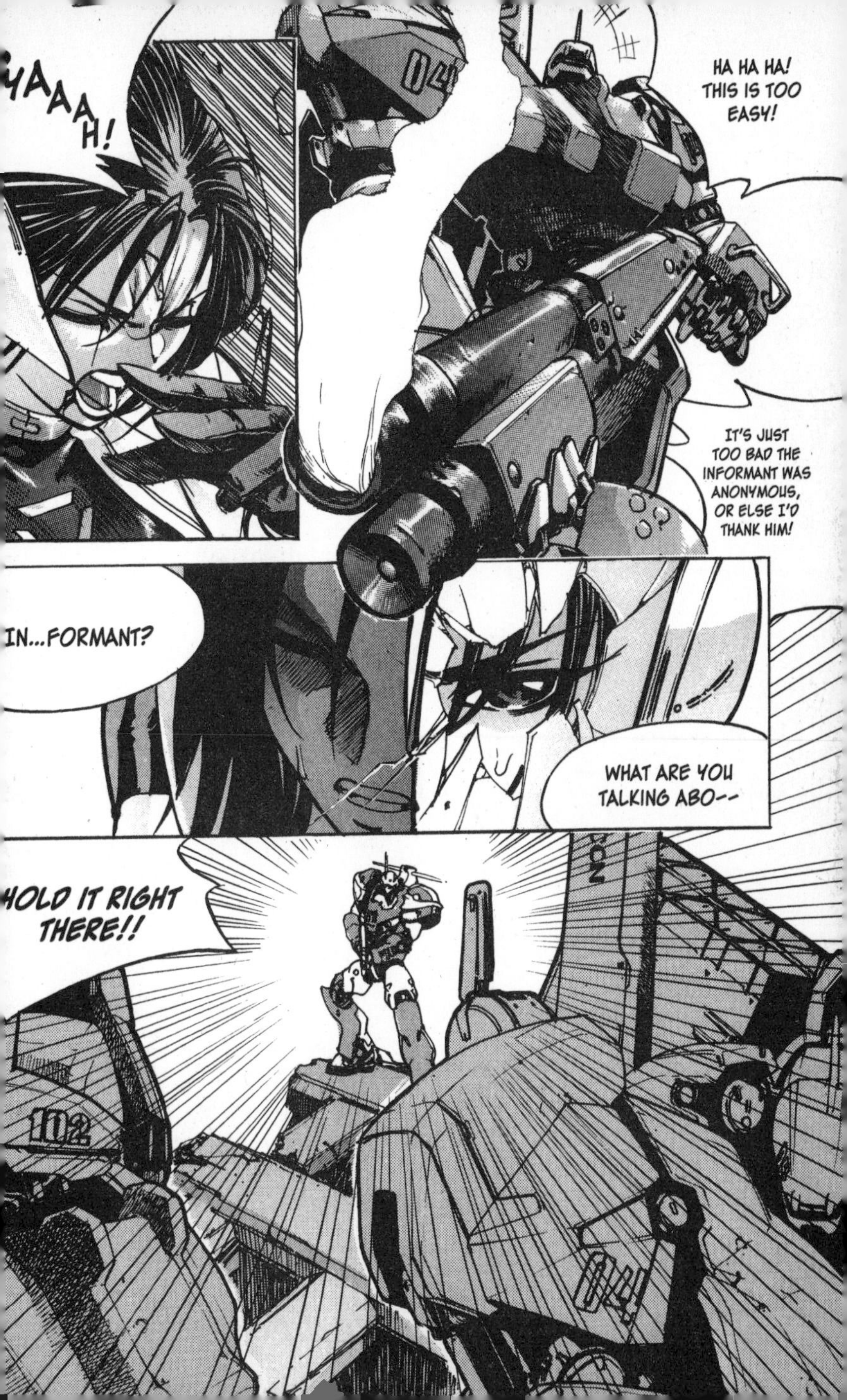
YAAAAH!
HA HA HA! THIS IS TOO EASY!
IT'S JUST TOO BAD THE INFORMANT WAS ANONYMOUS, OR ELSE I'D THANK HIM!
IN...FORMANT?
WHAT ARE YOU TALKING ABO--
HOLD IT RIGHT THERE!!

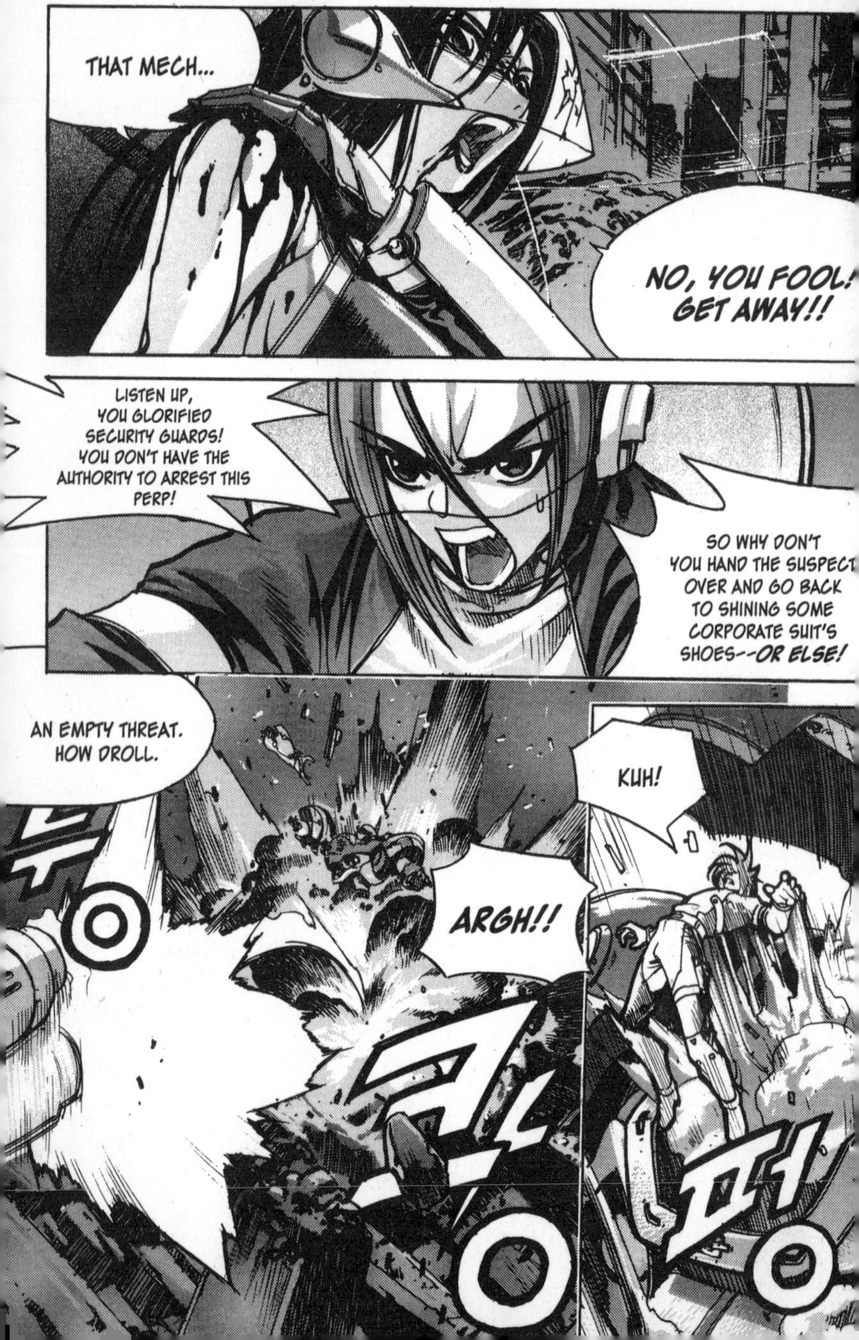
THAT MECH...
NO, YOU FOOL! GET AWAY!!
LISTEN UP, YOU GLORIFIED SECURITY GUARDS! YOU DON'T HAVE THE AUTHORITY TO ARREST THIS PERP!
SO WHY DON'T YOU HAND THE SUSPECT OVER AND GO BACK TO SHINING SOME CORPORATE SUIT'S SHOES--OR ELSE!
AN EMPTY THREAT. HOW DROLL.
ARGH!!
KUH!

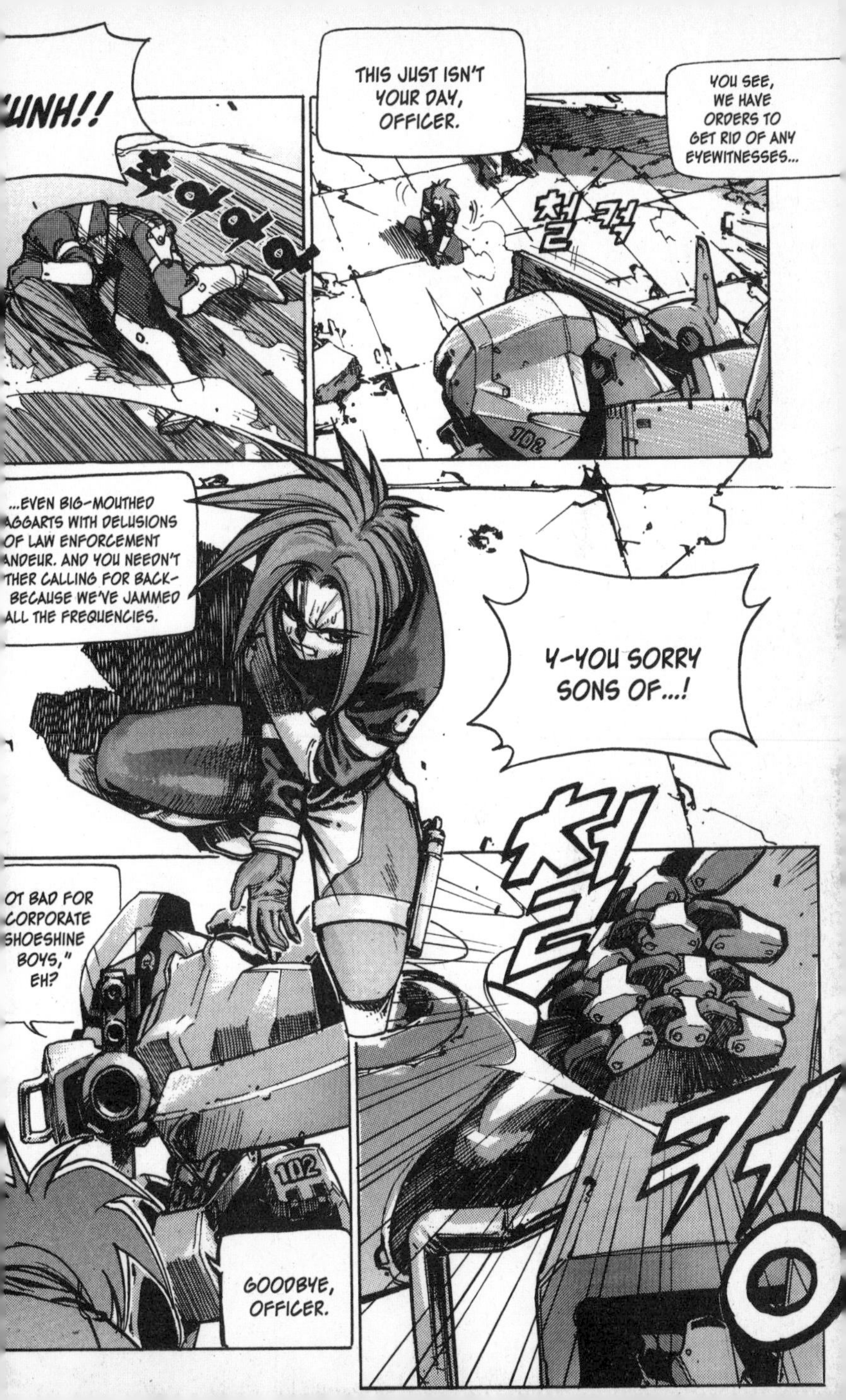

UNH!!
THIS JUST ISN'T YOUR DAY, OFFICER.
철컥
YOU SEE, WE HAVE ORDERS TO GET RID OF ANY EYEWITNESSES...
...EVEN BIG-MOUTHED AGGARTS WITH DELUSIONS OF LAW ENFORCEMENT ANDEUR. AND YOU NEEDN'T THER CALLING FOR BACK-BECAUSE WE'VE JAMMED ALL THE FREQUENCIES.
Y-YOU SORRY SONS OF...!
OT BAD FOR CORPORATE SHOESHINE BOYS," EH?
102
GOODBYE, OFFICER.

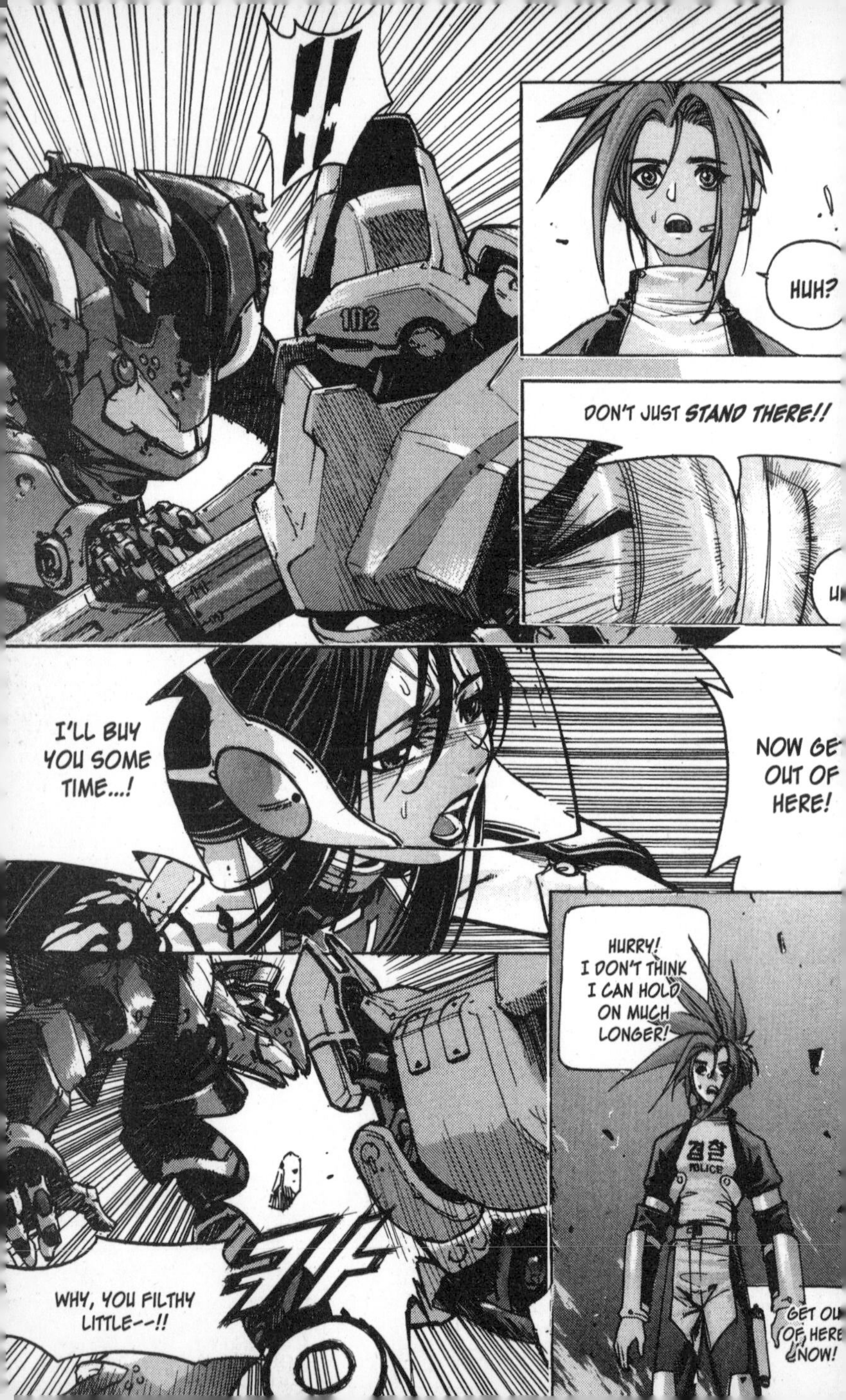
HUH?
DON'T JUST STAND THERE!!
I'LL BUY YOU SOME TIME...!
NOW GE
OUT OF HERE!
WHY, YOU FILTHY LITTLE--!!
HURRY! I DON'T THINK I CAN HOLD ON MUCH LONGER!
GET OU OF HERE NOW!

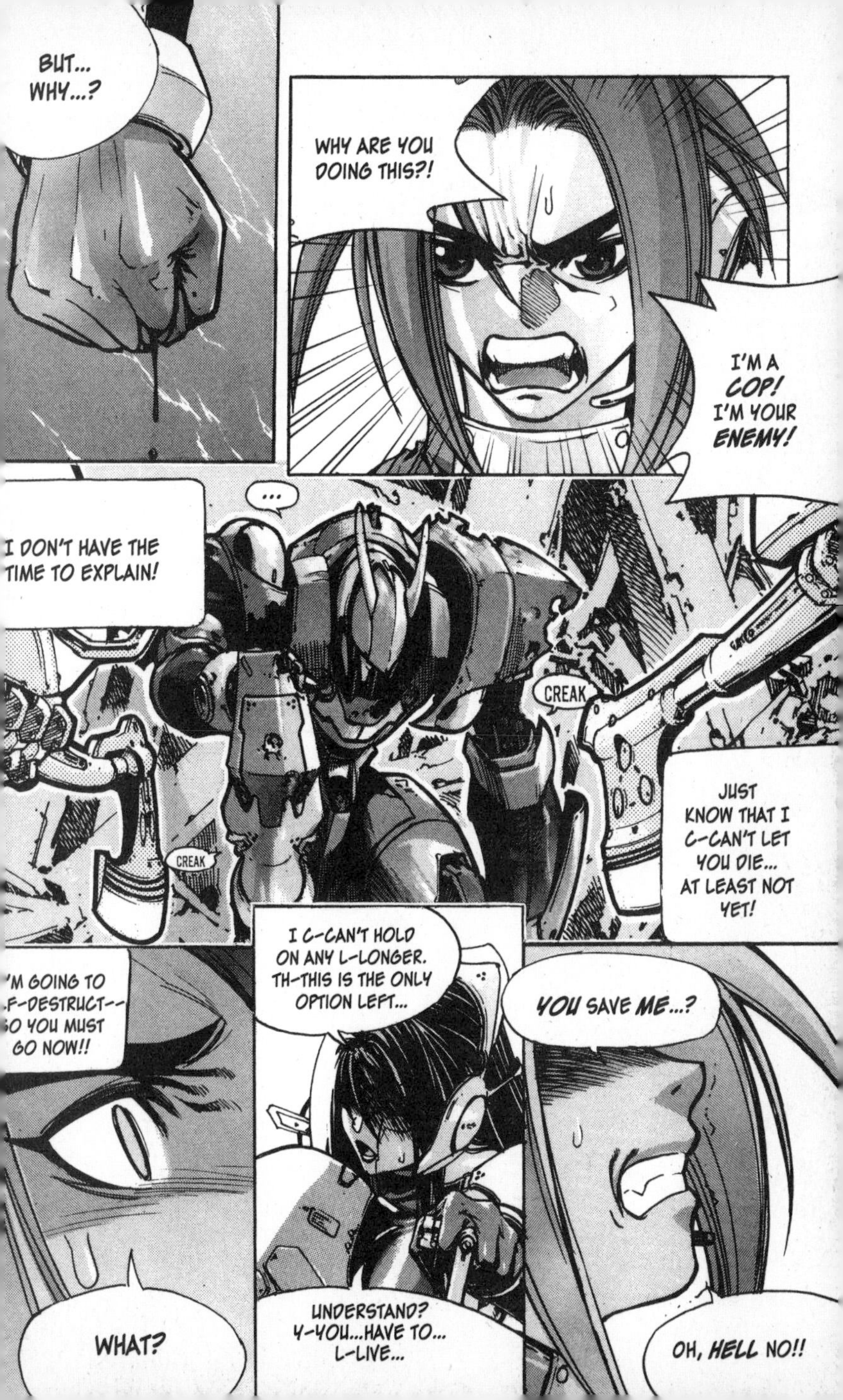

BUT... WHY...?
WHY ARE YOU DOING THIS?!
I'M A COP! I'M YOUR ENEMY!
...
I DON'T HAVE THE TIME TO EXPLAIN!
CREAK
CREAK
JUST KNOW THAT I C-CAN'T LET YOU DIE... AT LEAST NOT YET!
'M GOING TO F-DESTRUCT-- O YOU MUST GO NOW!!
WHAT?
I C-CAN'T HOLD ON ANY L-LONGER. TH-THIS IS THE ONLY OPTION LEFT...
UNDERSTAND? Y-YOU...HAVE TO... L-LIVE...
YOU SAVE ME...?
OH, HELL NO!!

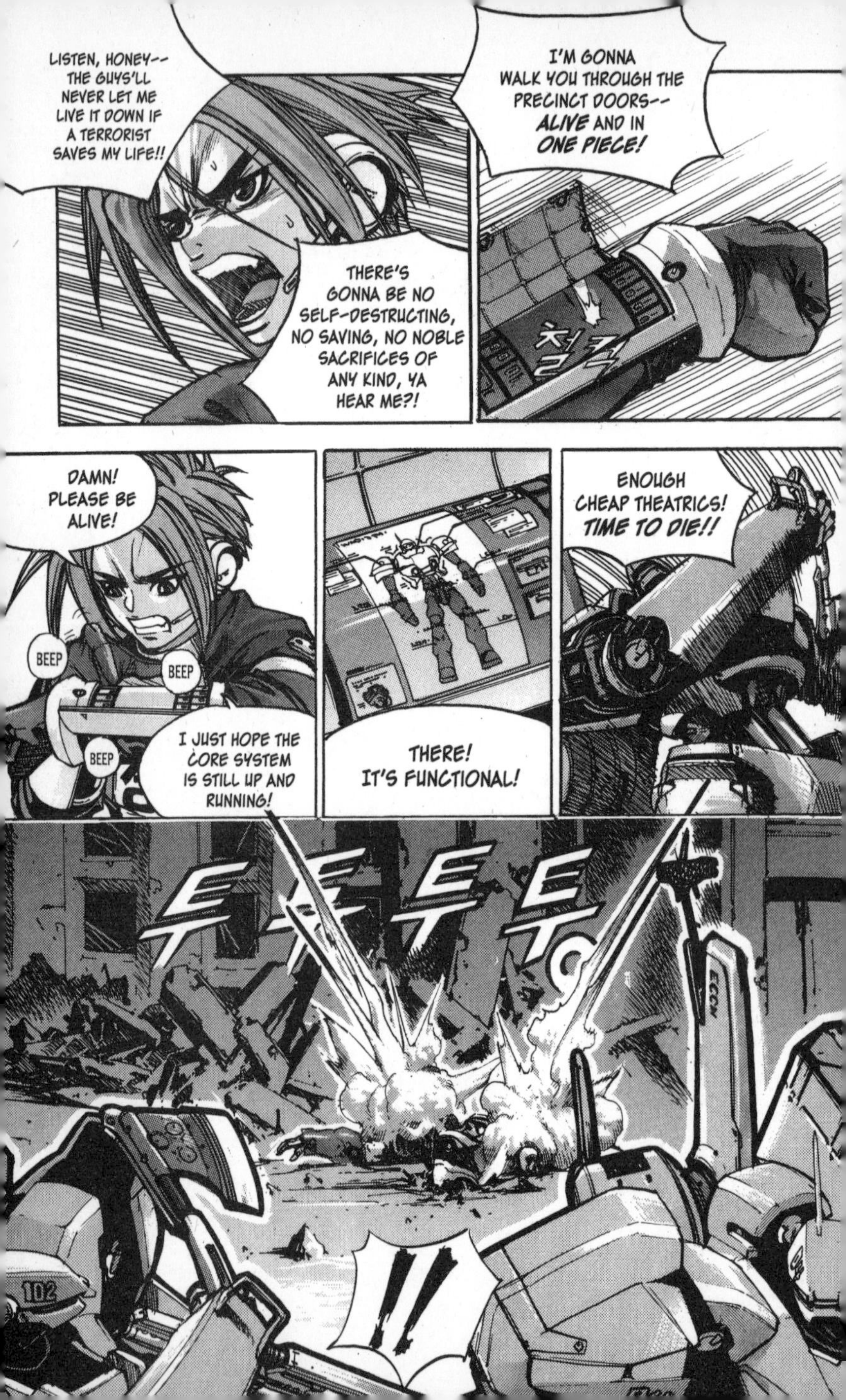

LISTEN, HONEY-- THE GUYS'LL NEVER LET ME LIVE IT DOWN IF A TERRORIST SAVES MY LIFE!!
THERE'S GONNA BE NO SELF-DESTRUCTING, NO SAVING, NO NOBLE SACRIFICES OF ANY KIND, YA HEAR ME?!
I'M GONNA WALK YOU THROUGH THE PRECINCT DOORS-- ALIVE AND IN ONE PIECE!
DAMN! PLEASE BE ALIVE!
BEEP
BEEP
BEEP
I JUST HOPE THE CORE SYSTEM IS STILL UP AND RUNNING!
THERE! IT'S FUNCTIONAL!
ENOUGH CHEAP THEATRICS! TIME TO DIE!!
!!

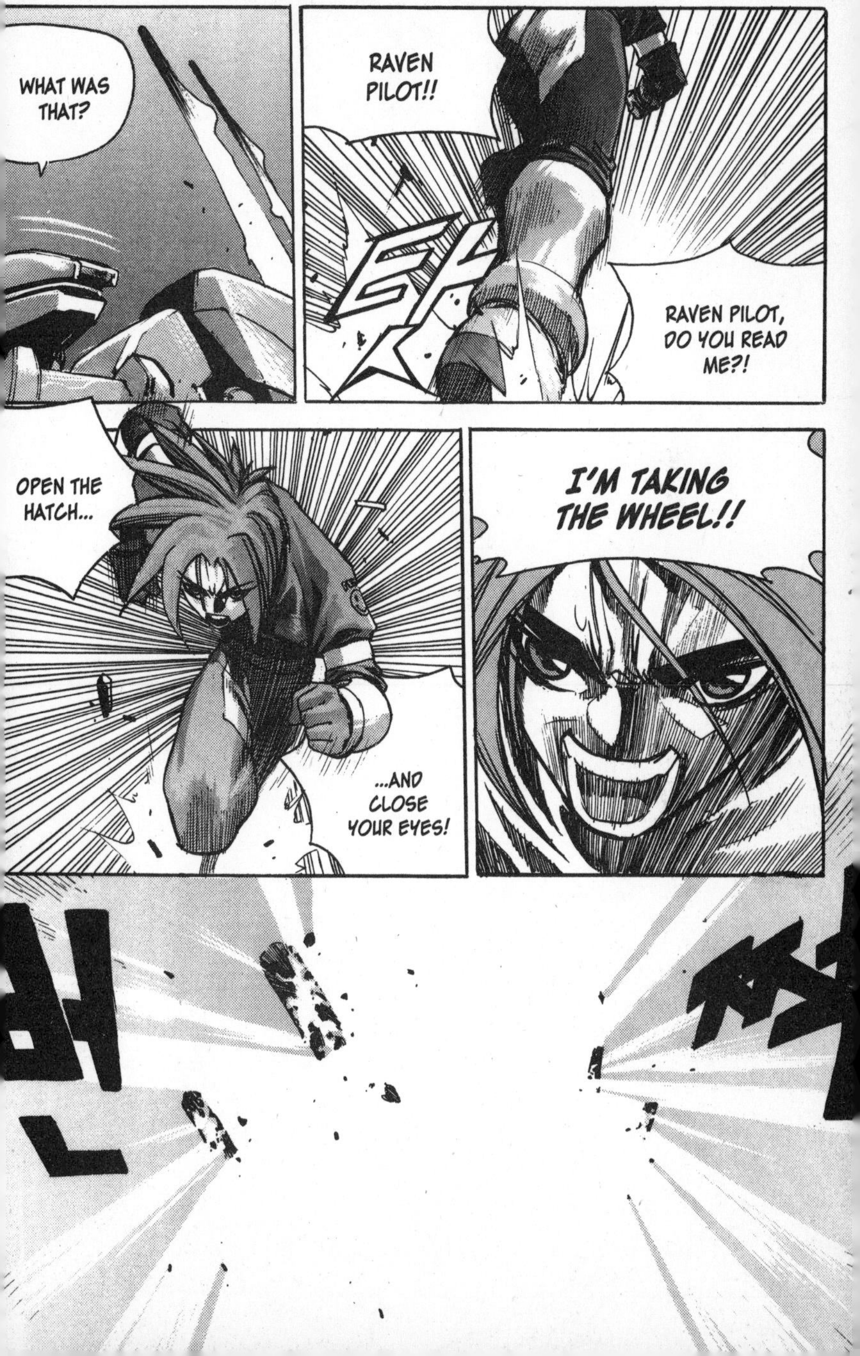
WHAT WAS THAT?
RAVEN PILOT!!
RAVEN PILOT, DO YOU READ ME?!
OPEN THE HATCH...
...AND CLOSE YOUR EYES!
I'M TAKING THE WHEEL!!

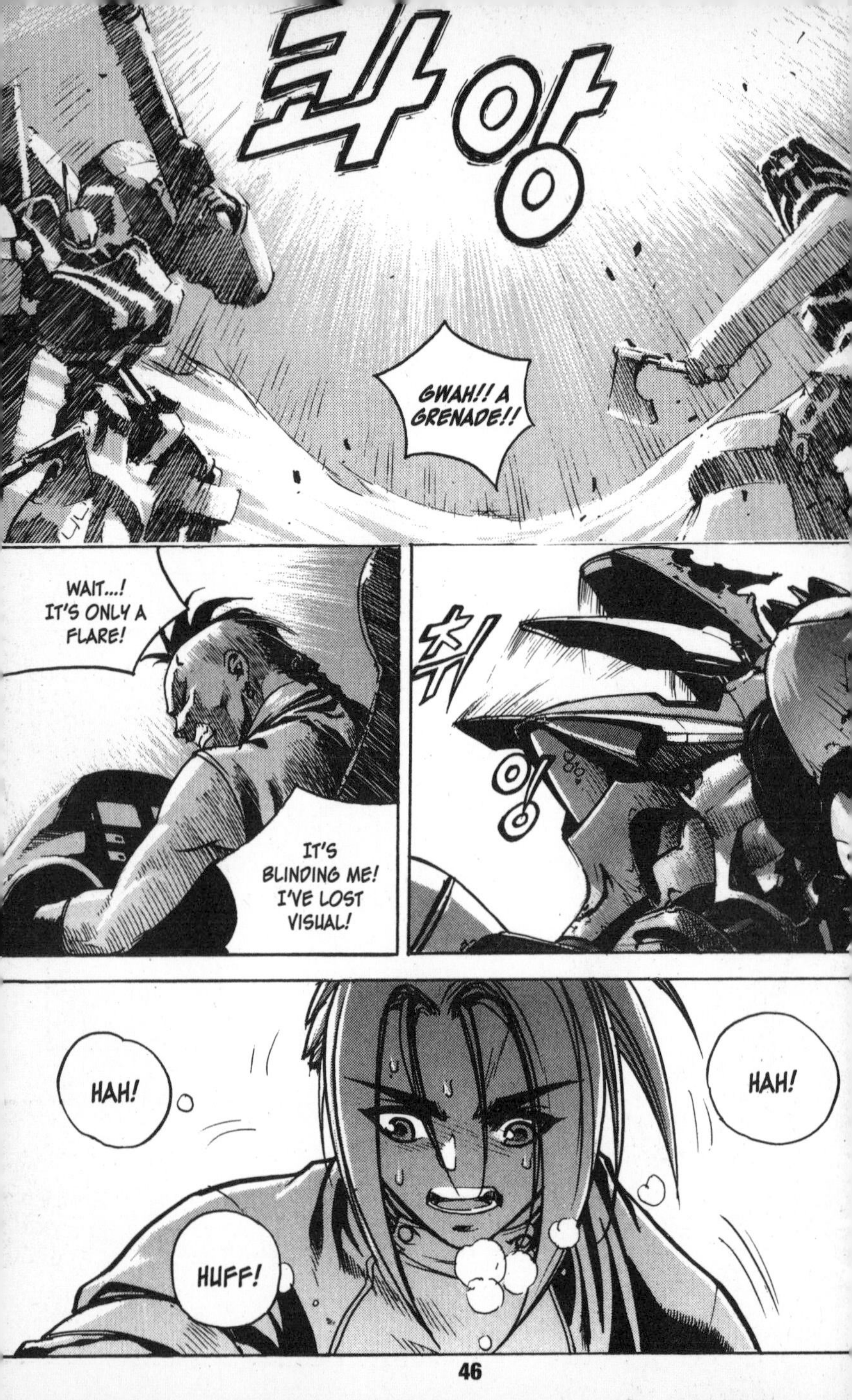
콰앙
GWAH!! A GRENADE!!
WAIT...! IT'S ONLY A FLARE!
IT'S BLINDING ME! I'VE LOST VISUAL!
HAH!
HAH!
HUFF!

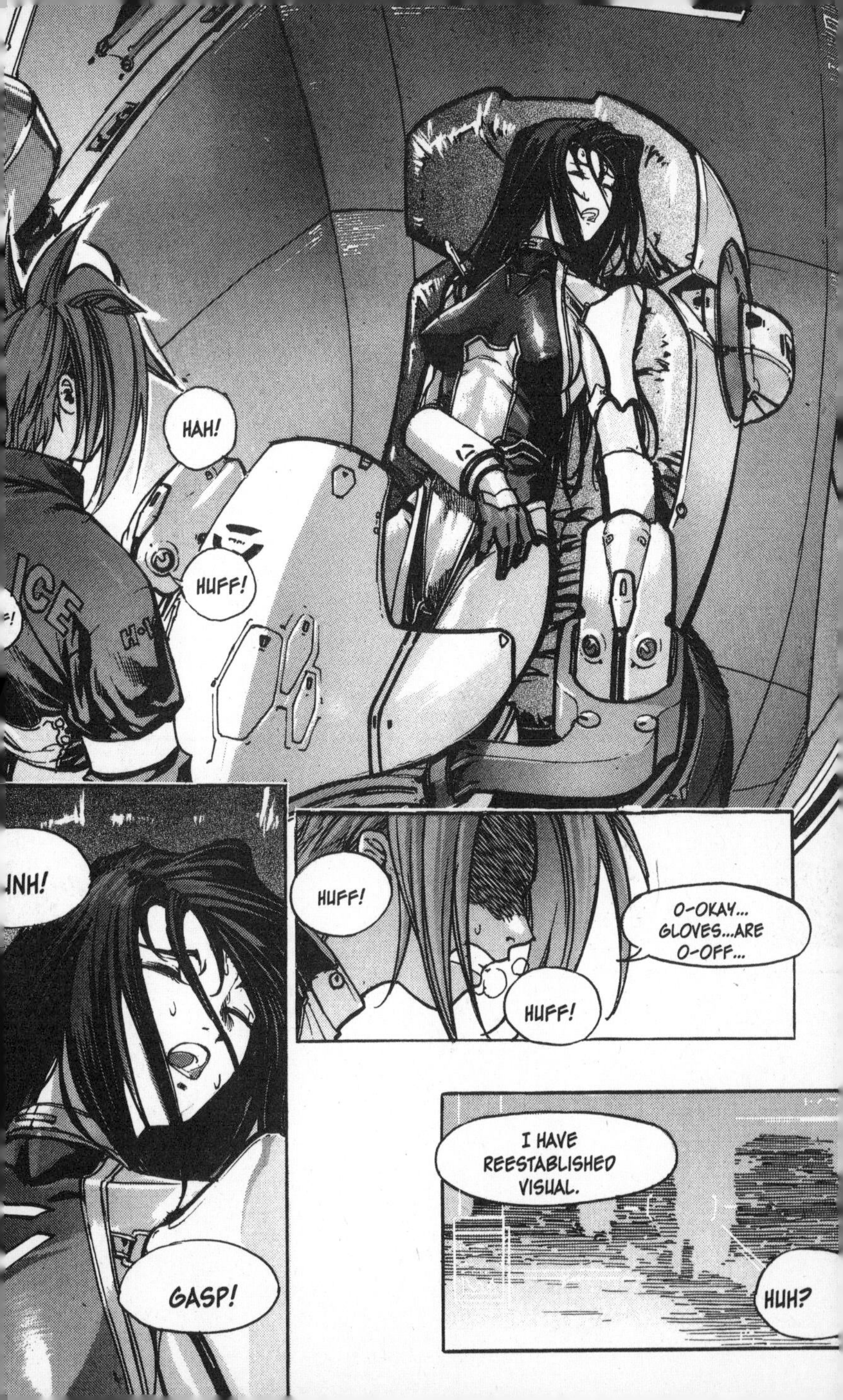
HAH!
HUFF!
GASP!
HUFF!
O-OKAY... GLOVES...ARE O-OFF...
HUFF!
I HAVE REESTABLISHED VISUAL.
HUH?

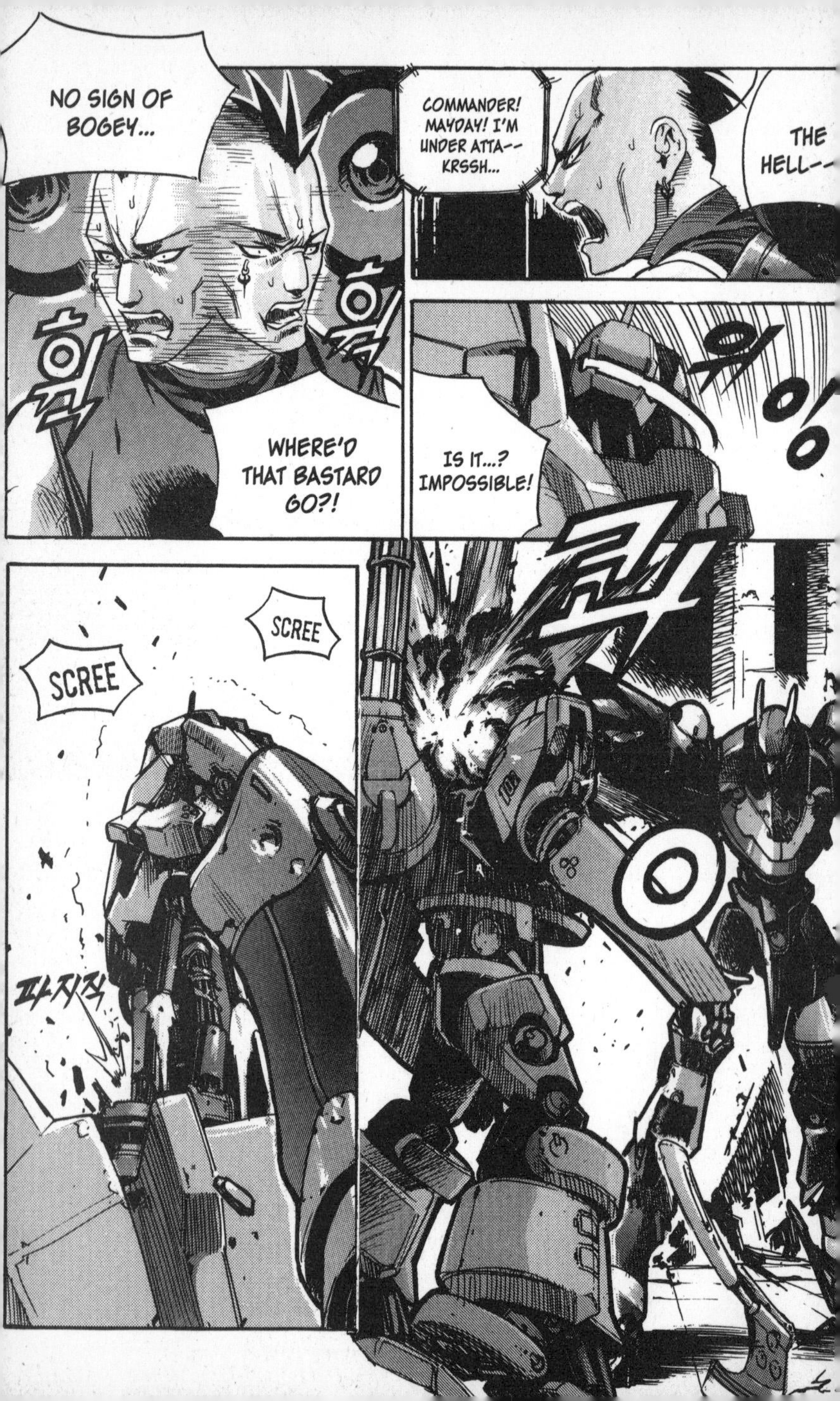
NO SIGN OF BOGEY...
WHERE'D THAT BASTARD GO?!
흐읍
흐읍
COMMANDER! MAYDAY! I'M UNDER ATTA-- KRSSH...
THE HELL--
IS IT...? IMPOSSIBLE!
와아아
SCREE
SCREE
파지직

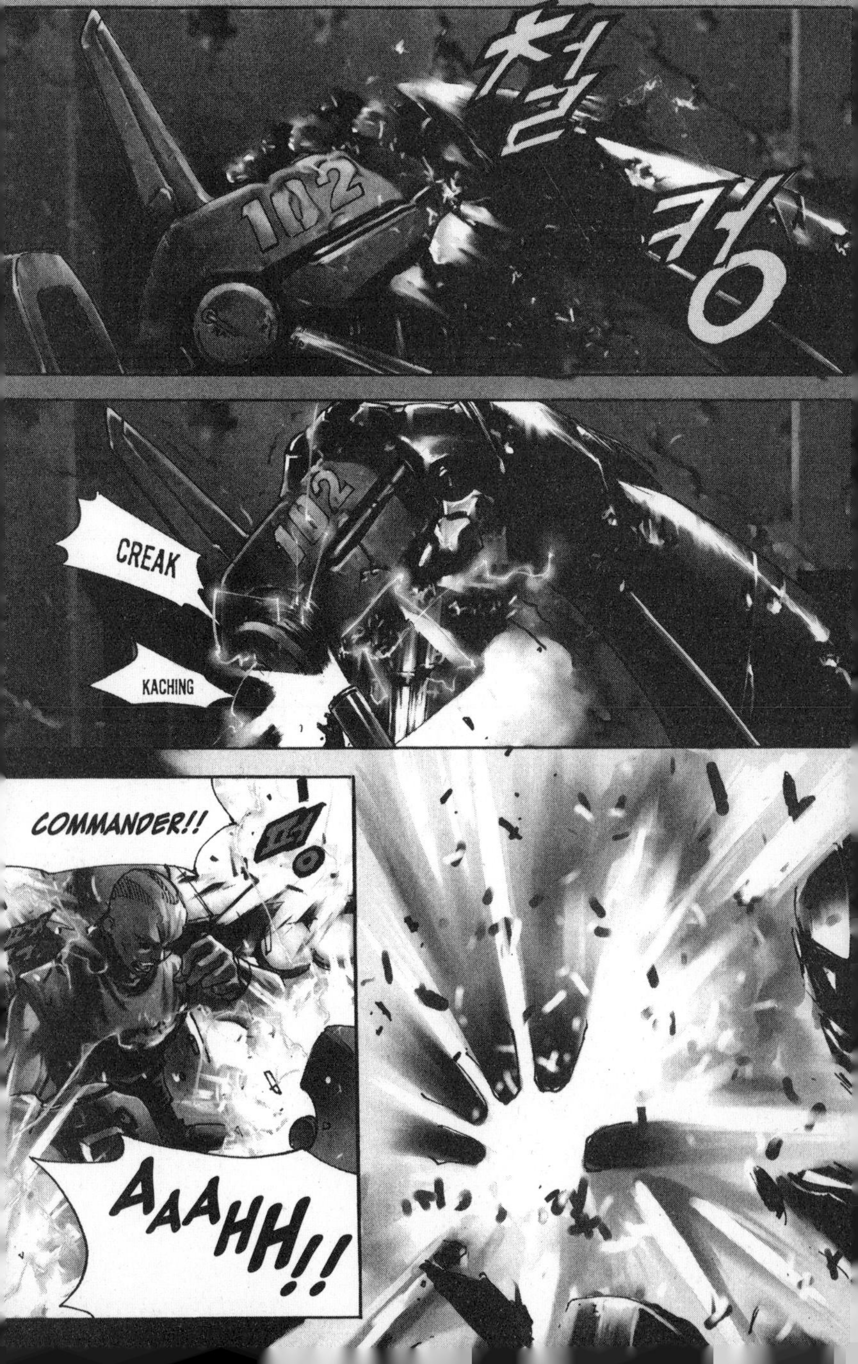
철컹
CREAK
KACHING
COMMANDER!!
AAAHH!!

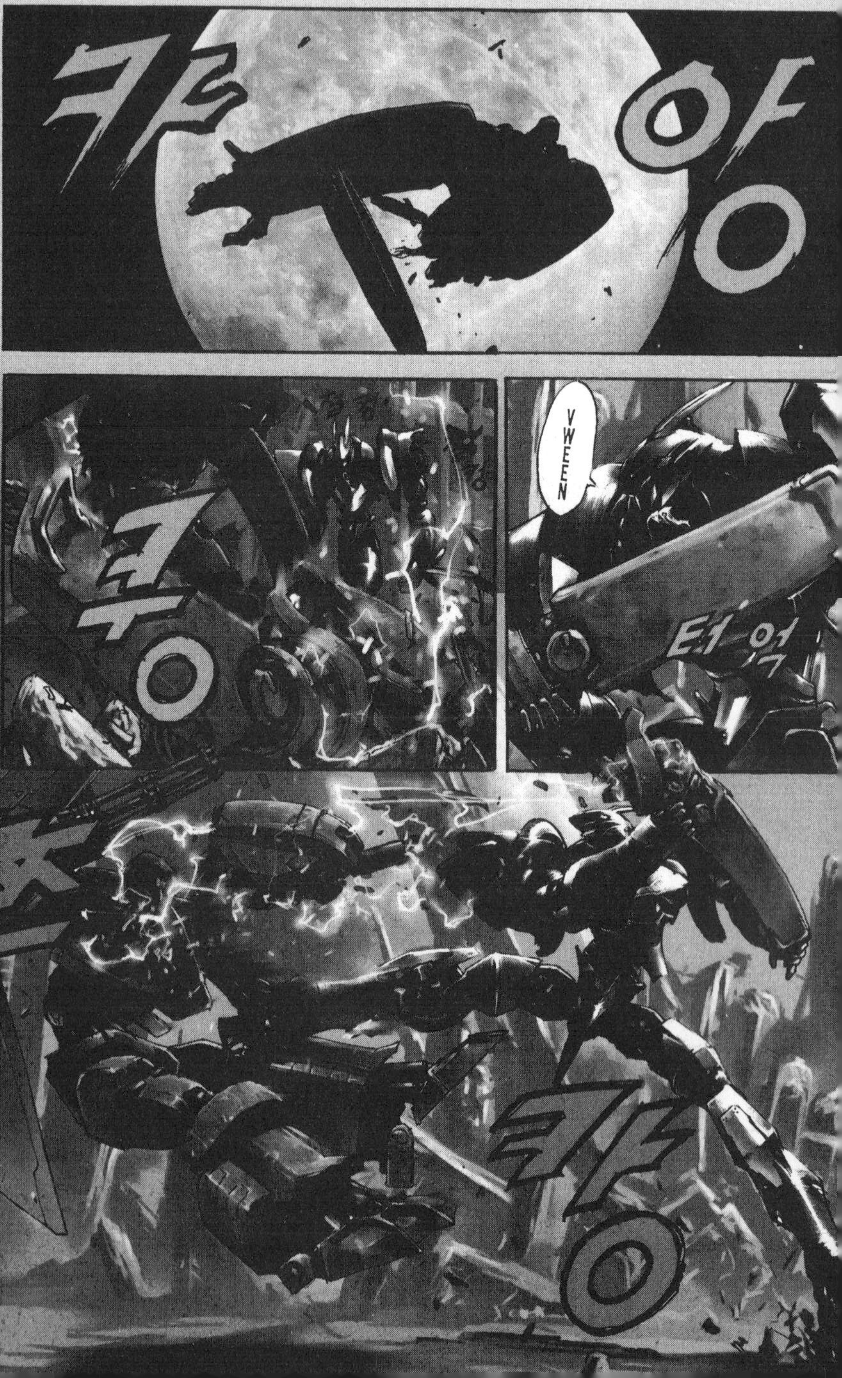
카앙
쿵
VWEEN
캉

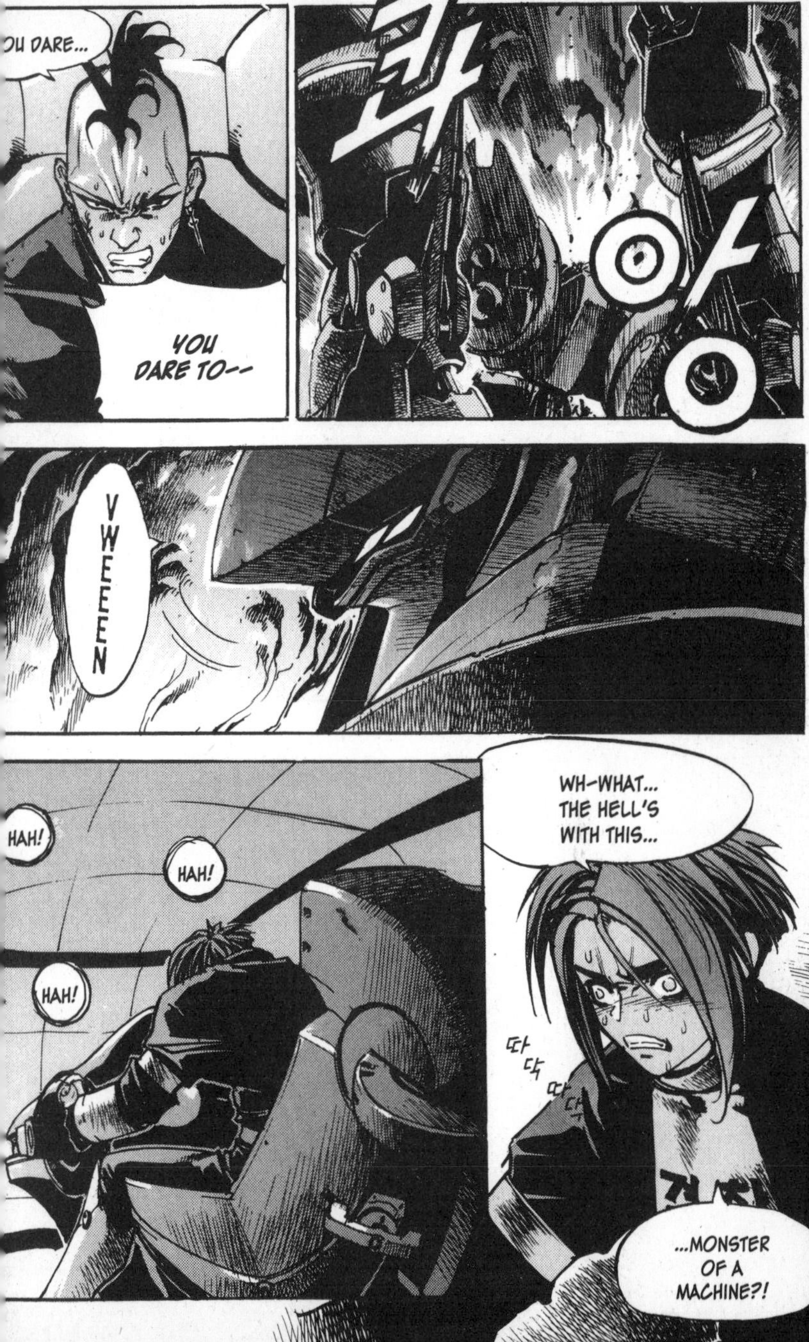
OU DARE...
YOU DARE TO--
콰앙
VWEEEEN
HAH!
HAH!
HAH!
WH-WHAT... THE HELL'S WITH THIS...
따닥 따닥
...MONSTER OF A MACHINE?!

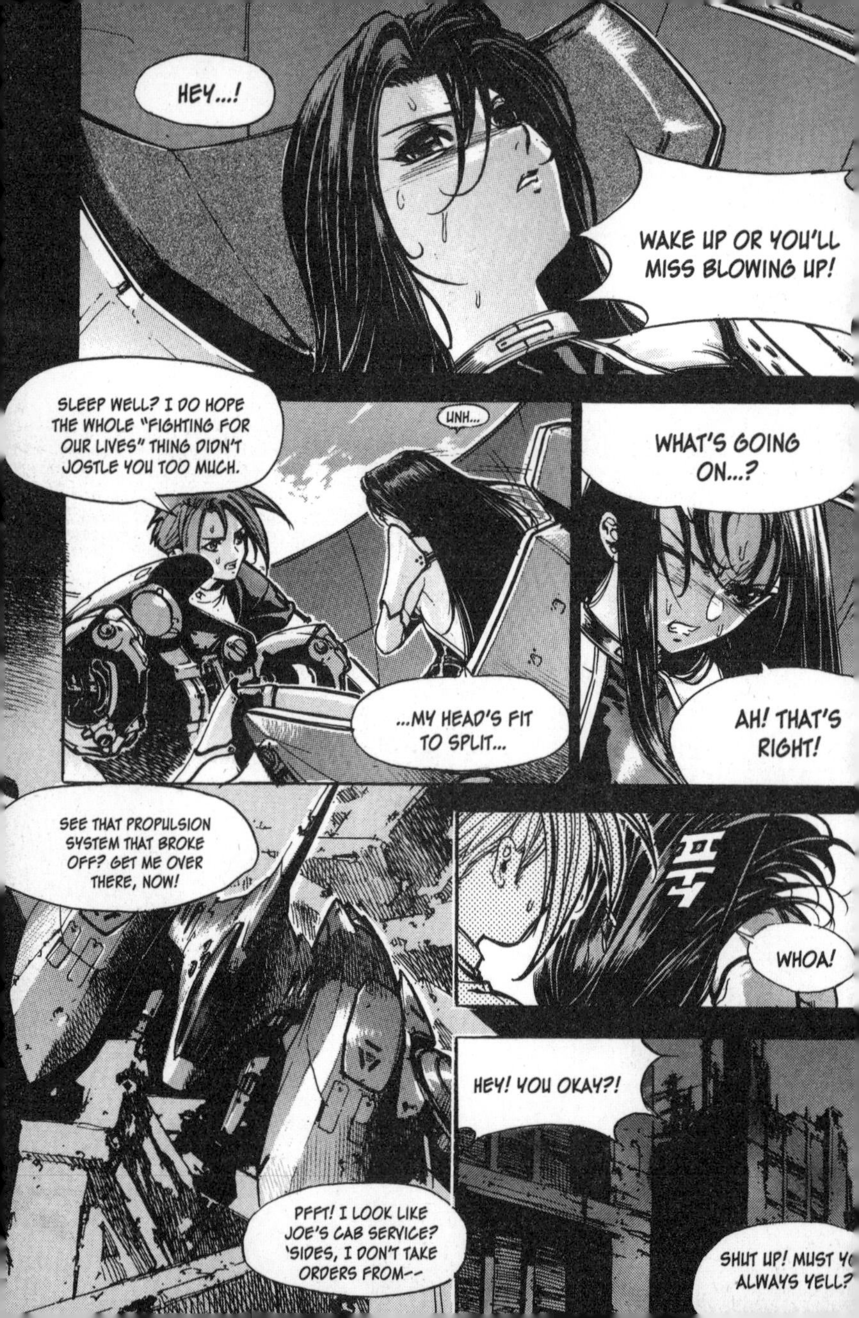
HEY...!
WAKE UP OR YOU'LL MISS BLOWING UP!
SLEEP WELL? I DO HOPE THE WHOLE "FIGHTING FOR OUR LIVES" THING DIDN'T JOSTLE YOU TOO MUCH.
UNH...
...MY HEAD'S FIT TO SPLIT...
WHAT'S GOING ON...?
AH! THAT'S RIGHT!
SEE THAT PROPULSION SYSTEM THAT BROKE OFF? GET ME OVER THERE, NOW!
WHOA!
HEY! YOU OKAY?!
PFFT! I LOOK LIKE JOE'S CAB SERVICE? 'SIDES, I DON'T TAKE ORDERS FROM--
SHUT UP! MUST YO ALWAYS YELL?

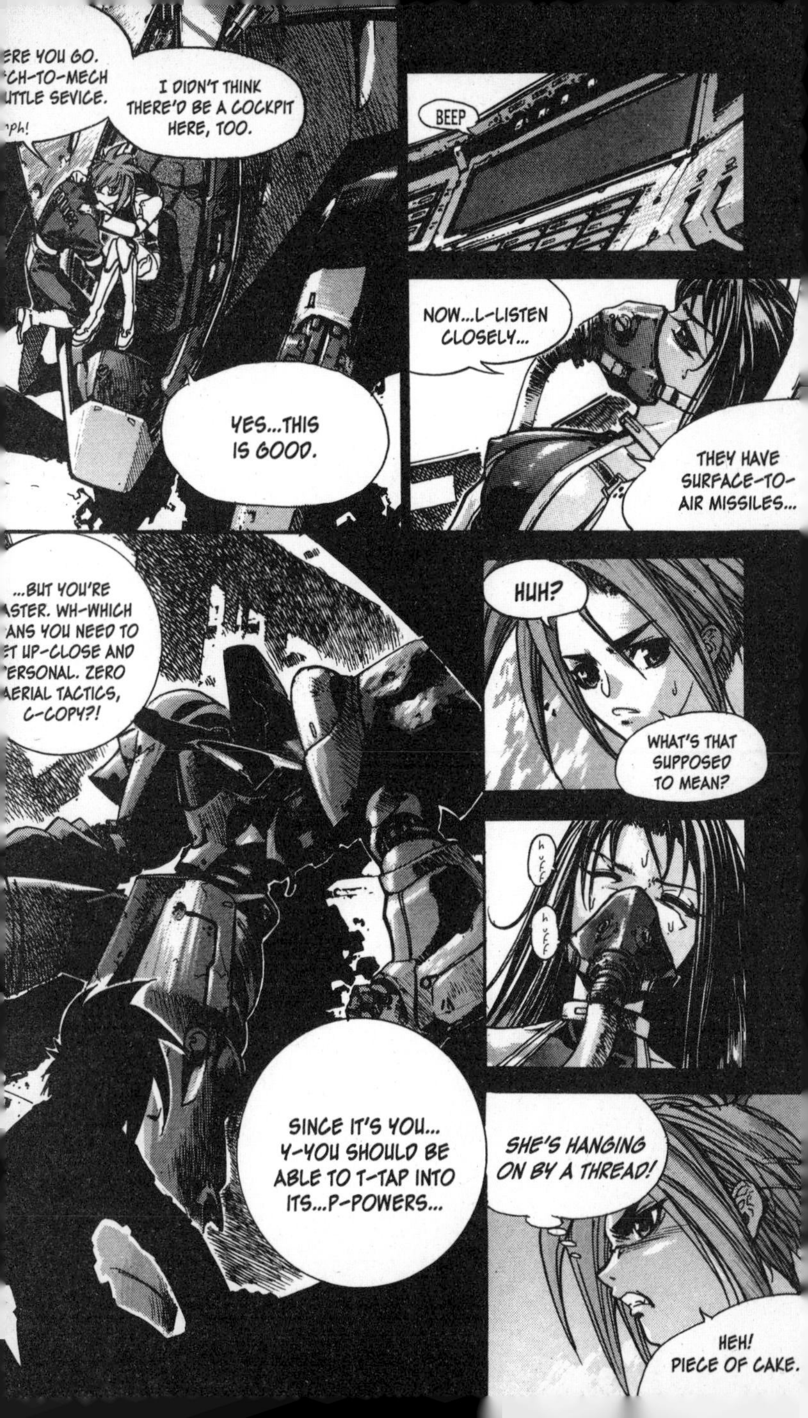

ERE YOU GO. CH-TO-MECH UTTLE SEVICE.
ph!
I DIDN'T THINK THERE'D BE A COCKPIT HERE, TOO.
YES...THIS IS GOOD.
BEEP
NOW...L-LISTEN CLOSELY...
THEY HAVE SURFACE-TO-AIR MISSILES...
...BUT YOU'RE ASTER. WH-WHICH ANS YOU NEED TO T UP-CLOSE AND ERSONAL. ZERO AERIAL TACTICS, C-COPY?!
SINCE IT'S YOU... Y-YOU SHOULD BE ABLE TO T-TAP INTO ITS...P-POWERS...
HUH?
WHAT'S THAT SUPPOSED TO MEAN?
huff
huff
SHE'S HANGING ON BY A THREAD!
HEH! PIECE OF CAKE.

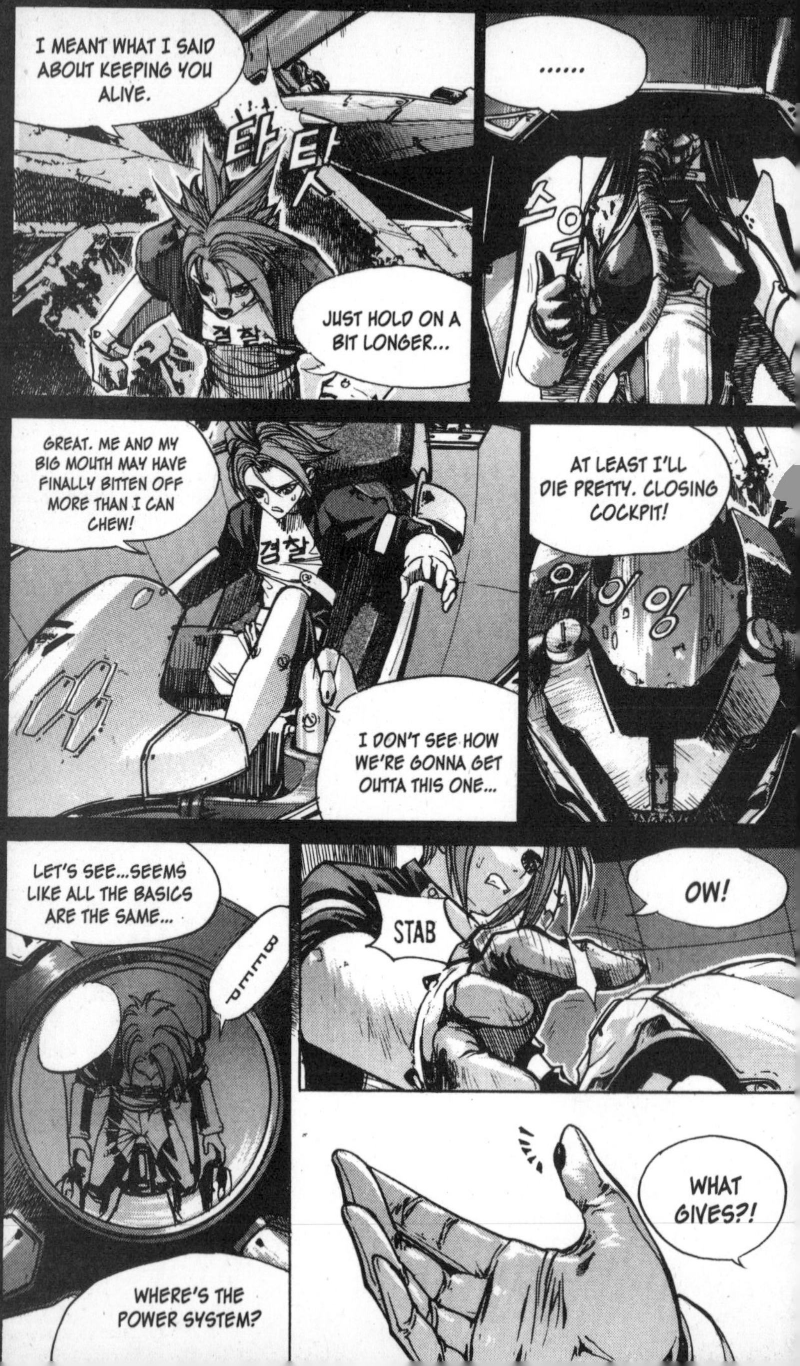
I MEANT WHAT I SAID ABOUT KEEPING YOU ALIVE.
타타
경찰
JUST HOLD ON A BIT LONGER...
......
GREAT. ME AND MY BIG MOUTH MAY HAVE FINALLY BITTEN OFF MORE THAN I CAN CHEW!
경찰
I DON'T SEE HOW WE'RE GONNA GET OUTTA THIS ONE...
AT LEAST I'LL DIE PRETTY. CLOSING COCKPIT!
위이잉
LET'S SEE...SEEMS LIKE ALL THE BASICS ARE THE SAME...
WHERE'S THE POWER SYSTEM?
STAB
OW!
WHAT GIVES?!

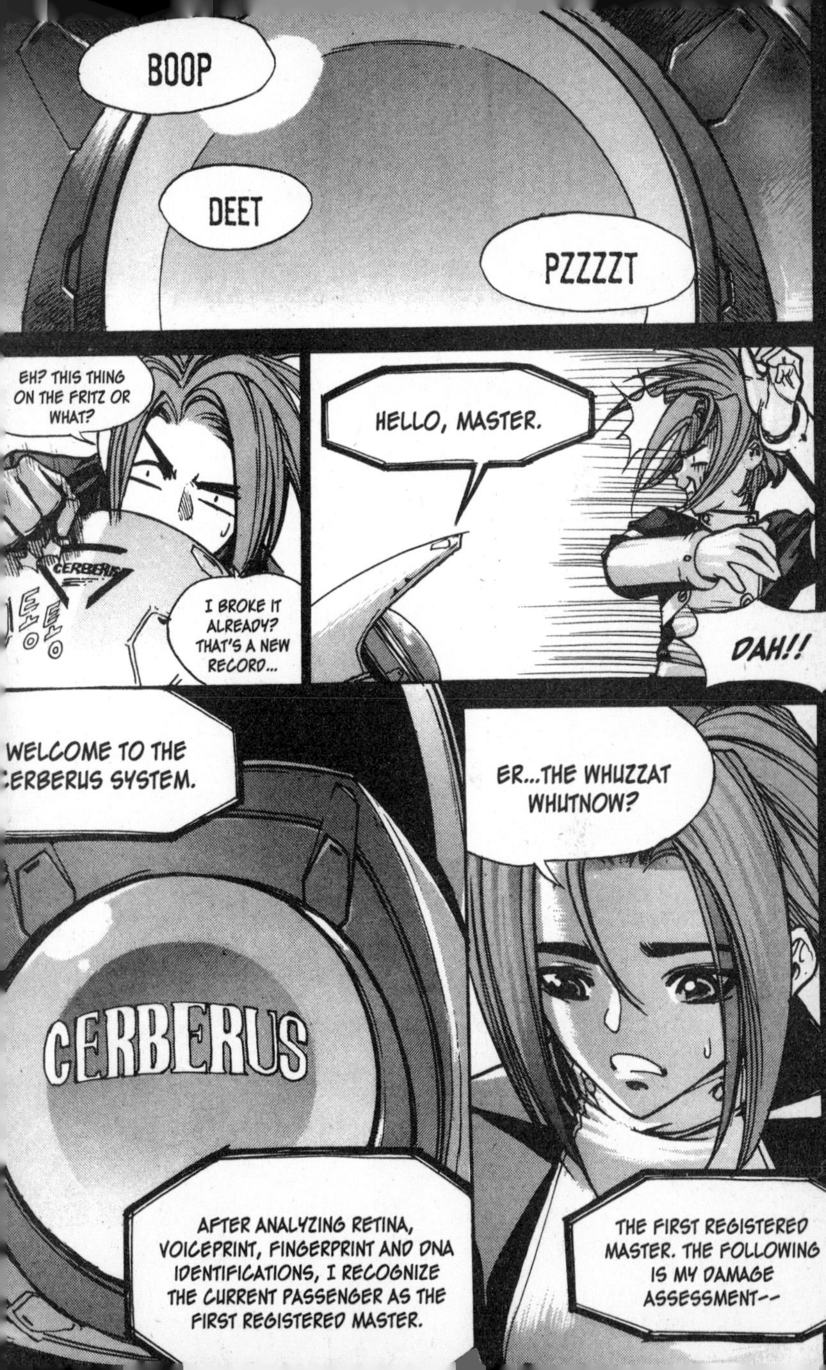
BOOP
DEET
PZZZZT
EH? THIS THING ON THE FRITZ OR WHAT?
I BROKE IT ALREADY? THAT'S A NEW RECORD...
HELLO, MASTER.
DAH!!
WELCOME TO THE ERBERUS SYSTEM.
CERBERUS
ER...THE WHUZZAT WHUTNOW?
AFTER ANALYZING RETINA, VOICEPRINT, FINGERPRINT AND DNA IDENTIFICATIONS, I RECOGNIZE THE CURRENT PASSENGER AS THE FIRST REGISTERED MASTER.
THE FIRST REGISTERED MASTER. THE FOLLOWING IS MY DAMAGE ASSESSMENT--

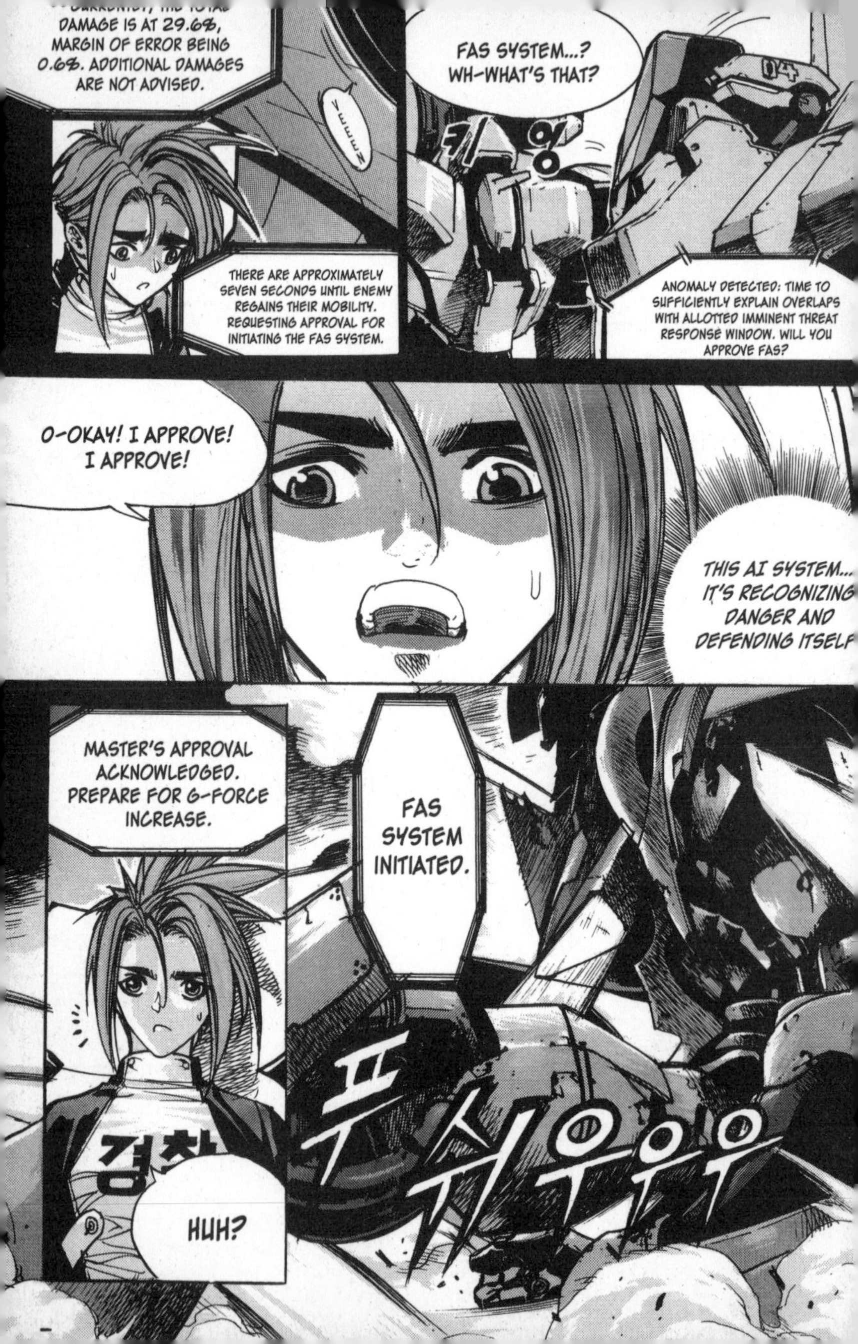
DAMAGE IS AT 29.6%, MARGIN OF ERROR BEING 0.6%. ADDITIONAL DAMAGES ARE NOT ADVISED.
VEEEEN
THERE ARE APPROXIMATELY SEVEN SECONDS UNTIL ENEMY REGAINS THEIR MOBILITY. REQUESTING APPROVAL FOR INITIATING THE FAS SYSTEM.
FAS SYSTEM...? WH-WHAT'S THAT?
ANOMALY DETECTED: TIME TO SUFFICIENTLY EXPLAIN OVERLAPS WITH ALLOTTED IMMINENT THREAT RESPONSE WINDOW. WILL YOU APPROVE FAS?
O-OKAY! I APPROVE! I APPROVE!
THIS AI SYSTEM... IT'S RECOGNIZING DANGER AND DEFENDING ITSELF
MASTER'S APPROVAL ACKNOWLEDGED. PREPARE FOR G-FORCE INCREASE.
FAS SYSTEM INITIATED.
HUH?

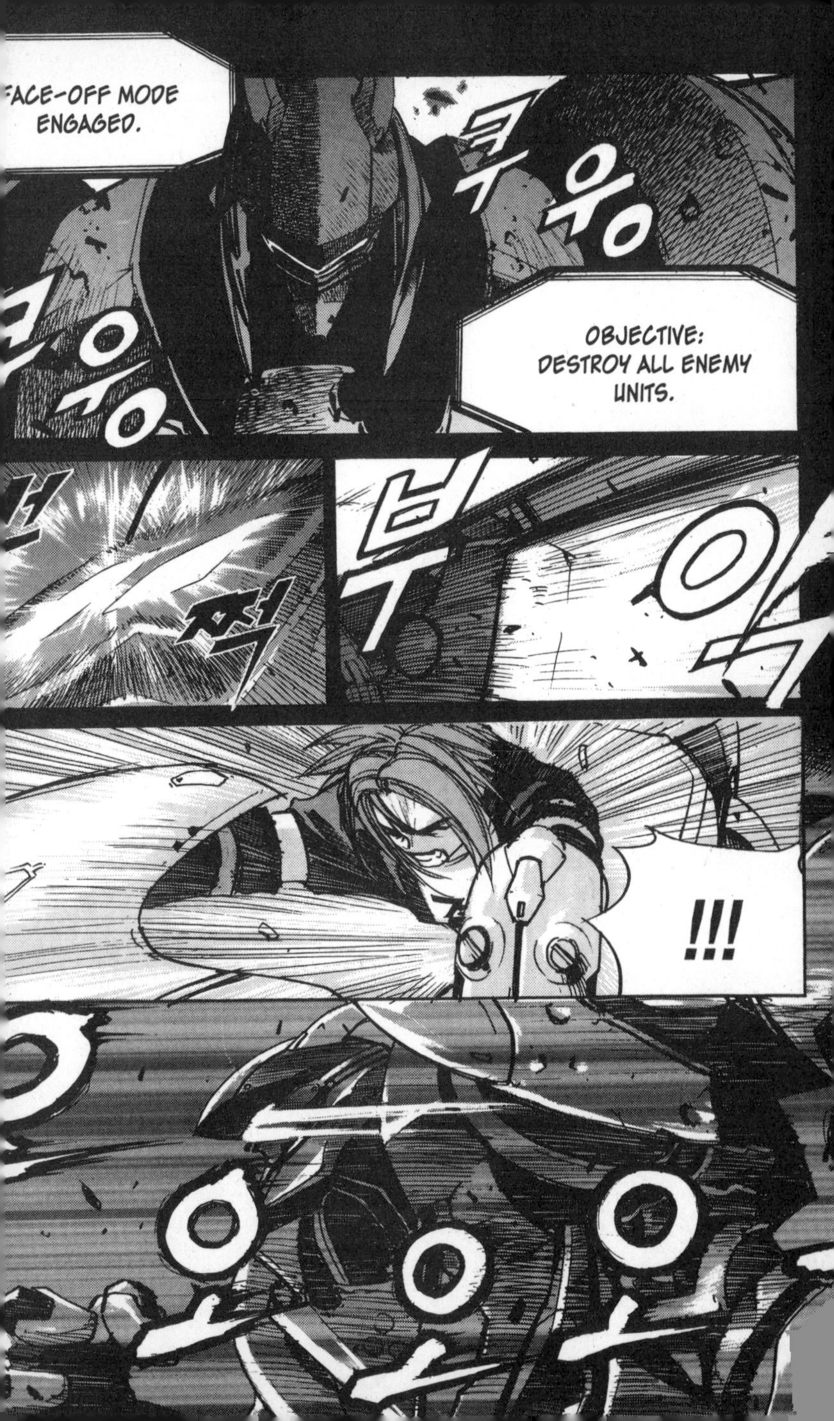
FACE-OFF MODE ENGAGED.
OBJECTIVE: DESTROY ALL ENEMY UNITS.
!!!

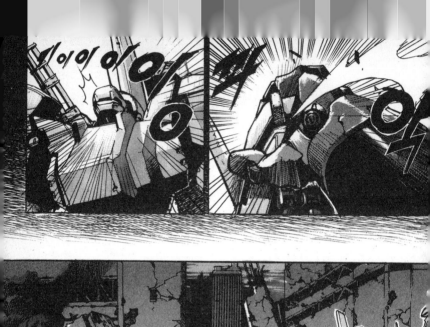

HEY! WHAT ARE YOU DOING JUST STANDING THERE?!

YAAAHH!!

SHOOT IT ALREADY! PUNCH THAT IRON LUNG FULL OF HOLES!!

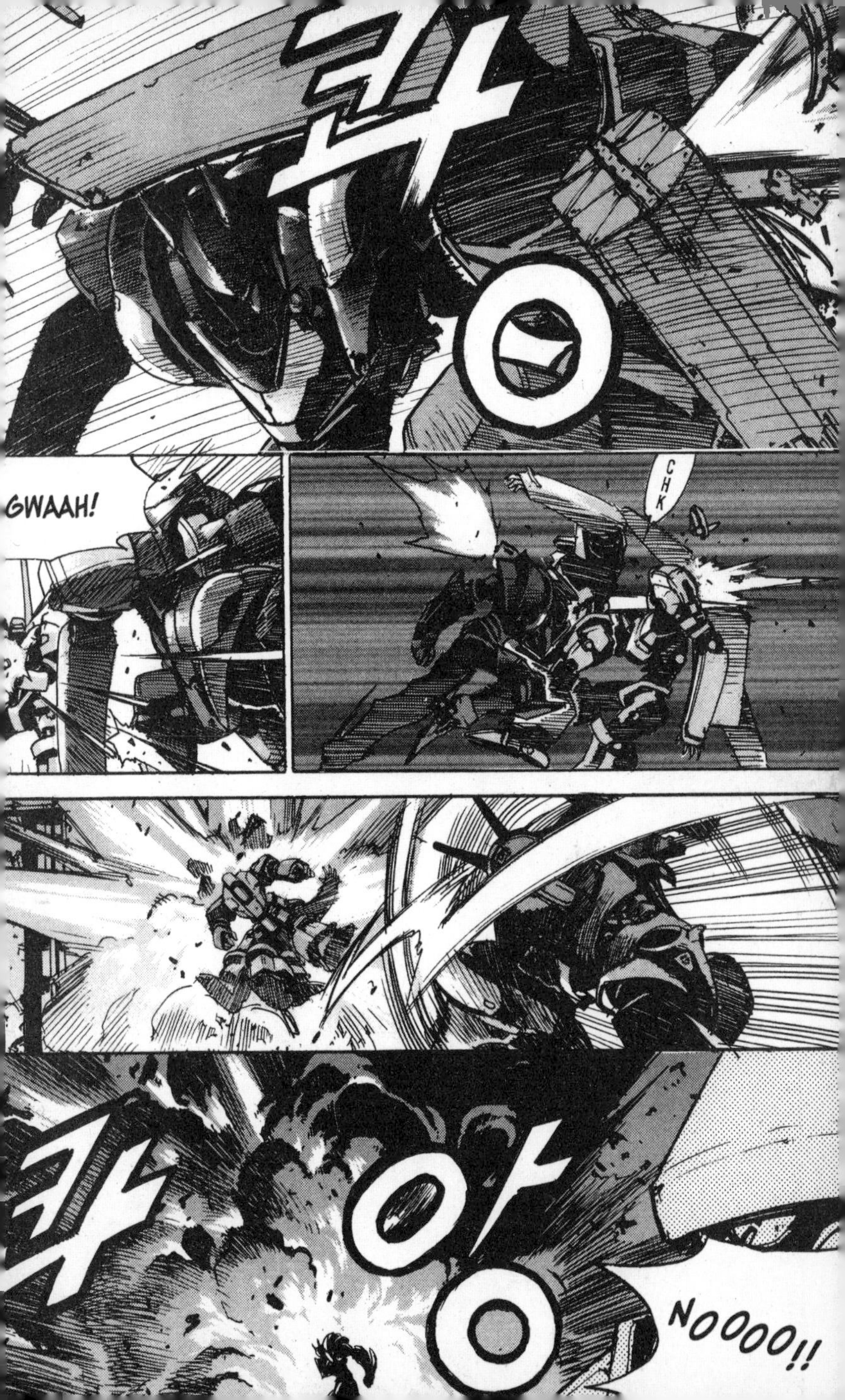
GWAAH!
CHK
NOOOO!!

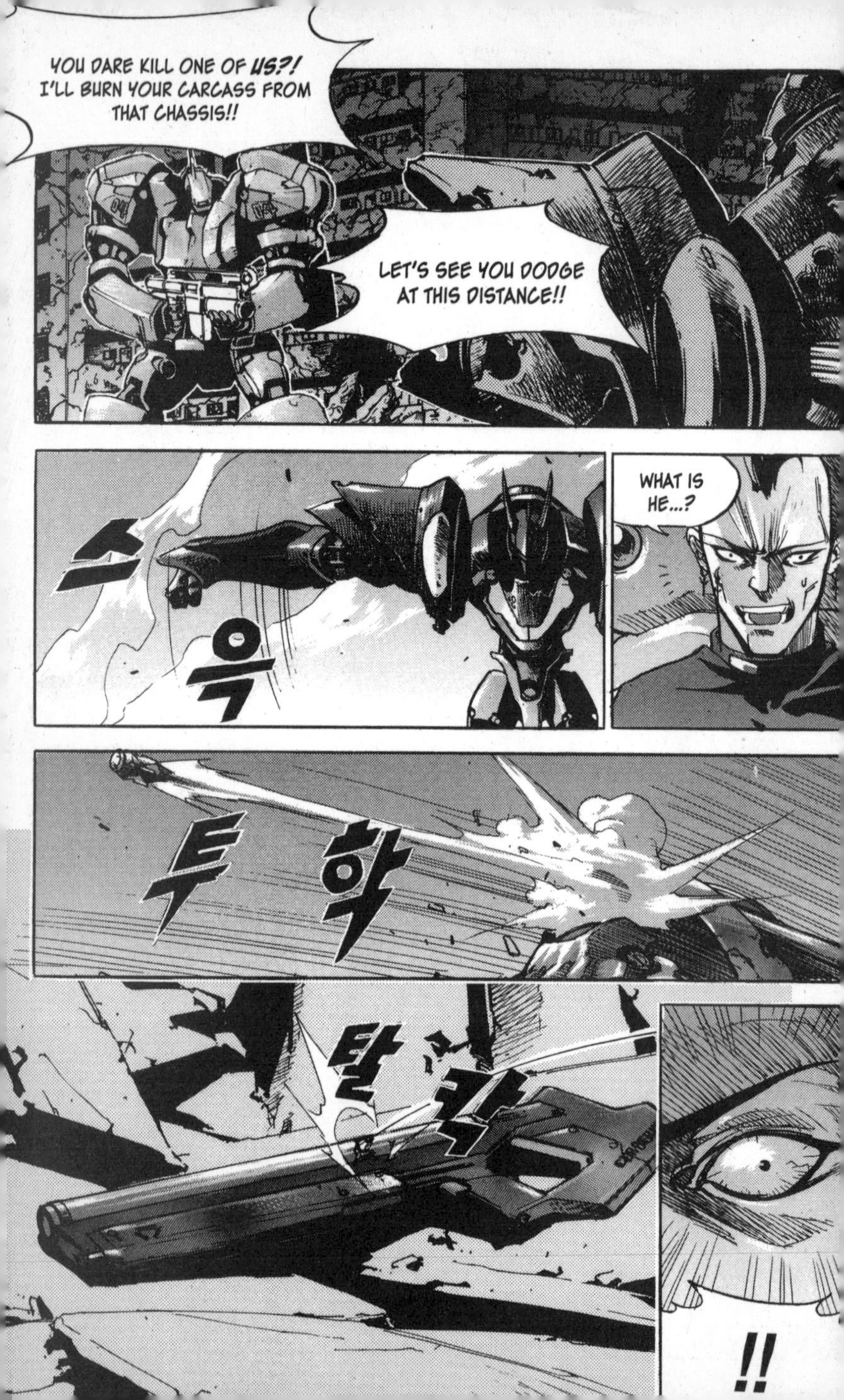
YOU DARE KILL ONE OF US?! I'LL BURN YOUR CARCASS FROM THAT CHASSIS!!
LET'S SEE YOU DODGE AT THIS DISTANCE!!
WHAT IS HE...?
!!

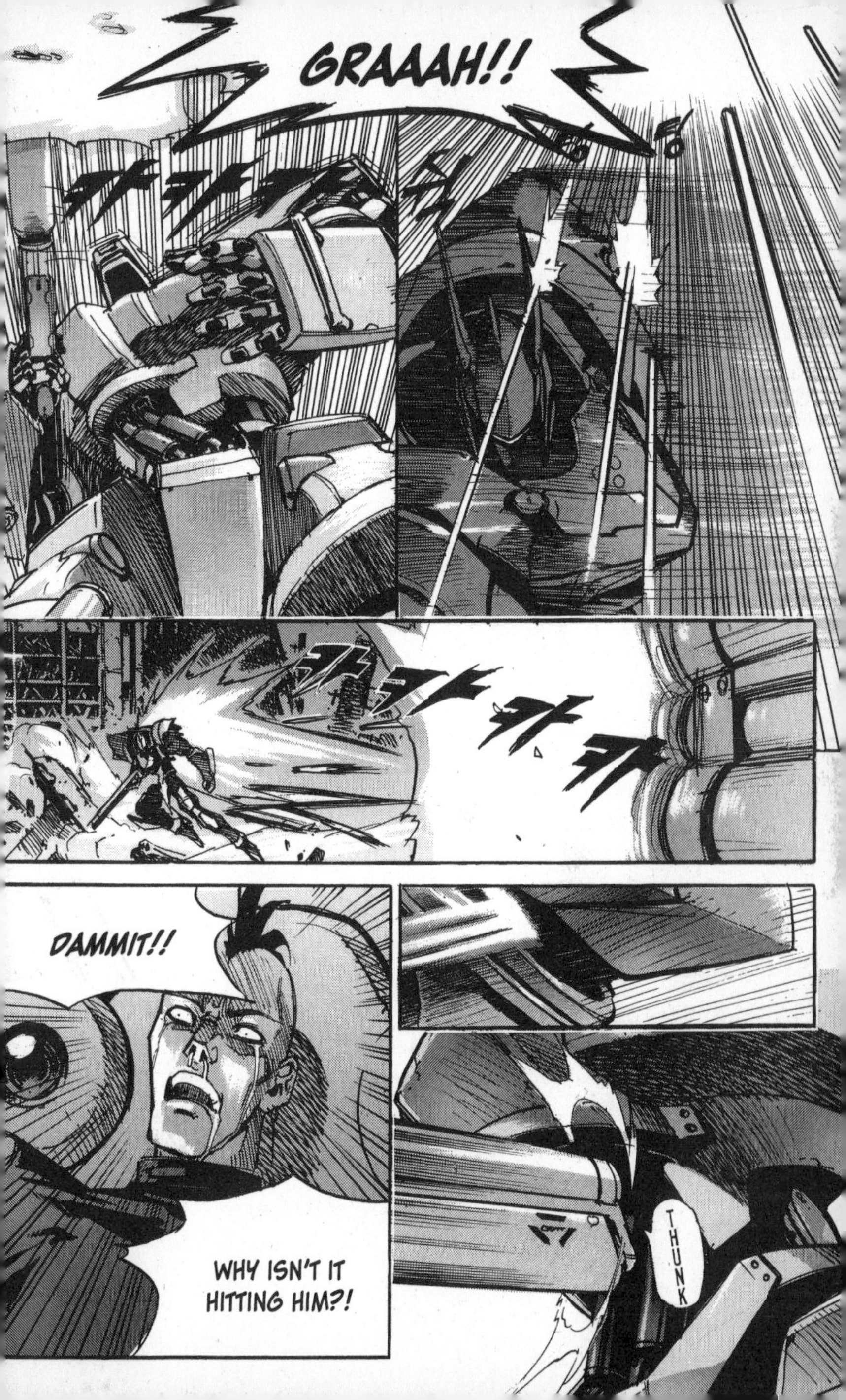
GRAAAH!!
DAMMIT!!
WHY ISN'T IT HITTING HIM?!
THUNK

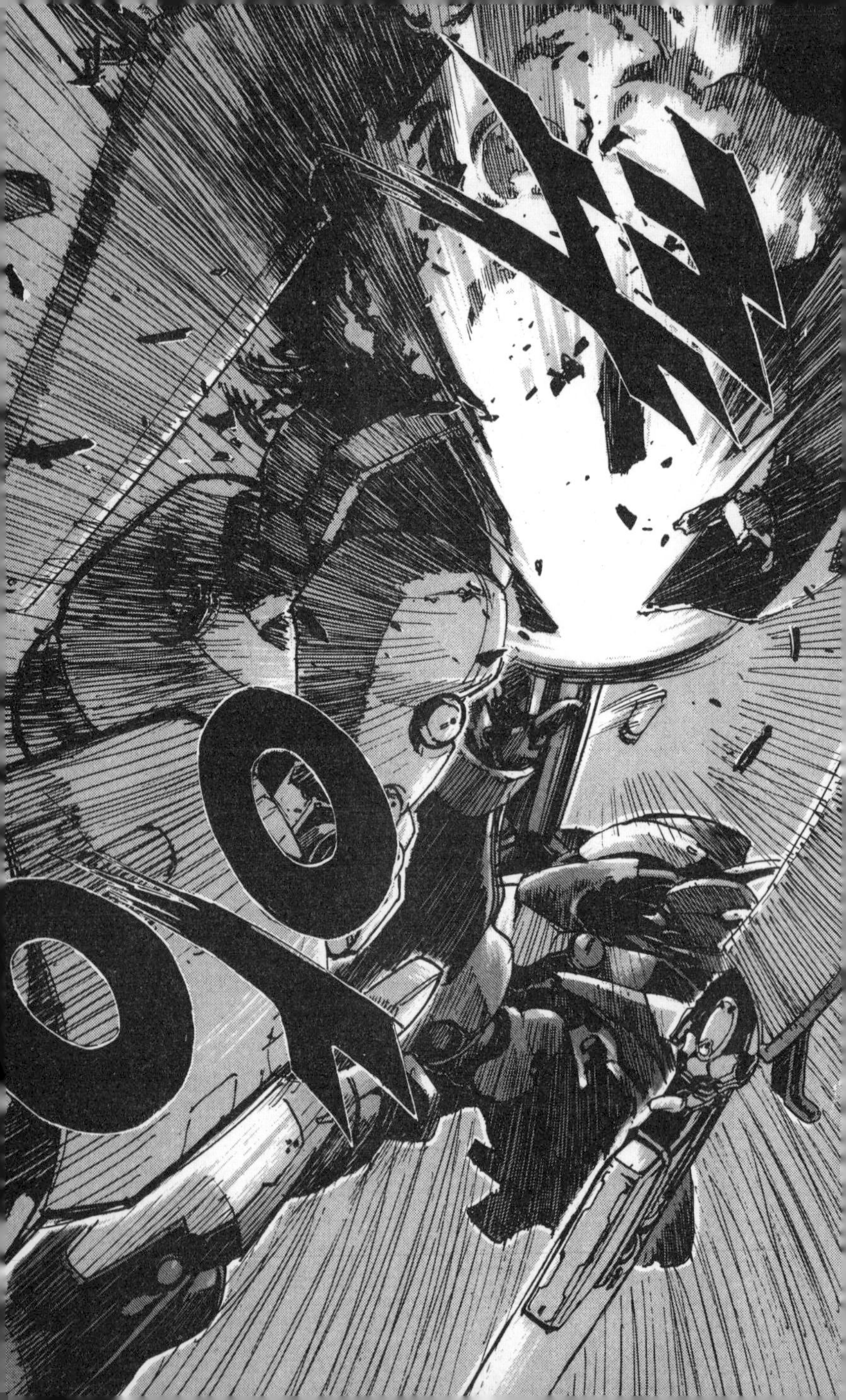

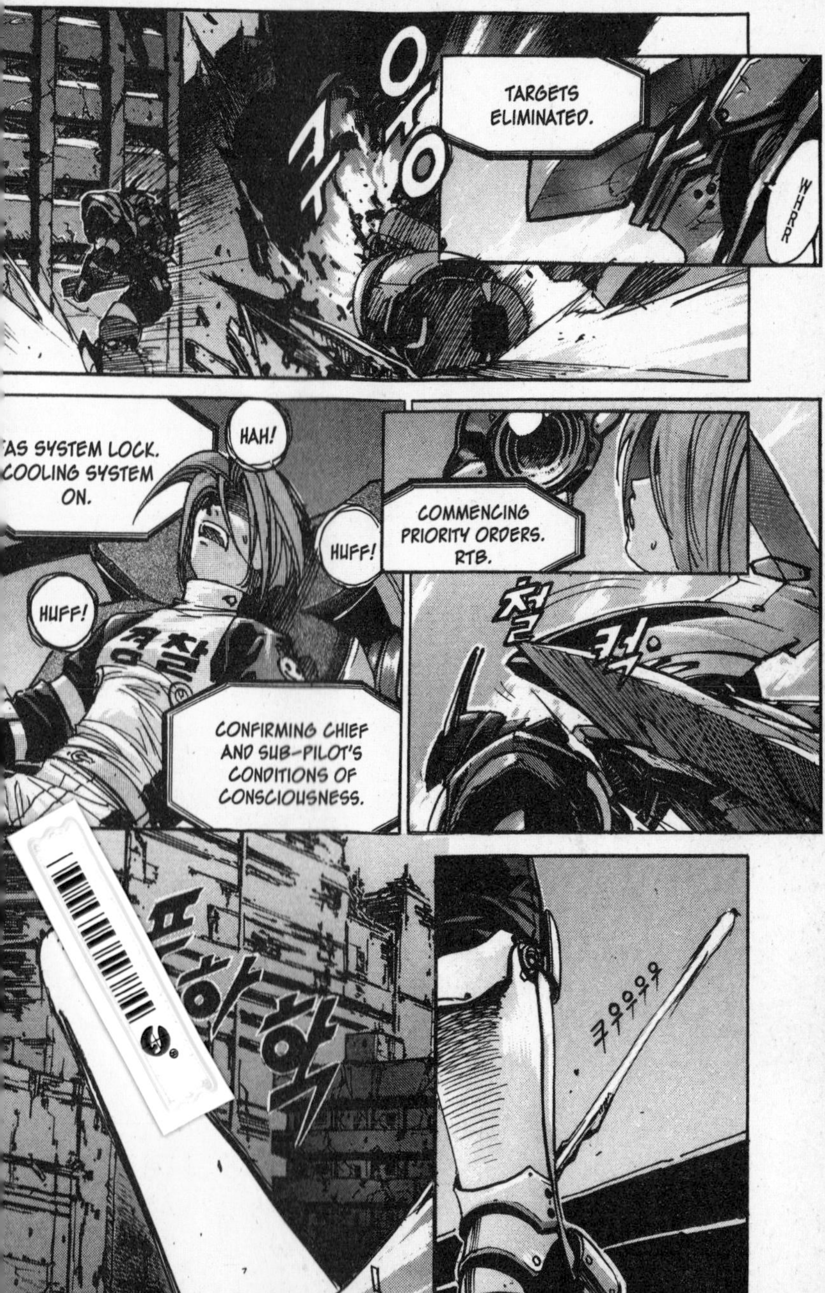
TARGETS ELIMINATED.
WHRRR
AS SYSTEM LOCK. COOLING SYSTEM ON.
HAH!
HUFF!
HUFF!
CONFIRMING CHIEF AND SUB-PILOT'S CONDITIONS OF CONSCIOUSNESS.
COMMENCING PRIORITY ORDERS. RTB.
철컥
쿠우우우우

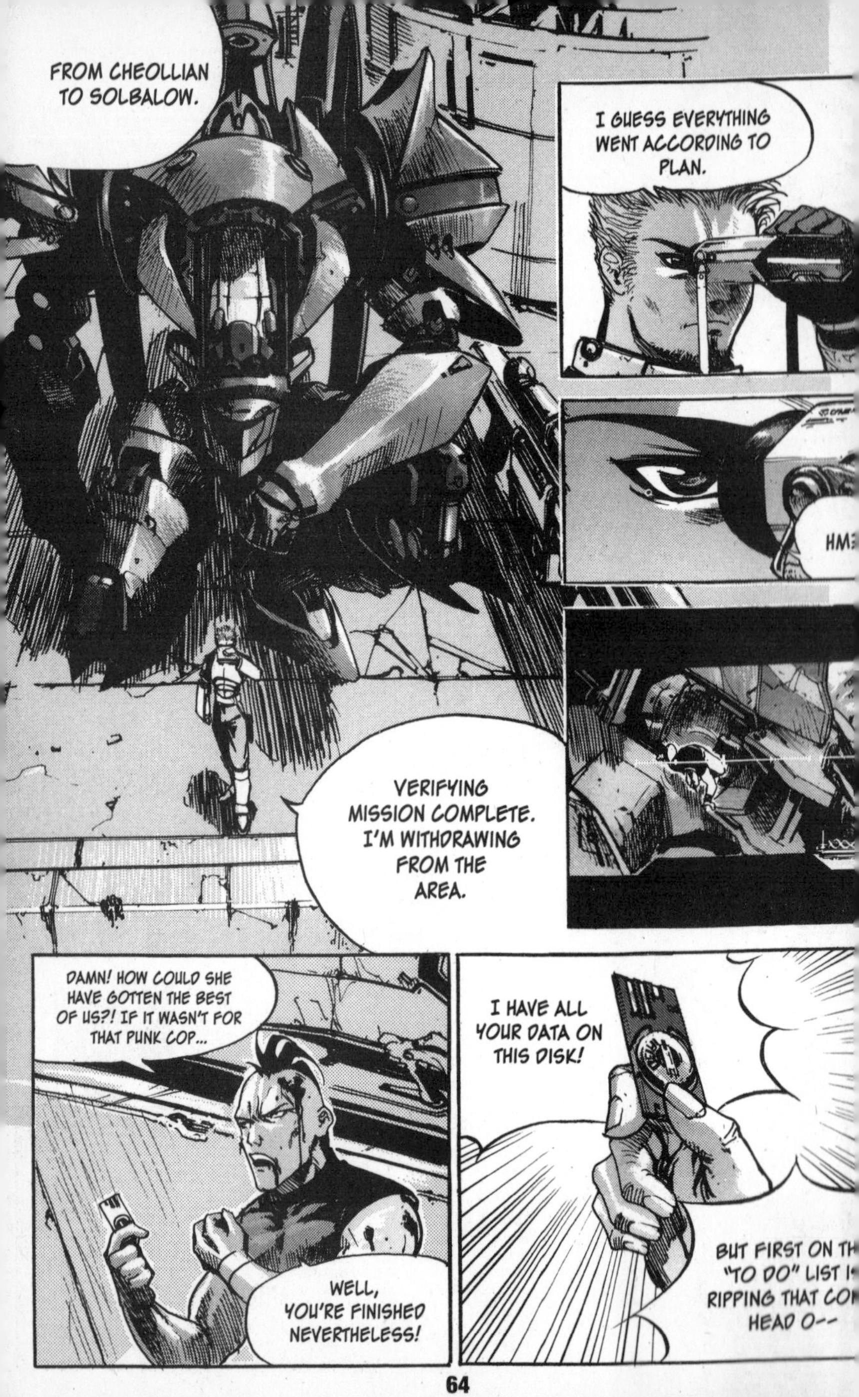
FROM CHEOLLIAN TO SOLBALOW.
VERIFYING MISSION COMPLETE. I'M WITHDRAWING FROM THE AREA.
I GUESS EVERYTHING WENT ACCORDING TO PLAN.
HM
DAMN! HOW COULD SHE HAVE GOTTEN THE BEST OF US?! IF IT WASN'T FOR THAT PUNK COP...
WELL, YOU'RE FINISHED NEVERTHELESS!
I HAVE ALL YOUR DATA ON THIS DISK!
BUT FIRST ON TH "TO DO" LIST I RIPPING THAT CO HEAD O--

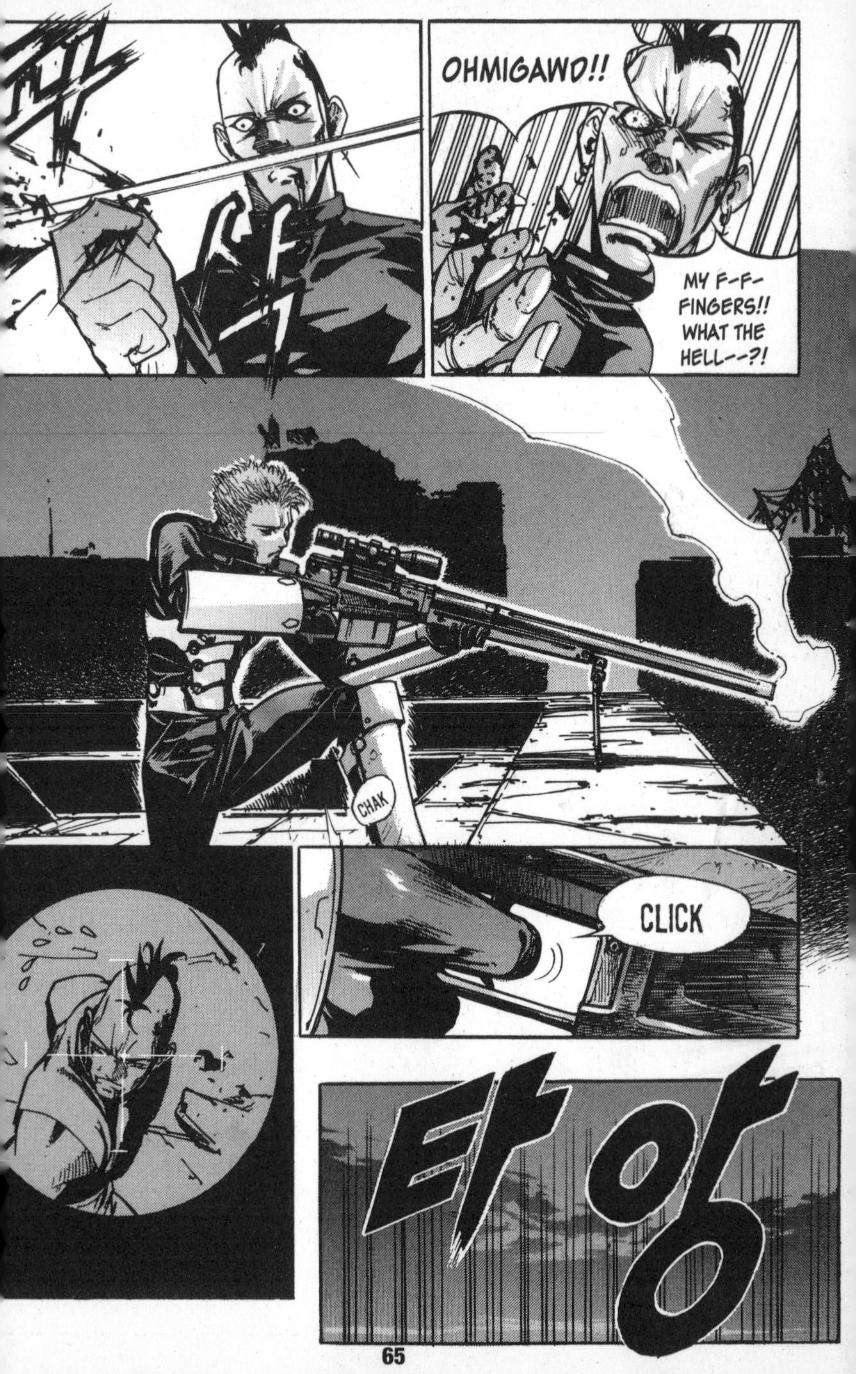
OHMIGAWD!!
MY F-F-FINGERS!! WHAT THE HELL--?!
CHAK
CLICK
타앙

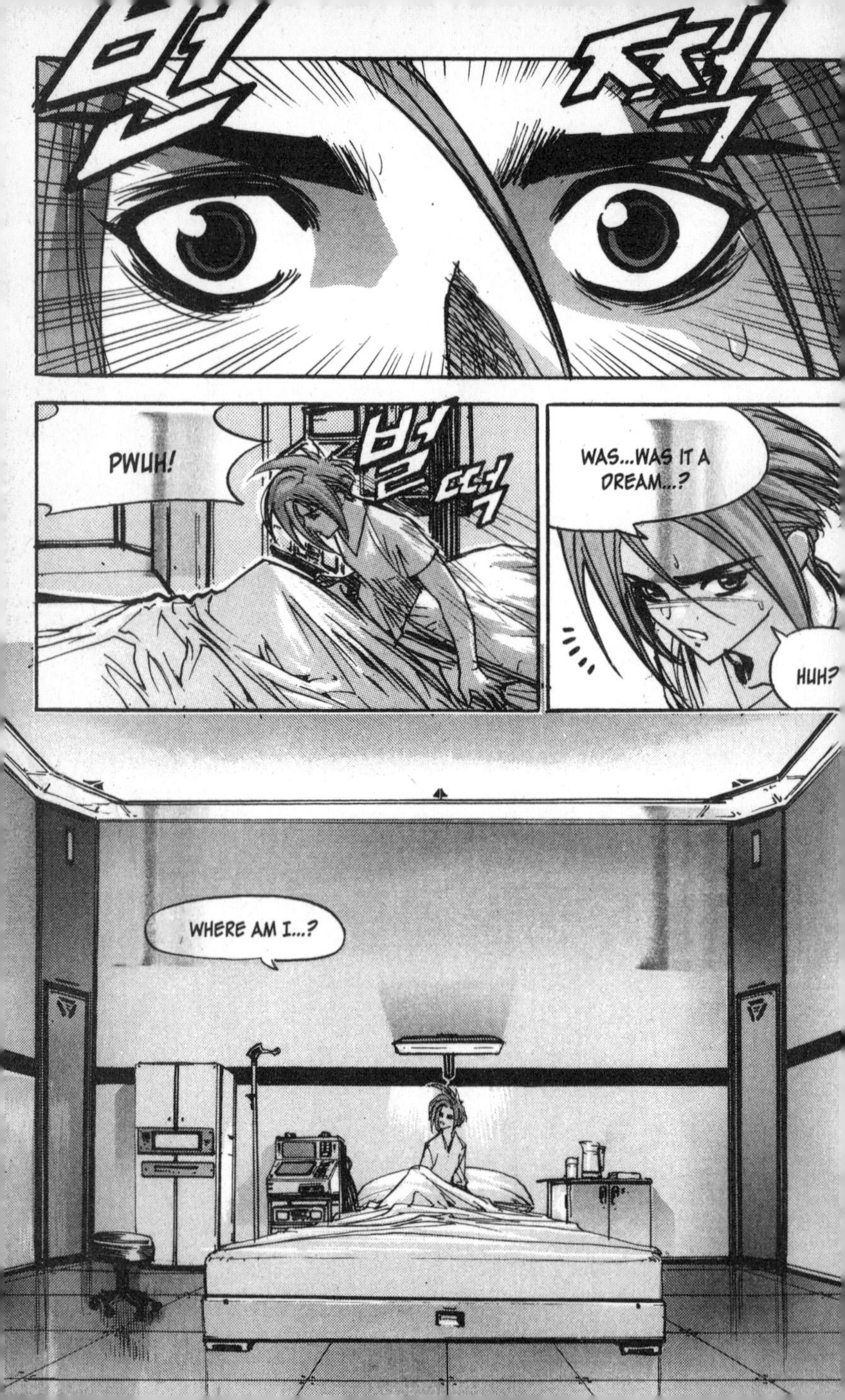
번쩍
PWUH!
벌떡
WAS...WAS IT A DREAM...?
HUH?
WHERE AM I...?

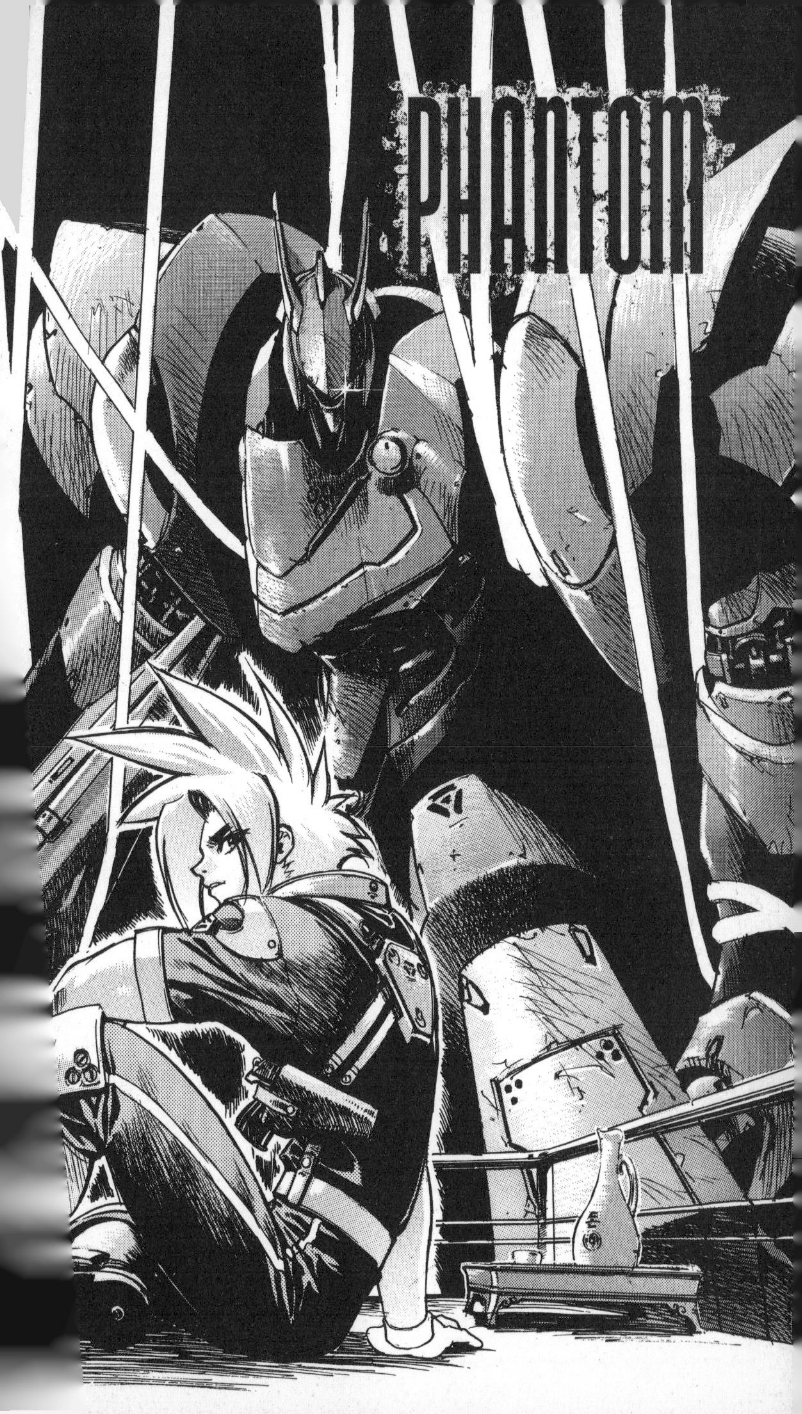
PHANTOM

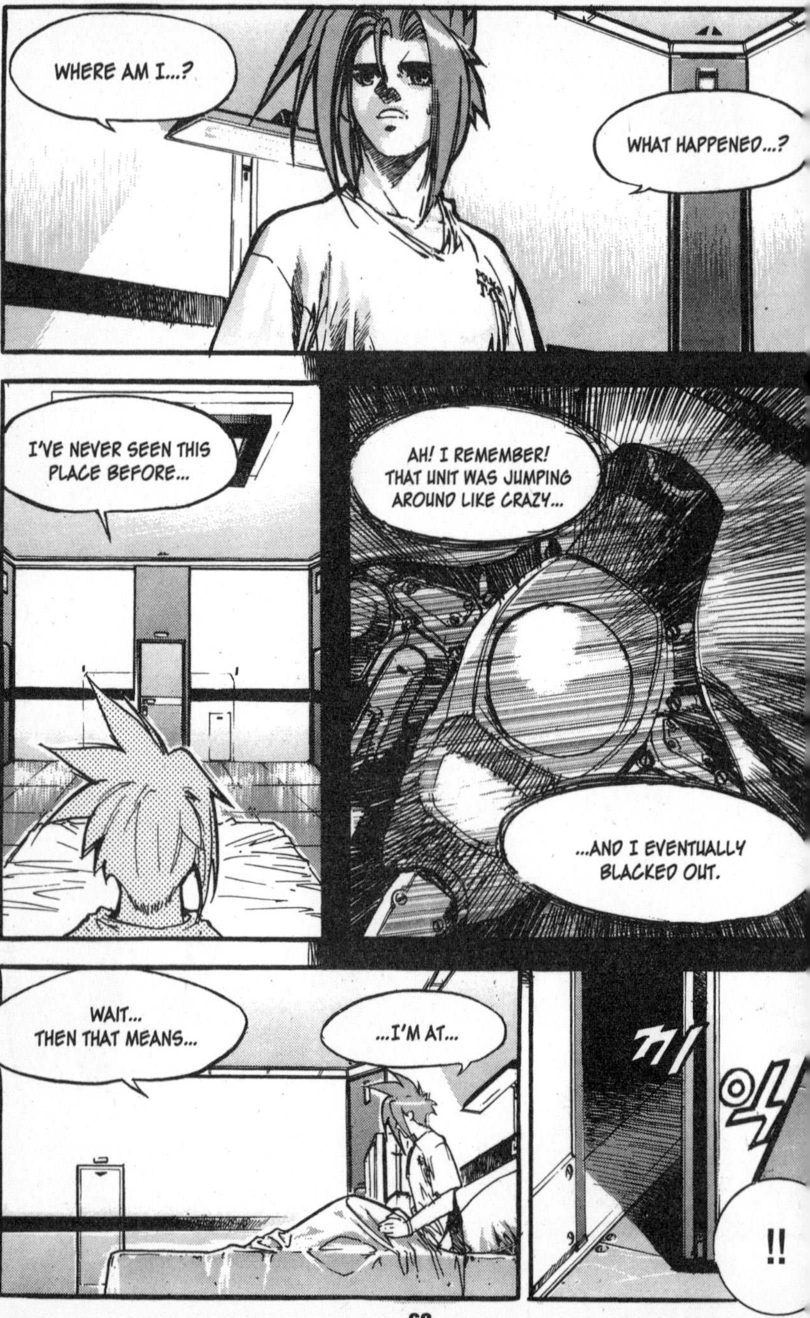
WHERE AM I...?
WHAT HAPPENED...?
I'VE NEVER SEEN THIS PLACE BEFORE...
AH! I REMEMBER! THAT UNIT WAS JUMPING AROUND LIKE CRAZY...
...AND I EVENTUALLY BLACKED OUT.
WAIT... THEN THAT MEANS...
...I'M AT...
!!

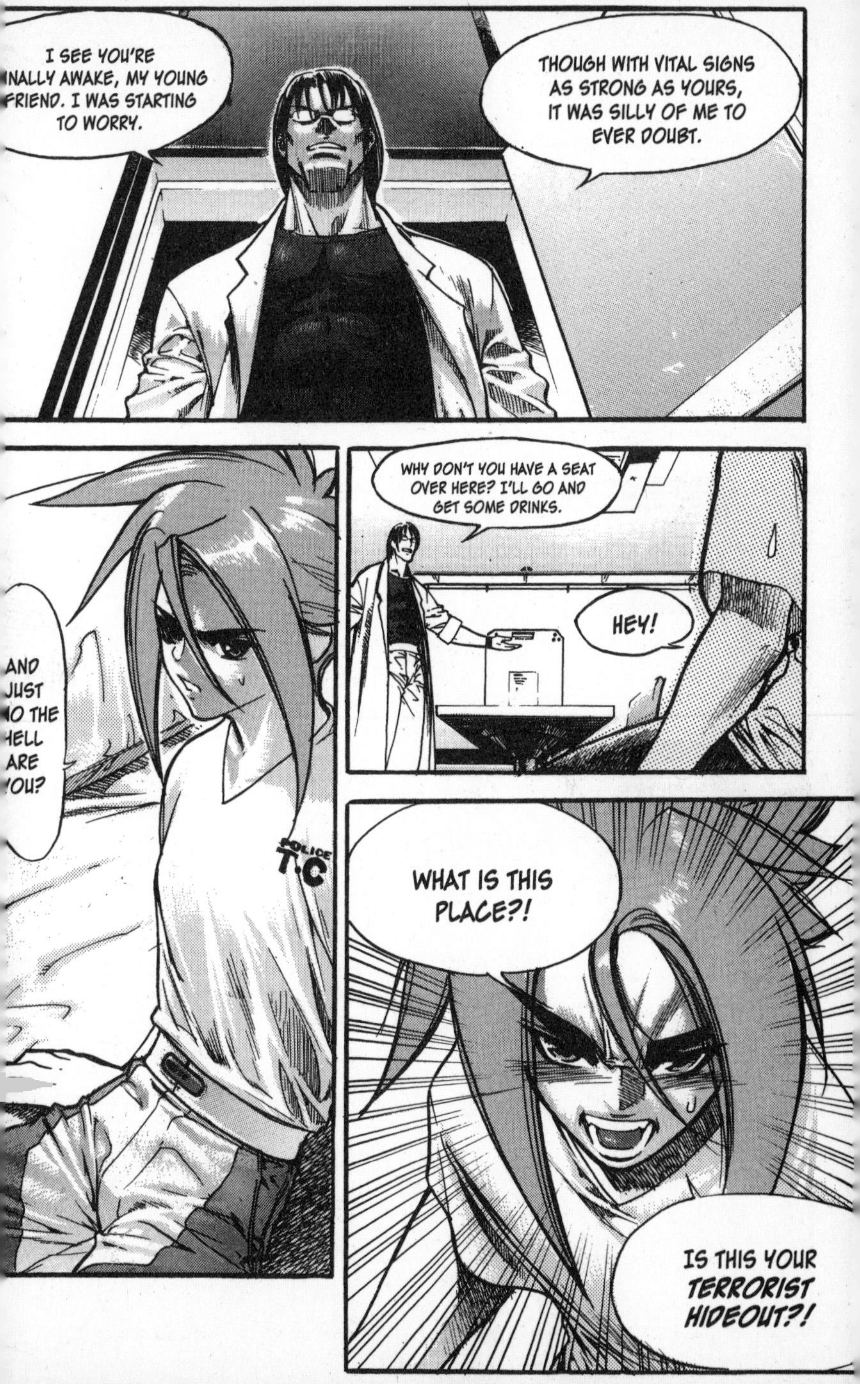
I SEE YOU'RE NALLY AWAKE, MY YOUNG FRIEND. I WAS STARTING TO WORRY.
THOUGH WITH VITAL SIGNS AS STRONG AS YOURS, IT WAS SILLY OF ME TO EVER DOUBT.
AND JUST HO THE HELL ARE OU?
POLICE T·C
WHY DON'T YOU HAVE A SEAT OVER HERE? I'LL GO AND GET SOME DRINKS.
HEY!
WHAT IS THIS PLACE?!
IS THIS YOUR TERRORIST HIDEOUT?!

"TERRORIST," HUH? INDEED. WE'LL LEAVE THAT ONE ALONE FOR NOW.

FIRST THINGS FIRST-- I WISH TO THANK YOU.

WHAT?

DID YOU NOT RESCUE OUR COMRADE?

COMRADE?

OH! HER!

IS SHE OKAY...? N-NOT THAT I *CARE* OR ANYTHING...

BEEP

BEEP

BEEP

FORTUNATELY, HER LIFE IS NOT DANGER.

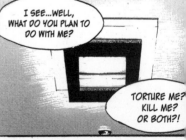

I SEE...WELL, WHAT DO YOU PLAN TO DO WITH ME?

TORTURE ME? KILL ME? OR BOTH?!

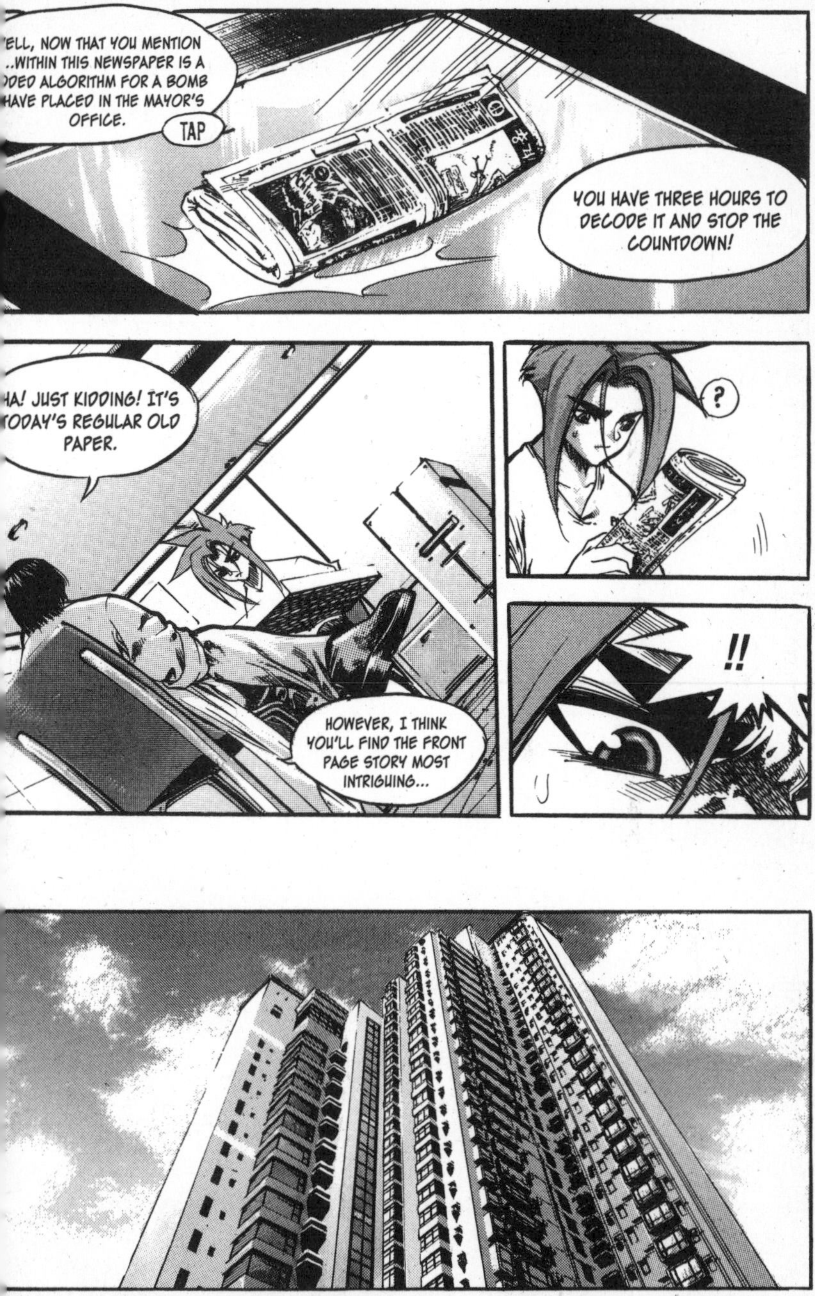
'ELL, NOW THAT YOU MENTION ..WITHIN THIS NEWSPAPER IS A ODED ALGORITHM FOR A BOMB HAVE PLACED IN THE MAYOR'S OFFICE.
TAP
YOU HAVE THREE HOURS TO DECODE IT AND STOP THE COUNTDOWN!
HA! JUST KIDDING! IT'S TODAY'S REGULAR OLD PAPER.
HOWEVER, I THINK YOU'LL FIND THE FRONT PAGE STORY MOST INTRIGUING...
?
!!

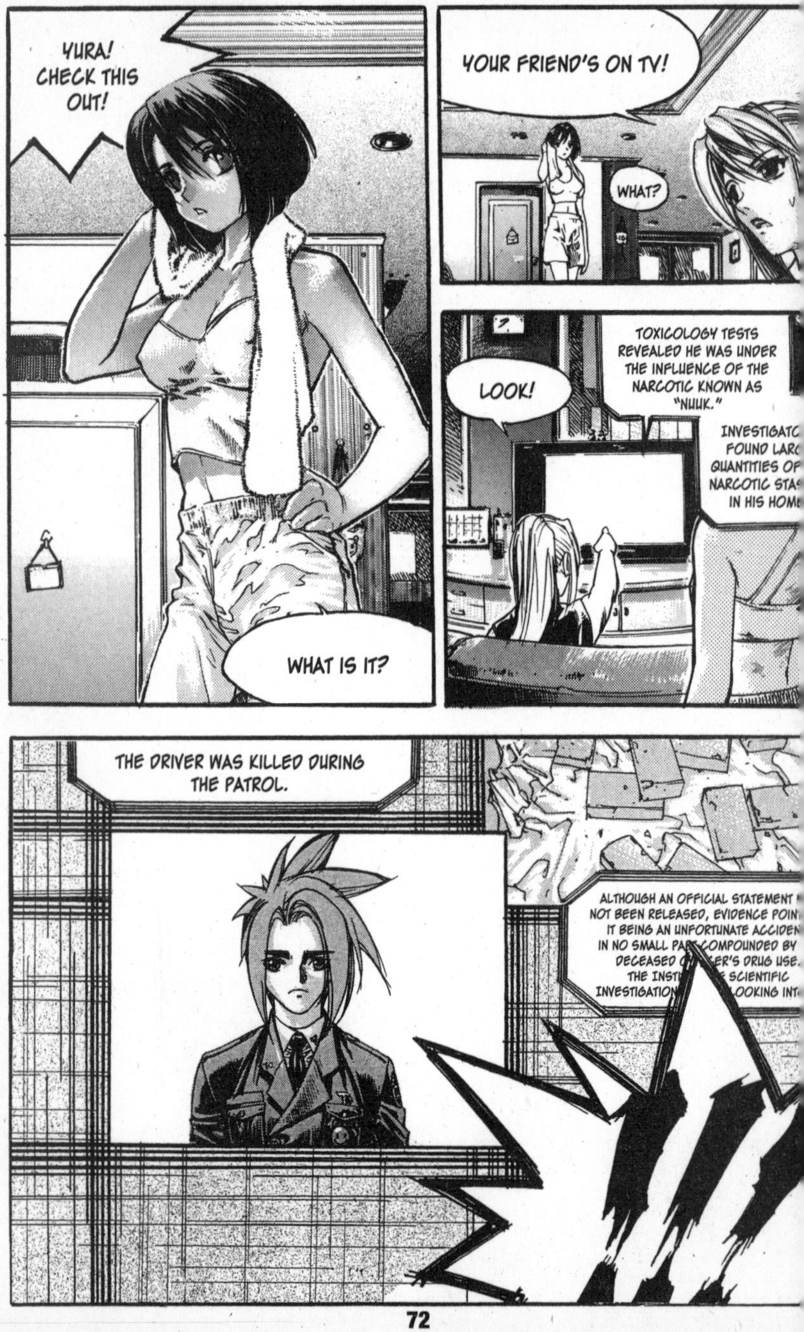
YURA! CHECK THIS OUT!
WHAT IS IT?
YOUR FRIEND'S ON TV!
WHAT?
LOOK!
TOXICOLOGY TESTS REVEALED HE WAS UNDER THE INFLUENCE OF THE NARCOTIC KNOWN AS "NUUK."
THE DRIVER WAS KILLED DURING THE PATROL.

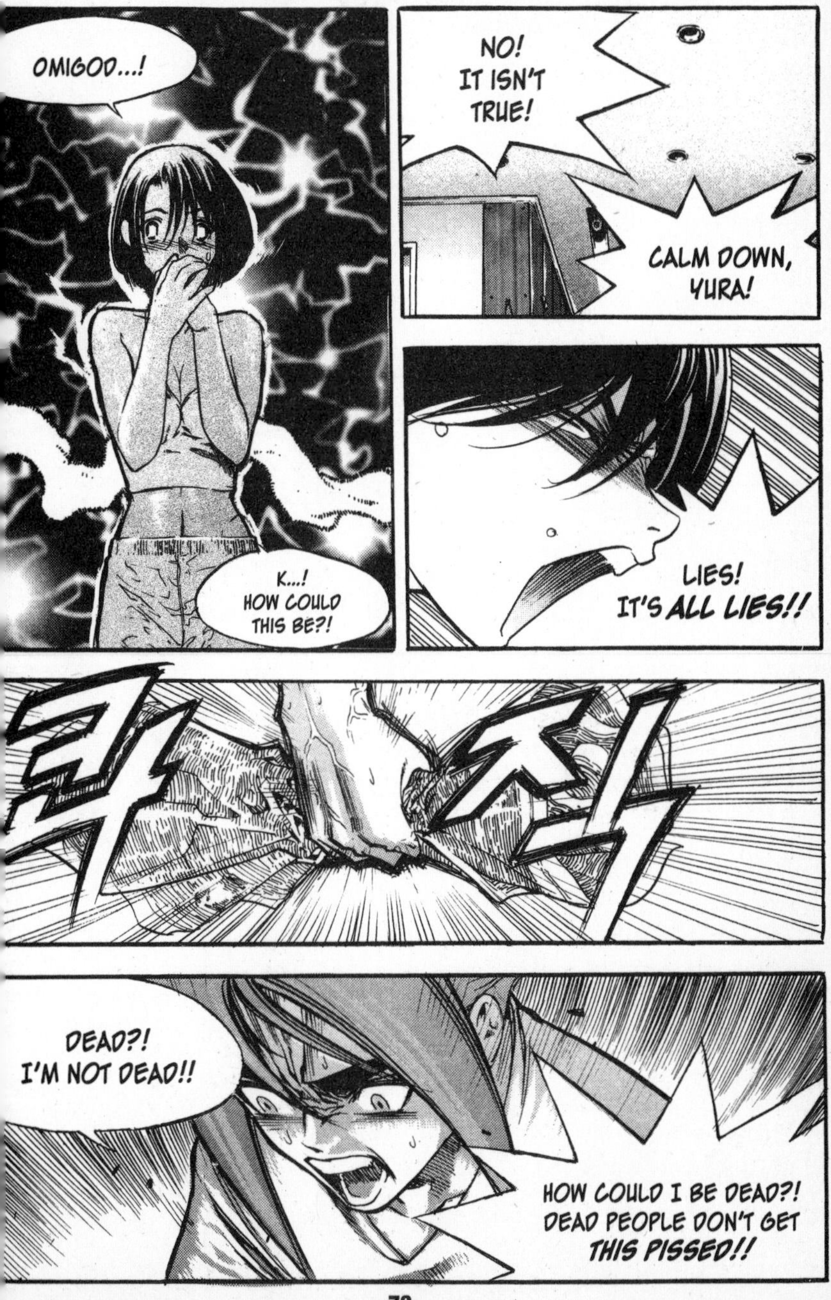
OMIGOD...!
K...! HOW COULD THIS BE?!
NO! IT ISN'T TRUE!
CALM DOWN, YURA!
LIES! IT'S ALL LIES!!
DEAD?! I'M NOT DEAD!!
HOW COULD I BE DEAD?! DEAD PEOPLE DON'T GET THIS PISSED!!

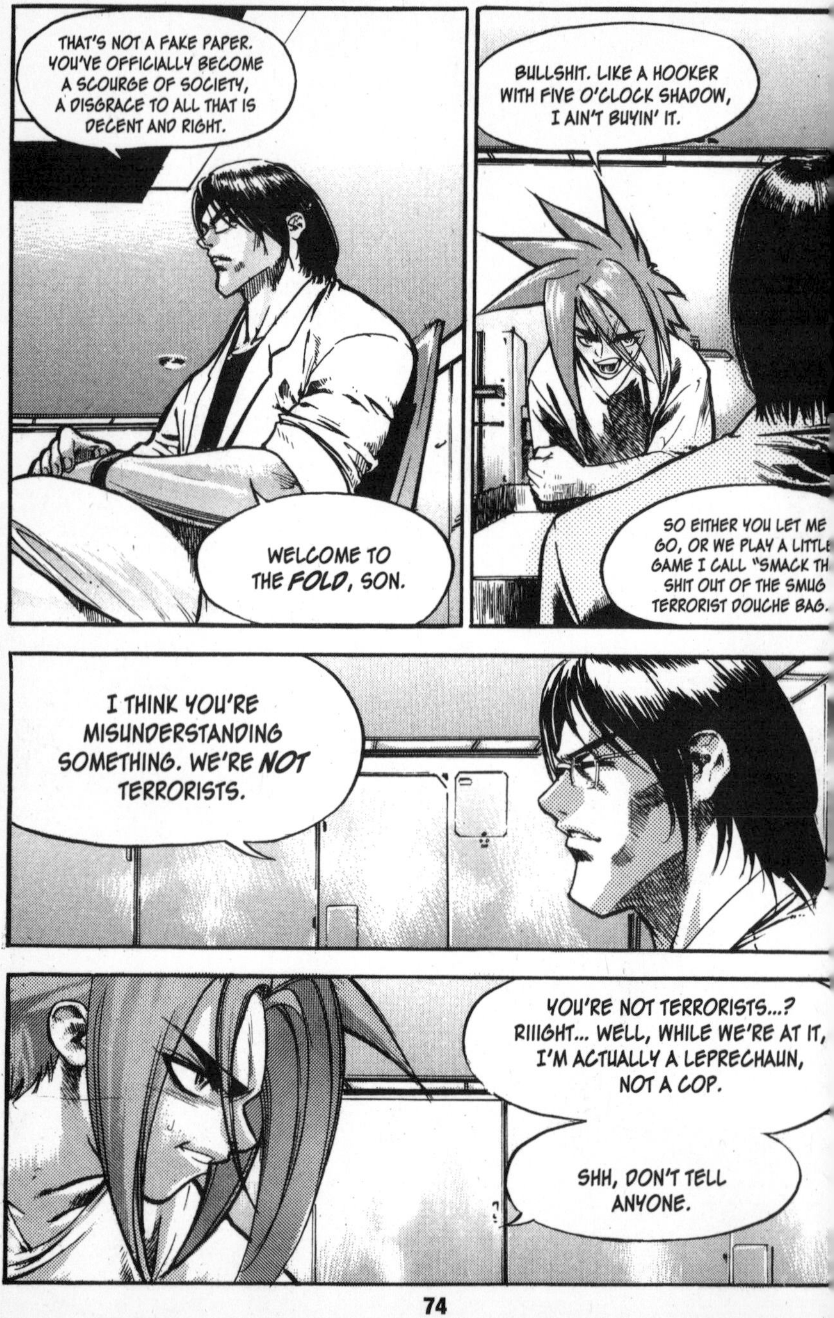
THAT'S NOT A FAKE PAPER. YOU'VE OFFICIALLY BECOME A SCOURGE OF SOCIETY, A DISGRACE TO ALL THAT IS DECENT AND RIGHT.
WELCOME TO THE *FOLD*, SON.
BULLSHIT. LIKE A HOOKER WITH FIVE O'CLOCK SHADOW, I AIN'T BUYIN' IT.
SO EITHER YOU LET ME GO, OR WE PLAY A LITTL GAME I CALL "SMACK TH SHIT OUT OF THE SMUG TERRORIST DOUCHE BAG.
I THINK YOU'RE MISUNDERSTANDING SOMETHING. WE'RE *NOT* TERRORISTS.
YOU'RE NOT TERRORISTS...? RIIIGHT... WELL, WHILE WE'RE AT IT, I'M ACTUALLY A LEPRECHAUN, NOT A COP.
SHH, DON'T TELL ANYONE.

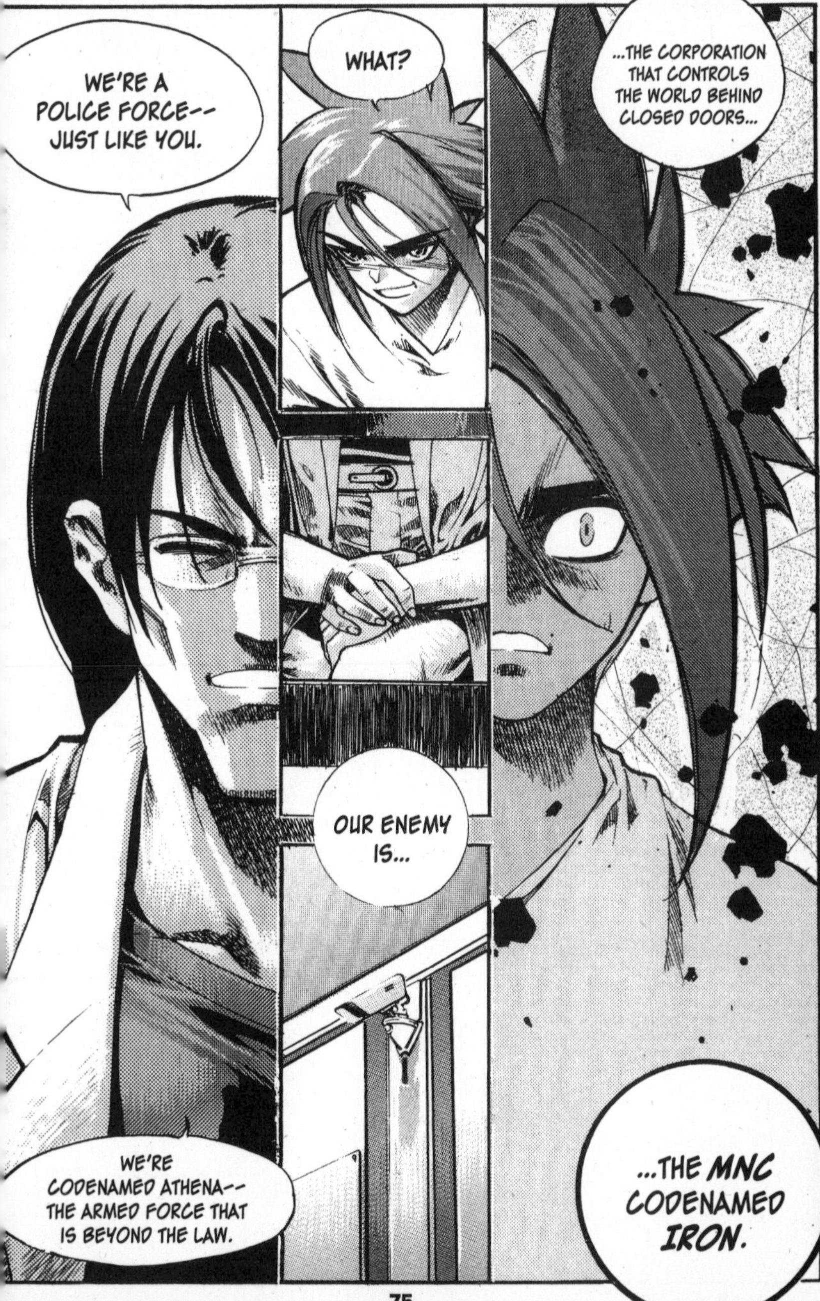
WE'RE A POLICE FORCE-- JUST LIKE YOU.
WE'RE CODENAMED ATHENA-- THE ARMED FORCE THAT IS BEYOND THE LAW.
WHAT?
OUR ENEMY IS...
...THE CORPORATION THAT CONTROLS THE WORLD BEHIND CLOSED DOORS...
...THE *MNC* CODENAMED *IRON*.

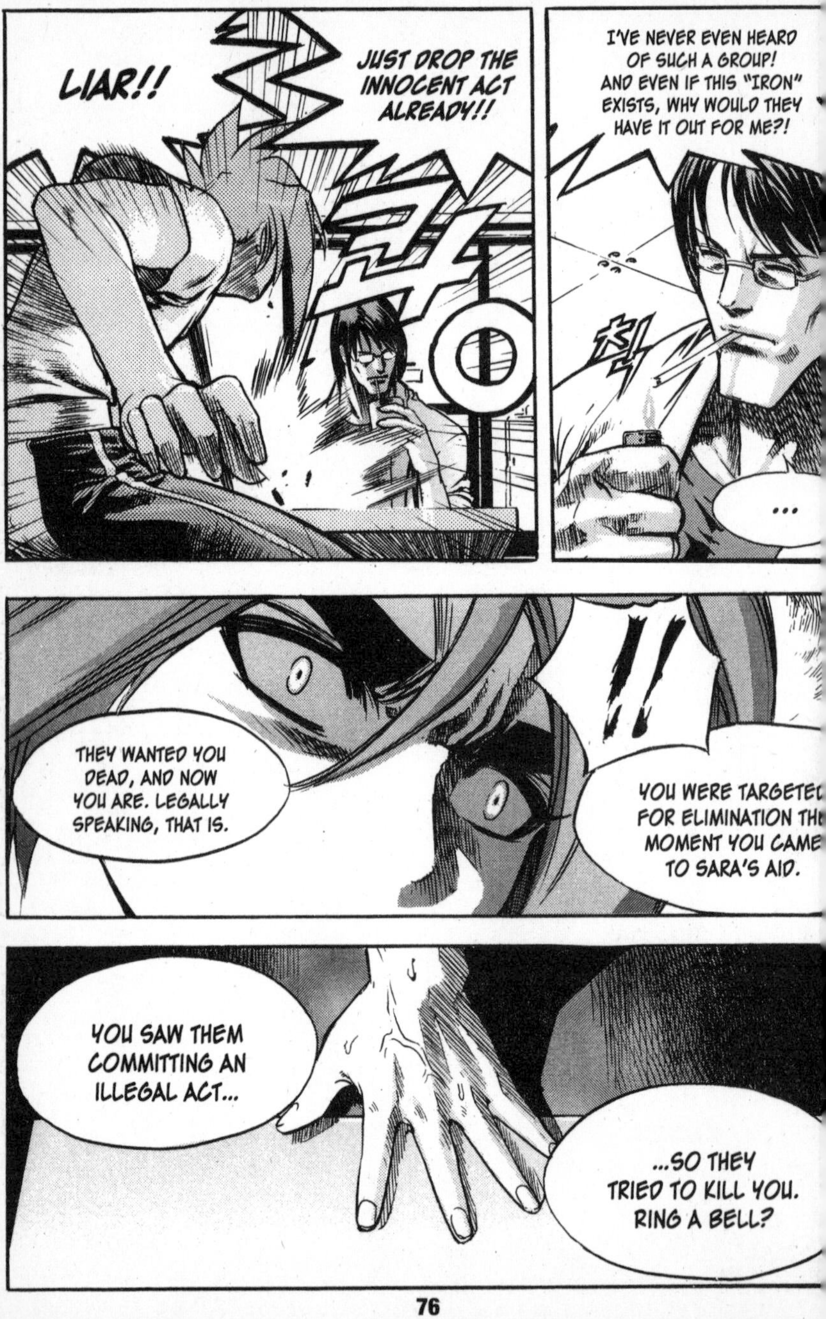
LIAR!!
JUST DROP THE INNOCENT ACT ALREADY!!
I'VE NEVER EVEN HEARD OF SUCH A GROUP! AND EVEN IF THIS "IRON" EXISTS, WHY WOULD THEY HAVE IT OUT FOR ME?!
...
THEY WANTED YOU DEAD, AND NOW YOU ARE. LEGALLY SPEAKING, THAT IS.
YOU WERE TARGETED FOR ELIMINATION THE MOMENT YOU CAME TO SARA'S AID.
YOU SAW THEM COMMITTING AN ILLEGAL ACT...
...SO THEY TRIED TO KILL YOU. RING A BELL?

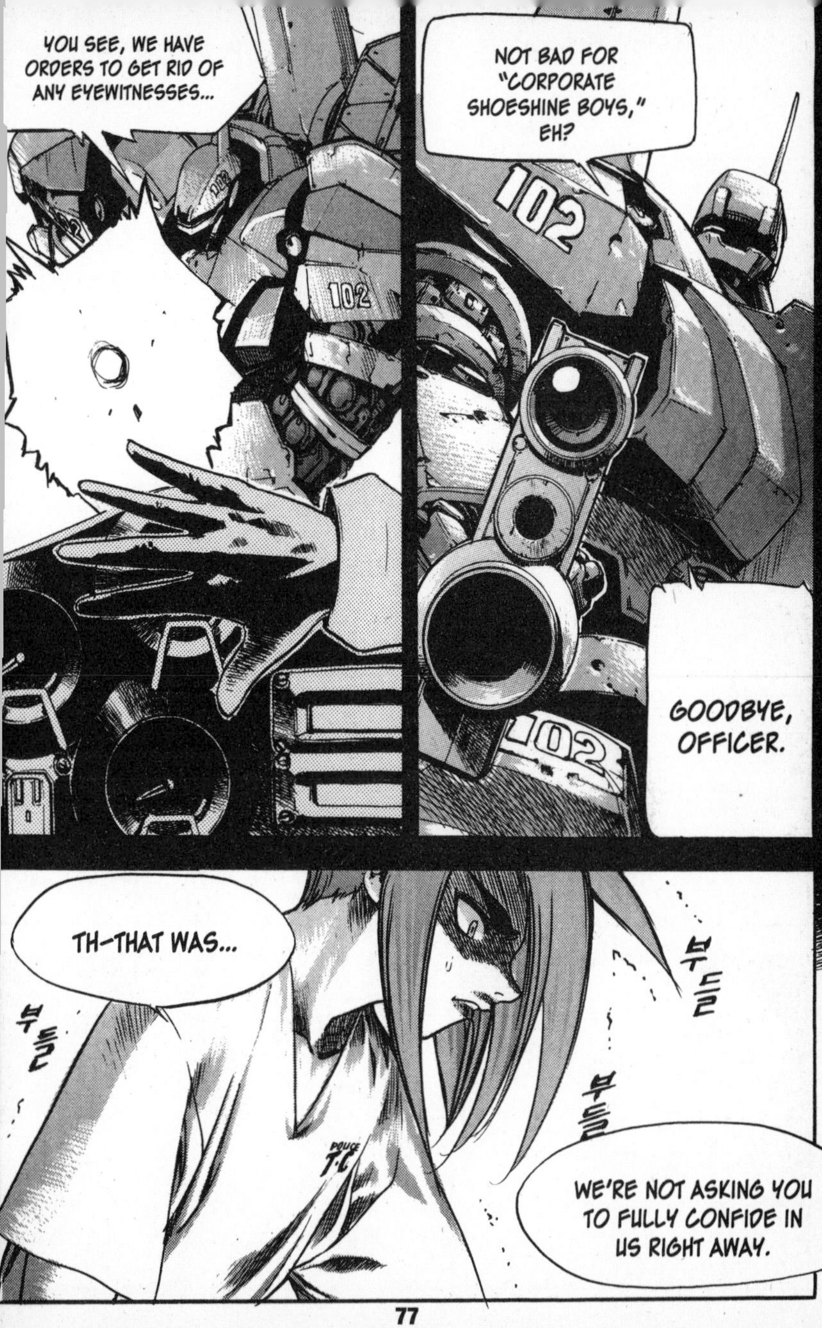
YOU SEE, WE HAVE ORDERS TO GET RID OF ANY EYEWITNESSES...
NOT BAD FOR "CORPORATE SHOESHINE BOYS," EH?
102
GOODBYE, OFFICER.
TH-THAT WAS...
부들
부들
부들
WE'RE NOT ASKING YOU TO FULLY CONFIDE IN US RIGHT AWAY.

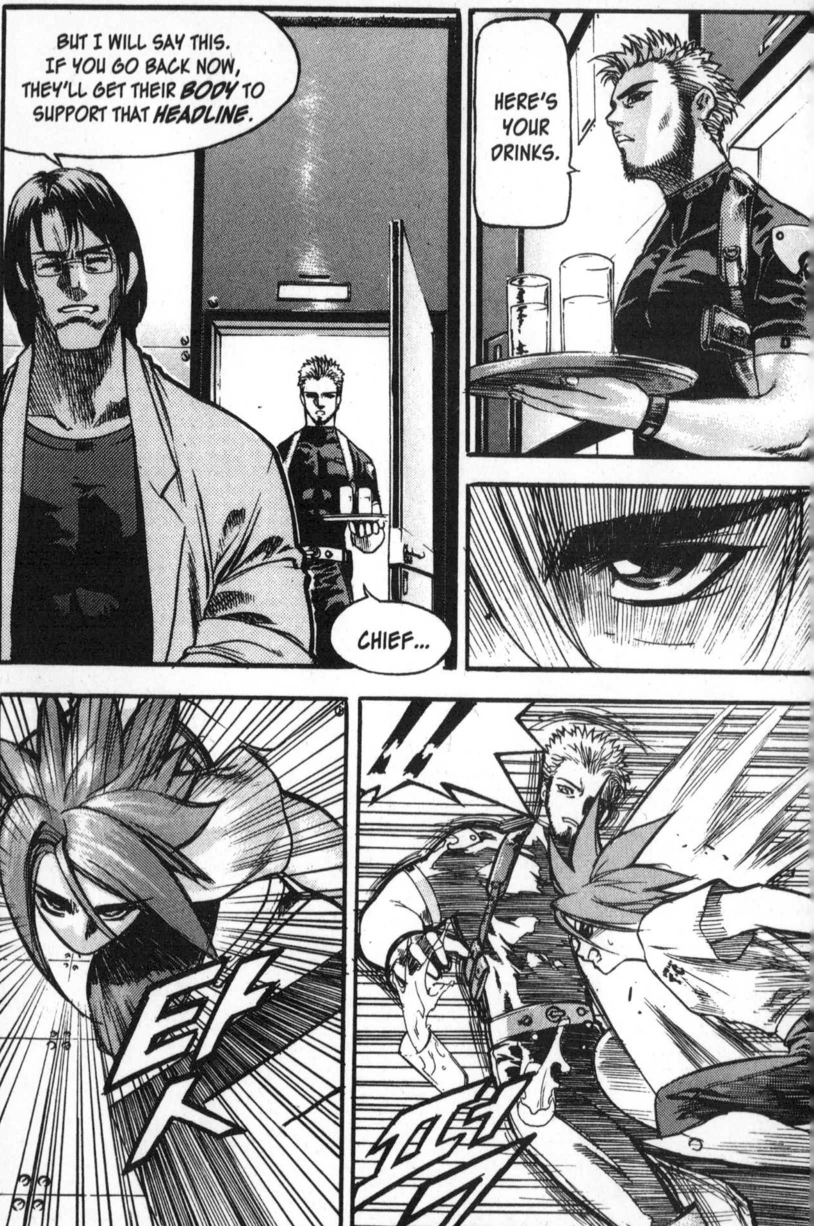
BUT I WILL SAY THIS. IF YOU GO BACK NOW, THEY'LL GET THEIR ***BODY*** TO SUPPORT THAT ***HEADLINE***.
CHIEF...
HERE'S YOUR DRINKS.

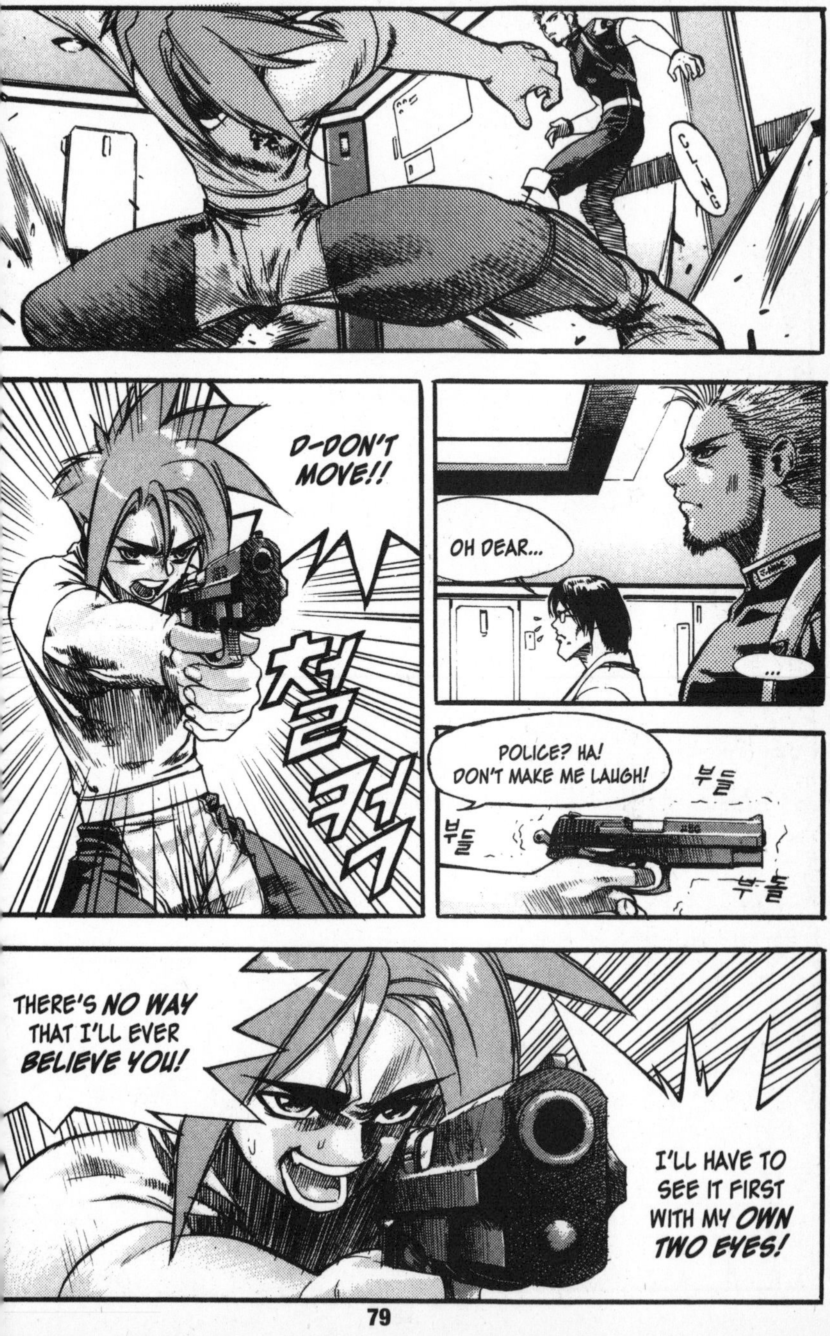
CLING
D-DON'T MOVE!!
OH DEAR...
...
POLICE? HA! DON'T MAKE ME LAUGH!
부들
부들
부들
THERE'S NO WAY THAT I'LL EVER BELIEVE YOU!
I'LL HAVE TO SEE IT FIRST WITH MY OWN TWO EYES!

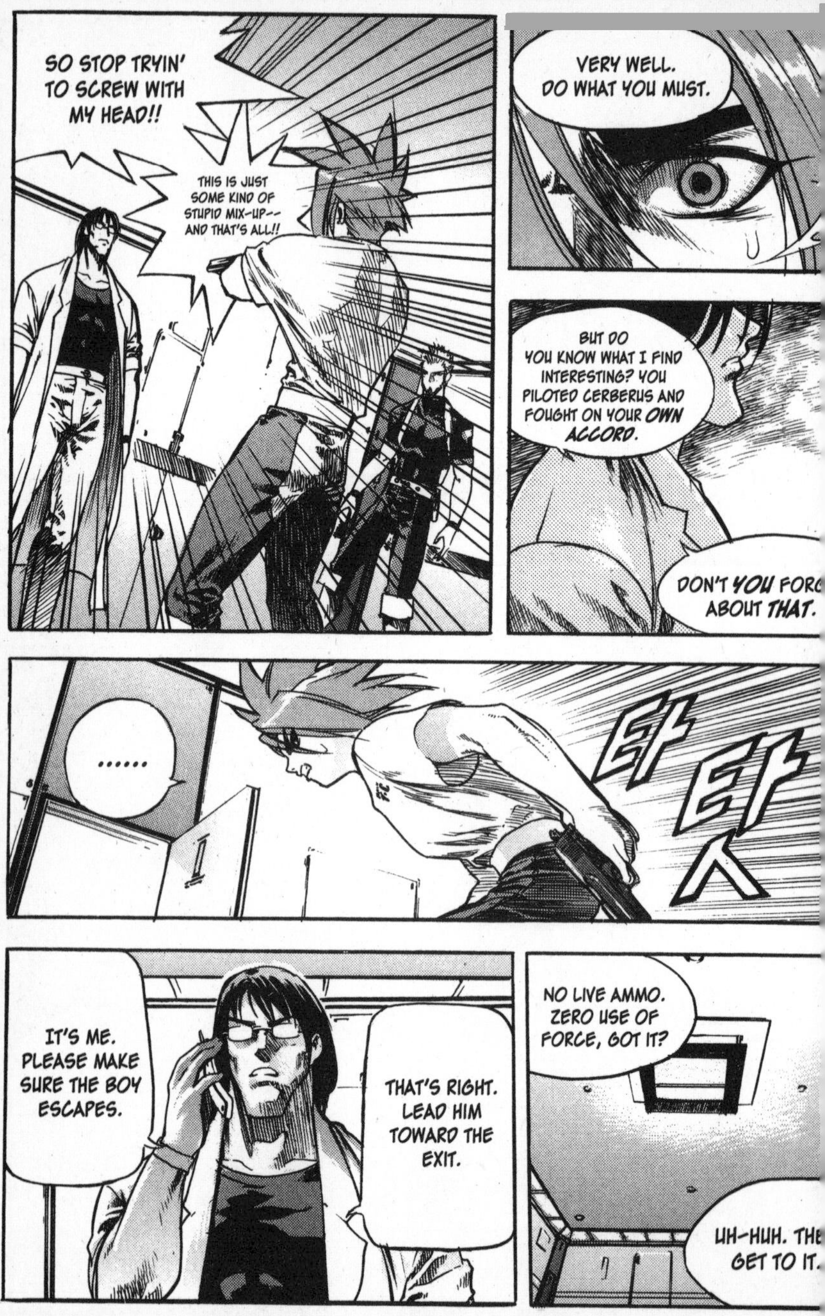
SO STOP TRYIN' TO SCREW WITH MY HEAD!!
THIS IS JUST SOME KIND OF STUPID MIX-UP-- AND THAT'S ALL!!
VERY WELL. DO WHAT YOU MUST.
BUT DO YOU KNOW WHAT I FIND INTERESTING? YOU PILOTED CERBERUS AND FOUGHT ON YOUR *OWN ACCORD*.
DON'T *YOU* FORC
ABOUT *THAT*.
......
IT'S ME. PLEASE MAKE SURE THE BOY ESCAPES.
THAT'S RIGHT. LEAD HIM TOWARD THE EXIT.
NO LIVE AMMO. ZERO USE OF FORCE, GOT IT?
UH-HUH. THE
GET TO IT.

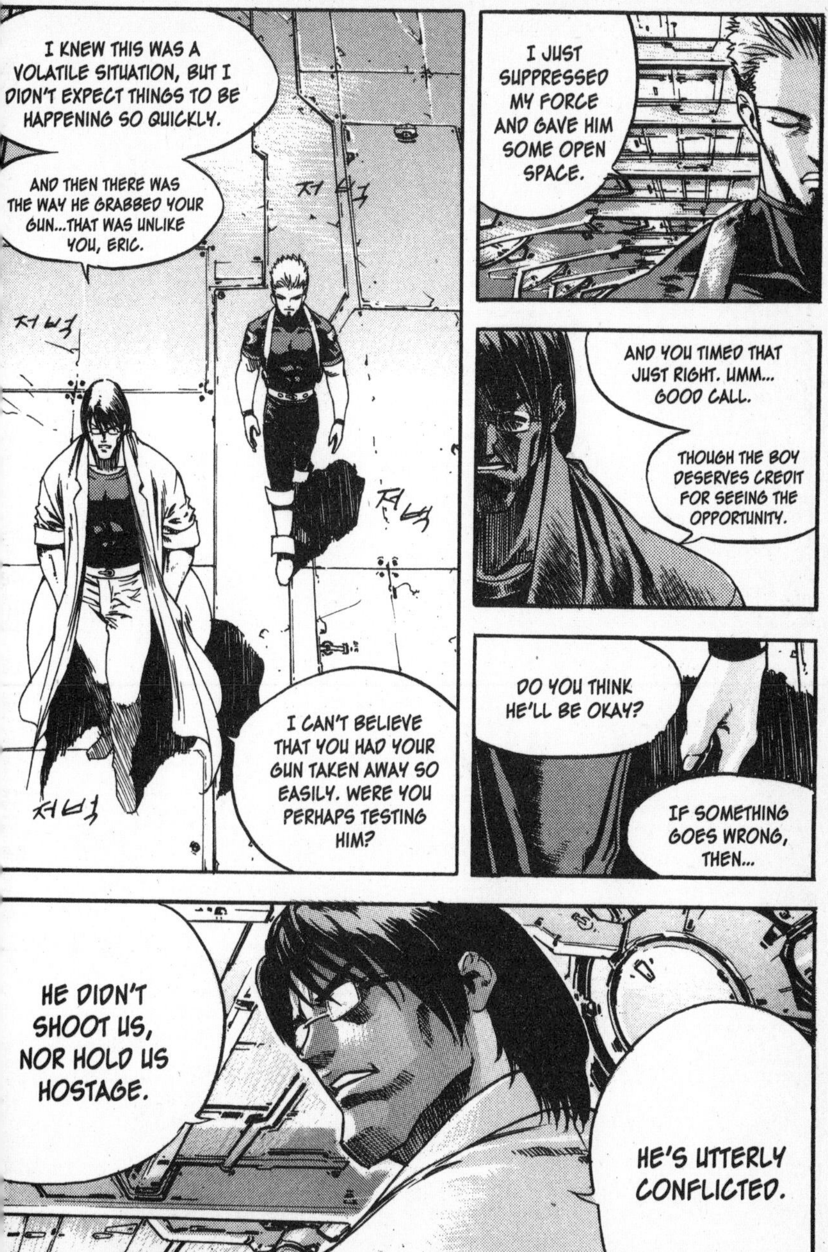
I KNEW THIS WAS A VOLATILE SITUATION, BUT I DIDN'T EXPECT THINGS TO BE HAPPENING SO QUICKLY.
AND THEN THERE WAS THE WAY HE GRABBED YOUR GUN...THAT WAS UNLIKE YOU, ERIC.
저벅
저벅
저벅
저벅
I CAN'T BELIEVE THAT YOU HAD YOUR GUN TAKEN AWAY SO EASILY. WERE YOU PERHAPS TESTING HIM?
I JUST SUPPRESSED MY FORCE AND GAVE HIM SOME OPEN SPACE.
AND YOU TIMED THAT JUST RIGHT. UMM... GOOD CALL.
THOUGH THE BOY DESERVES CREDIT FOR SEEING THE OPPORTUNITY.
DO YOU THINK HE'LL BE OKAY?
IF SOMETHING GOES WRONG, THEN...
HE DIDN'T SHOOT US, NOR HOLD US HOSTAGE.
HE'S UTTERLY CONFLICTED.

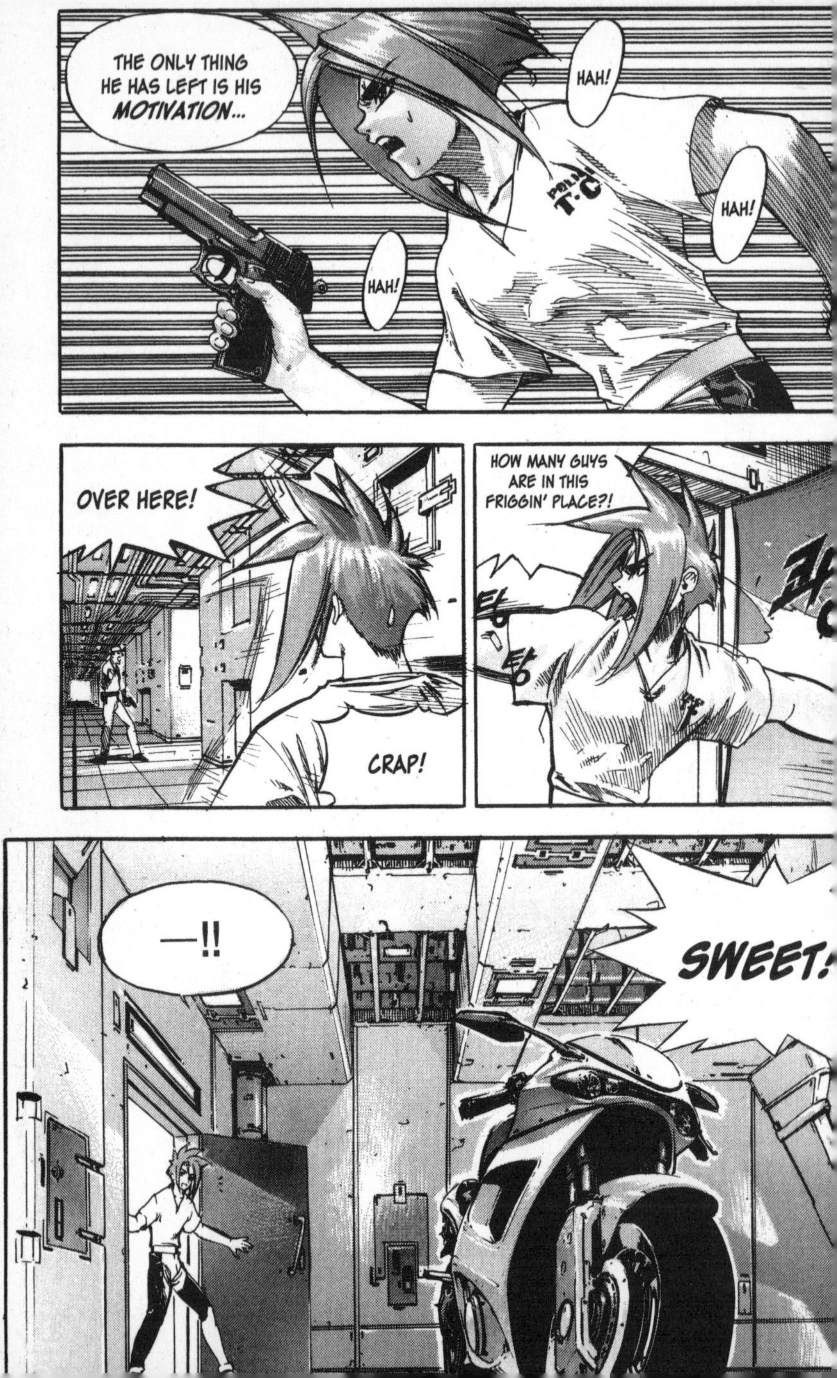
THE ONLY THING HE HAS LEFT IS HIS MOTIVATION...
HAH!
HAH!
HAH!
OVER HERE!
CRAP!
HOW MANY GUYS ARE IN THIS FRIGGIN' PLACE?!
—!!
SWEET!

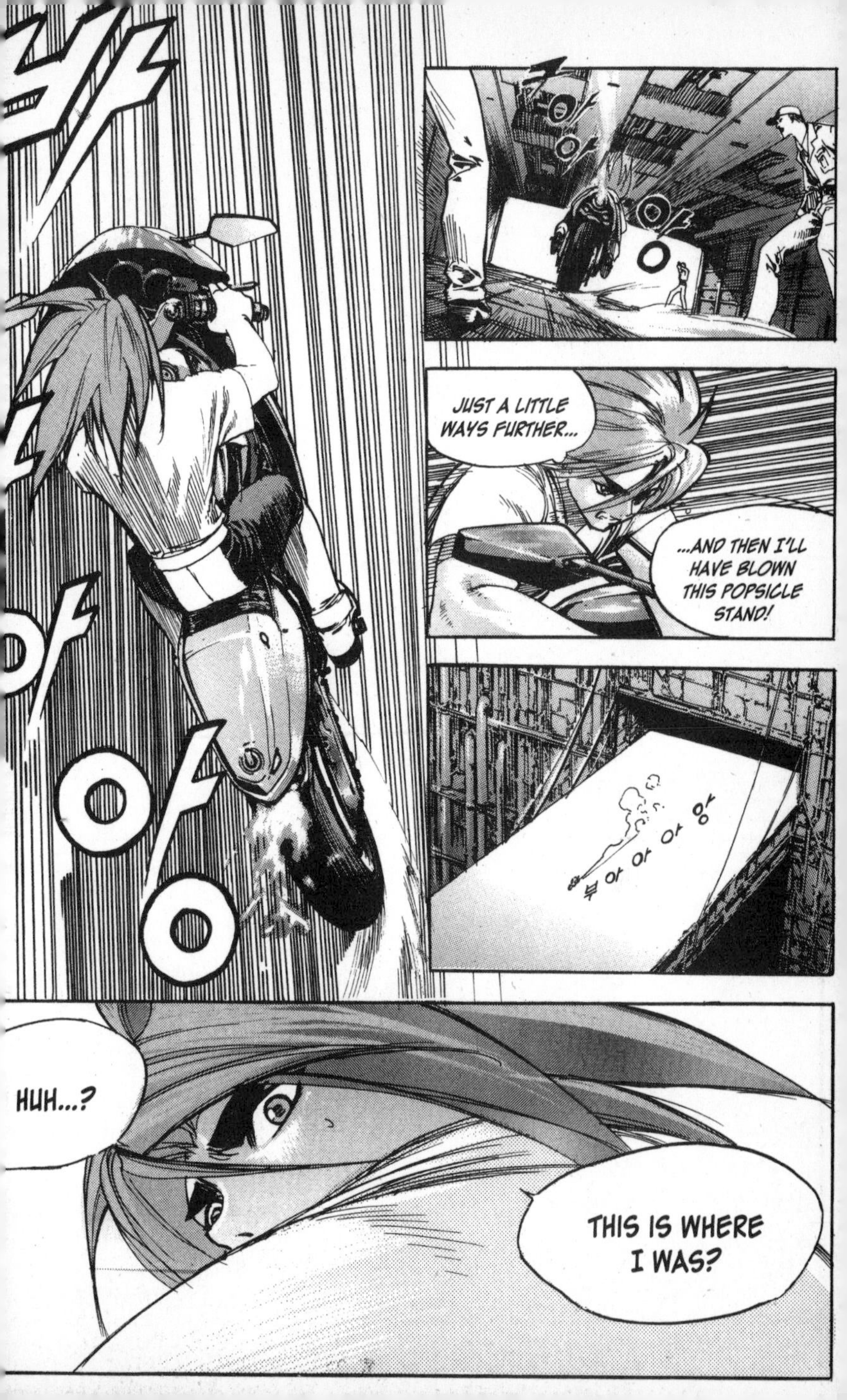
JUST A LITTLE WAYS FURTHER...
...AND THEN I'LL HAVE BLOWN THIS POPSICLE STAND!
HUH...?
THIS IS WHERE I WAS?

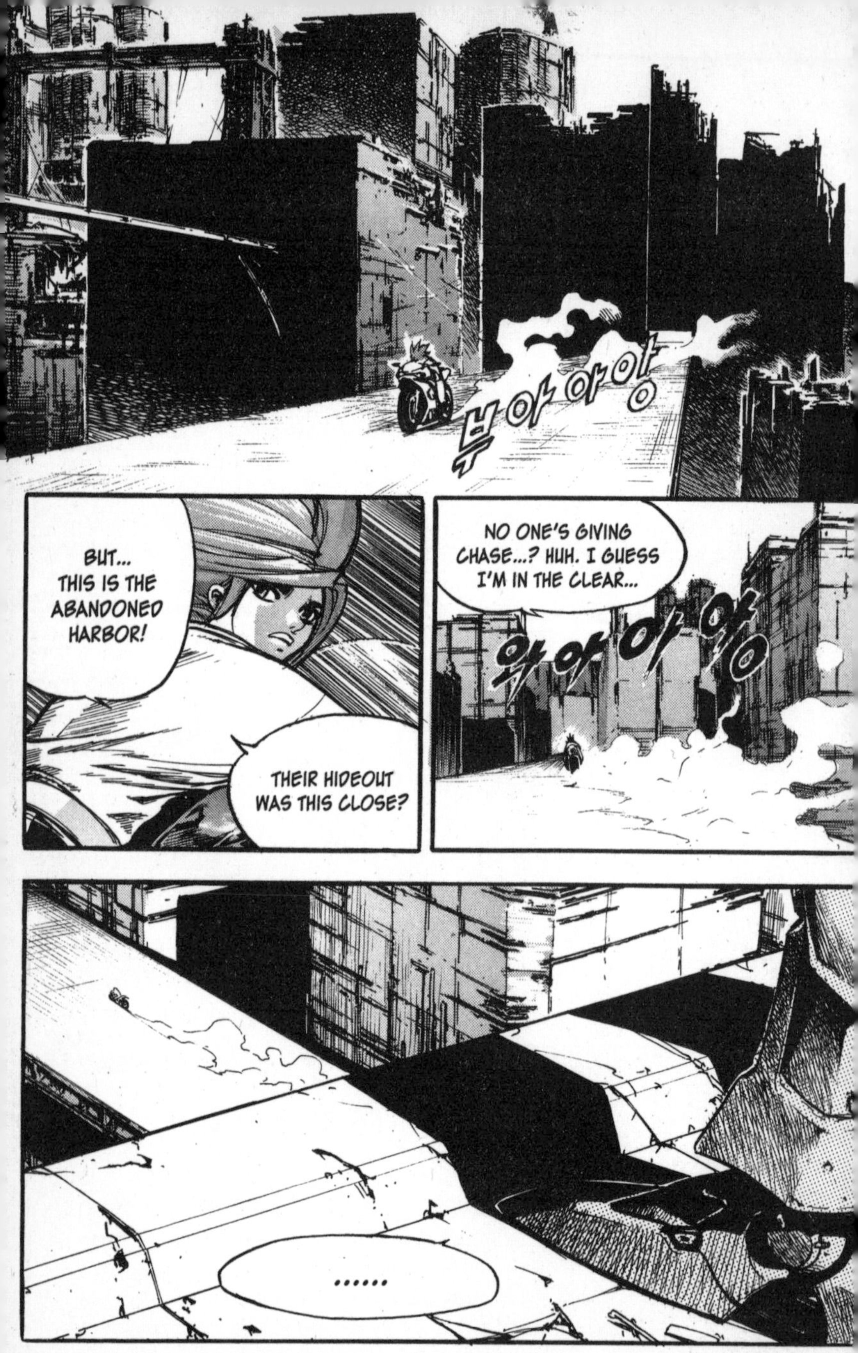

부아아아앙
BUT... THIS IS THE ABANDONED HARBOR!
THEIR HIDEOUT WAS THIS CLOSE?
NO ONE'S GIVING CHASE...? HUH. I GUESS I'M IN THE CLEAR...
와아아아앙
......

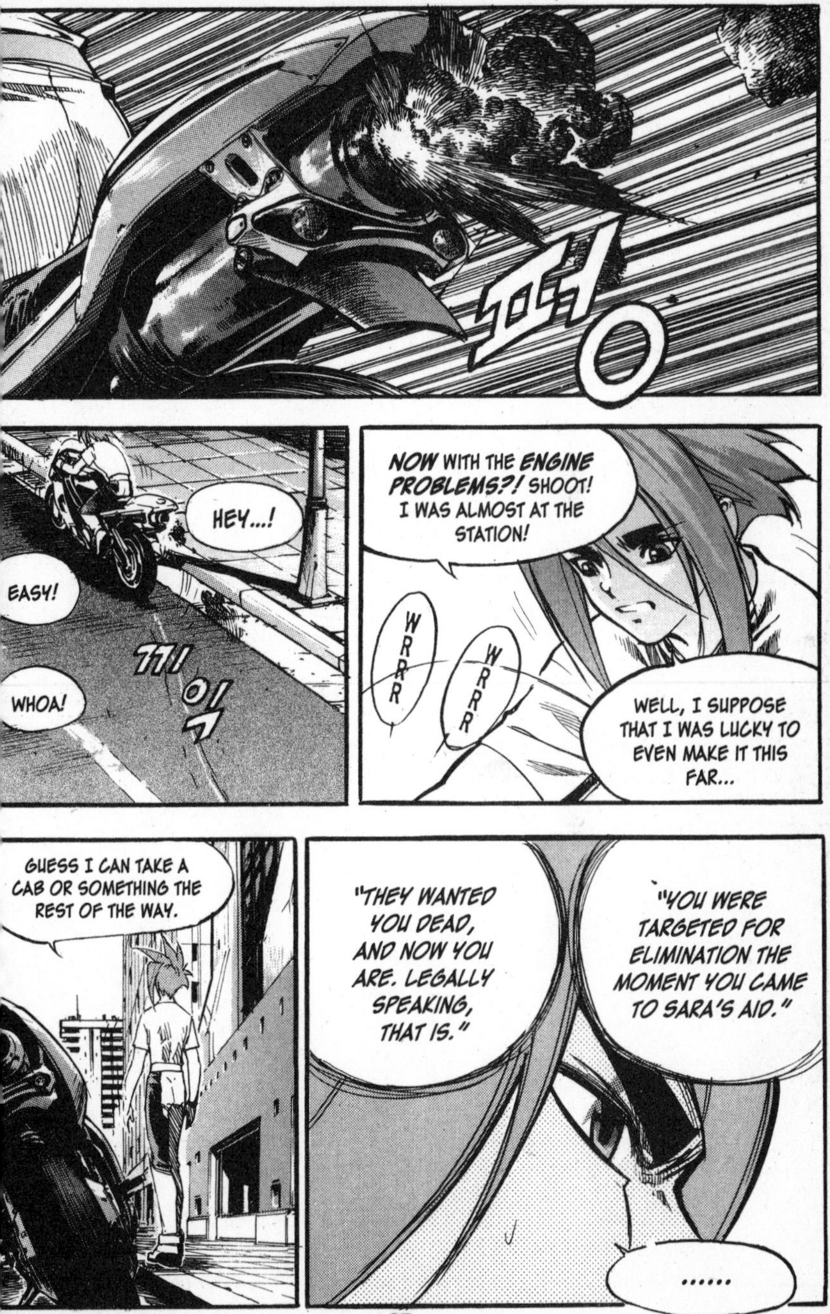
SOCH
HEY...!
EASY!
WHOA!
NOW WITH THE ENGINE PROBLEMS?! SHOOT! I WAS ALMOST AT THE STATION!
WRRR
WRRR
WELL, I SUPPOSE THAT I WAS LUCKY TO EVEN MAKE IT THIS FAR...
GUESS I CAN TAKE A CAB OR SOMETHING THE REST OF THE WAY.
"THEY WANTED YOU DEAD, AND NOW YOU ARE. LEGALLY SPEAKING, THAT IS."
"YOU WERE TARGETED FOR ELIMINATION THE MOMENT YOU CAME TO SARA'S AID."
......

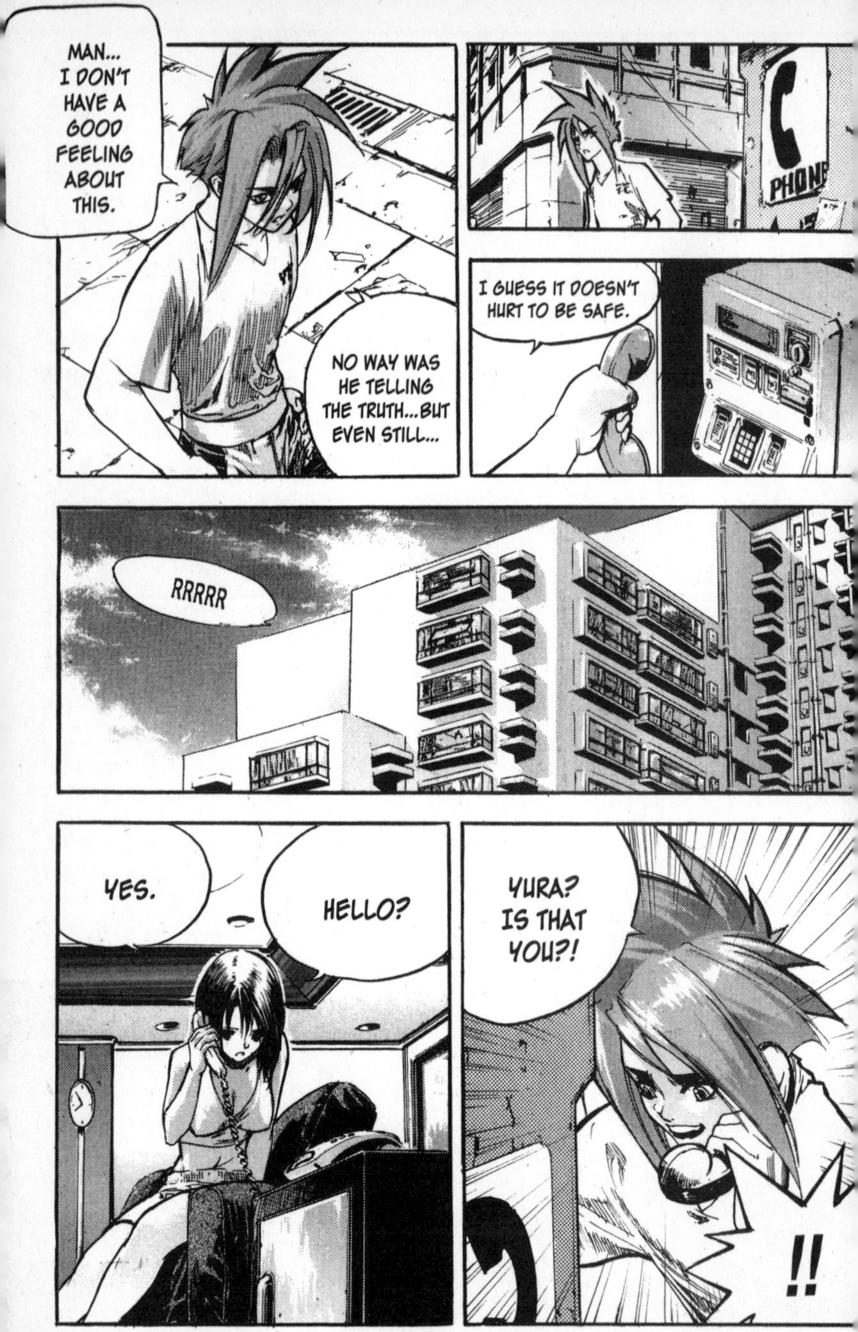
MAN... I DON'T HAVE A GOOD FEELING ABOUT THIS.
NO WAY WAS HE TELLING THE TRUTH...BUT EVEN STILL...
PHONE
I GUESS IT DOESN'T HURT TO BE SAFE.
RRRRR
YES.
HELLO?
YURA? IS THAT YOU?!
!!

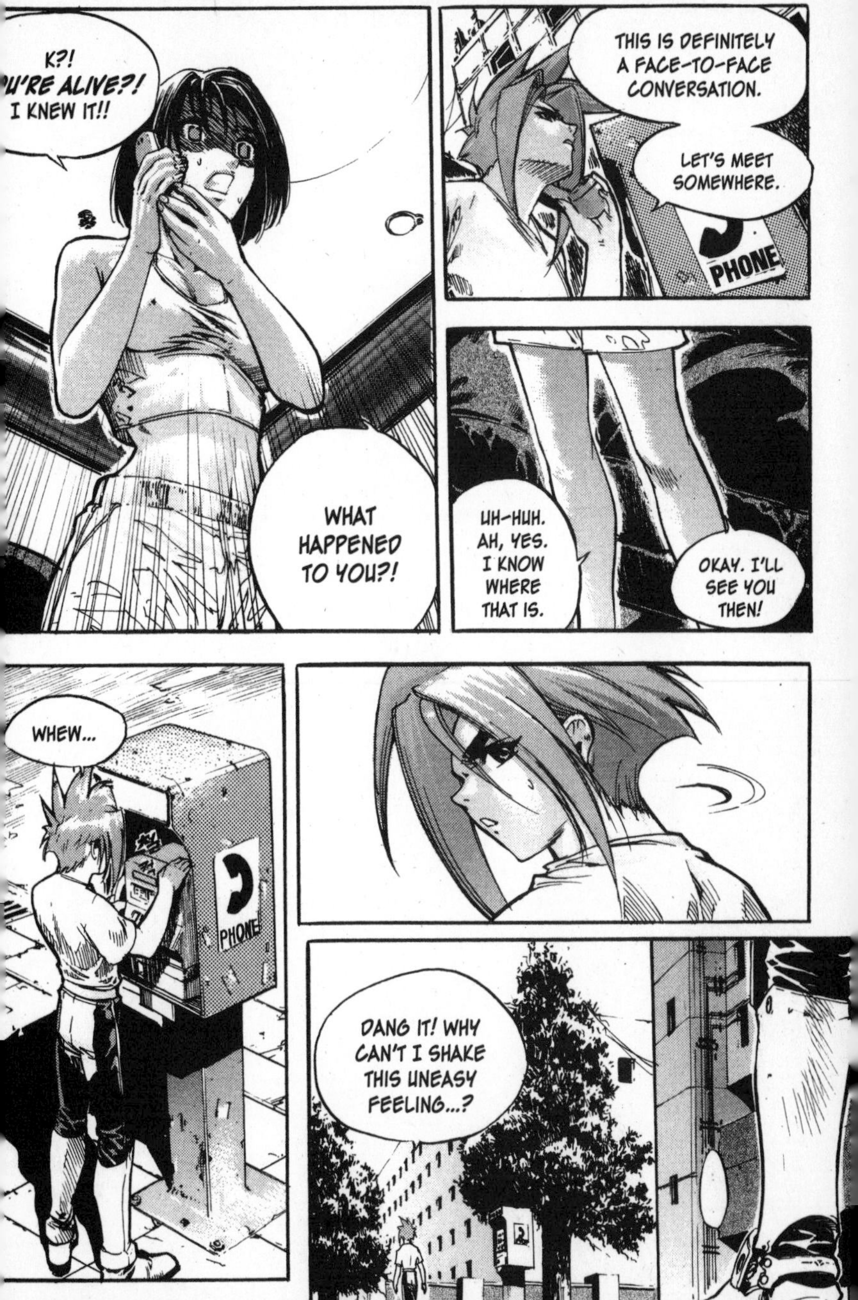
K?!
U'RE ALIVE?!
I KNEW IT!!
THIS IS DEFINITELY A FACE-TO-FACE CONVERSATION.
LET'S MEET SOMEWHERE.
PHONE
WHAT HAPPENED TO YOU?!
UH-HUH. AH, YES. I KNOW WHERE THAT IS.
OKAY. I'LL SEE YOU THEN!
WHEW...
PHONE
DANG IT! WHY CAN'T I SHAKE THIS UNEASY FEELING...?

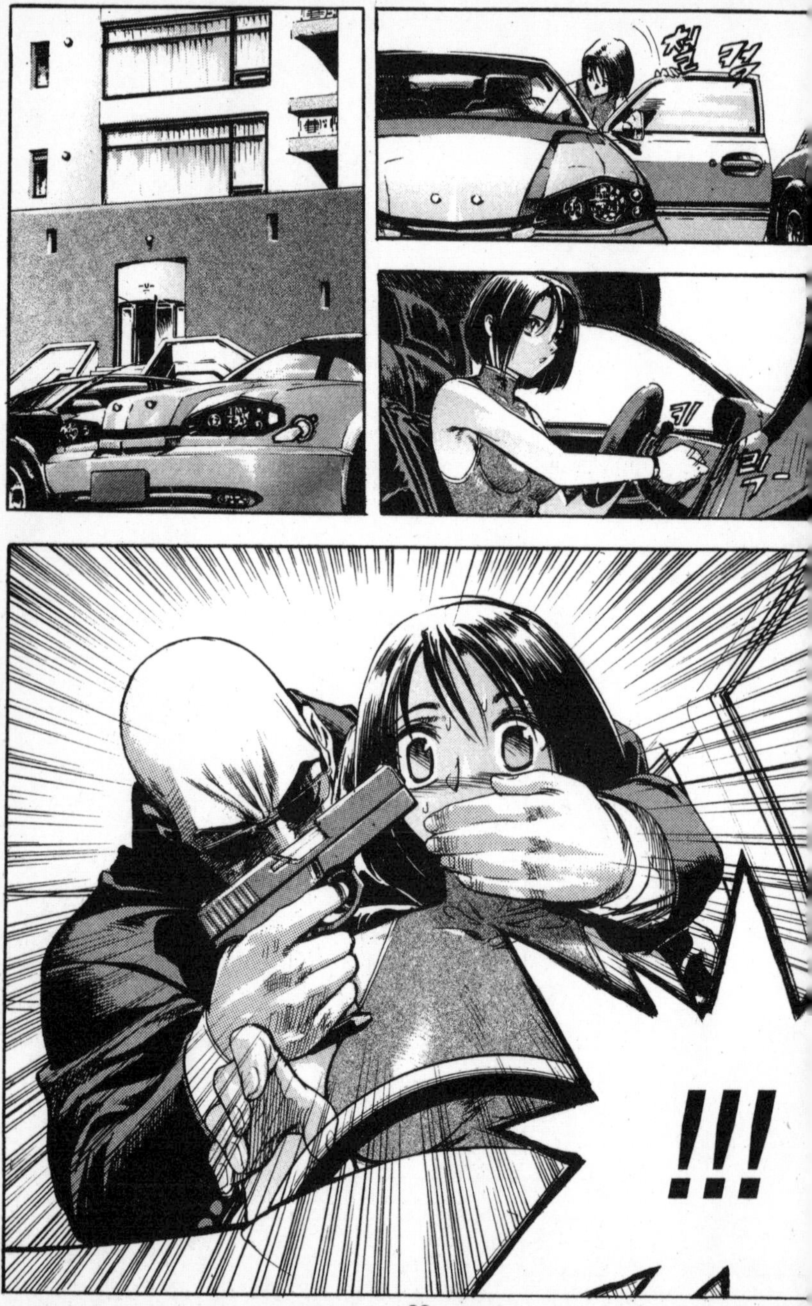
철컥
키
릭-
!!!

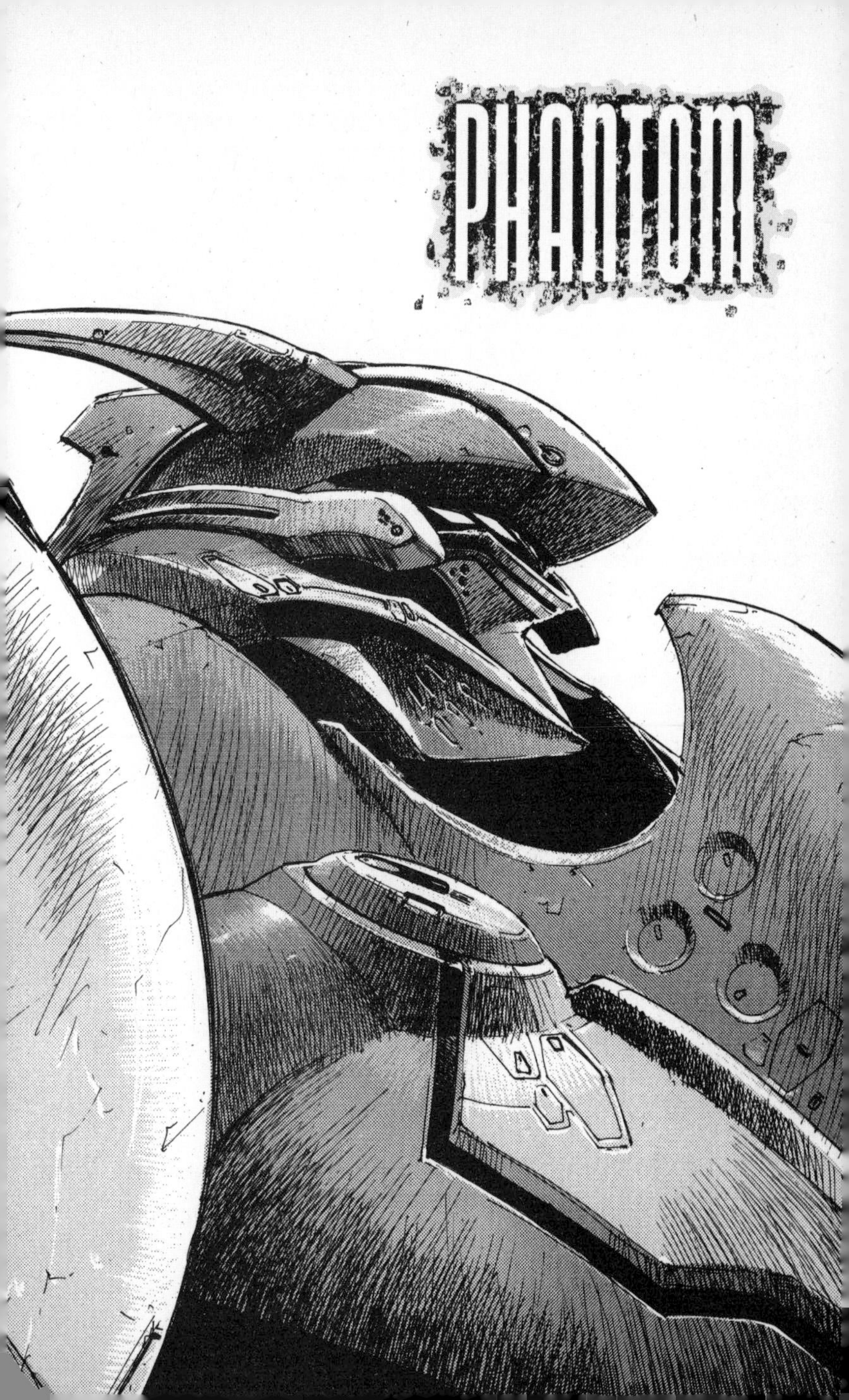
PHANTOM

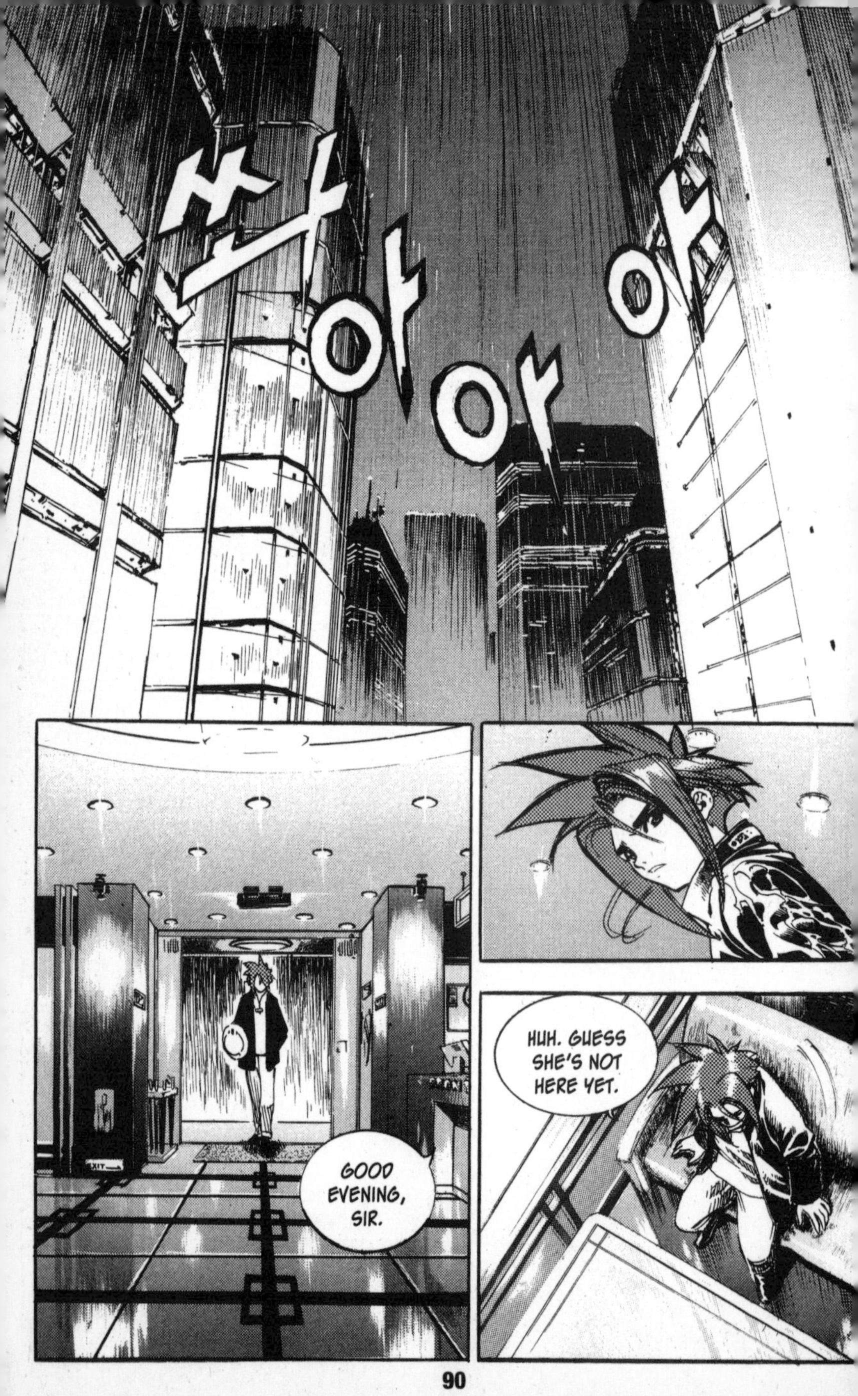
쏴아아아
GOOD EVENING, SIR.
HUH. GUESS SHE'S NOT HERE YET.

MAYBE THE
AIN'S DELAYING
HER.

IT'S COMING
DOWN IN BUCKETS
TONIGHT...

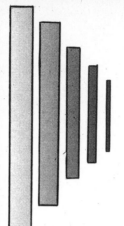

TICK

TICK

TICK

TICK

TICK

Cafe
Wagen

KAY, NOW I'M
OFFICIALLY
WORRIED.

SOMETHING
MUST'VE
HAPPENED TO
HER...!

91

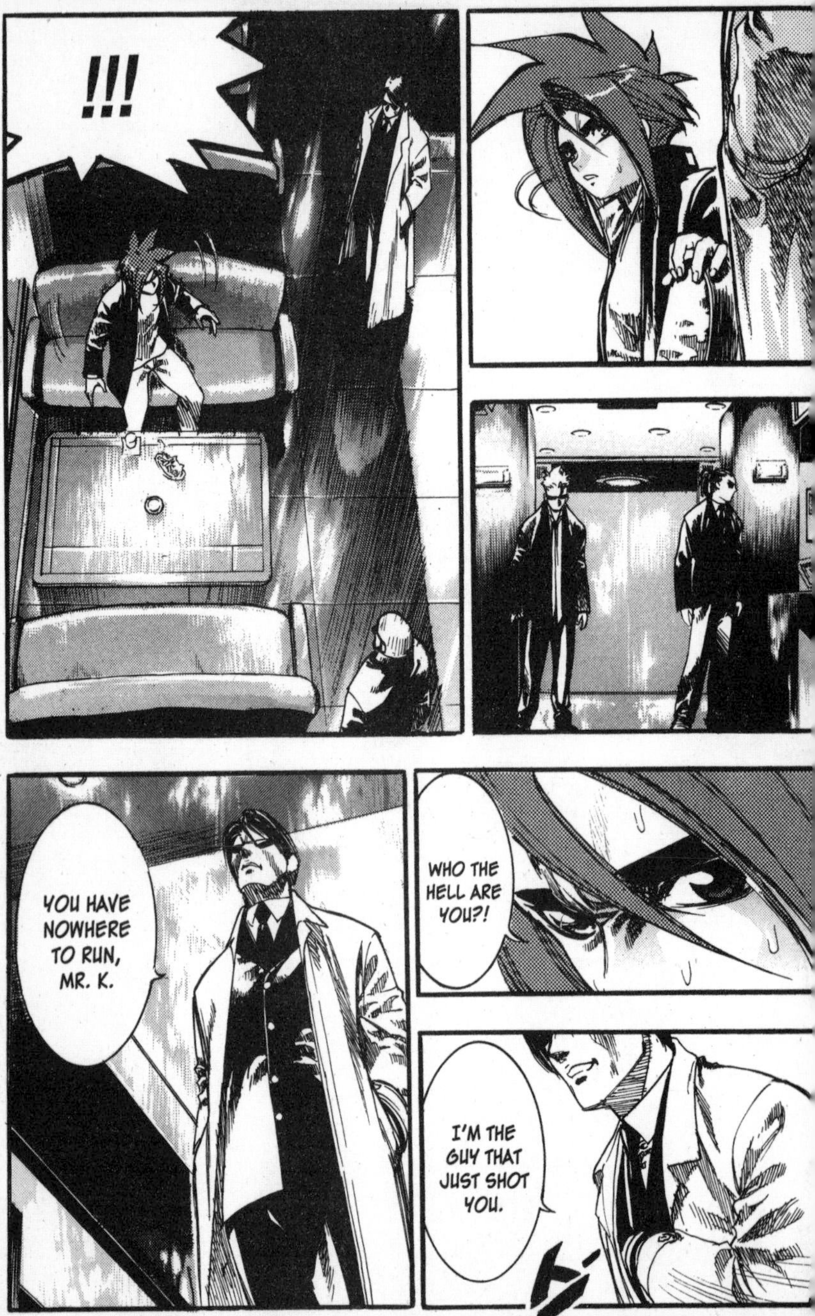
!!!
YOU HAVE NOWHERE TO RUN, MR. K.
WHO THE HELL ARE YOU?!
I'M THE GUY THAT JUST SHOT YOU.

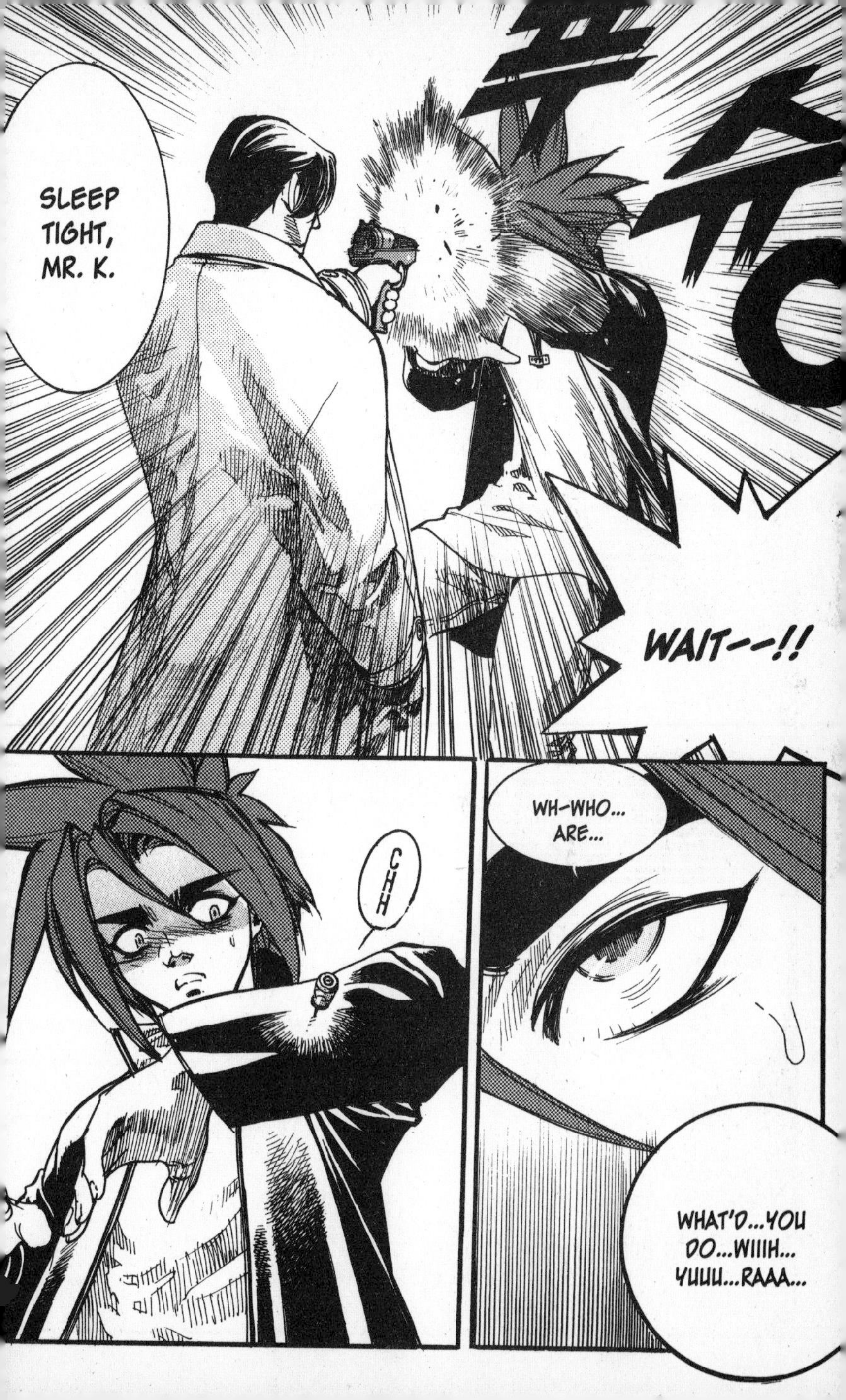
SLEEP TIGHT, MR. K.
WAIT--!!
CHH
WH-WHO... ARE...
WHAT'D...YOU DO...WIIIH... YUUU...RAAA...

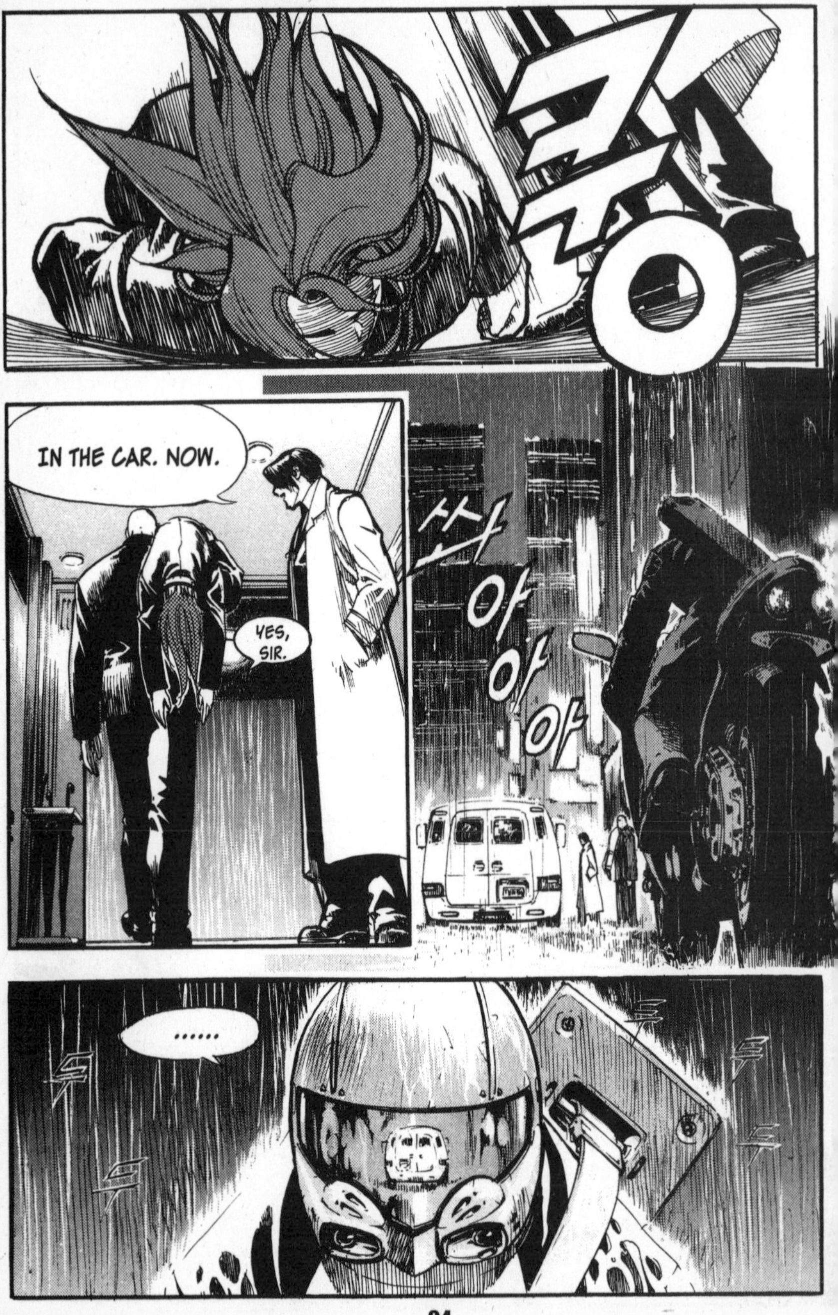
IN THE CAR. NOW.
YES, SIR.
쏴아아아
....

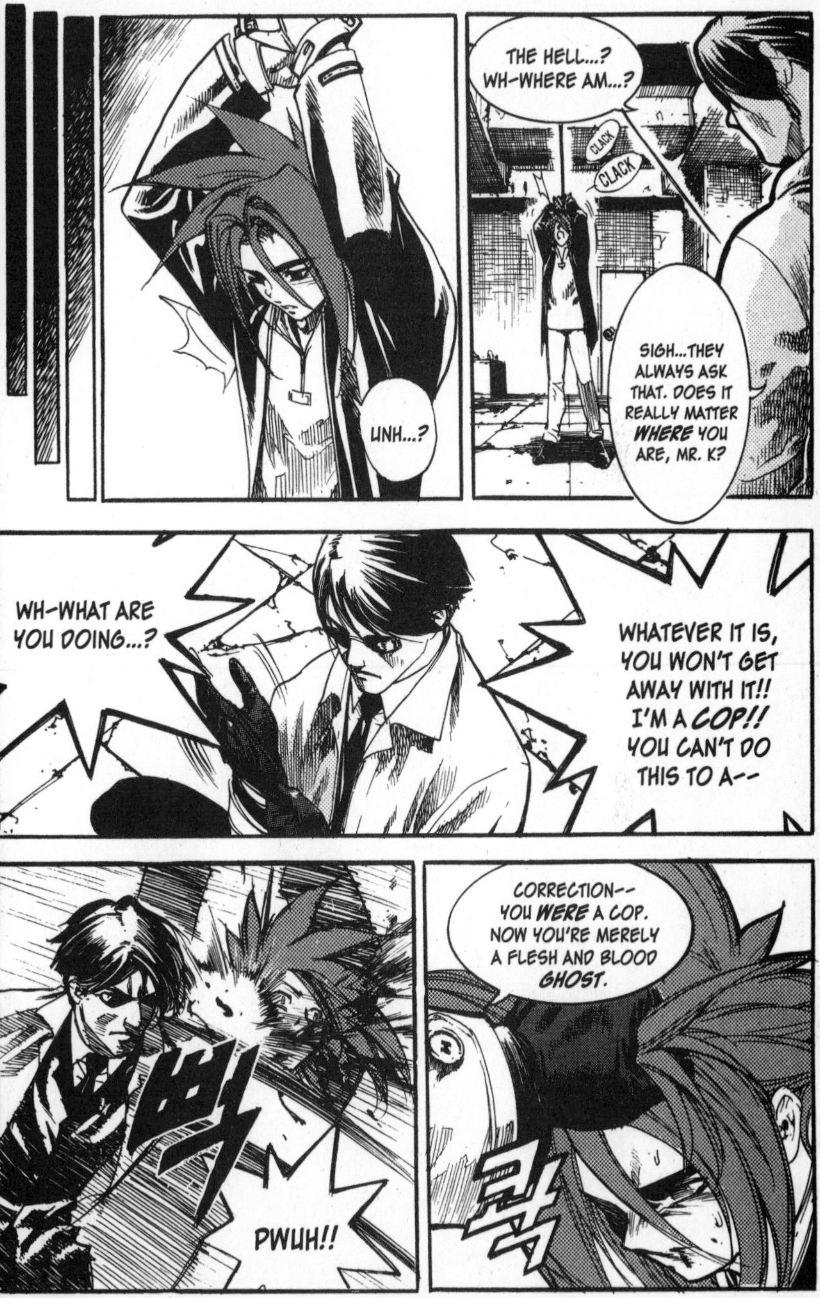
UNH...?
THE HELL...? WH-WHERE AM...?
CLACK
CLACK
SIGH...THEY ALWAYS ASK THAT. DOES IT REALLY MATTER *WHERE* YOU ARE, MR. K?
WH-WHAT ARE YOU DOING...?
WHATEVER IT IS, YOU WON'T GET AWAY WITH IT!! I'M A *COP!!* YOU CAN'T DO THIS TO A--
PWUH!!
CORRECTION-- YOU *WERE* A COP. NOW YOU'RE MERELY A FLESH AND BLOOD *GHOST*.

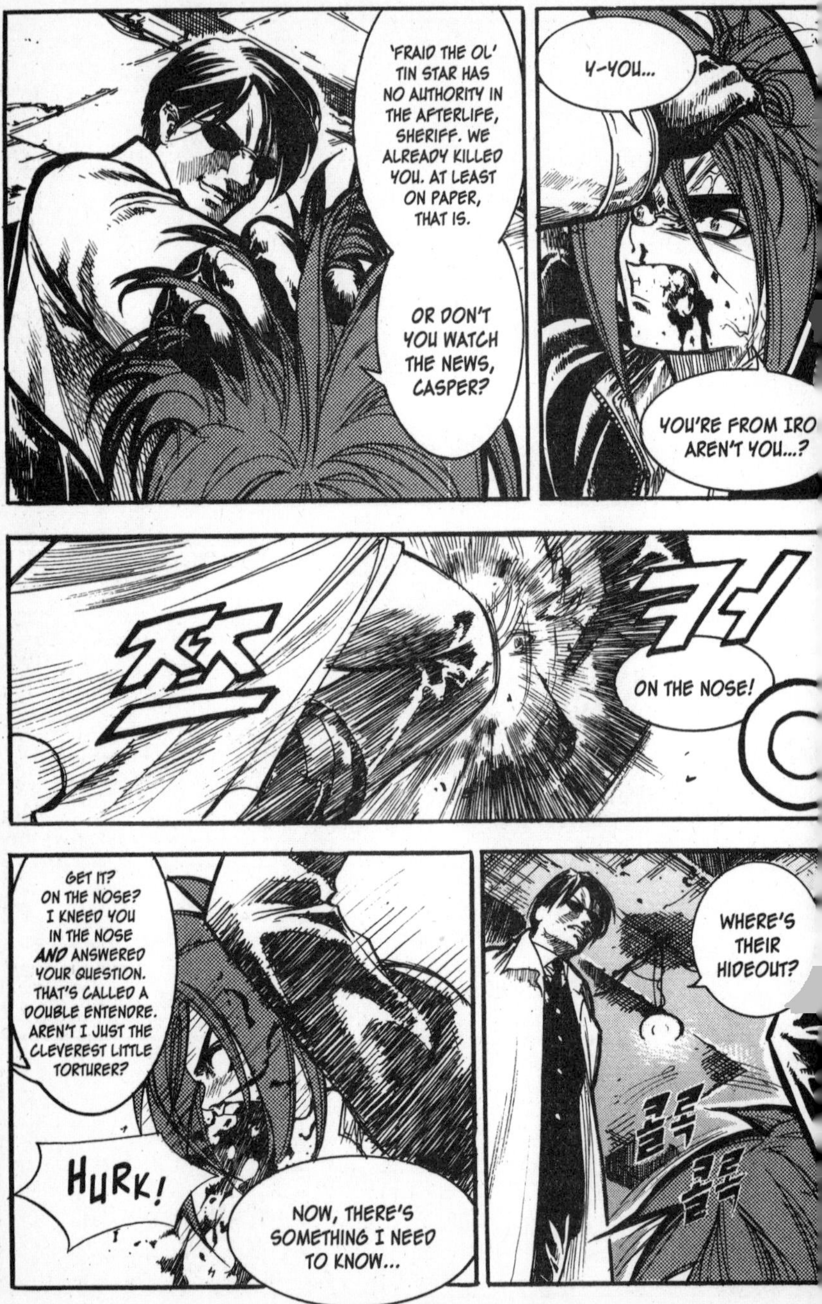
'FRAID THE OL' TIN STAR HAS NO AUTHORITY IN THE AFTERLIFE, SHERIFF. WE ALREADY KILLED YOU. AT LEAST ON PAPER, THAT IS.
OR DON'T YOU WATCH THE NEWS, CASPER?
Y-YOU...
YOU'RE FROM IRO AREN'T YOU...?
ON THE NOSE!
GET IT? ON THE NOSE? I KNEED YOU IN THE NOSE AND ANSWERED YOUR QUESTION. THAT'S CALLED A DOUBLE ENTENDRE. AREN'T I JUST THE CLEVEREST LITTLE TORTURER?
HURK!
NOW, THERE'S SOMETHING I NEED TO KNOW...
WHERE'S THEIR HIDEOUT?

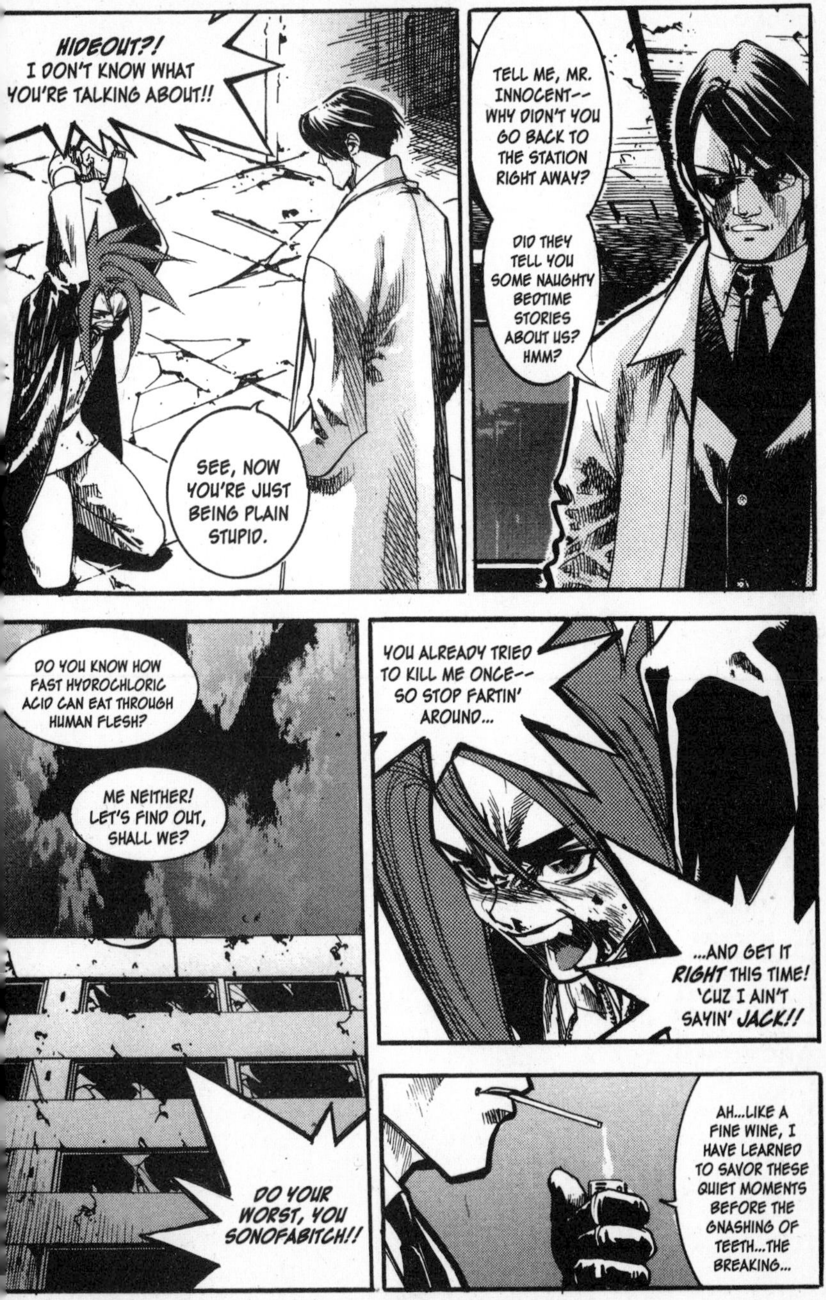
HIDEOUT?! I DON'T KNOW WHAT YOU'RE TALKING ABOUT!!
SEE, NOW YOU'RE JUST BEING PLAIN STUPID.
TELL ME, MR. INNOCENT-- WHY DIDN'T YOU GO BACK TO THE STATION RIGHT AWAY?
DID THEY TELL YOU SOME NAUGHTY BEDTIME STORIES ABOUT US? HMM?
DO YOU KNOW HOW FAST HYDROCHLORIC ACID CAN EAT THROUGH HUMAN FLESH?
ME NEITHER! LET'S FIND OUT, SHALL WE?
DO YOUR WORST, YOU SONOFABITCH!!
YOU ALREADY TRIED TO KILL ME ONCE-- SO STOP FARTIN' AROUND...
...AND GET IT RIGHT THIS TIME! 'CUZ I AIN'T SAYIN' JACK!!
AH...LIKE A FINE WINE, I HAVE LEARNED TO SAVOR THESE QUIET MOMENTS BEFORE THE GNASHING OF TEETH...THE BREAKING...

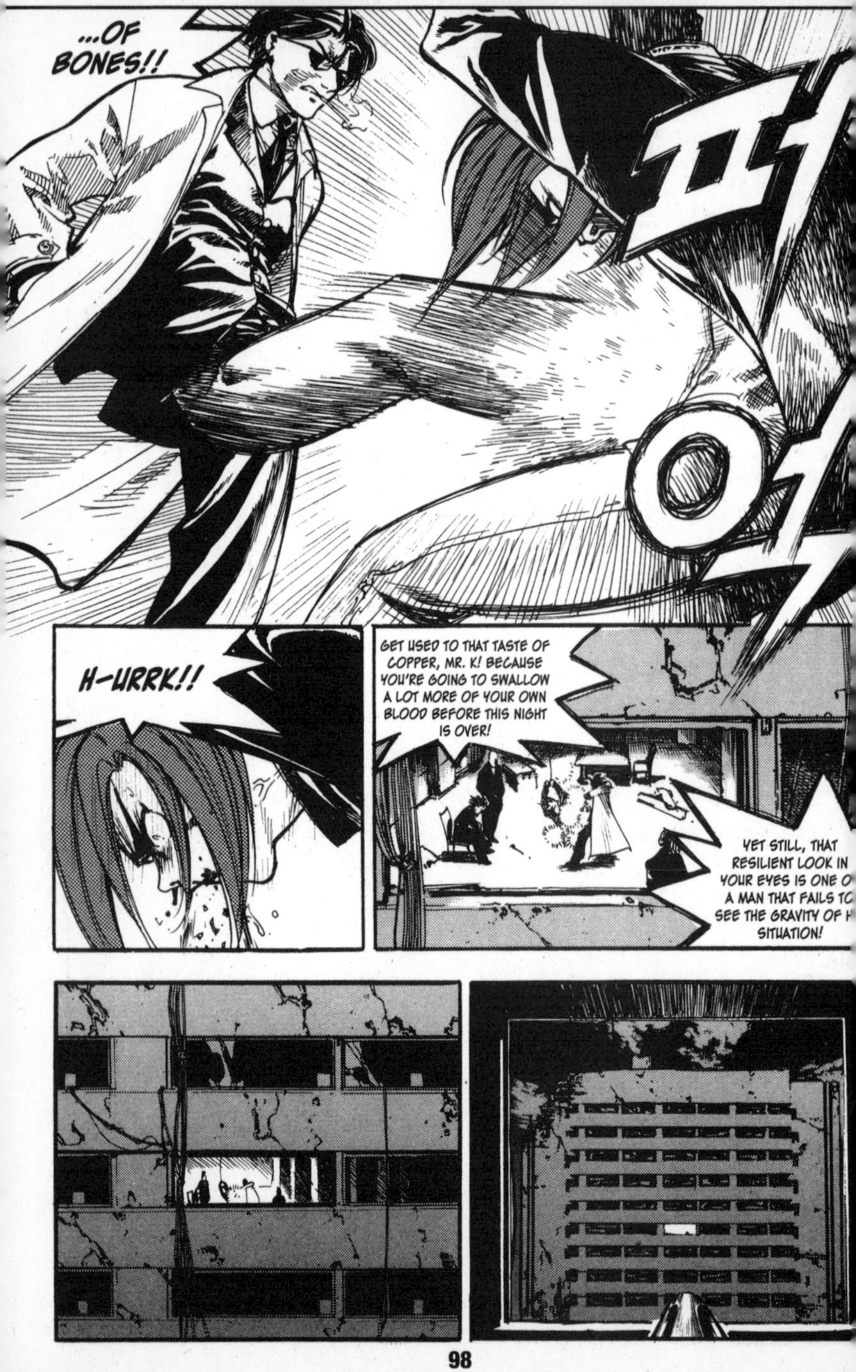

...OF BONES!!
H-URRK!!
GET USED TO THAT TASTE OF COPPER, MR. K! BECAUSE YOU'RE GOING TO SWALLOW A LOT MORE OF YOUR OWN BLOOD BEFORE THIS NIGHT IS OVER!
YET STILL, THAT RESILIENT LOOK IN YOUR EYES IS ONE O A MAN THAT FAILS TO SEE THE GRAVITY OF H SITUATION!

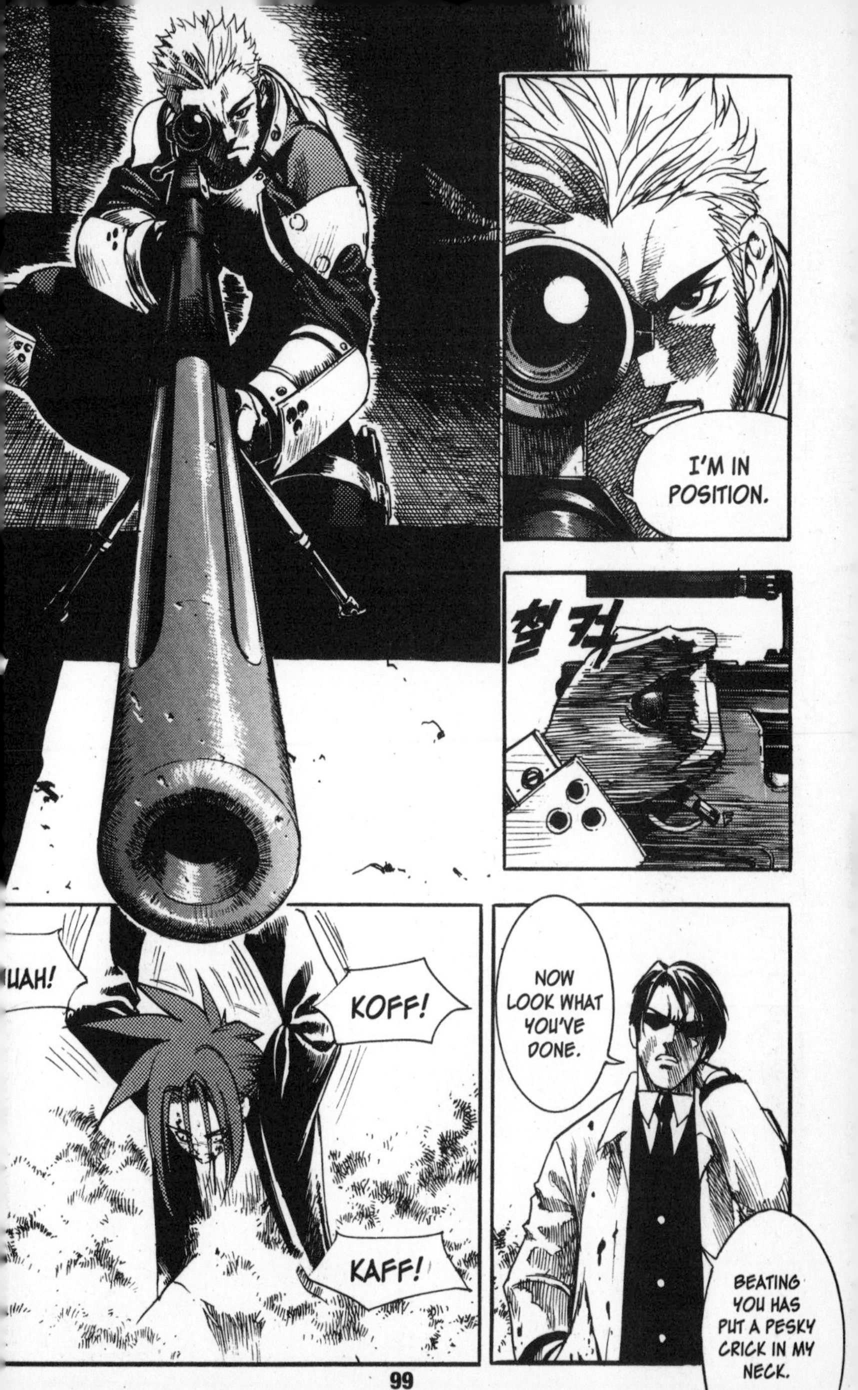
I'M IN POSITION.
철컥
UAH!
KOFF!
KAFF!
NOW LOOK WHAT YOU'VE DONE.
BEATING YOU HAS PUT A PESKY CRICK IN MY NECK.

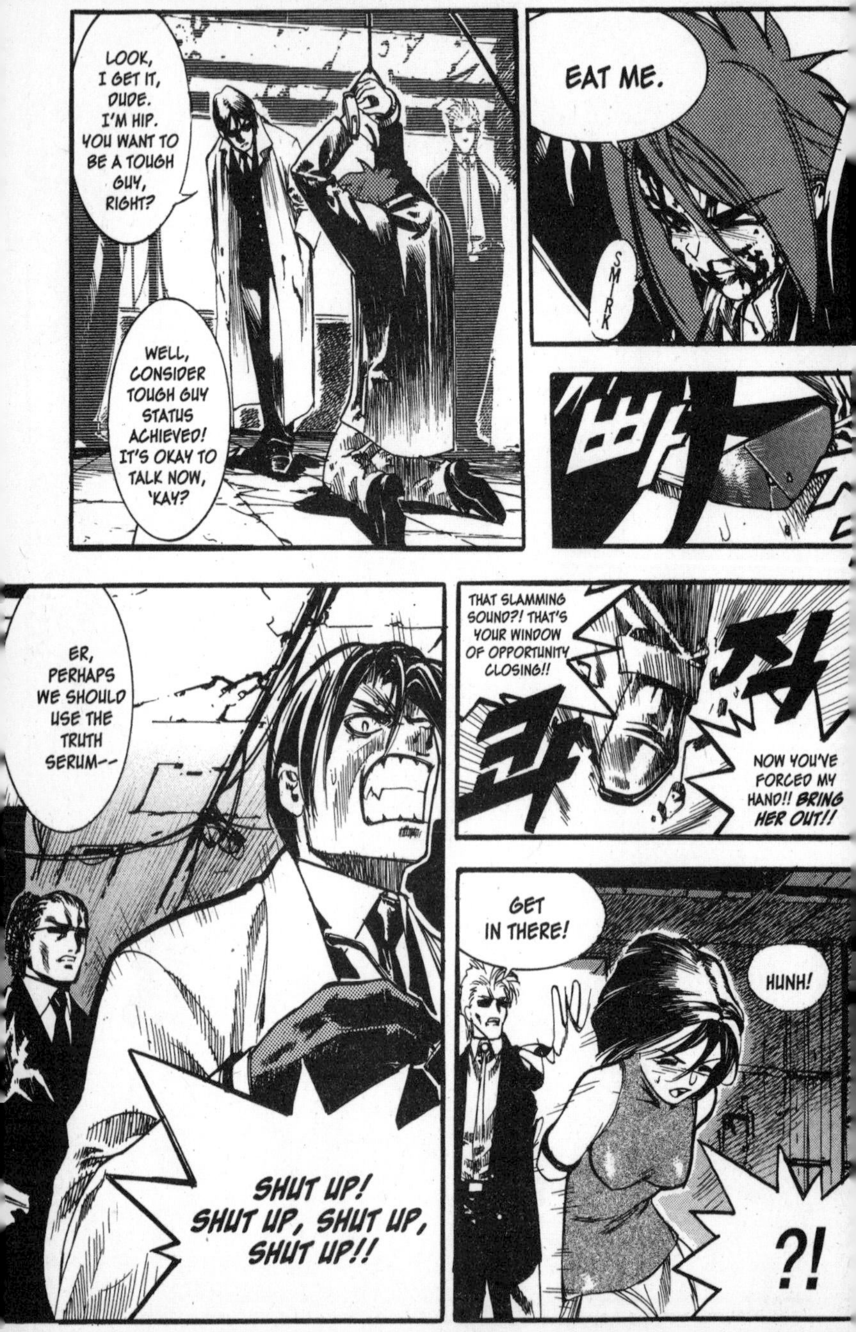
LOOK, I GET IT, DUDE. I'M HIP. YOU WANT TO BE A TOUGH GUY, RIGHT?
WELL, CONSIDER TOUGH GUY STATUS ACHIEVED! IT'S OKAY TO TALK NOW, 'KAY?
EAT ME.
SMIRK
ER, PERHAPS WE SHOULD USE THE TRUTH SERUM--
SHUT UP! SHUT UP, SHUT UP, SHUT UP!!
THAT SLAMMING SOUND?! THAT'S YOUR WINDOW OF OPPORTUNITY CLOSING!!
NOW YOU'VE FORCED MY HAND!! BRING HER OUT!!
GET IN THERE!
HUNH!
?!

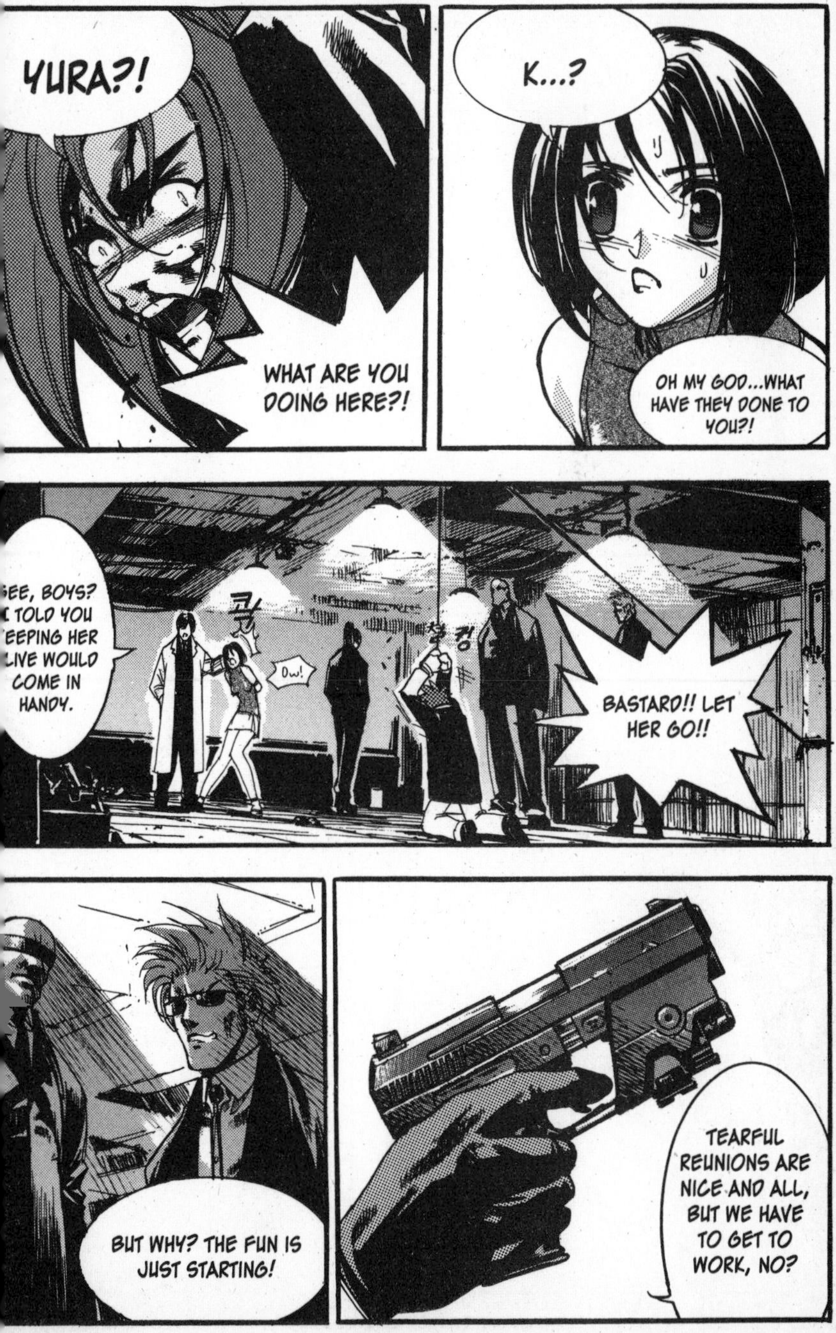
YURA?!
WHAT ARE YOU DOING HERE?!
K...?
OH MY GOD...WHAT HAVE THEY DONE TO YOU?!
EE, BOYS? TOLD YOU EEPING HER LIVE WOULD COME IN HANDY.
Ow!
BASTARD!! LET HER GO!!
BUT WHY? THE FUN IS JUST STARTING!
TEARFUL REUNIONS ARE NICE AND ALL, BUT WE HAVE TO GET TO WORK, NO?

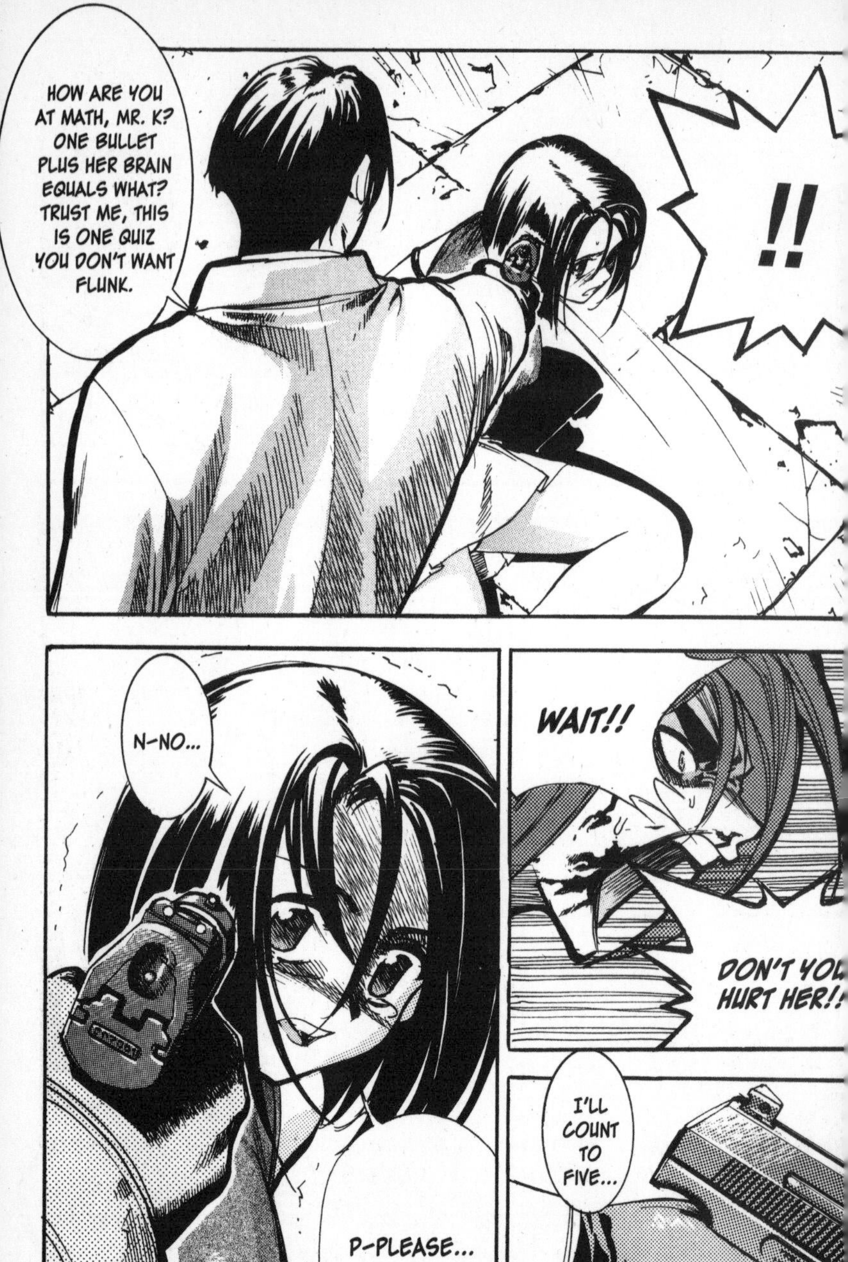
HOW ARE YOU AT MATH, MR. K? ONE BULLET PLUS HER BRAIN EQUALS WHAT? TRUST ME, THIS IS ONE QUIZ YOU DON'T WANT FLUNK.
!!
N-NO...
P-PLEASE...
WAIT!!
DON'T YOU HURT HER!!
I'LL COUNT TO FIVE...

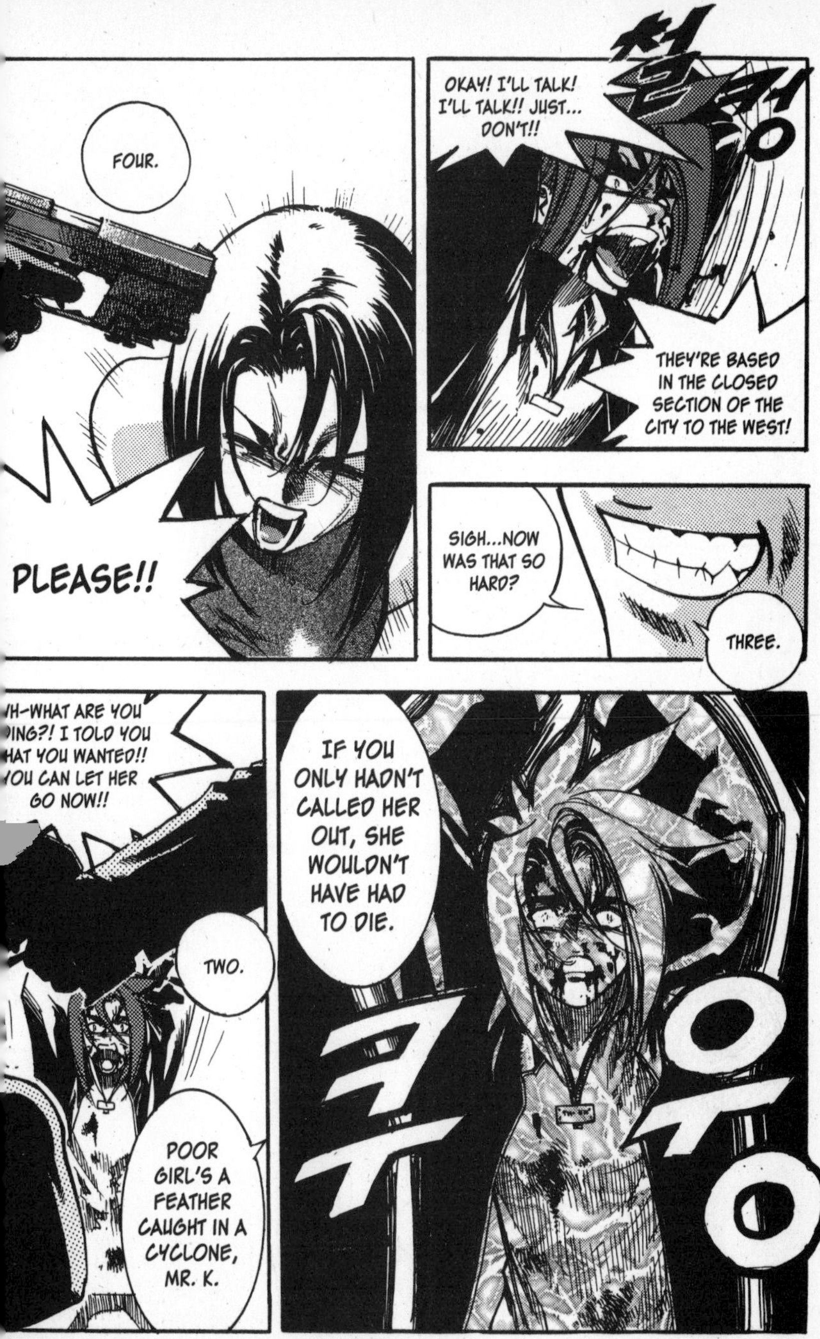
FOUR.
PLEASE!!
OKAY! I'LL TALK! I'LL TALK!! JUST... DON'T!!
THEY'RE BASED IN THE CLOSED SECTION OF THE CITY TO THE WEST!
SIGH...NOW WAS THAT SO HARD?
THREE.
H-WHAT ARE YOU ING?! I TOLD YOU HAT YOU WANTED!! OU CAN LET HER GO NOW!!
TWO.
POOR GIRL'S A FEATHER CAUGHT IN A CYCLONE, MR. K.
IF YOU ONLY HADN'T CALLED HER OUT, SHE WOULDN'T HAVE HAD TO DIE.

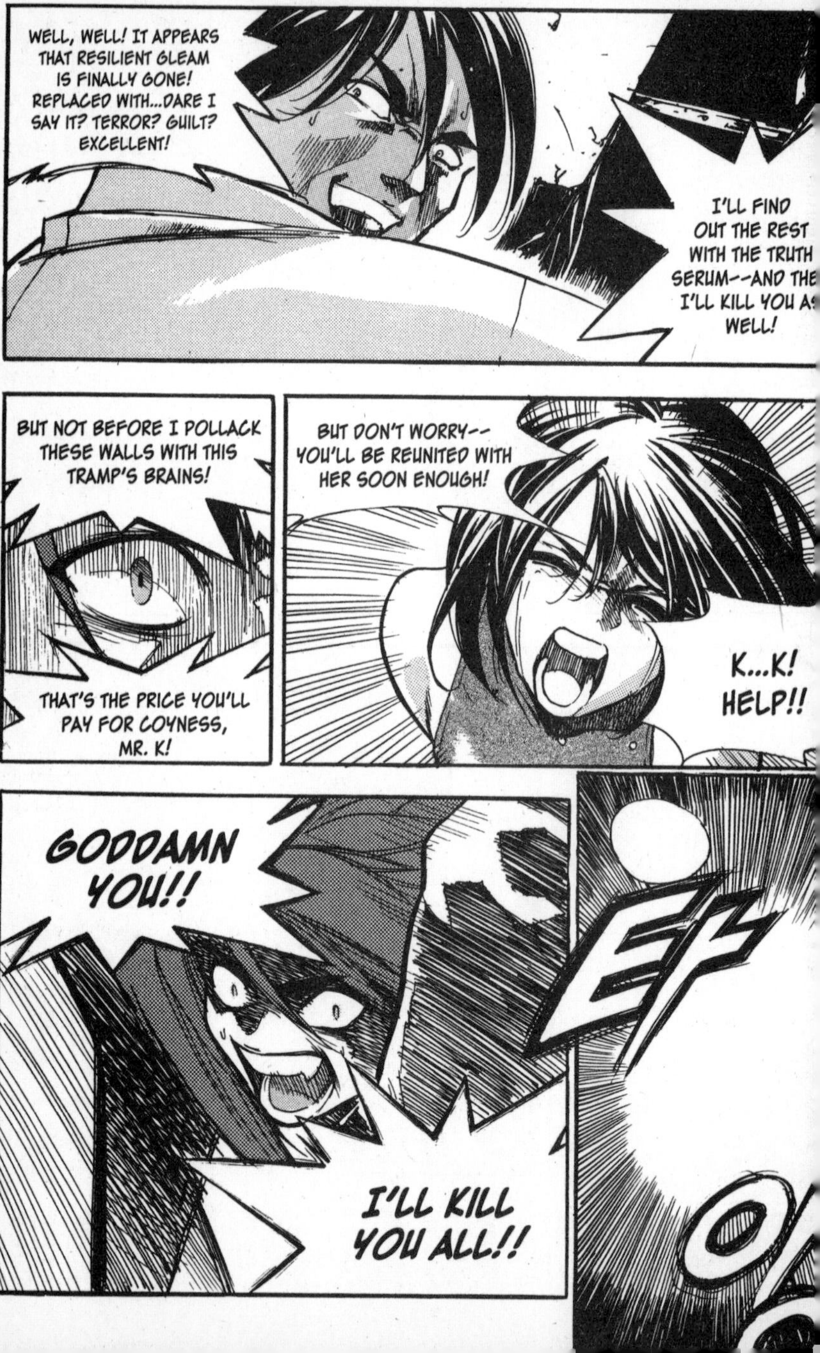
WELL, WELL! IT APPEARS THAT RESILIENT GLEAM IS FINALLY GONE! REPLACED WITH...DARE I SAY IT? TERROR? GUILT? EXCELLENT!
I'LL FIND OUT THE REST WITH THE TRUTH SERUM--AND THE I'LL KILL YOU A WELL!
BUT NOT BEFORE I POLLACK THESE WALLS WITH THIS TRAMP'S BRAINS!
THAT'S THE PRICE YOU'LL PAY FOR COYNESS, MR. K!
BUT DON'T WORRY-- YOU'LL BE REUNITED WITH HER SOON ENOUGH!
K...K! HELP!!
GODDAMN YOU!!
I'LL KILL YOU ALL!!

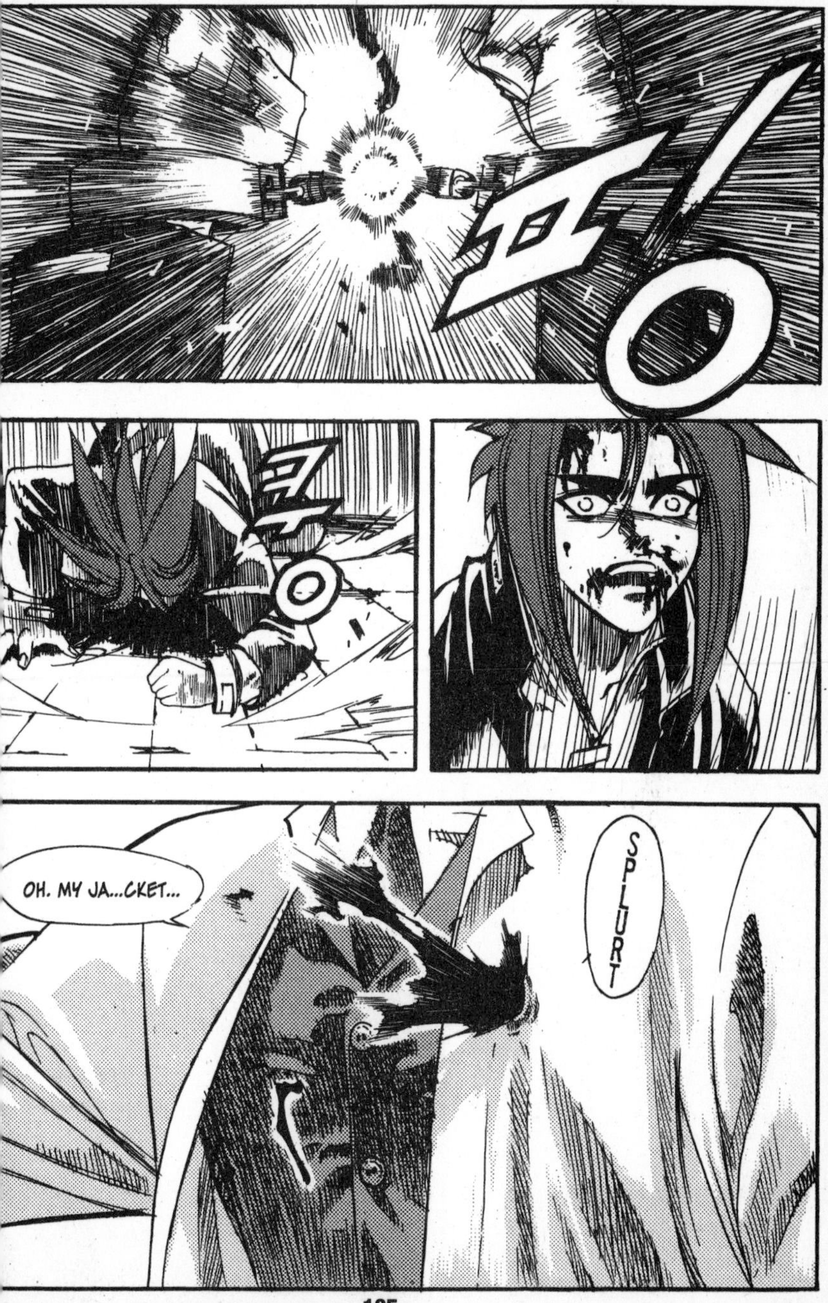
OH. MY JA...CKET...
SPLURT

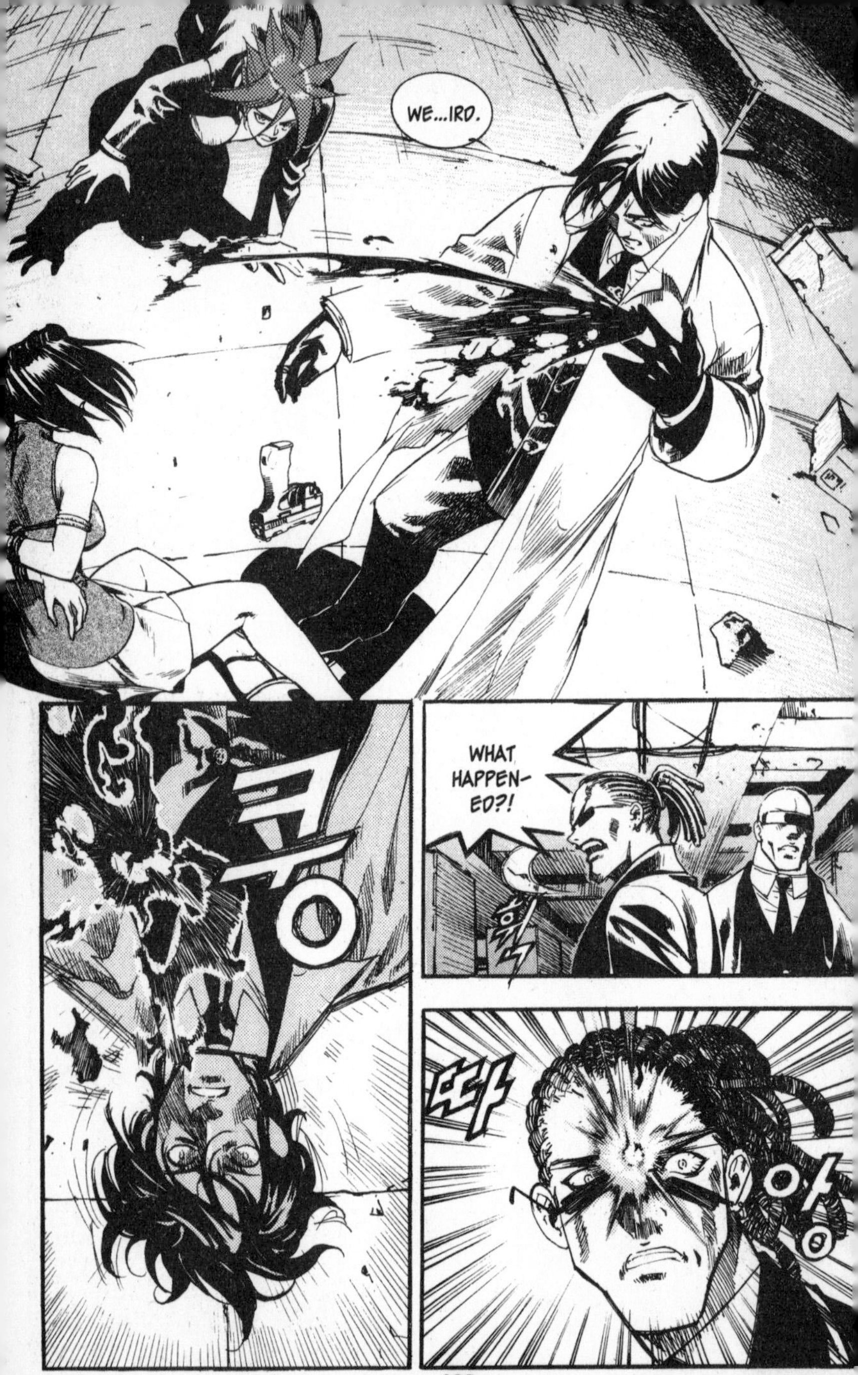
WE...IRD.
WHAT HAPPEN-ED?!

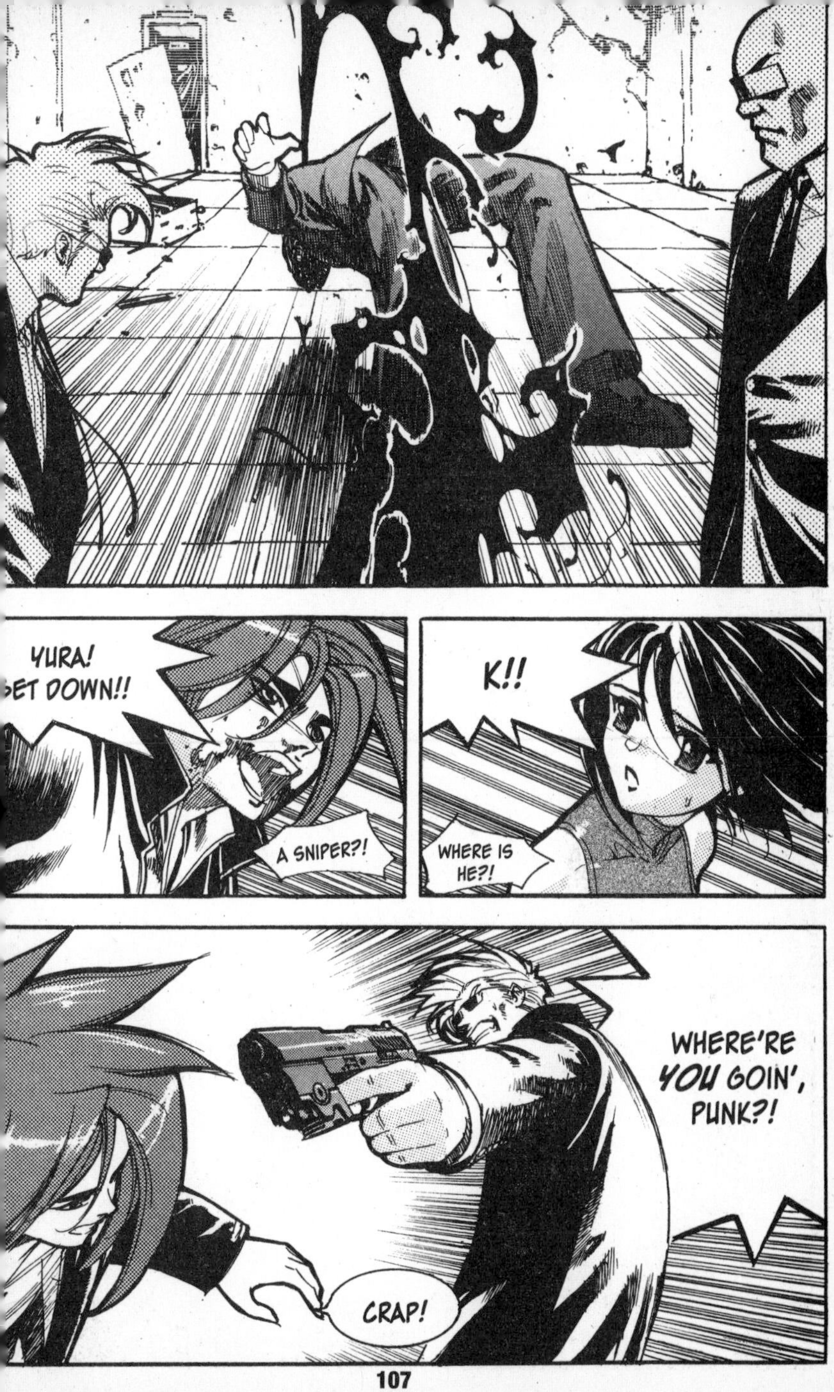
YURA! GET DOWN!!
A SNIPER?!
K!!
WHERE IS HE?!
WHERE'RE YOU GOIN', PUNK?!
CRAP!

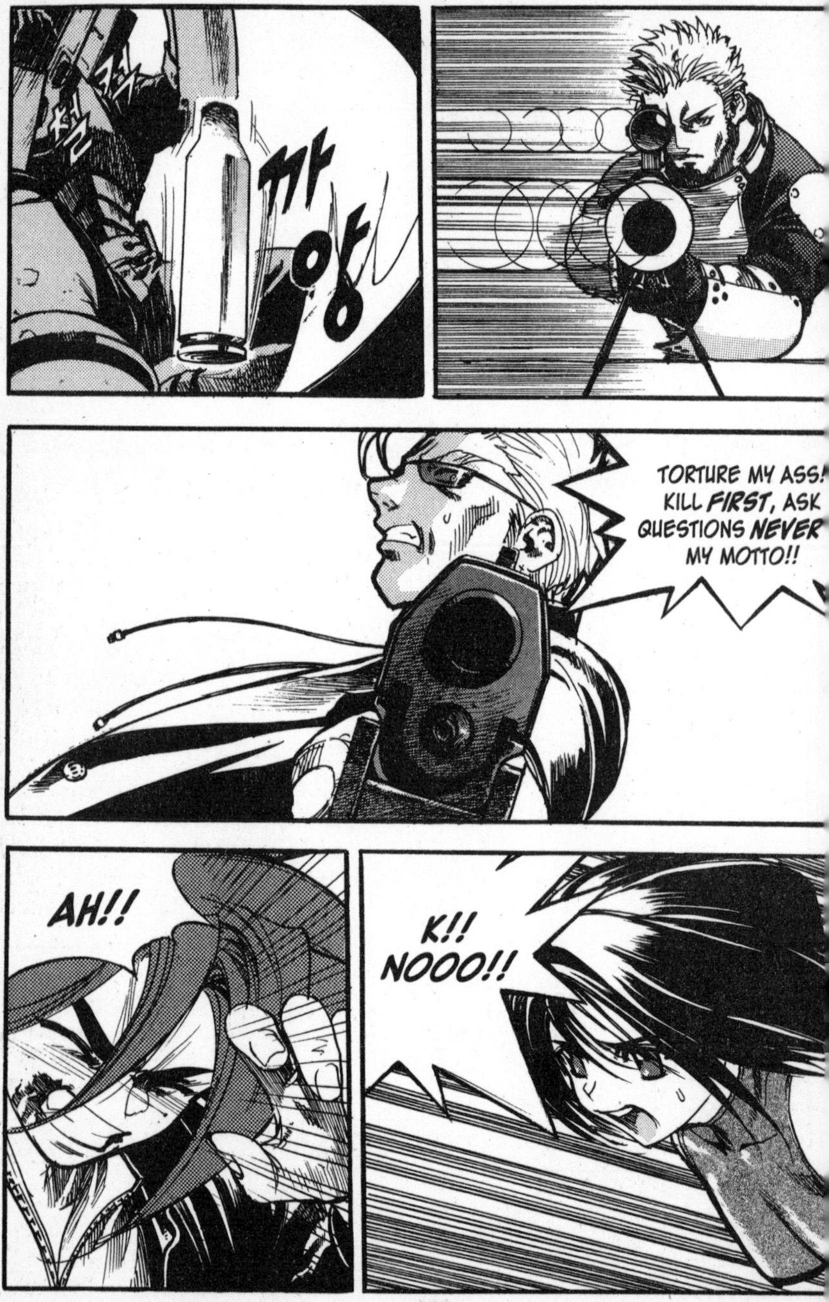
까앙
TORTURE MY ASS! KILL FIRST, ASK QUESTIONS NEVER MY MOTTO!!
AH!!
K!! NOOO!!

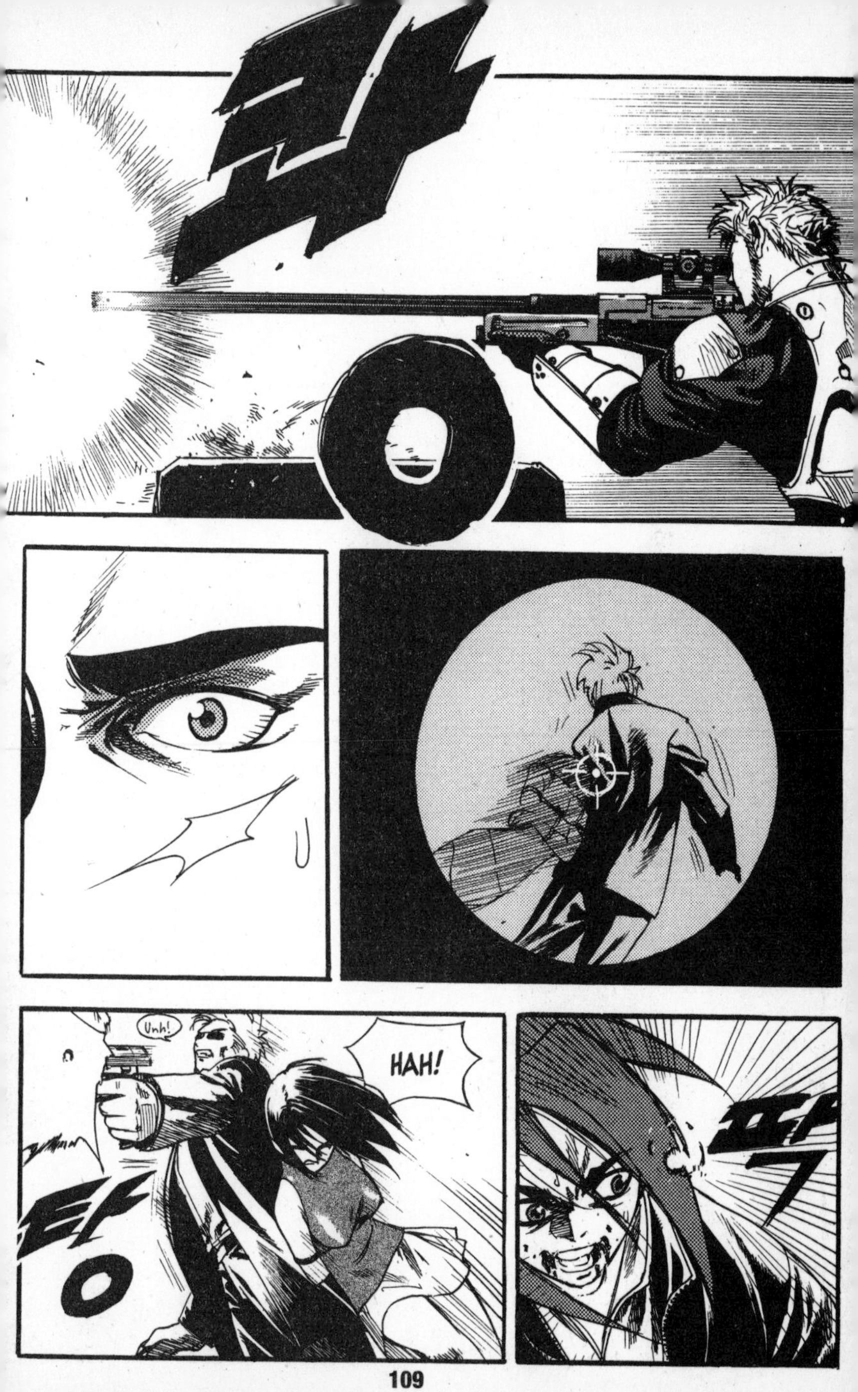
Unh!
HAH!

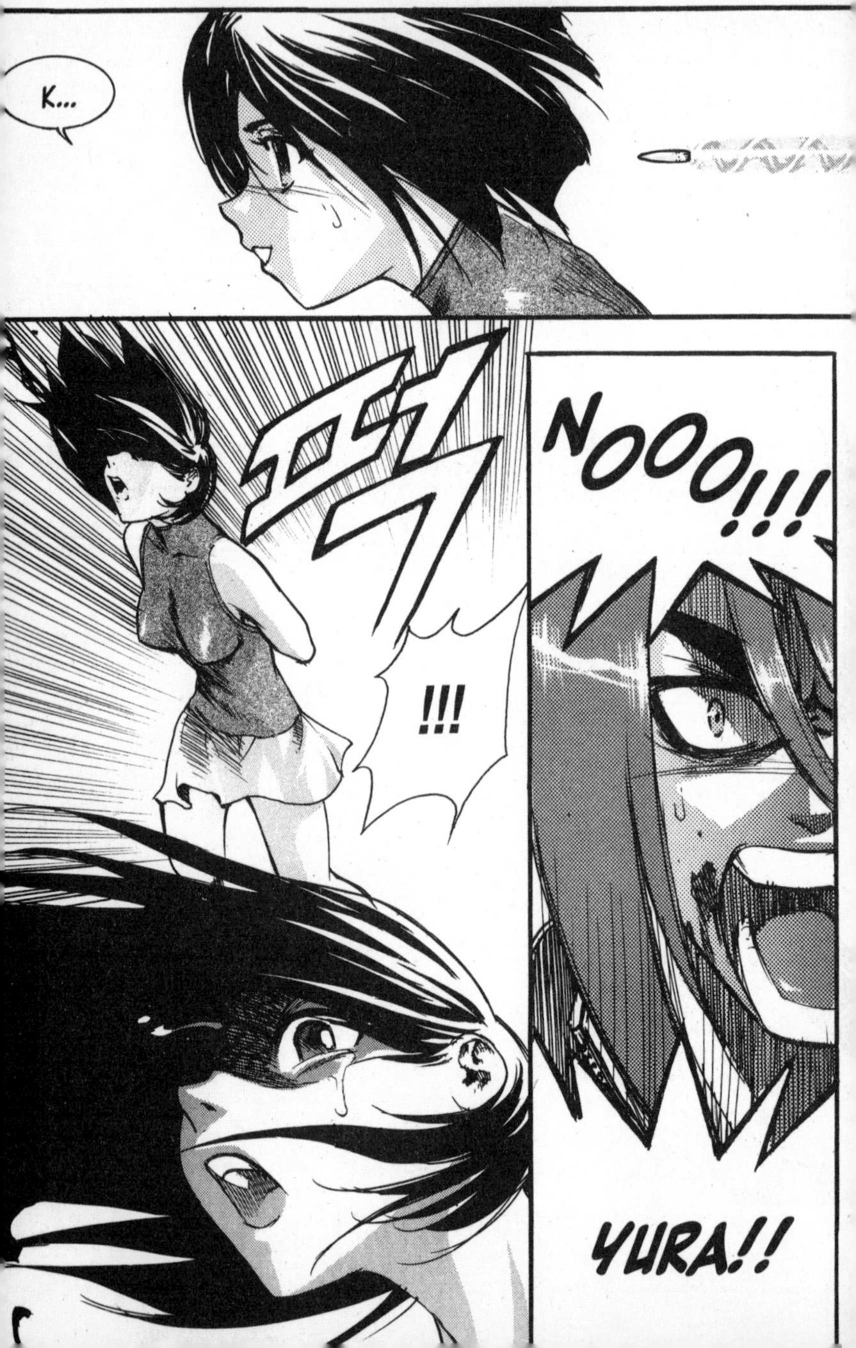
K...
!!!
NOOO!!!
YURA!!

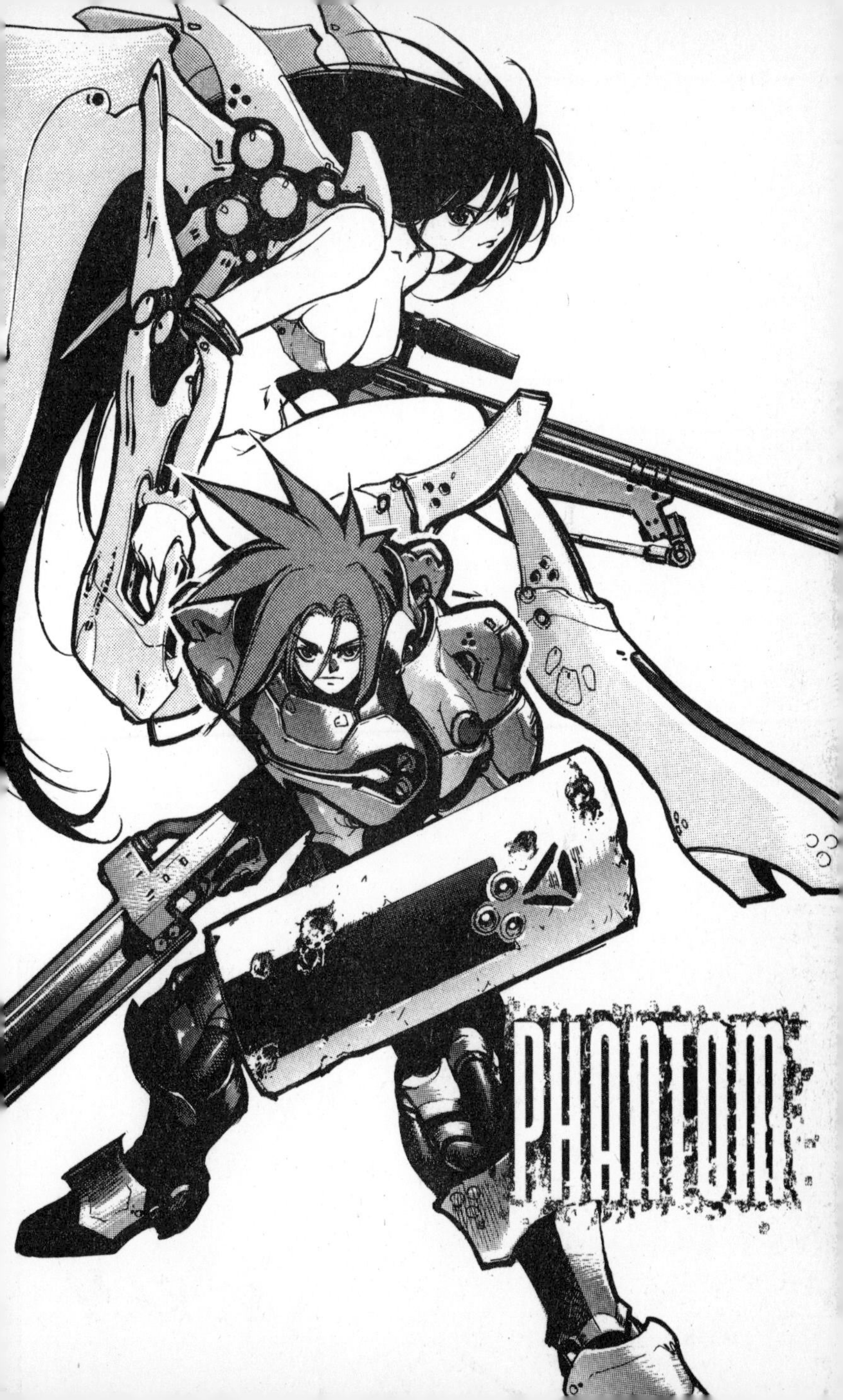
PHANTOM

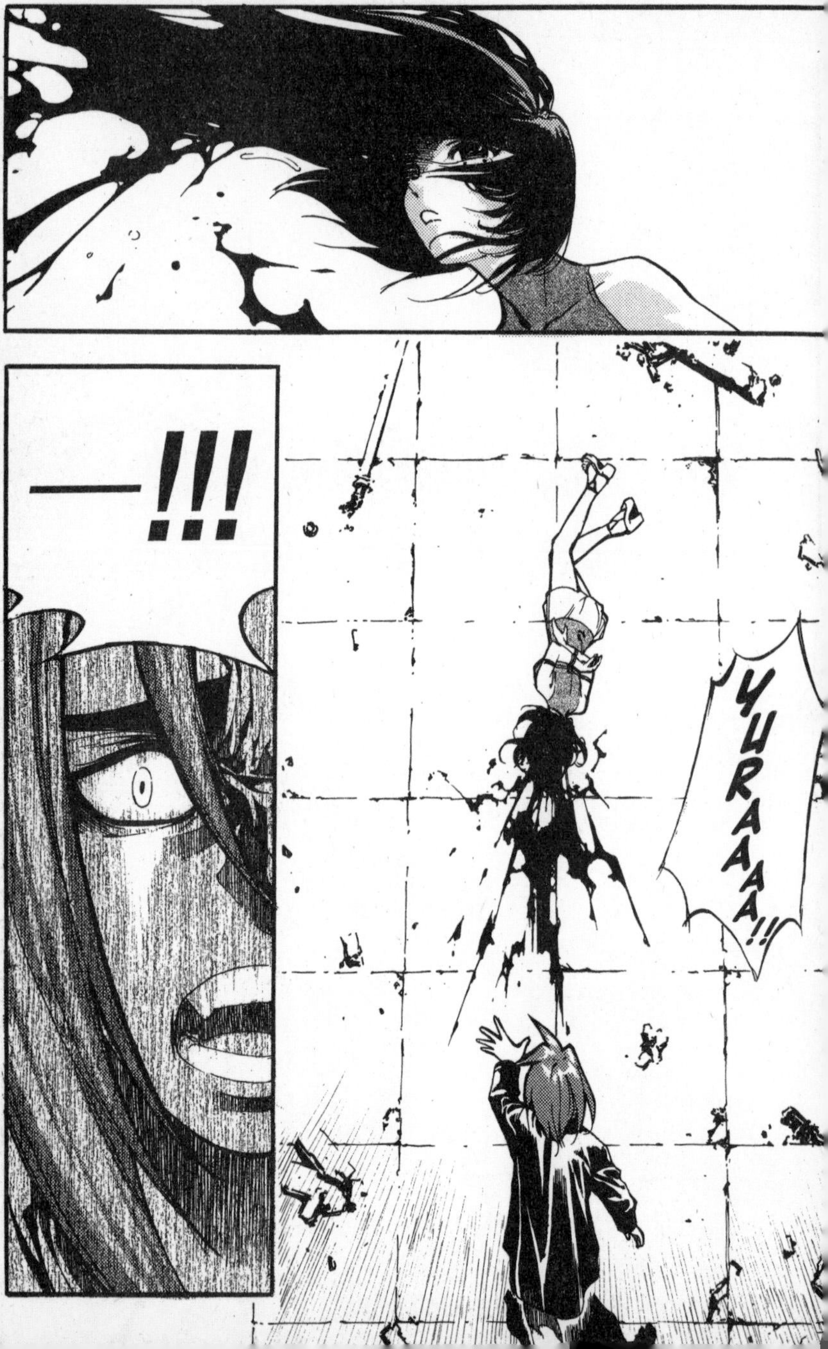
—!!!
YURAAAA!!

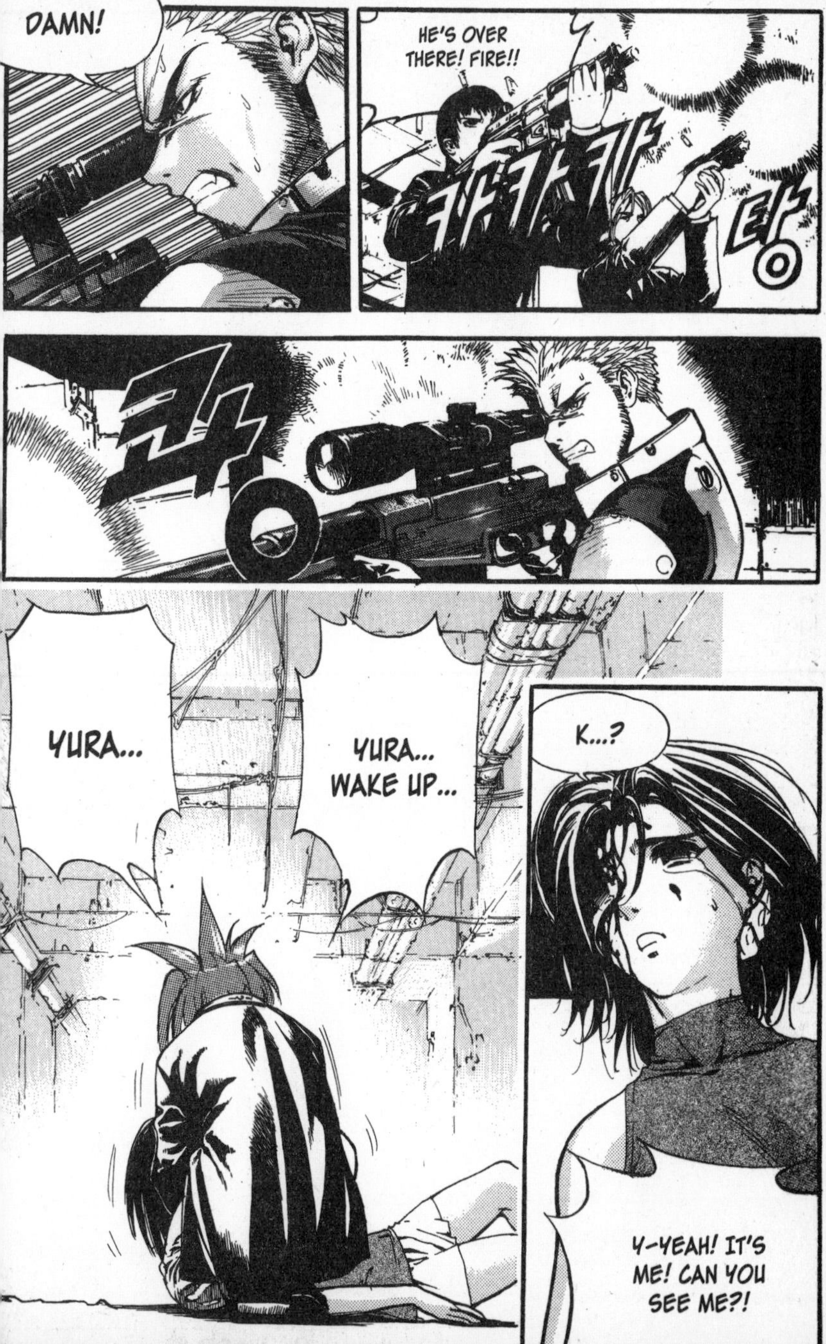
DAMN!
HE'S OVER THERE! FIRE!!
YURA...
YURA... WAKE UP...
K...?
Y-YEAH! IT'S ME! CAN YOU SEE ME?!

I-IT...IT'S S-STRANGE...I...

...FEEL L-LIKE... I'M F-FALLING...

JUST HANG IN THERE! I'LL GET YOU TO A HOSPITAL!

HOLD ON, OKAY?!

KUH!

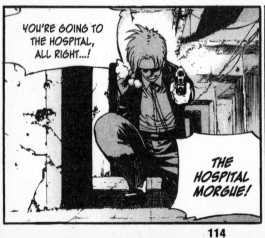

YOU'RE GOING TO THE HOSPITAL, ALL RIGHT...!

THE HOSPITAL MORGUE!

GAH!

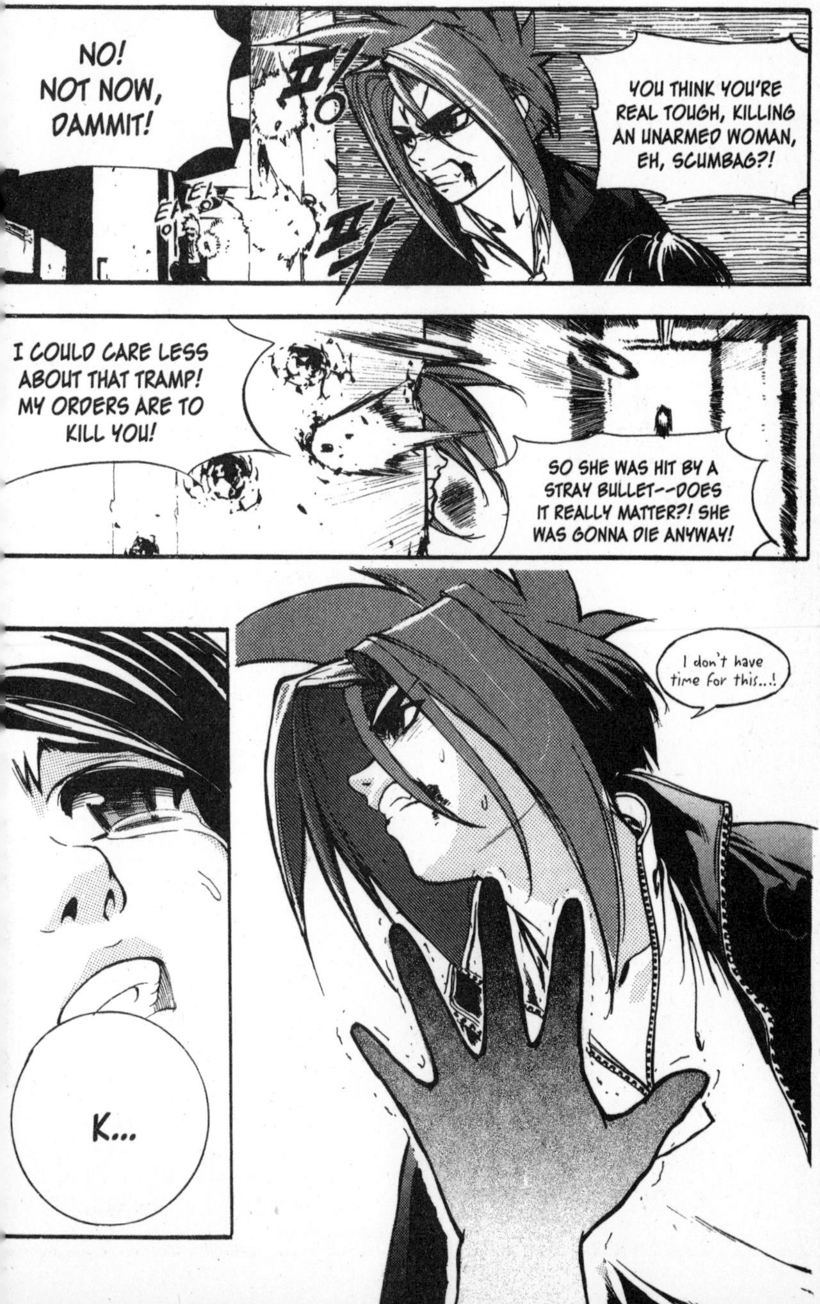
NO! NOT NOW, DAMMIT!
YOU THINK YOU'RE REAL TOUGH, KILLING AN UNARMED WOMAN, EH, SCUMBAG?!
I COULD CARE LESS ABOUT THAT TRAMP! MY ORDERS ARE TO KILL YOU!
SO SHE WAS HIT BY A STRAY BULLET--DOES IT REALLY MATTER?! SHE WAS GONNA DIE ANYWAY!
K...
I don't have time for this...!

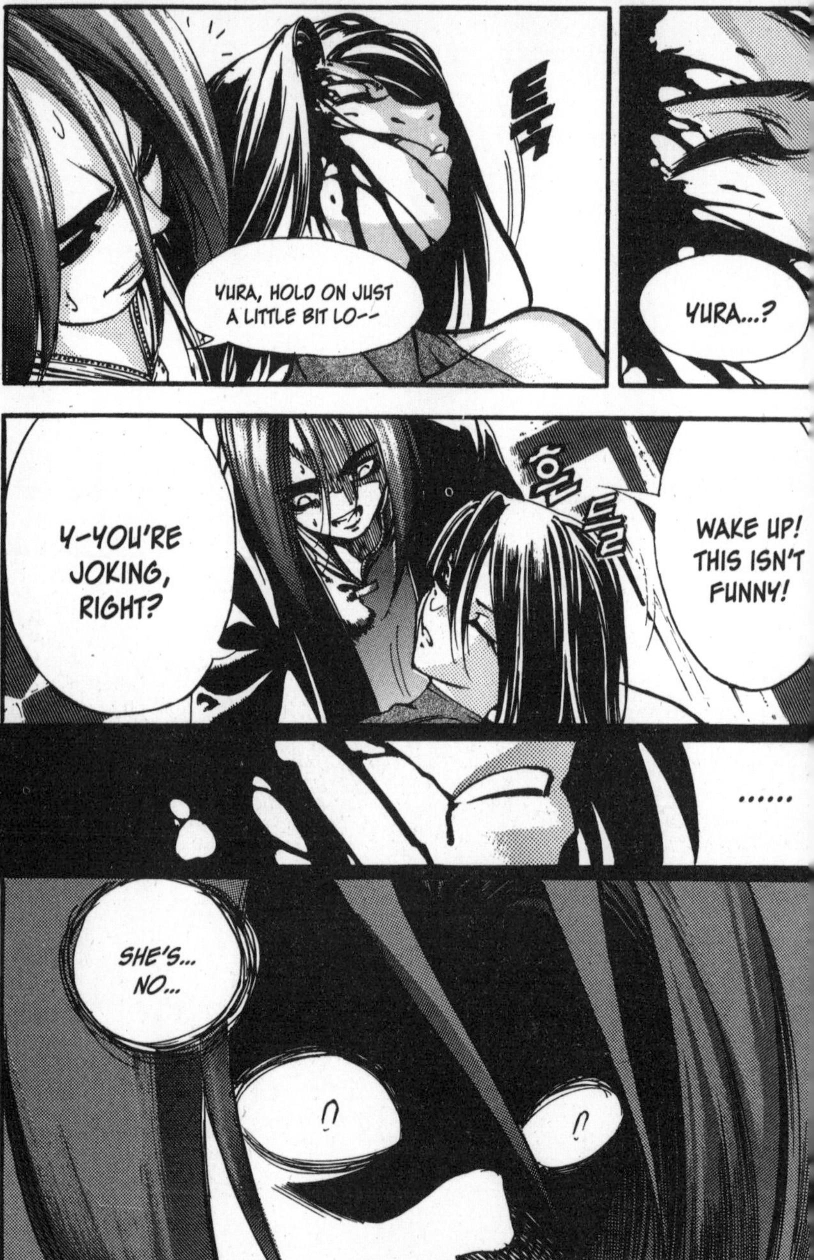

YURA, HOLD ON JUST A LITTLE BIT LO--
YURA...?
Y-YOU'RE JOKING, RIGHT?
WAKE UP! THIS ISN'T FUNNY!
......
SHE'S... NO...

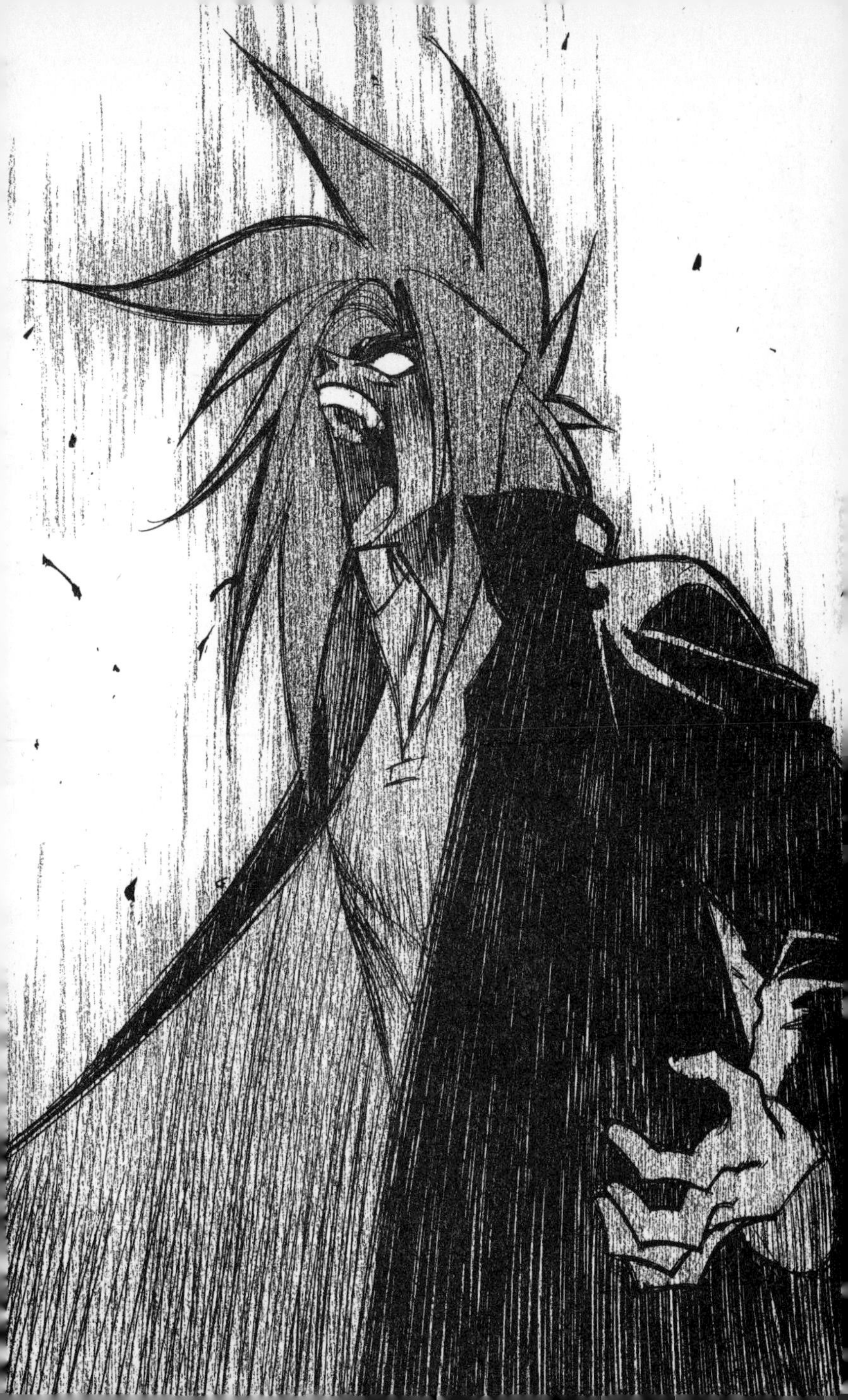

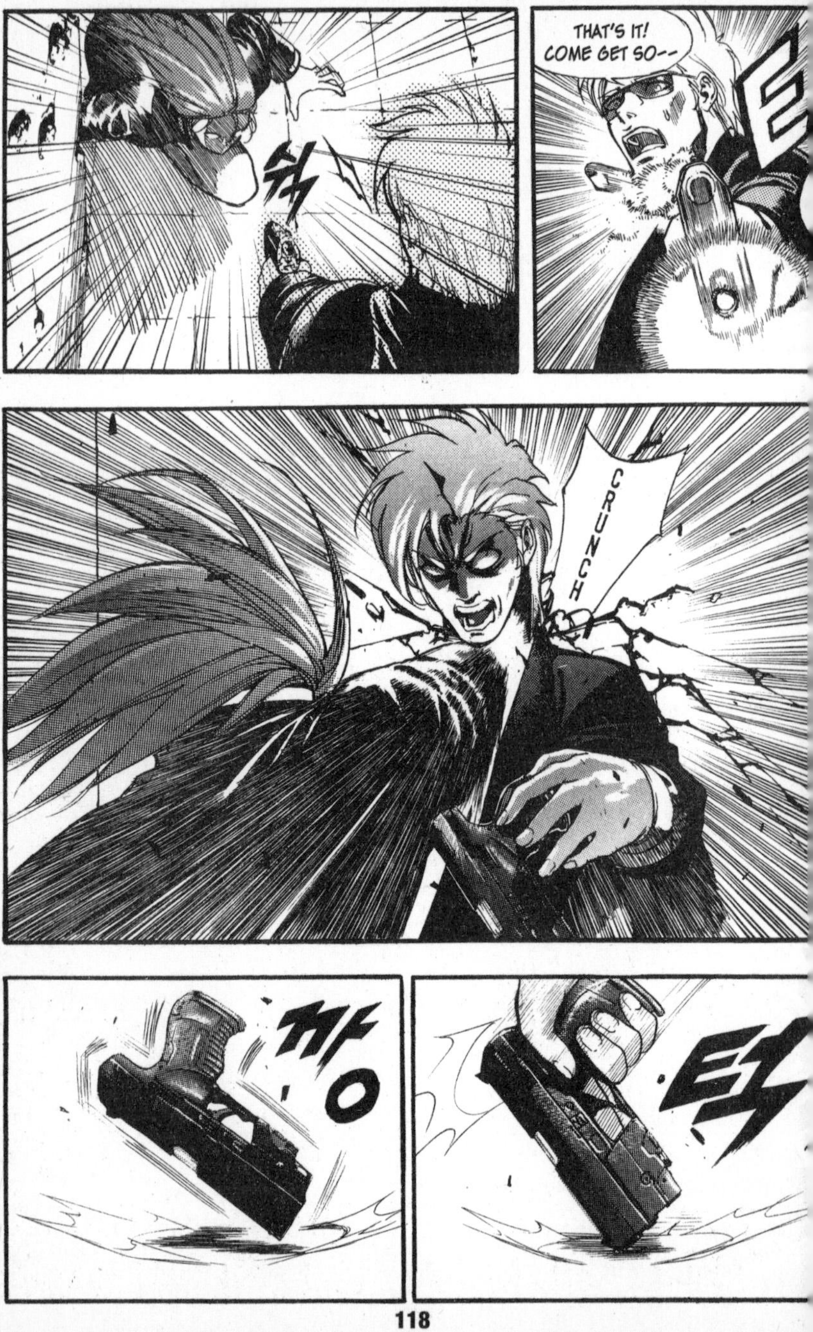
THAT'S IT!
COME GET SO--
CRUNCH

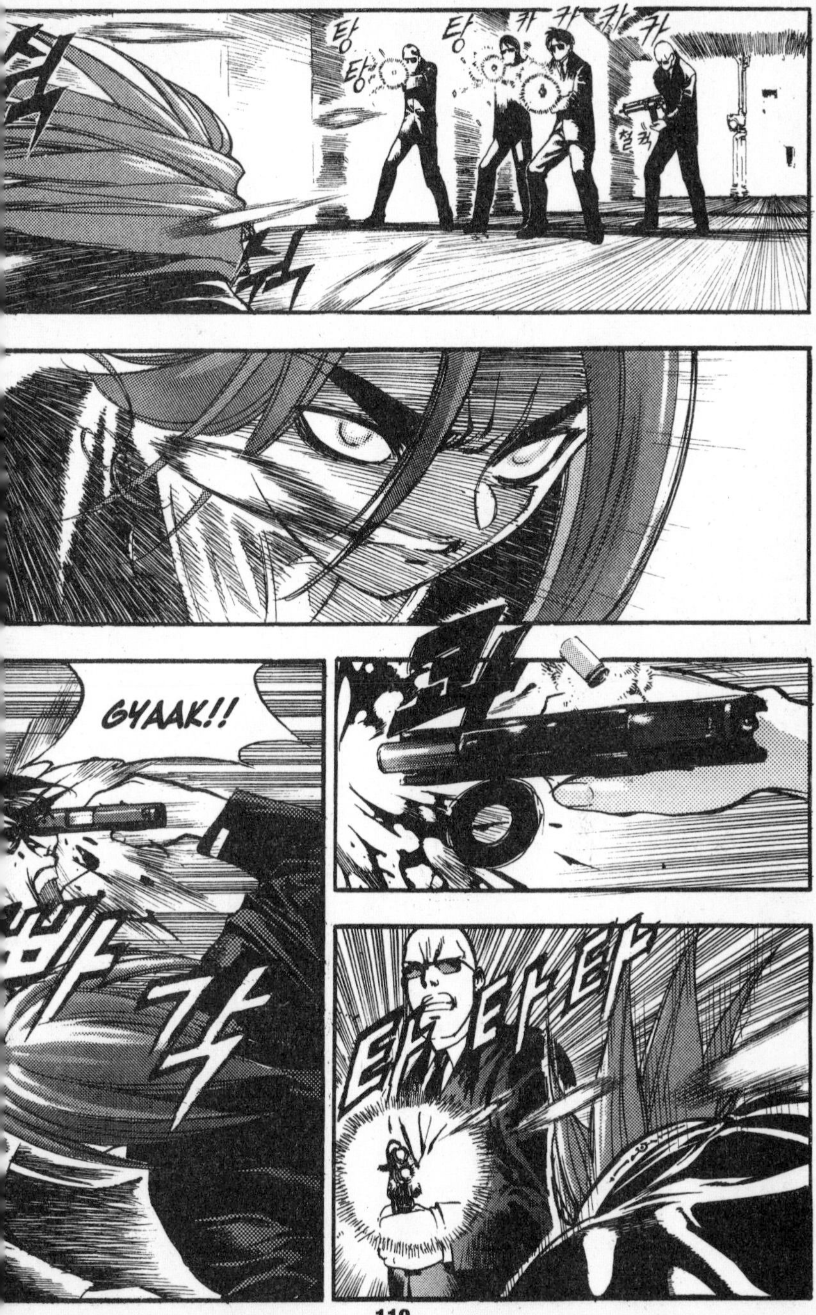
탕
탕
탕
카 카 카 카
철컥
GYAAK!!
빠각

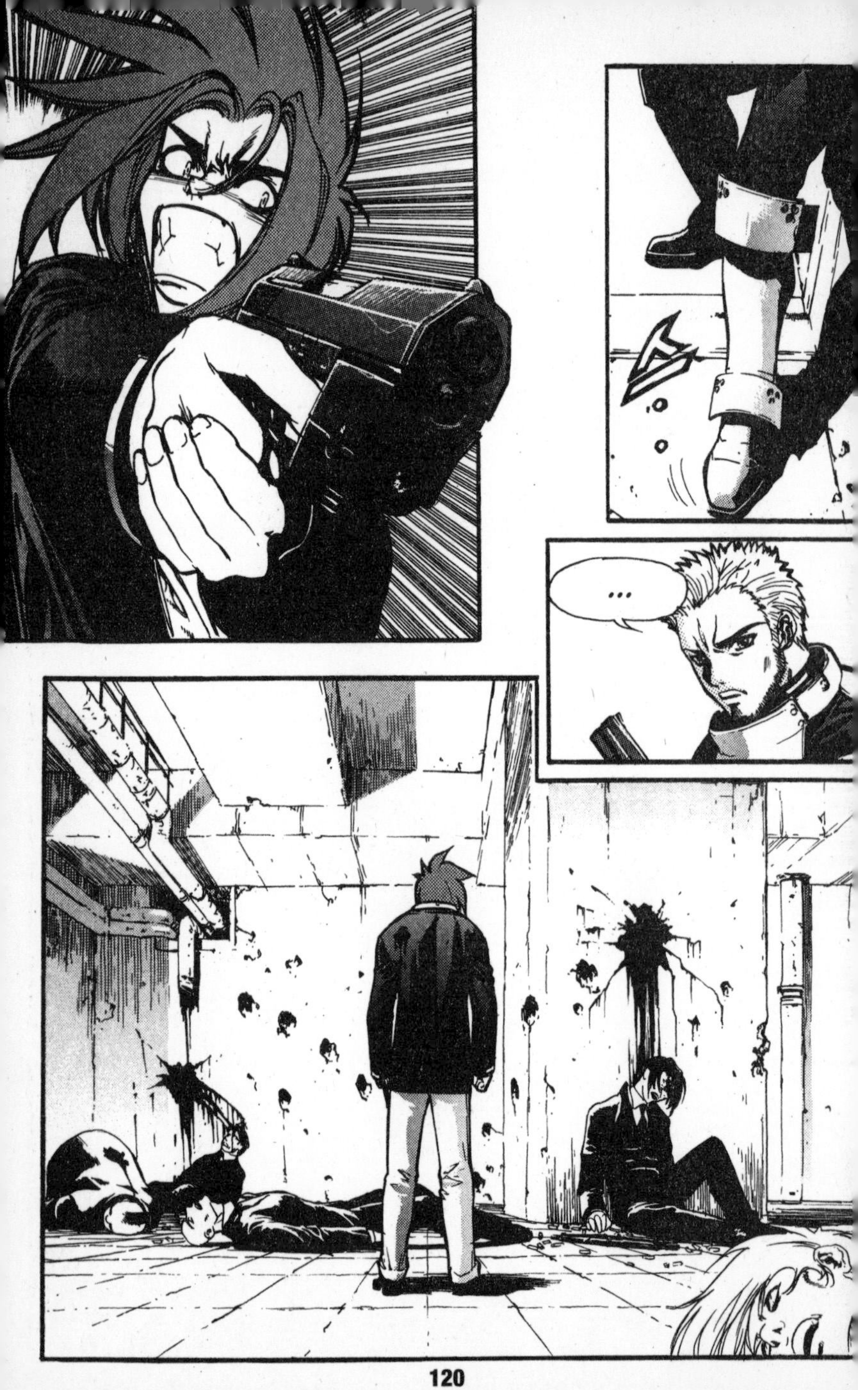
...

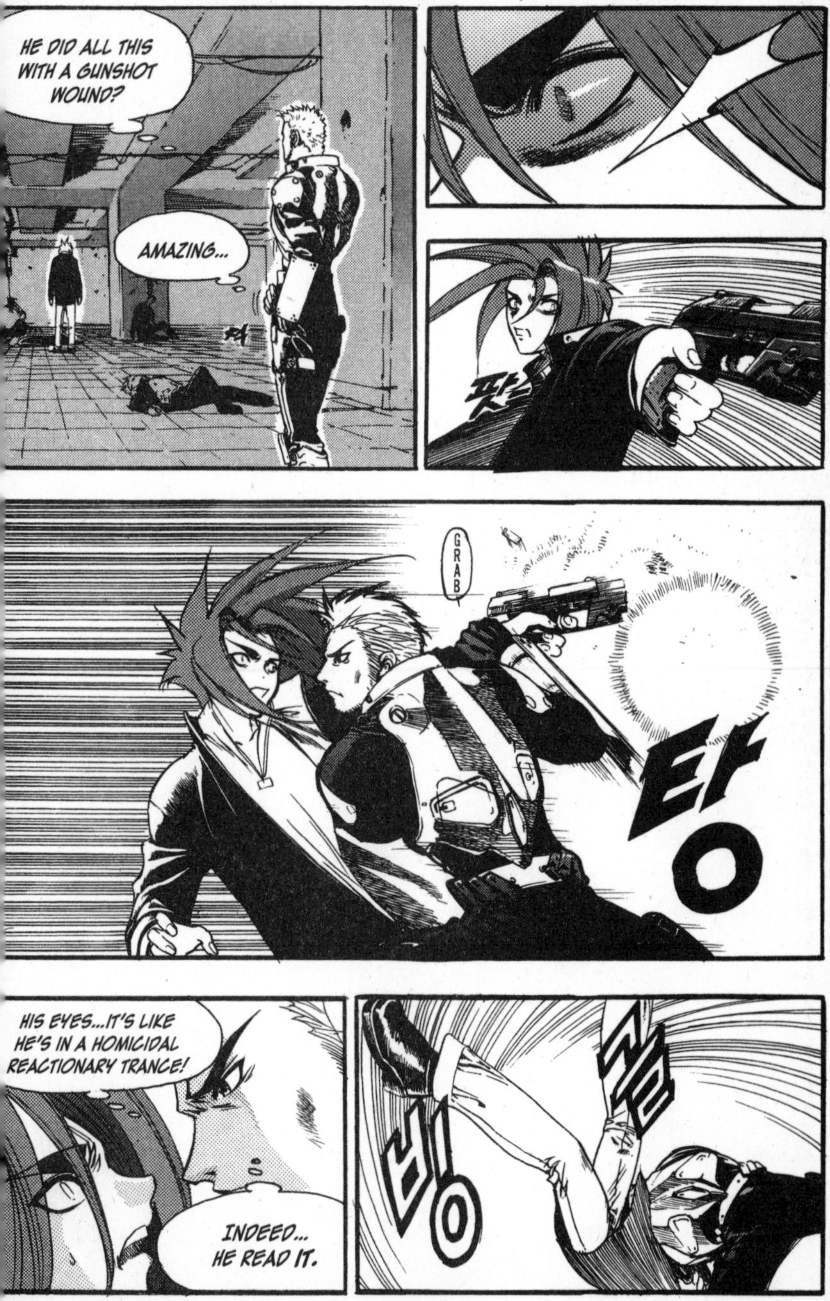
HE DID ALL THIS WITH A GUNSHOT WOUND?
AMAZING...
GRAB
HIS EYES...IT'S LIKE HE'S IN A HOMICIDAL REACTIONARY TRANCE!
INDEED... HE READ IT.

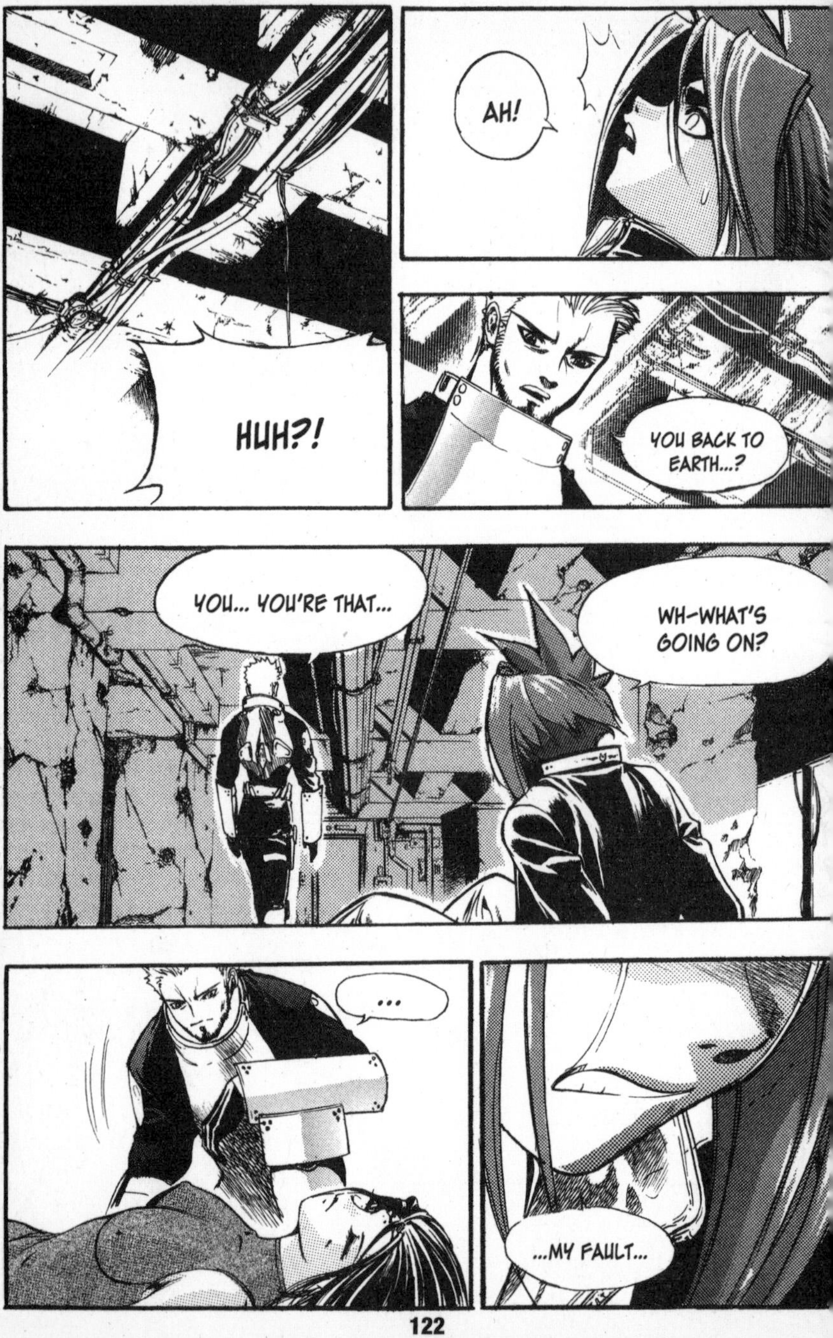
HUH?!
AH!
YOU BACK TO EARTH...?
YOU... YOU'RE THAT...
WH-WHAT'S GOING ON?
...
...MY FAULT...

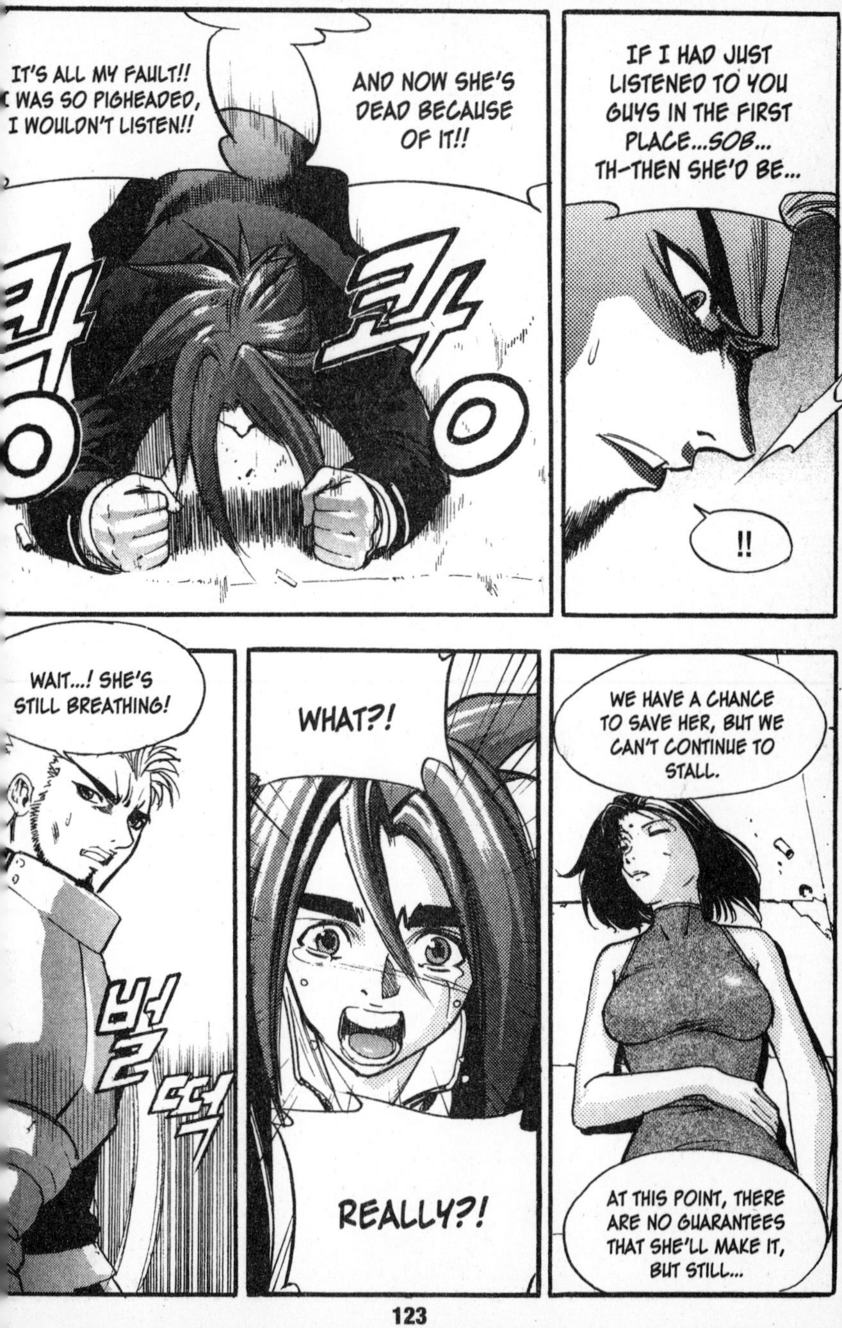
IT'S ALL MY FAULT!! I WAS SO PIGHEADED, I WOULDN'T LISTEN!!
AND NOW SHE'S DEAD BECAUSE OF IT!!
IF I HAD JUST LISTENED TO YOU GUYS IN THE FIRST PLACE...SOB... TH-THEN SHE'D BE...
!!
WAIT...! SHE'S STILL BREATHING!
WHAT?!
REALLY?!
WE HAVE A CHANCE TO SAVE HER, BUT WE CAN'T CONTINUE TO STALL.
AT THIS POINT, THERE ARE NO GUARANTEES THAT SHE'LL MAKE IT, BUT STILL...

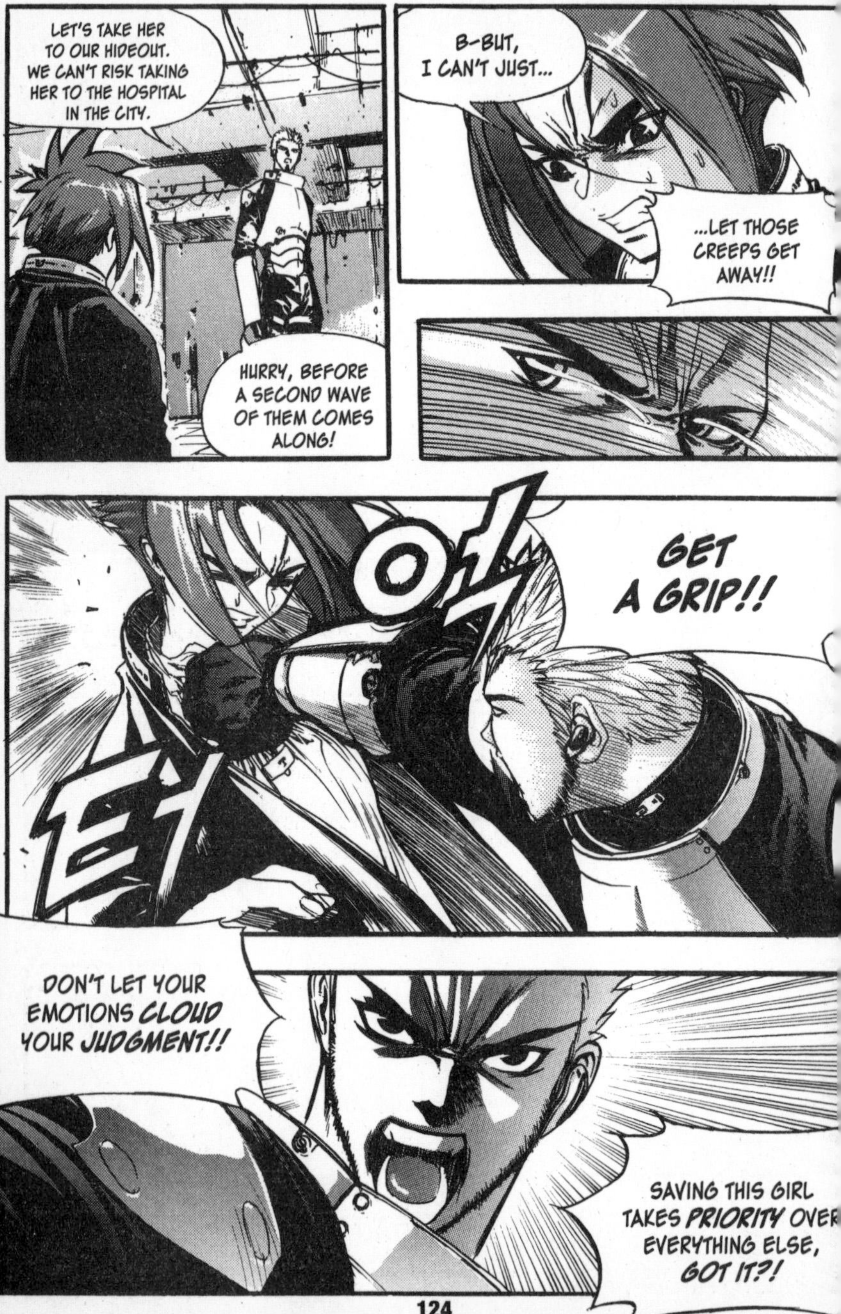
LET'S TAKE HER TO OUR HIDEOUT. WE CAN'T RISK TAKING HER TO THE HOSPITAL IN THE CITY.
HURRY, BEFORE A SECOND WAVE OF THEM COMES ALONG!
B-BUT, I CAN'T JUST...
...LET THOSE CREEPS GET AWAY!!
GET A GRIP!!
DON'T LET YOUR EMOTIONS CLOUD YOUR JUDGMENT!!
SAVING THIS GIRL TAKES PRIORITY OVER EVERYTHING ELSE, GOT IT?!

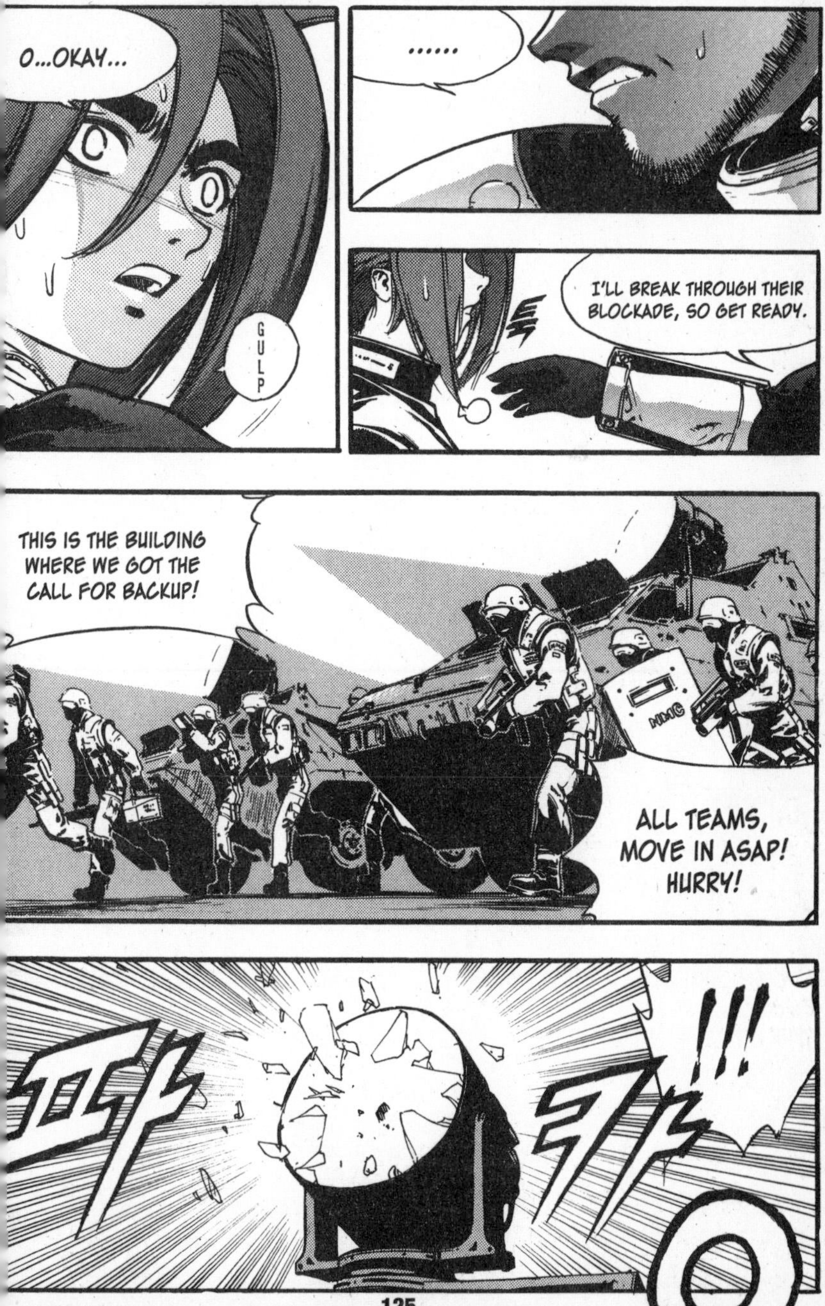
......
I'LL BREAK THROUGH THEIR BLOCKADE, SO GET READY.
O...OKAY...
GULP
THIS IS THE BUILDING WHERE WE GOT THE CALL FOR BACKUP!
ALL TEAMS, MOVE IN ASAP! HURRY!

SIR, WE LOST THE LIGHTS!

WHAT'S GOING ON?

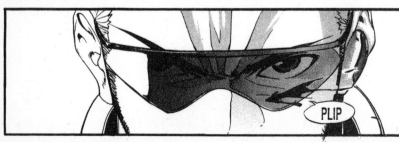

PLIP

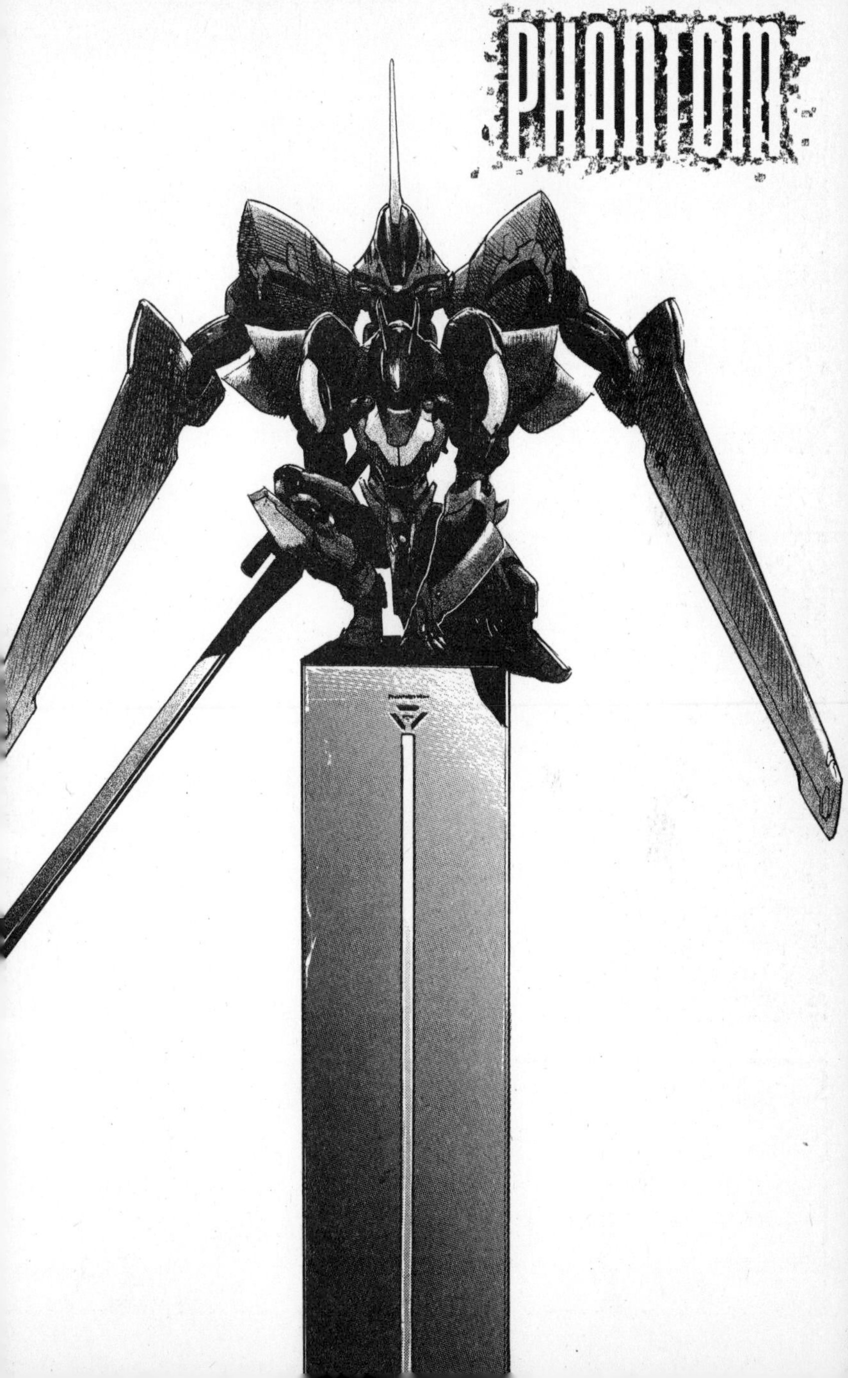
PHANTOM

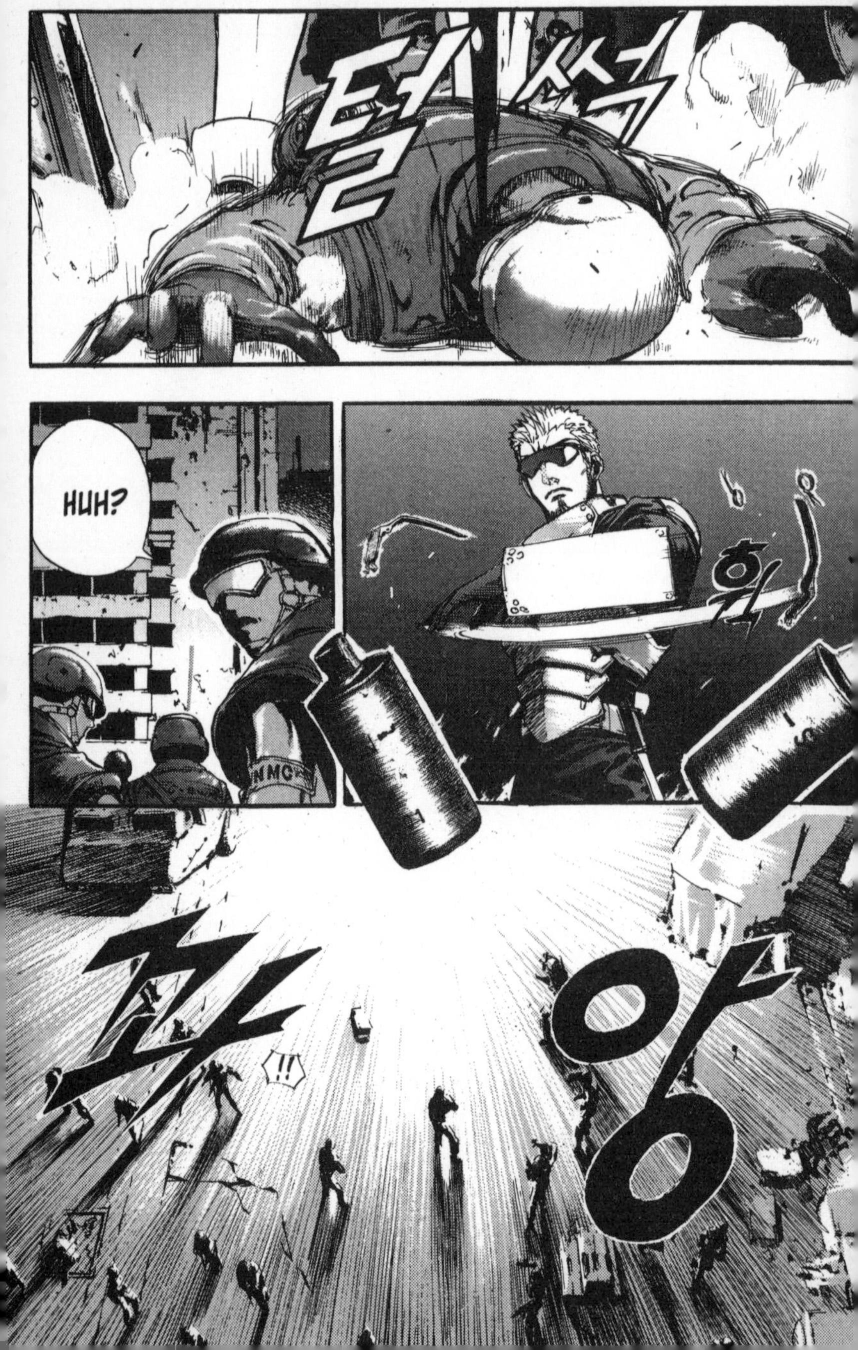
털썩
HUH?
휙
!!
쾅

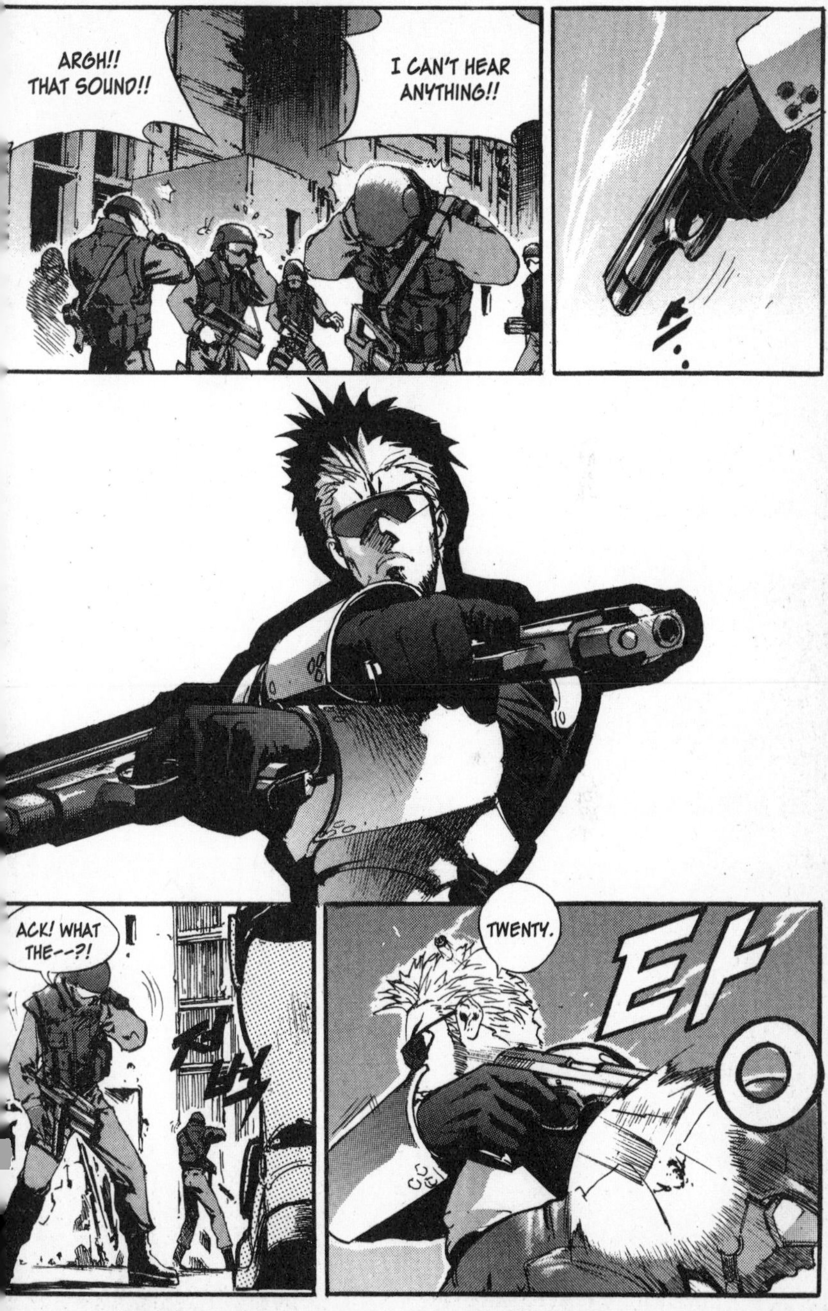
ARGH!! THAT SOUND!!
I CAN'T HEAR ANYTHING!!
ACK! WHAT THE--?!
TWENTY.

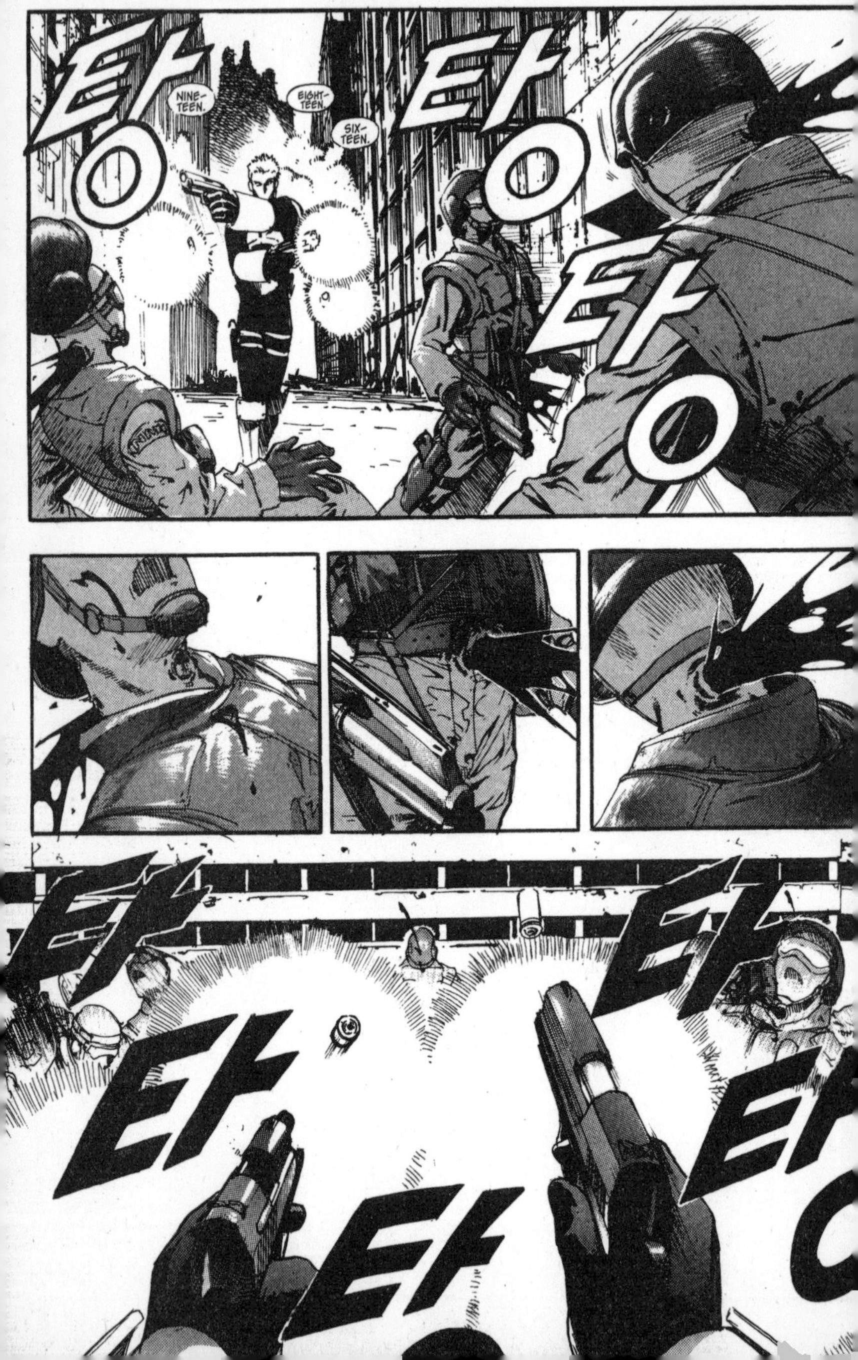
NINE-TEEN.
EIGHT-TEEN.
SIX-TEEN.

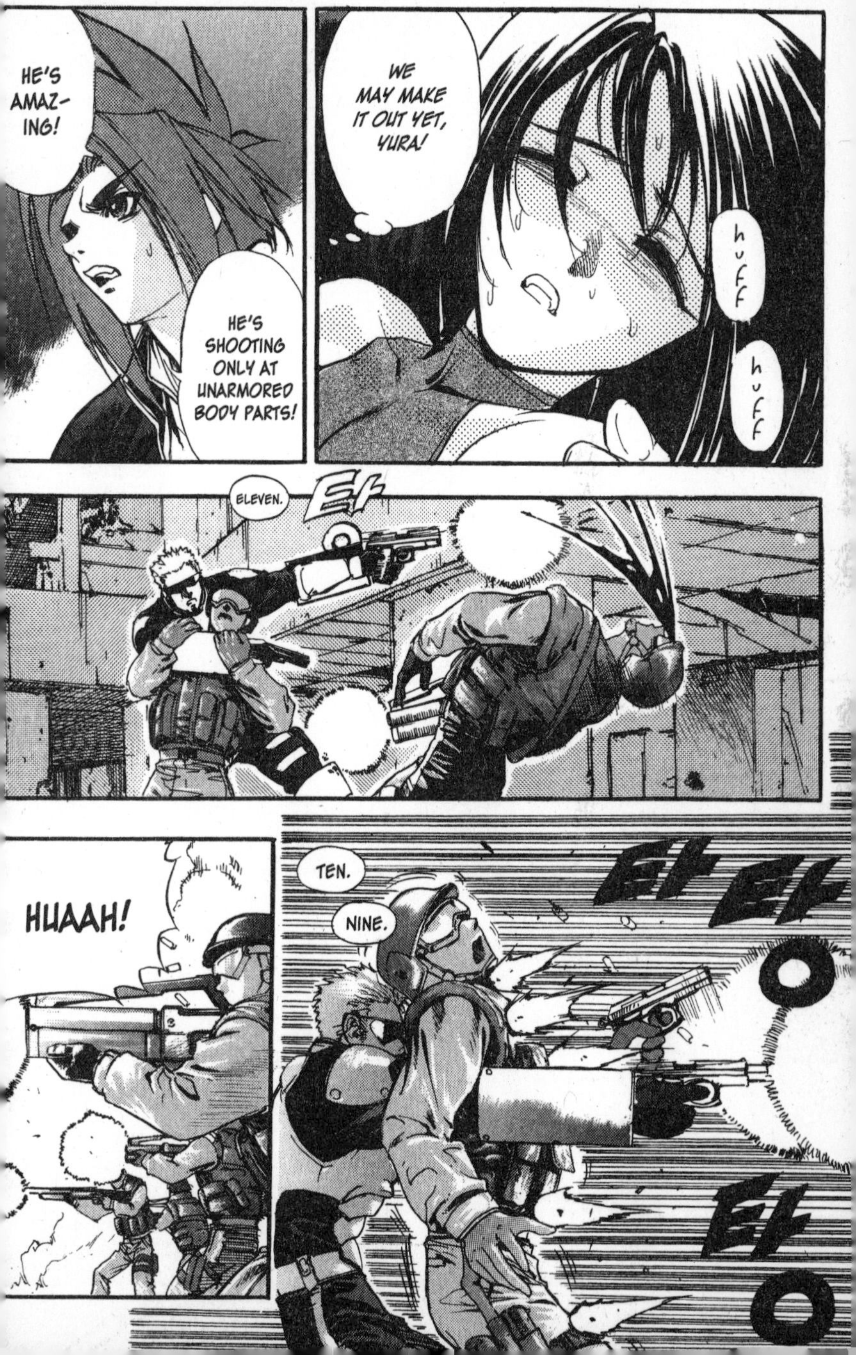

HE'S AMAZ-ING!
HE'S SHOOTING ONLY AT UNARMORED BODY PARTS!
WE MAY MAKE IT OUT YET, YURA!
huff
huff
ELEVEN.
HUAAH!
TEN.
NINE.

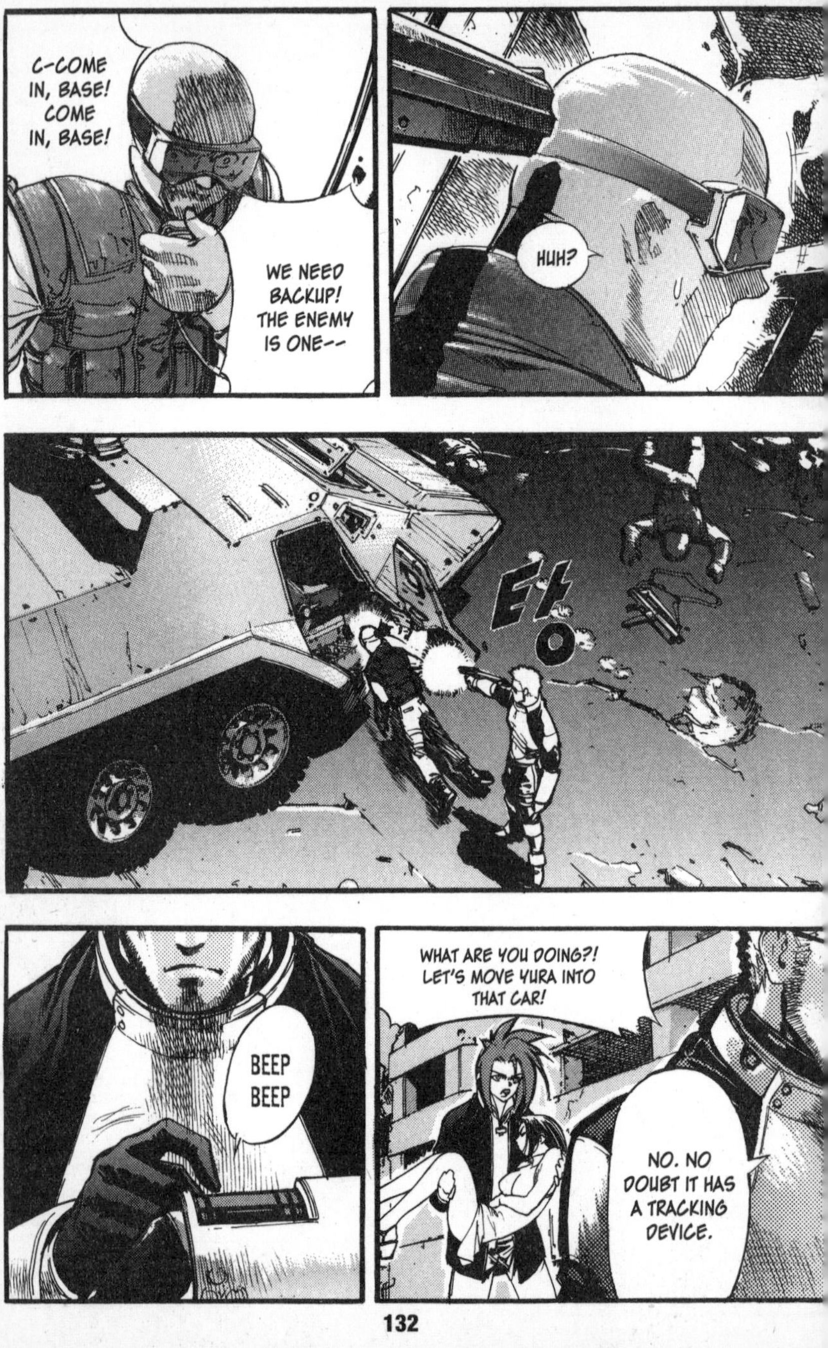
C-COME IN, BASE! COME IN, BASE!
WE NEED BACKUP! THE ENEMY IS ONE--
HUH?
BEEP BEEP
WHAT ARE YOU DOING?! LET'S MOVE YURA INTO THAT CAR!
NO. NO DOUBT IT HAS A TRACKING DEVICE.

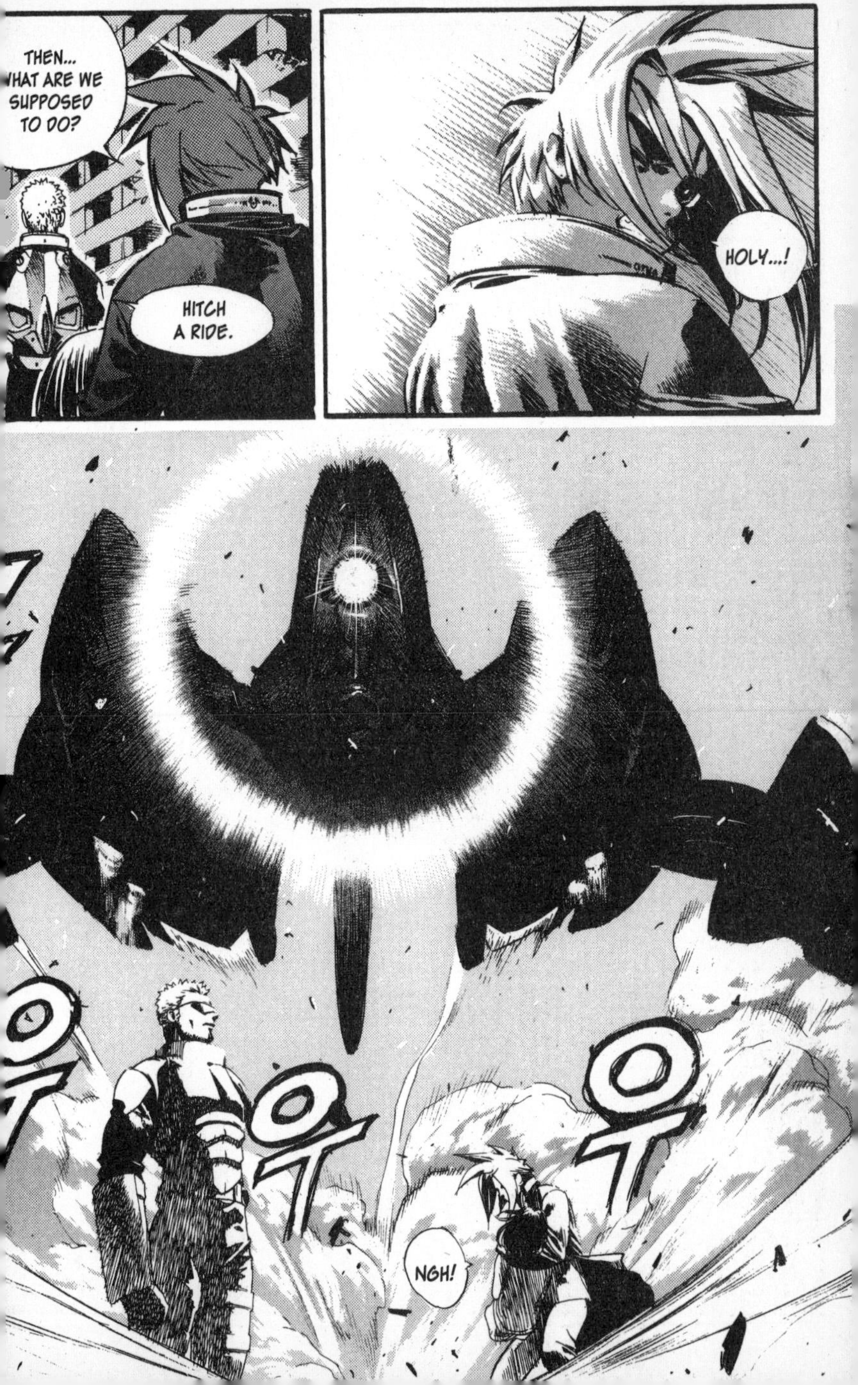
THEN... WHAT ARE WE SUPPOSED TO DO?
HITCH A RIDE.
HOLY...!
NGH!

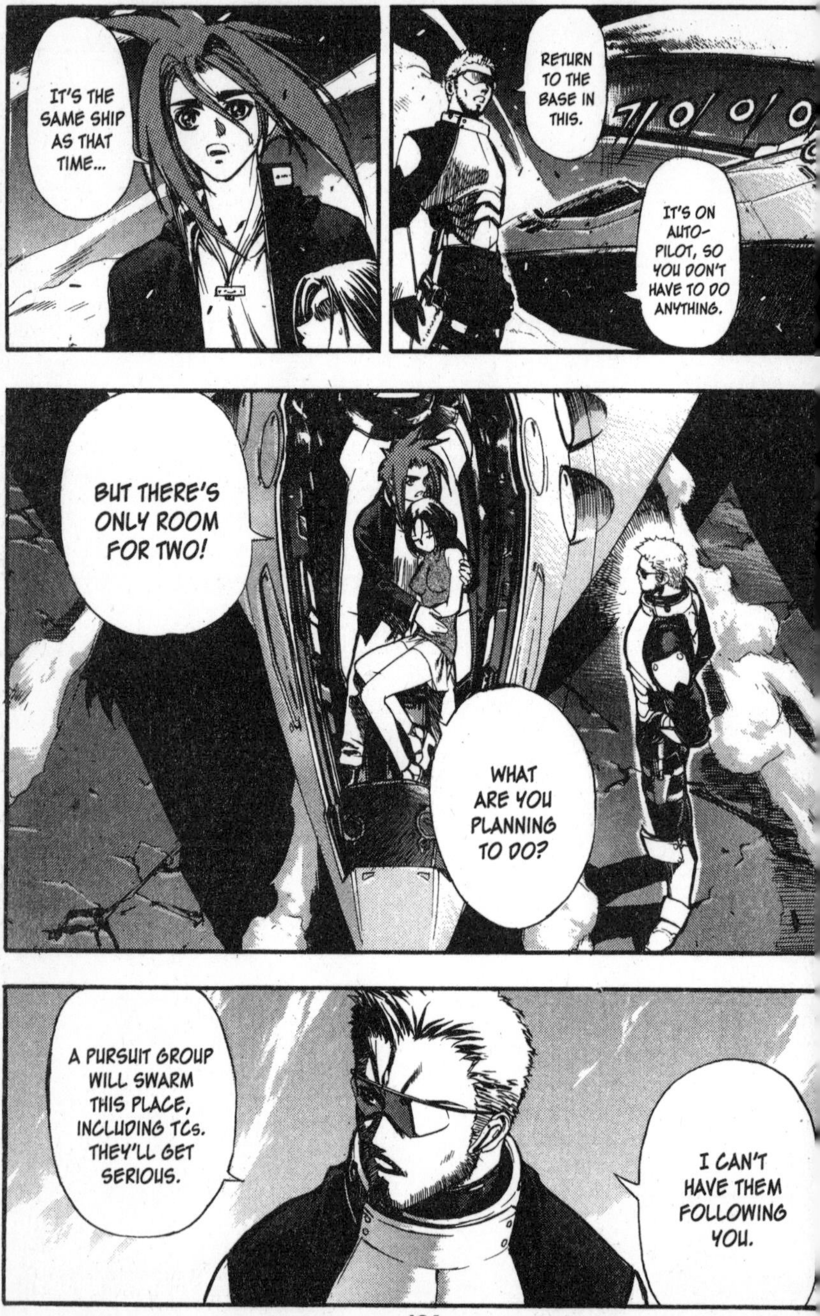
IT'S THE SAME SHIP AS THAT TIME...
RETURN TO THE BASE IN THIS.
IT'S ON AUTO-PILOT, SO YOU DON'T HAVE TO DO ANYTHING.
BUT THERE'S ONLY ROOM FOR TWO!
WHAT ARE YOU PLANNING TO DO?
A PURSUIT GROUP WILL SWARM THIS PLACE, INCLUDING TCs. THEY'LL GET SERIOUS.
I CAN'T HAVE THEM FOLLOWING YOU.

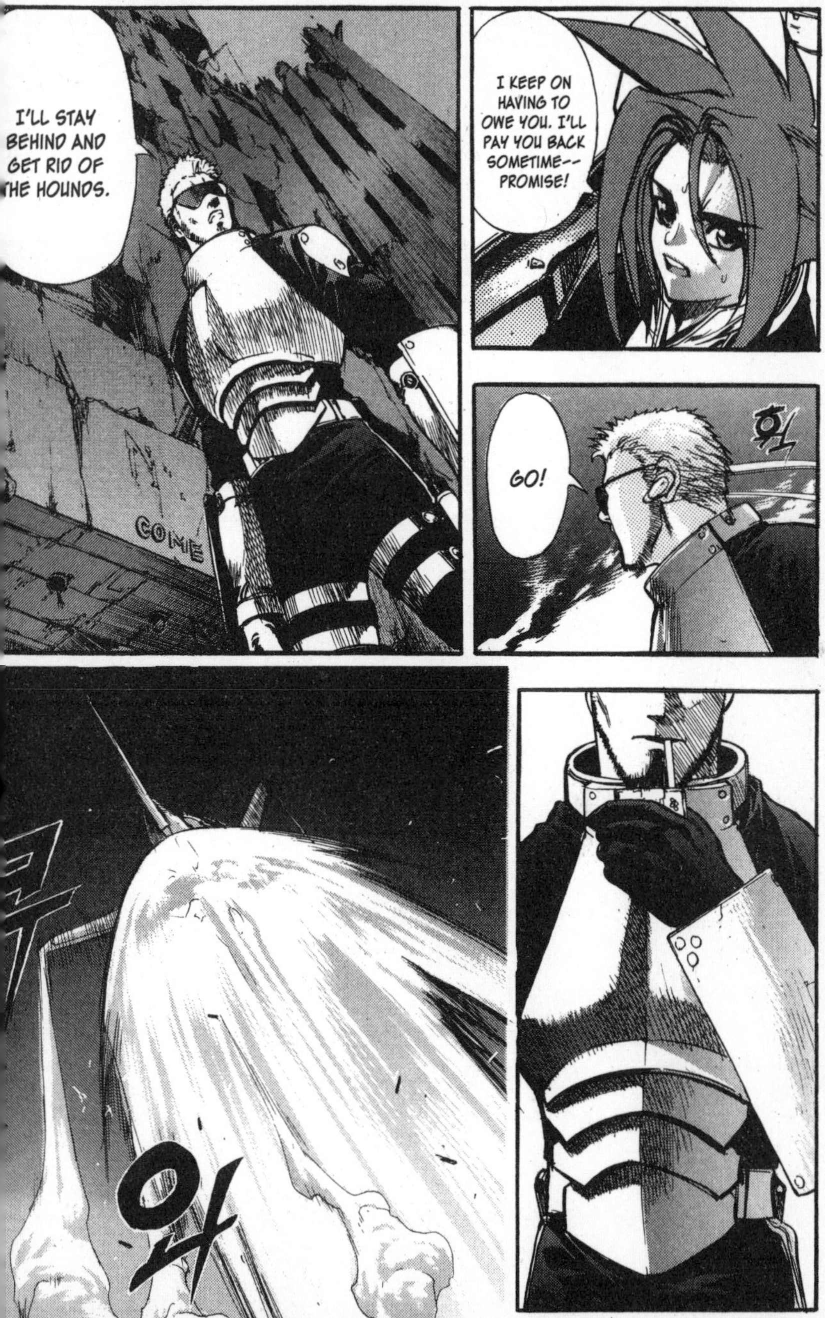
I'LL STAY BEHIND AND GET RID OF THE HOUNDS.
COME
I KEEP ON HAVING TO OWE YOU. I'LL PAY YOU BACK SOMETIME-- PROMISE!
GO!

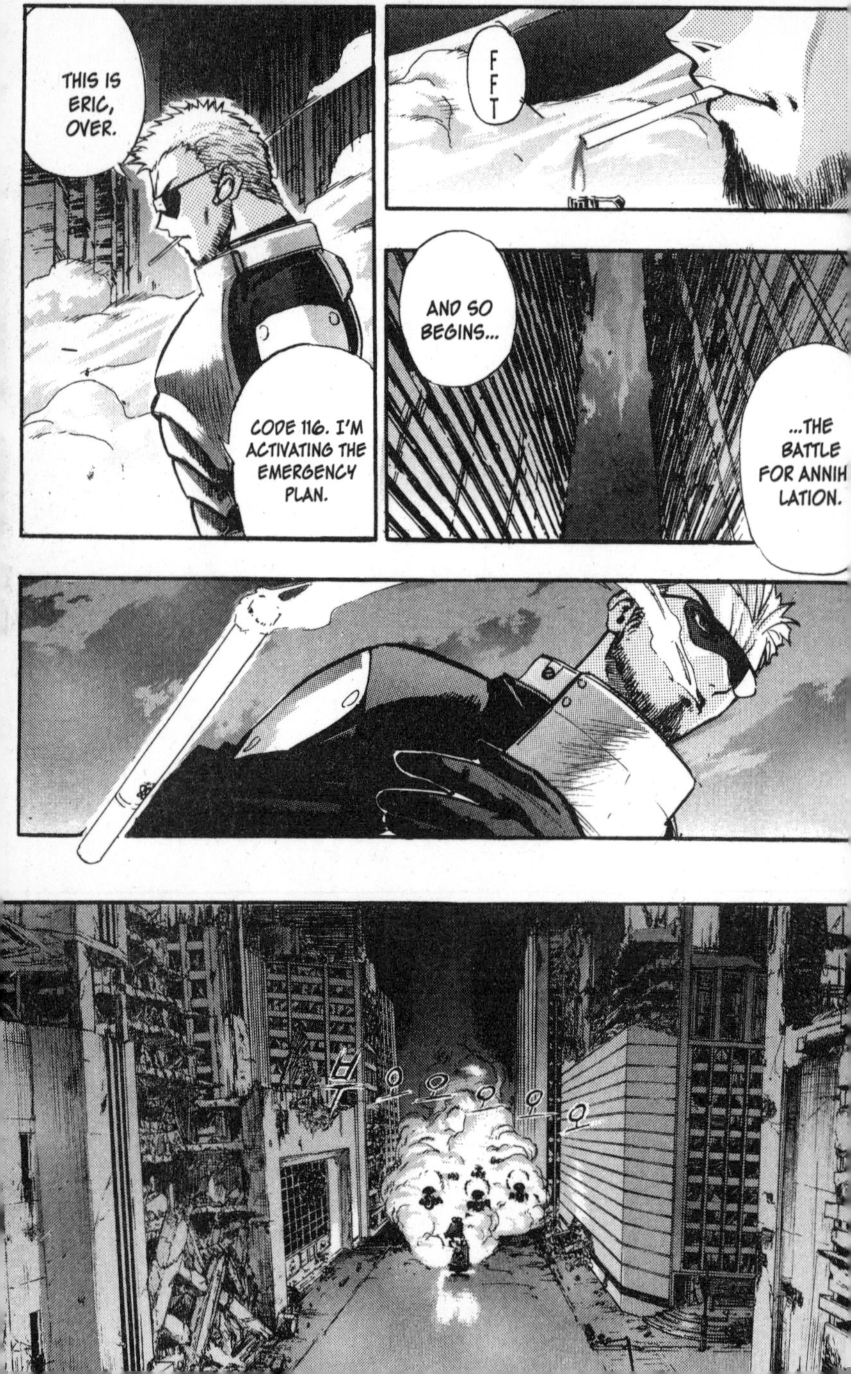
THIS IS ERIC, OVER.
CODE 116. I'M ACTIVATING THE EMERGENCY PLAN.
FFT
AND SO BEGINS...
...THE BATTLE FOR ANNIH LATION.

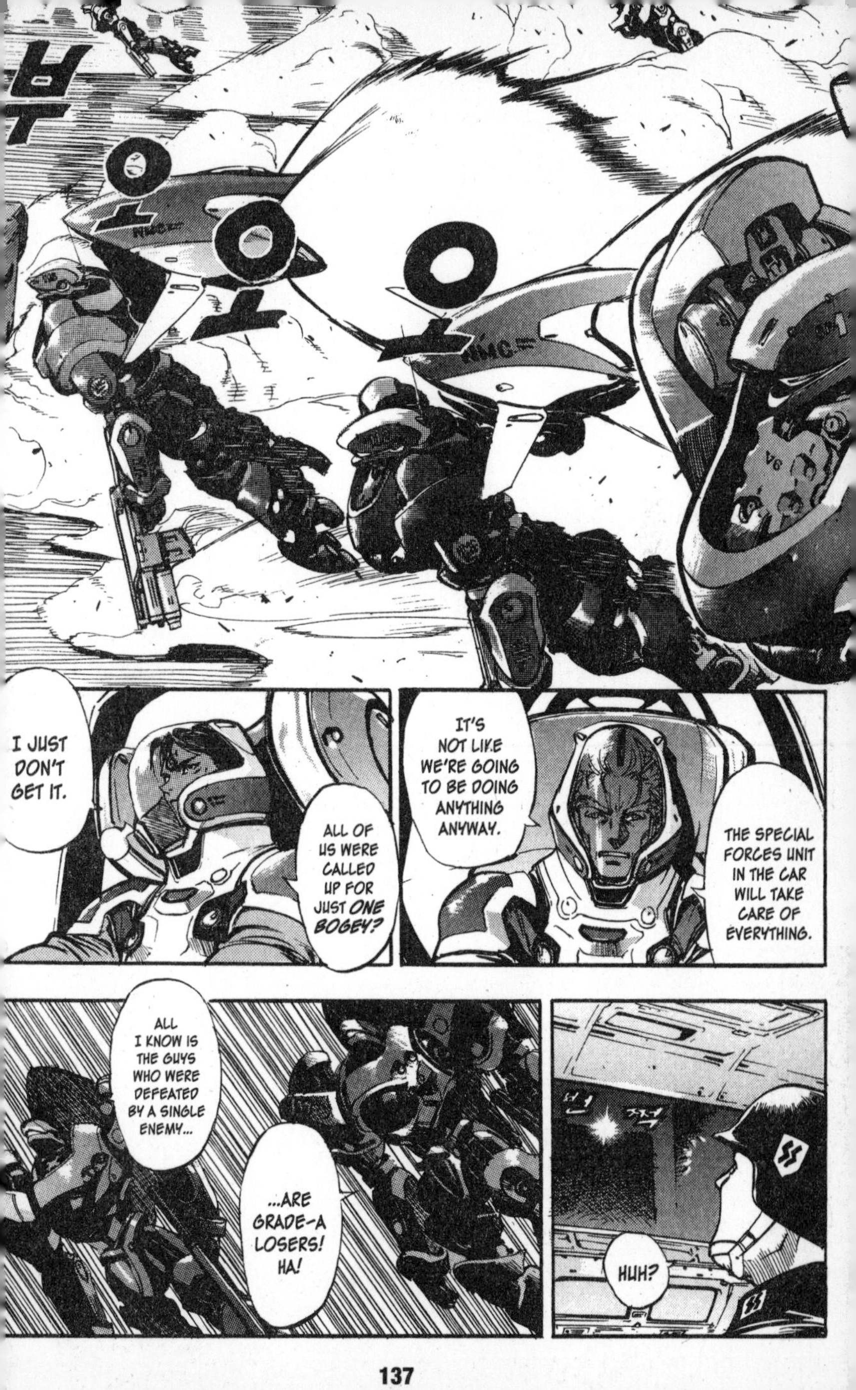
I JUST DON'T GET IT.
ALL OF US WERE CALLED UP FOR JUST *ONE BOGEY?*
IT'S NOT LIKE WE'RE GOING TO BE DOING ANYTHING ANYWAY.
THE SPECIAL FORCES UNIT IN THE CAR WILL TAKE CARE OF EVERYTHING.
ALL I KNOW IS THE GUYS WHO WERE DEFEATED BY A SINGLE ENEMY...
...ARE GRADE-A LOSERS! HA!
번쩍
HUH?

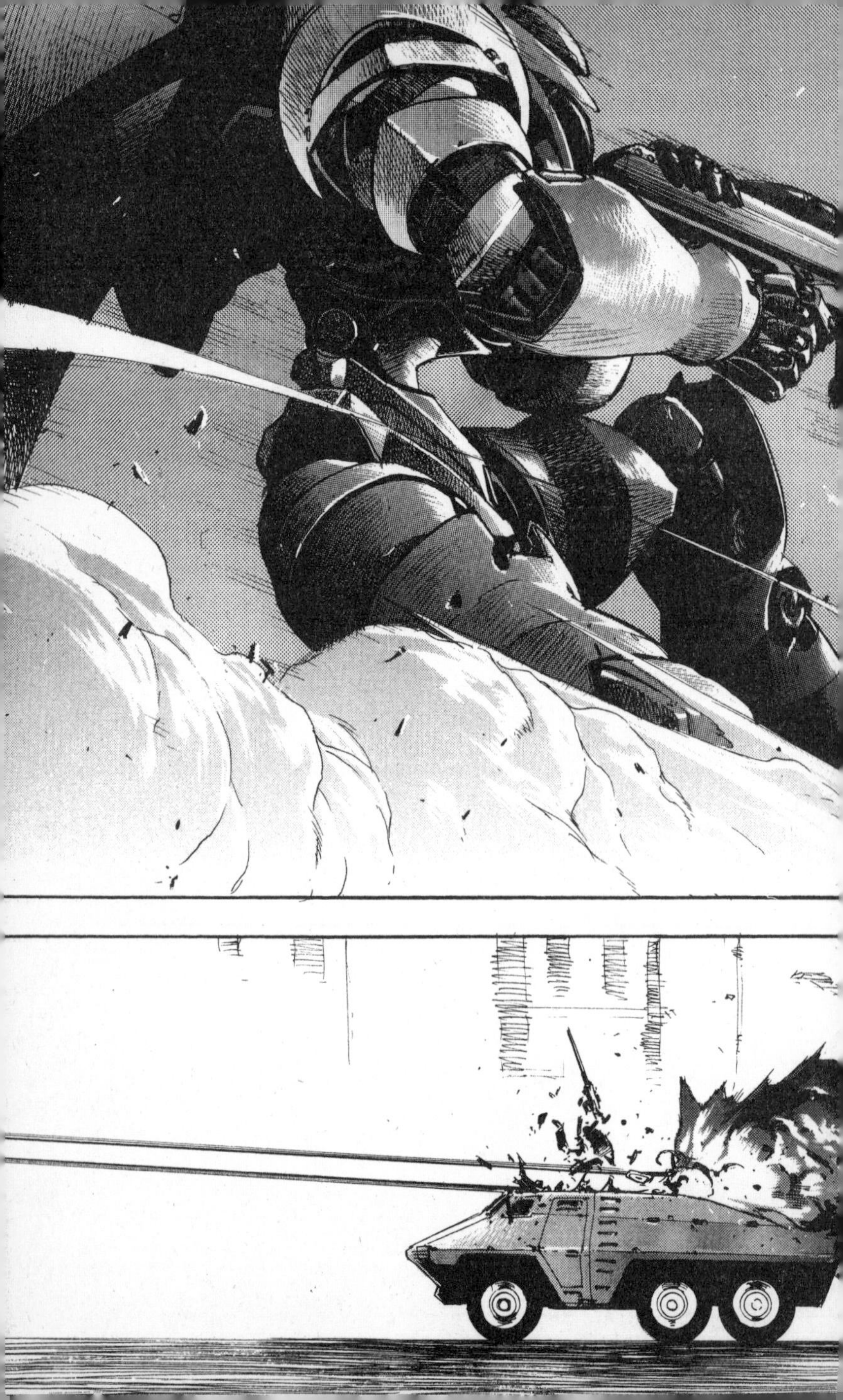

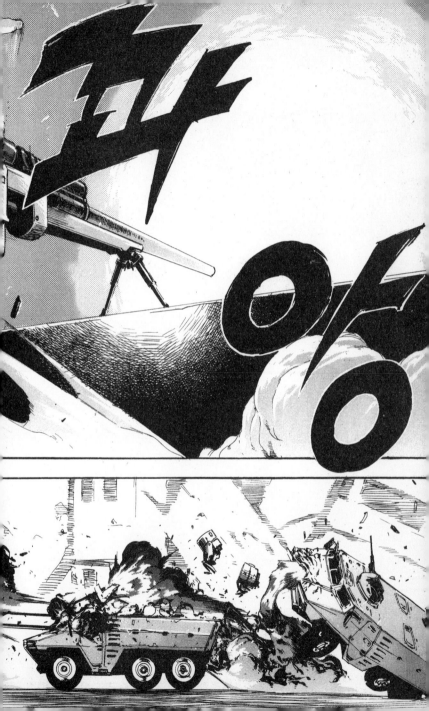

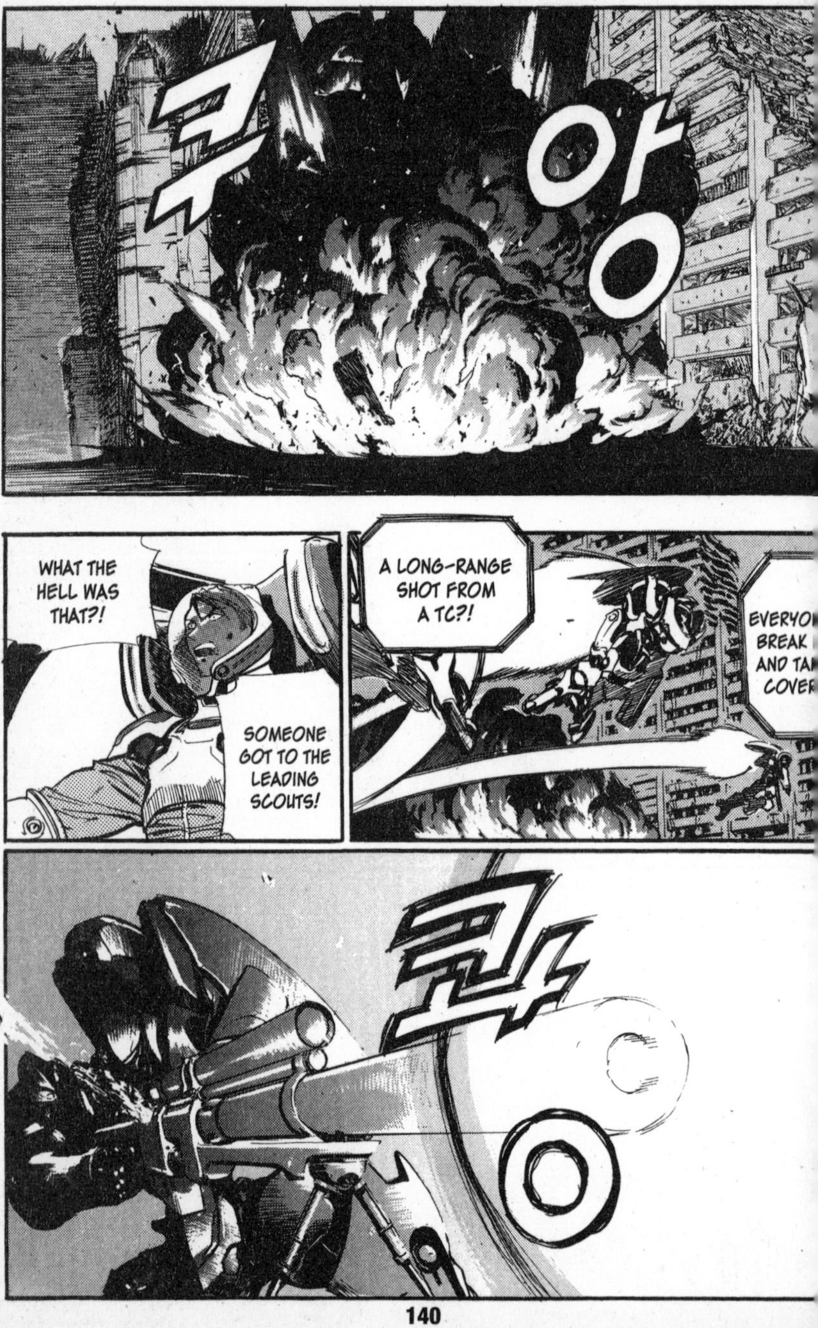
WHAT THE HELL WAS THAT?!
SOMEONE GOT TO THE LEADING SCOUTS!
A LONG-RANGE SHOT FROM A TC?!
EVERYO BREAK AND TA COVER

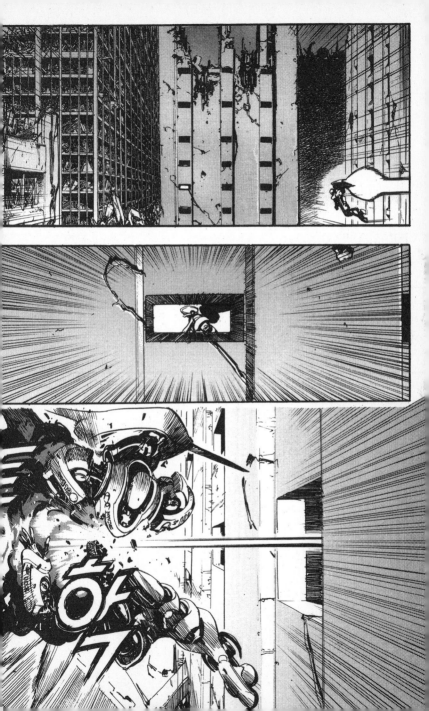

HE PREDICTED OUR FORMATION AND SHOT THROUGH THE BUILDINGS?!

WHAT KIND OF PILOT ARE WE UP AGAINST?!

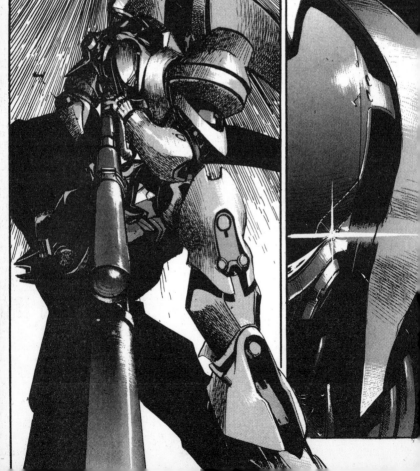

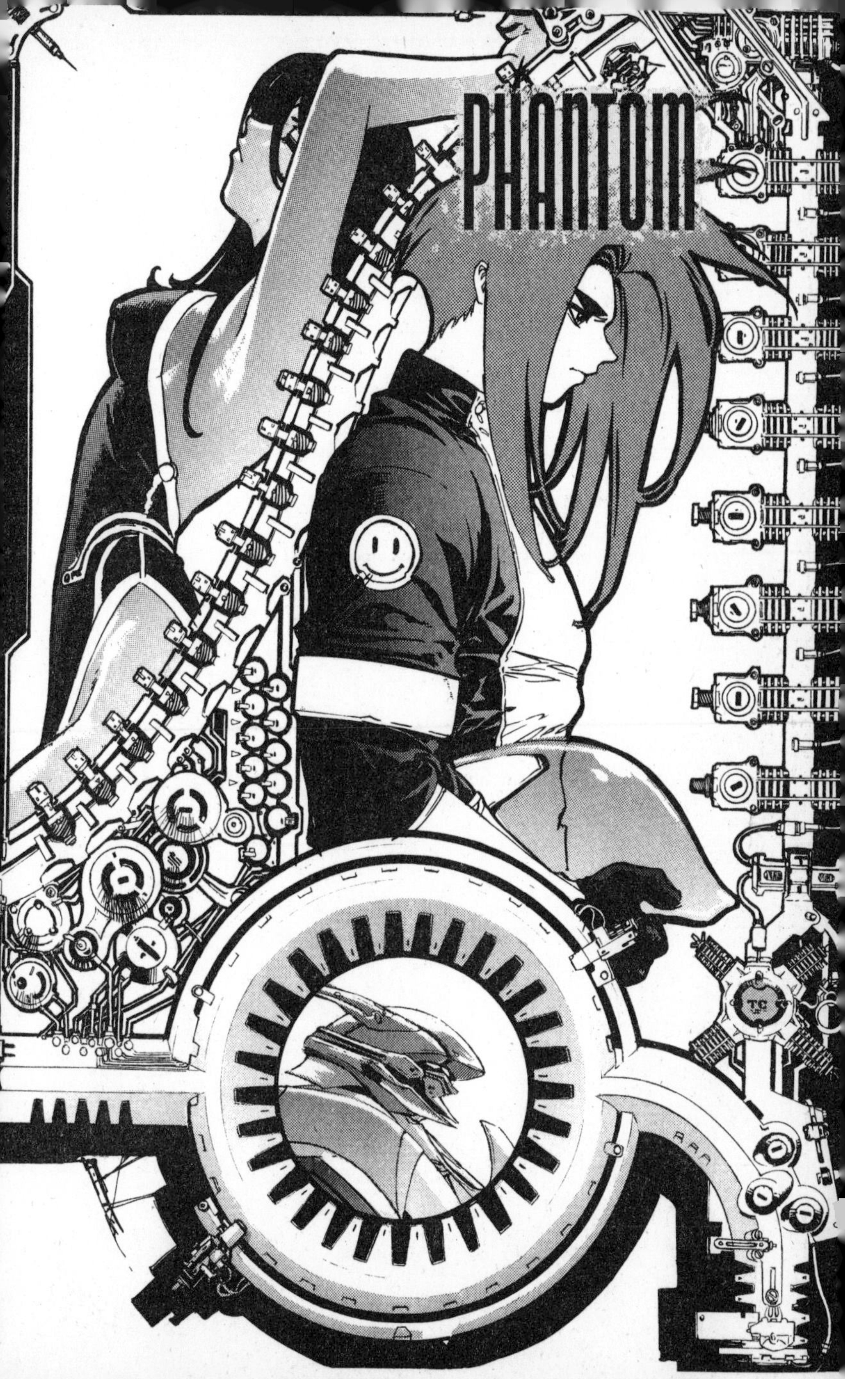
PHANTOM

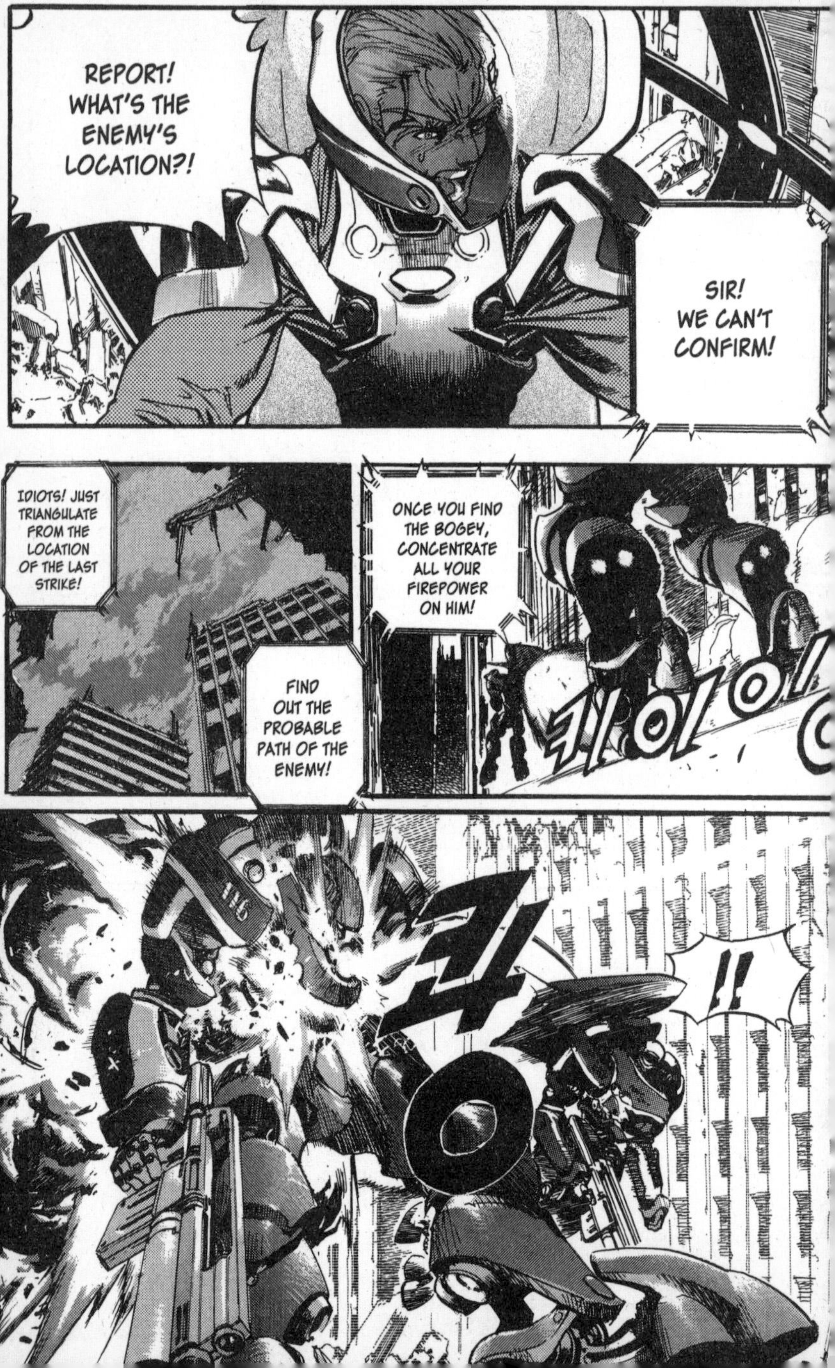
REPORT! WHAT'S THE ENEMY'S LOCATION?!
SIR! WE CAN'T CONFIRM!
IDIOTS! JUST TRIANGULATE FROM THE LOCATION OF THE LAST STRIKE!
FIND OUT THE PROBABLE PATH OF THE ENEMY!
ONCE YOU FIND THE BOGEY, CONCENTRATE ALL YOUR FIREPOWER ON HIM!
!!

AST! THE TA'S ALL CREWY, MMANDER!

CLICK

THIS AREA'S A RADAR DEAD ZONE.

DON'T PANIC! REMEMBER, THE ENEMY IS ENCOUNTERING THE SAME TERRAIN AS YOU!

SO KEEP ON MOVING, OR ELSE YOU'LL GET SNIPED!

FIND OUT HIS POSITION MANUALLY!

SIR! WE FOUND HIM!

쿠 와 아 아 아

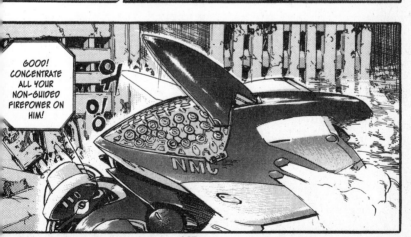

GOOD! CONCENTRATE ALL YOUR NON-GUIDED FIREPOWER ON HIM!

NMC

145

ALL
UNITS FIRE!!
REDUCE HIM
TO ASH!!

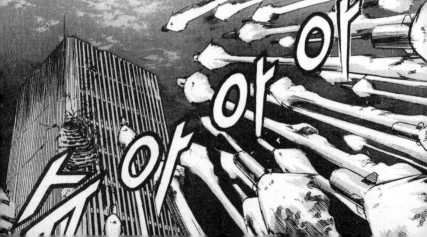

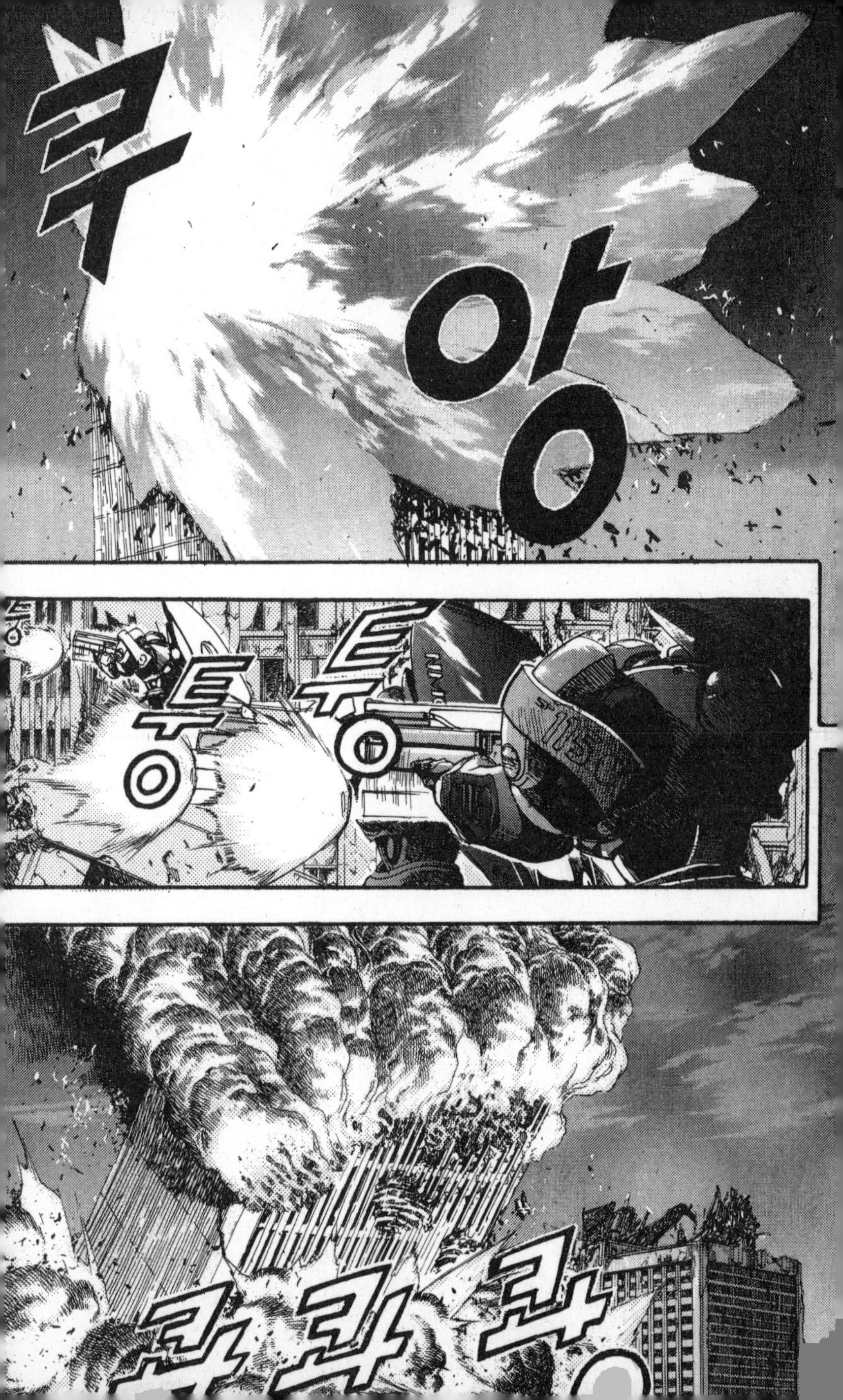
쿠앙
퉁
퉁
쿠쿠쾅

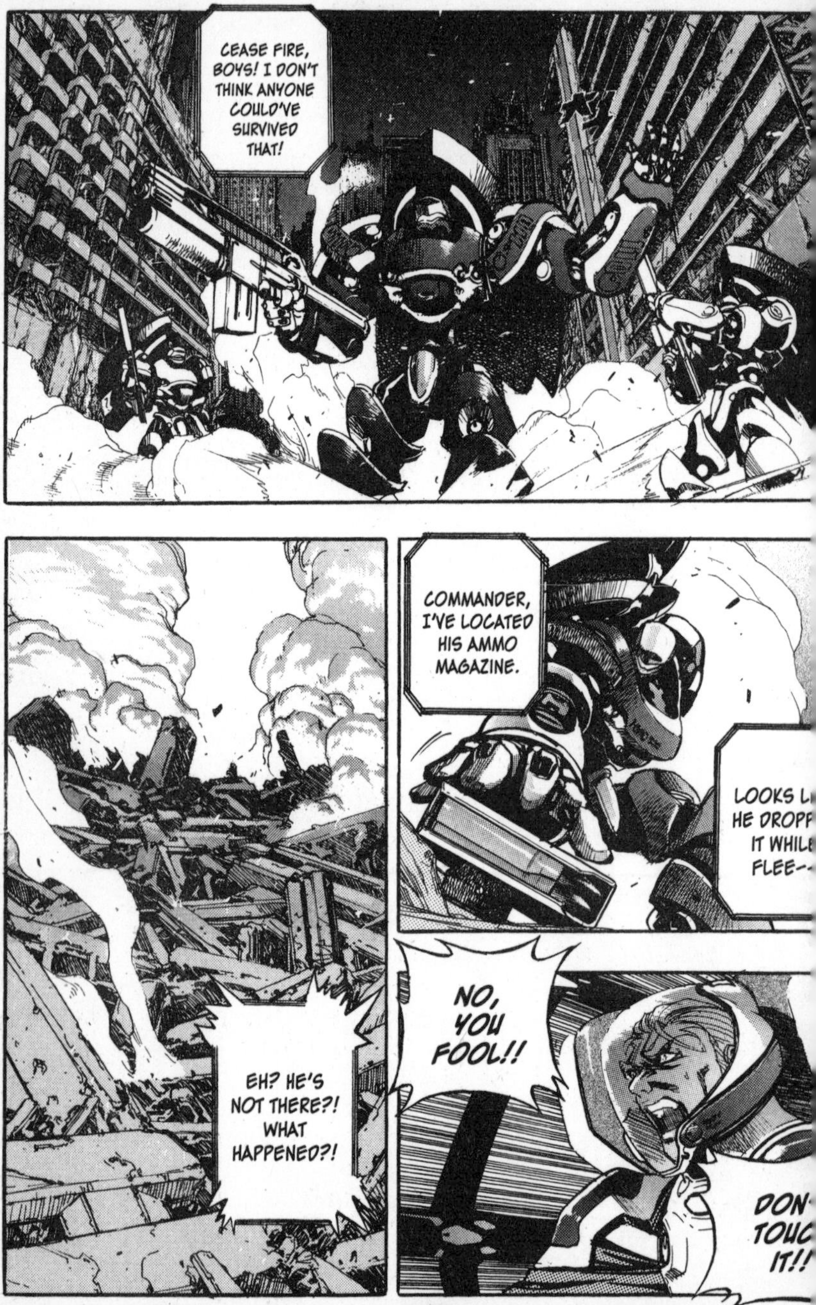
CEASE FIRE, BOYS! I DON'T THINK ANYONE COULD'VE SURVIVED THAT!
EH? HE'S NOT THERE?! WHAT HAPPENED?!
COMMANDER, I'VE LOCATED HIS AMMO MAGAZINE.
LOOKS L HE DROPP IT WHILE FLEE--
NO, YOU FOOL!!
DON- TOUC IT!!

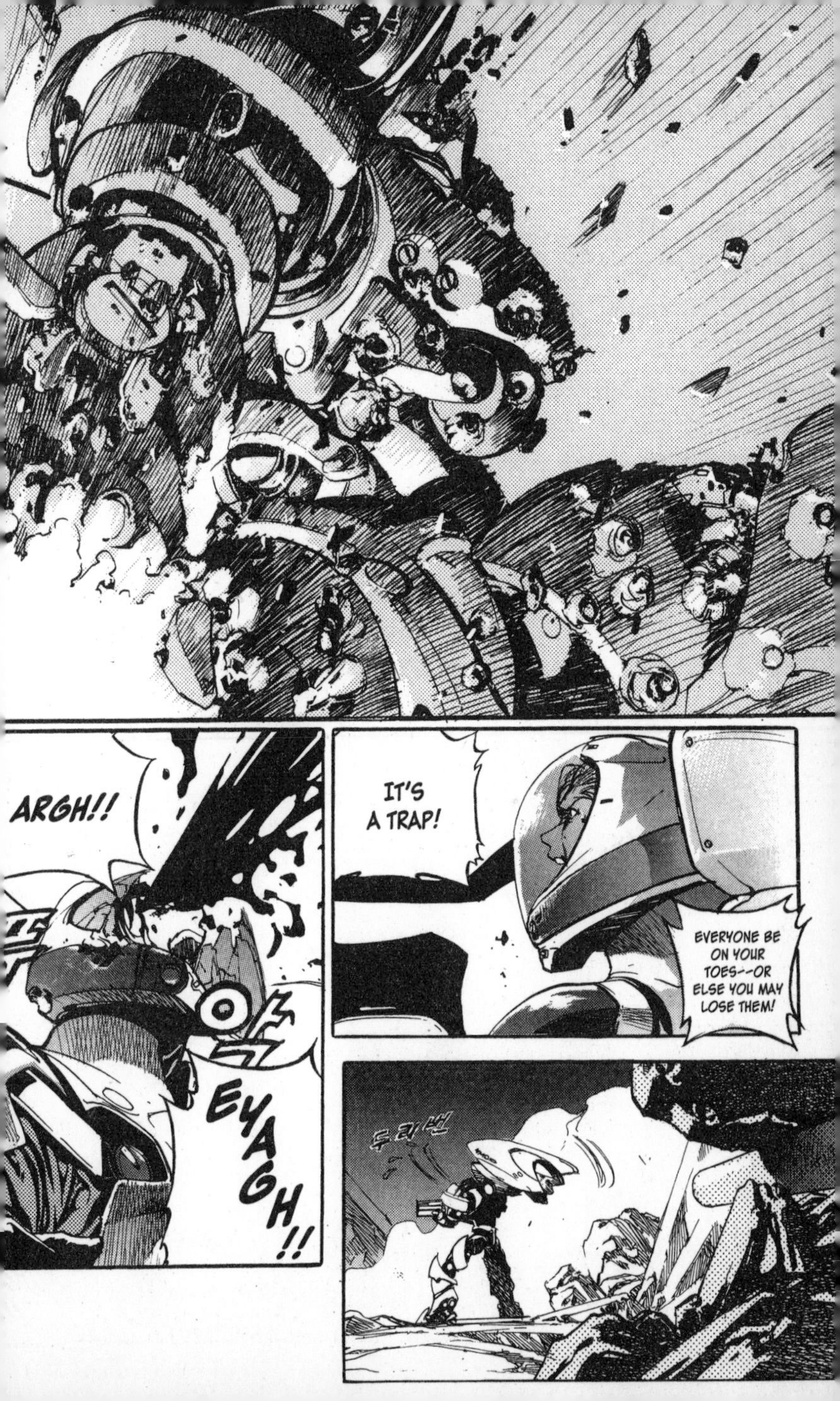

ARGH!!
EYAGH!!
IT'S A TRAP!
EVERYONE BE ON YOUR TOES--OR ELSE YOU MAY LOSE THEM!

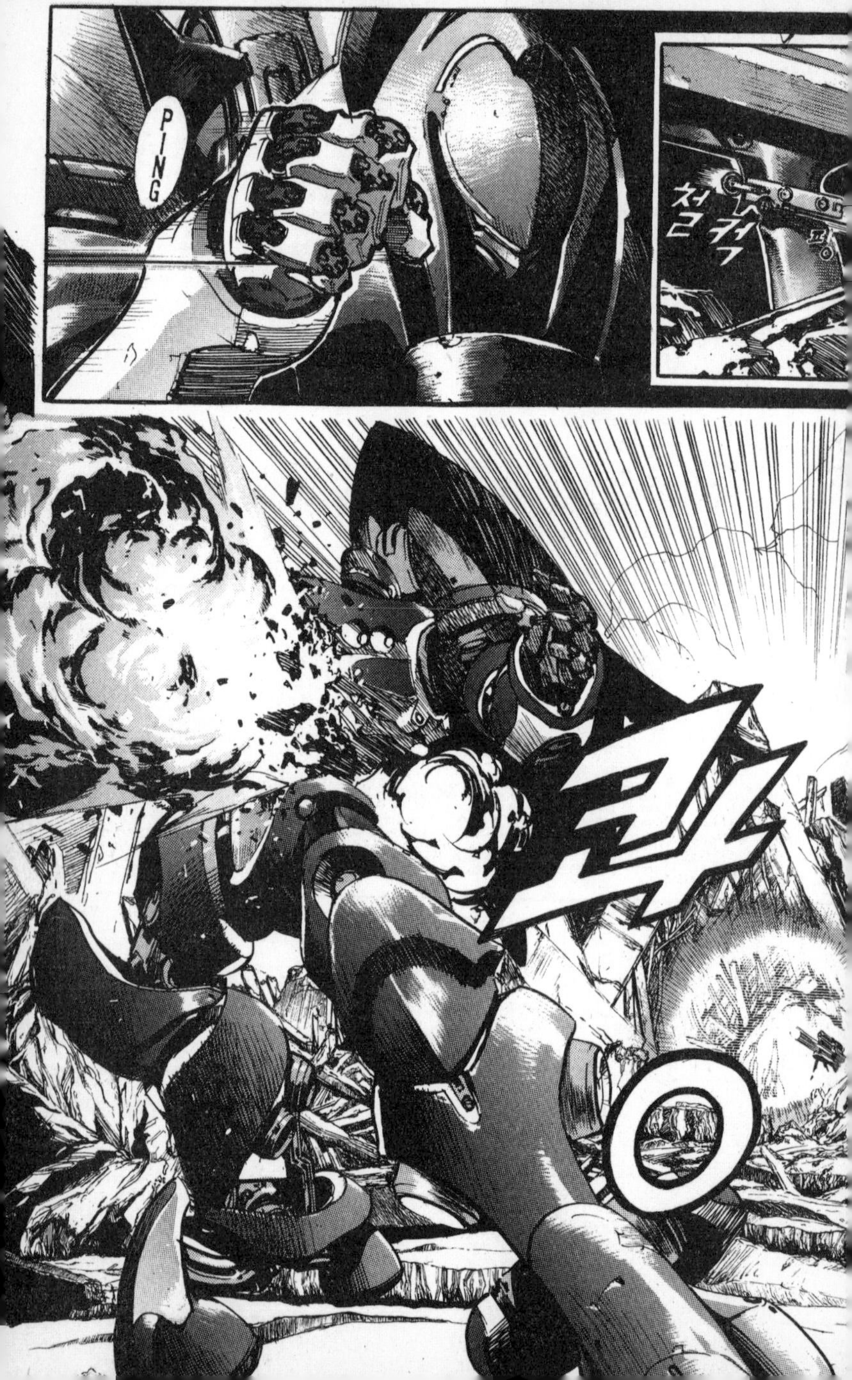
PING

NO! ANOTHER ONE?!

HE MUST BE NEAR!!

...

TWO TO GO.

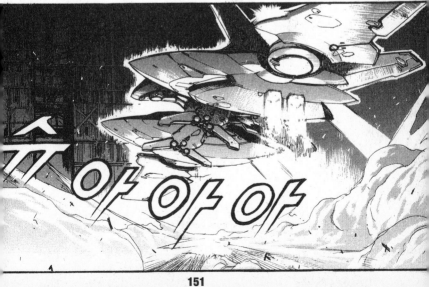

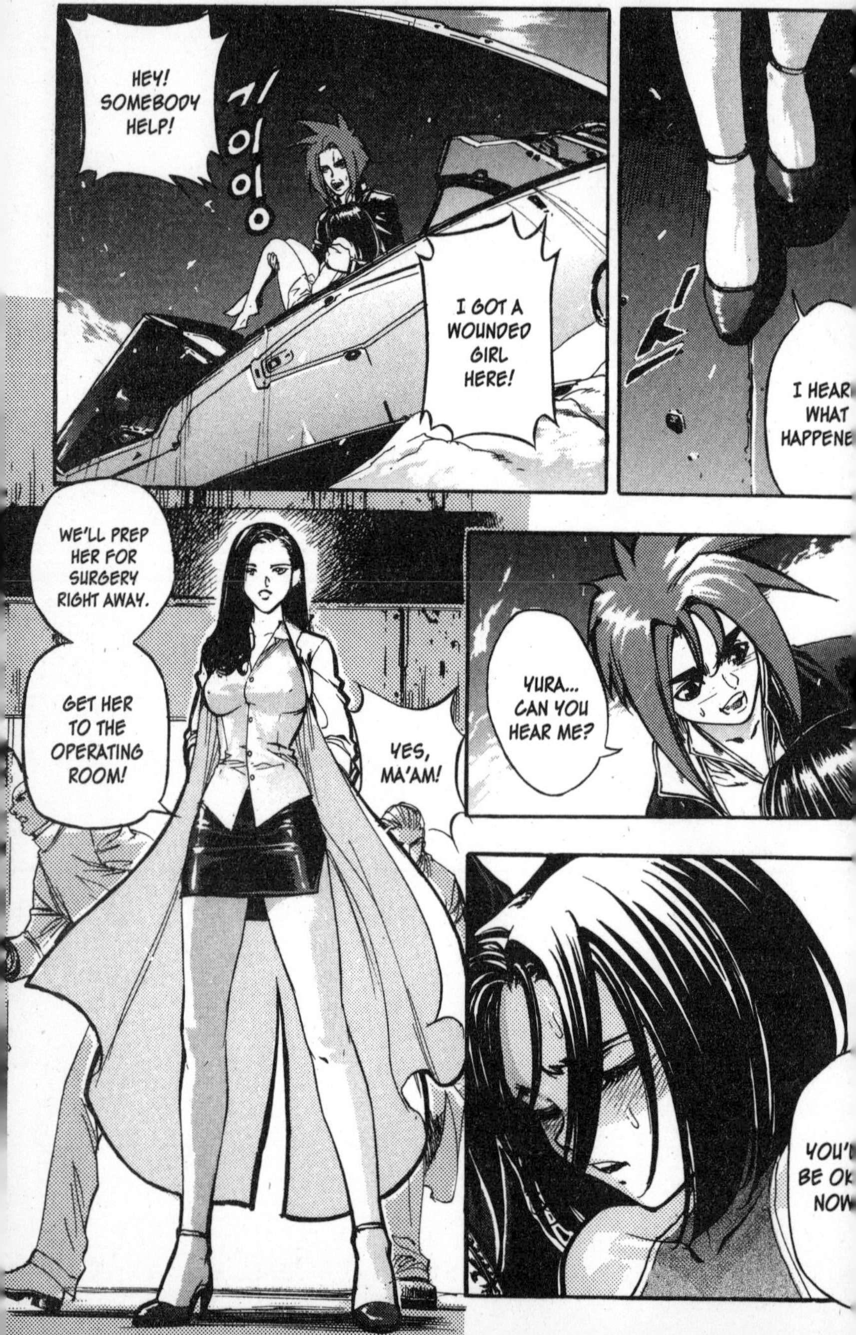
HEY! SOMEBODY HELP!
기이잉
I GOT A WOUNDED GIRL HERE!
I HEAR WHAT HAPPENE
WE'LL PREP HER FOR SURGERY RIGHT AWAY.
GET HER TO THE OPERATING ROOM!
YES, MA'AM!
YURA... CAN YOU HEAR ME?
YOU' BE OK NOW

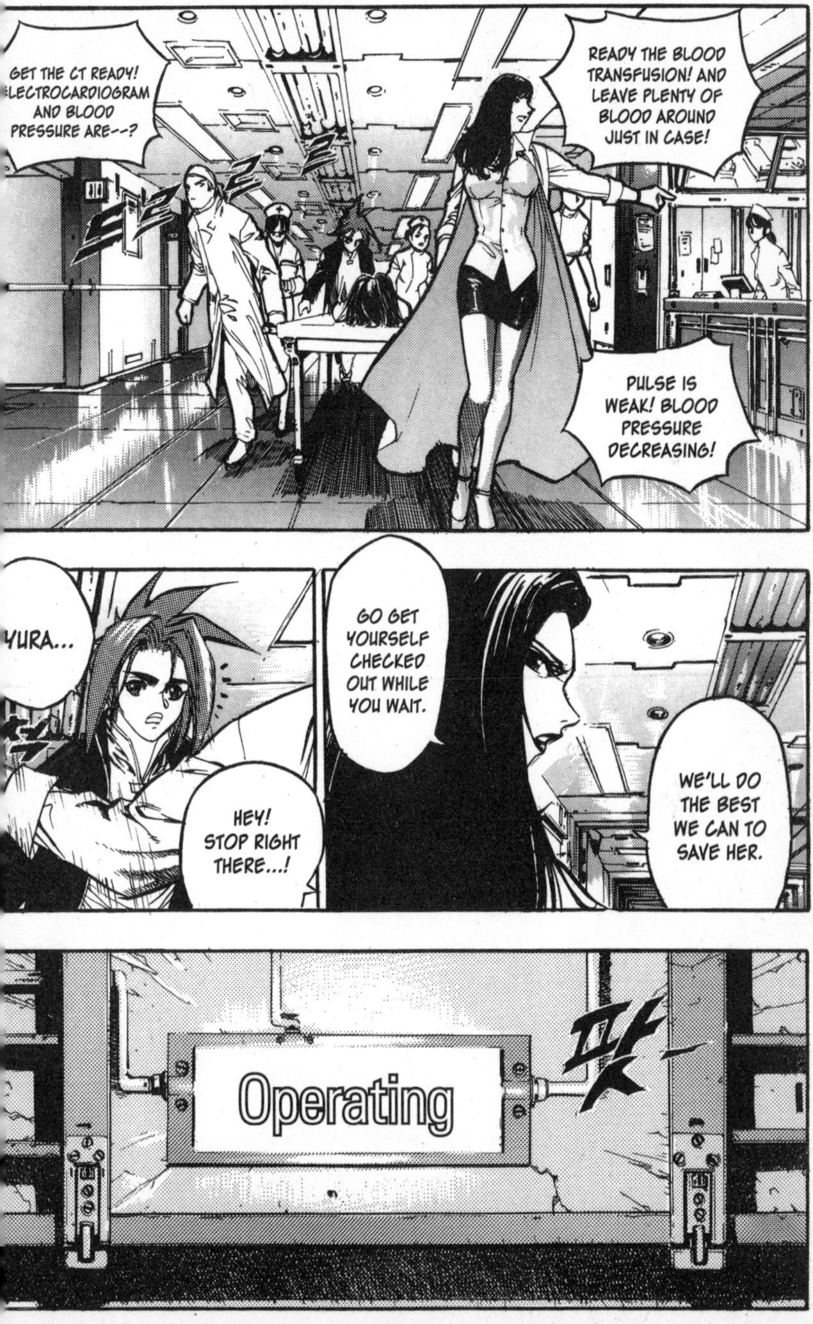
GET THE CT READY! ELECTROCARDIOGRAM AND BLOOD PRESSURE ARE--?
READY THE BLOOD TRANSFUSION! AND LEAVE PLENTY OF BLOOD AROUND JUST IN CASE!
PULSE IS WEAK! BLOOD PRESSURE DECREASING!
YURA...
HEY! STOP RIGHT THERE...!
GO GET YOURSELF CHECKED OUT WHILE YOU WAIT.
WE'LL DO THE BEST WE CAN TO SAVE HER.
Operating

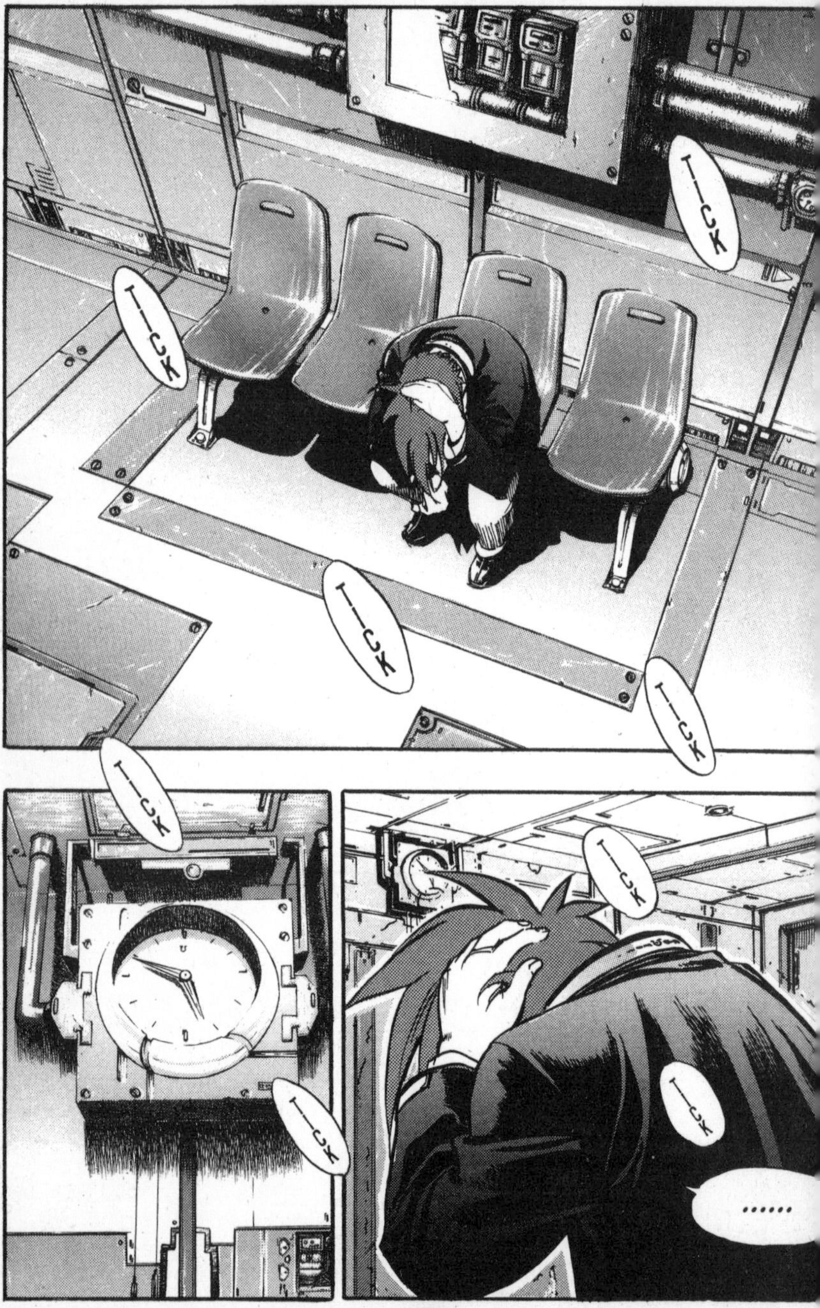
TICK
TICK
TICK
TICK
TICK
TICK
TICK
TICK
......

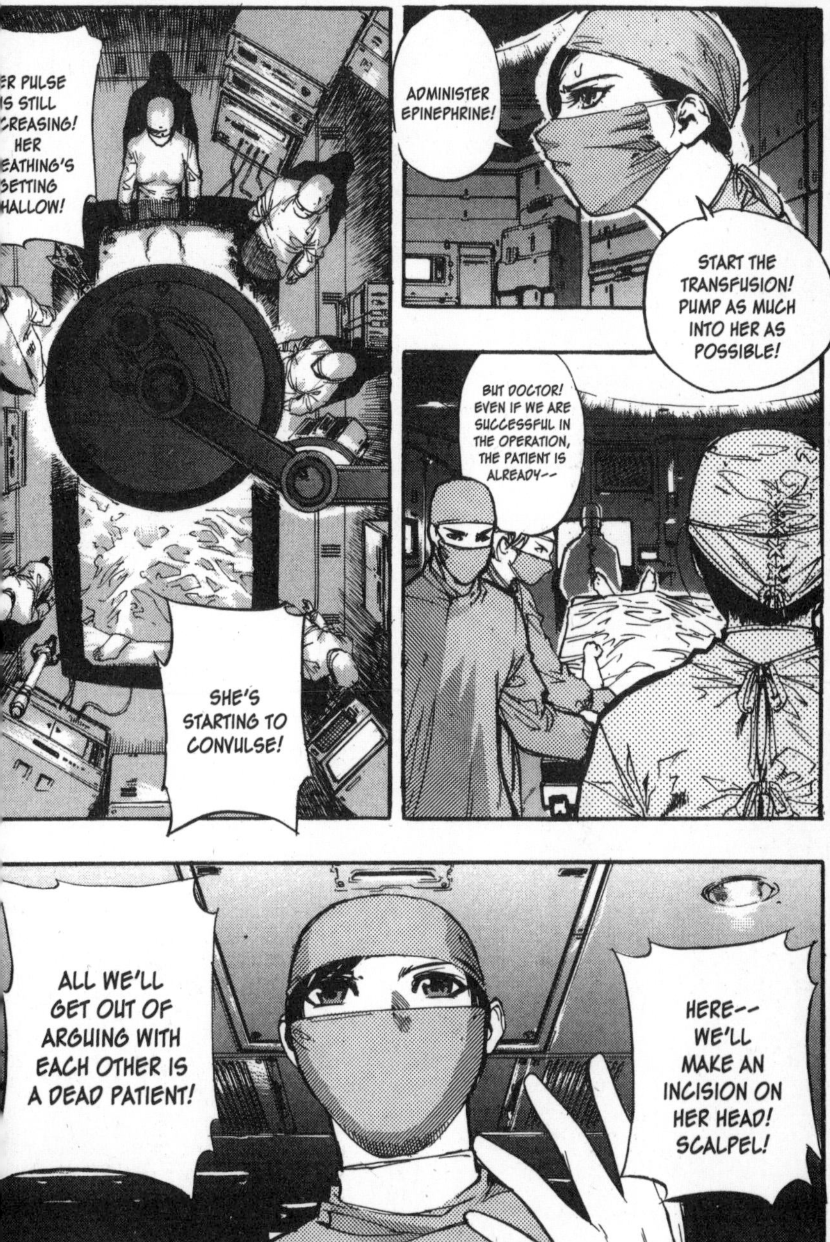
ER PULSE S STILL CREASING! HER EATHING'S SETTING HALLOW!
SHE'S STARTING TO CONVULSE!
ADMINISTER EPINEPHRINE!
START THE TRANSFUSION! PUMP AS MUCH INTO HER AS POSSIBLE!
BUT DOCTOR! EVEN IF WE ARE SUCCESSFUL IN THE OPERATION, THE PATIENT IS ALREADY--
ALL WE'LL GET OUT OF ARGUING WITH EACH OTHER IS A DEAD PATIENT!
HERE-- WE'LL MAKE AN INCISION ON HER HEAD! SCALPEL!

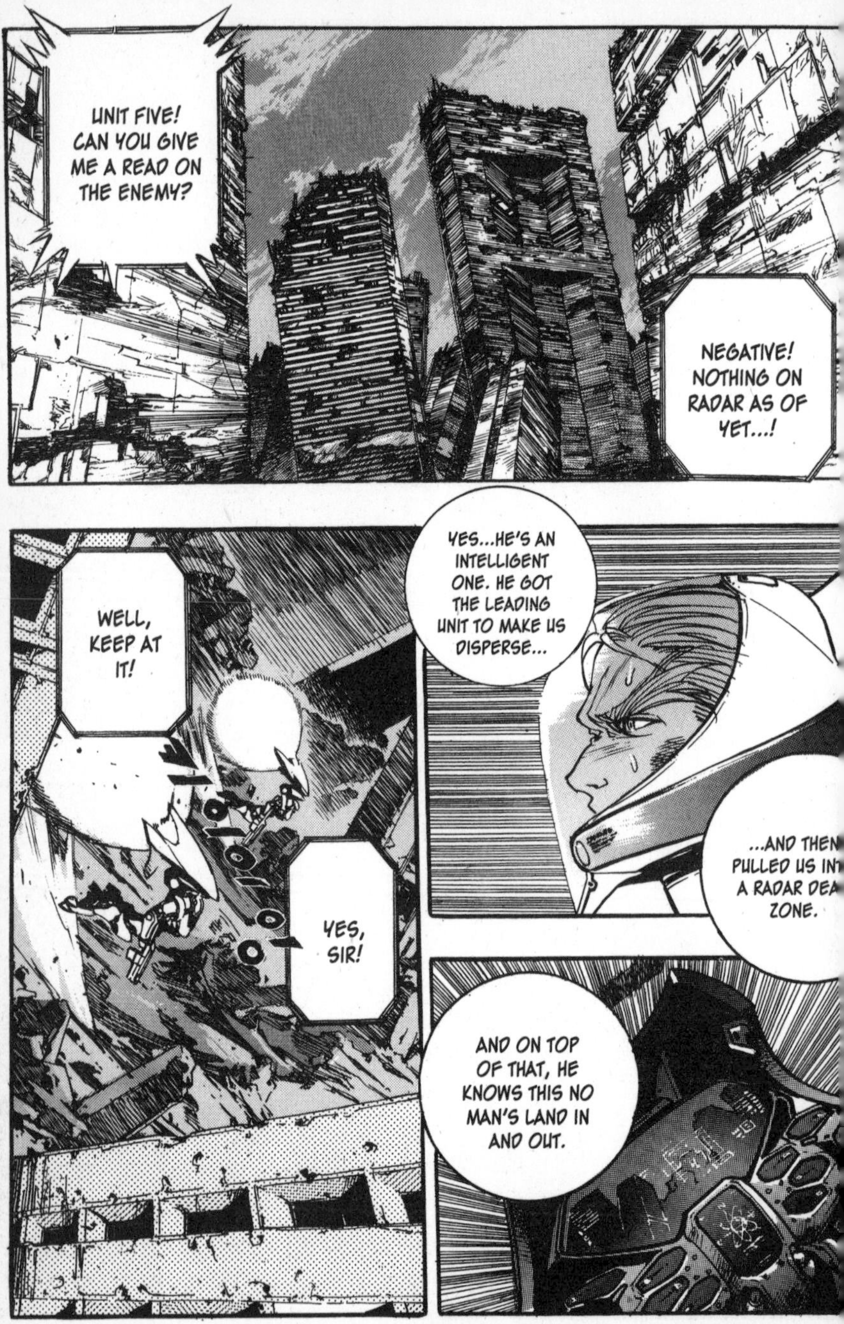
UNIT FIVE! CAN YOU GIVE ME A READ ON THE ENEMY?
NEGATIVE! NOTHING ON RADAR AS OF YET...!
WELL, KEEP AT IT!
YES, SIR!
YES...HE'S AN INTELLIGENT ONE. HE GOT THE LEADING UNIT TO MAKE US DISPERSE...
...AND THEN PULLED US IN A RADAR DEA ZONE.
AND ON TOP OF THAT, HE KNOWS THIS NO MAN'S LAND IN AND OUT.

IF IT WEREN'T FOR MY ORDERS TO KILL HIM, I'D ALMOST ADMIRE THE GUY!

TOO BAD!

UNIT 5! GO BACK TO BASE AND REQUEST ADDITIONAL UNITS!

I'LL TRY TO HOLD HIM HERE WHILE YOU'RE GONE!

YES, SIR! RIGHT AWAY, SIR!

팟

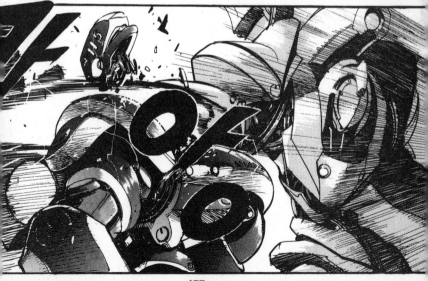

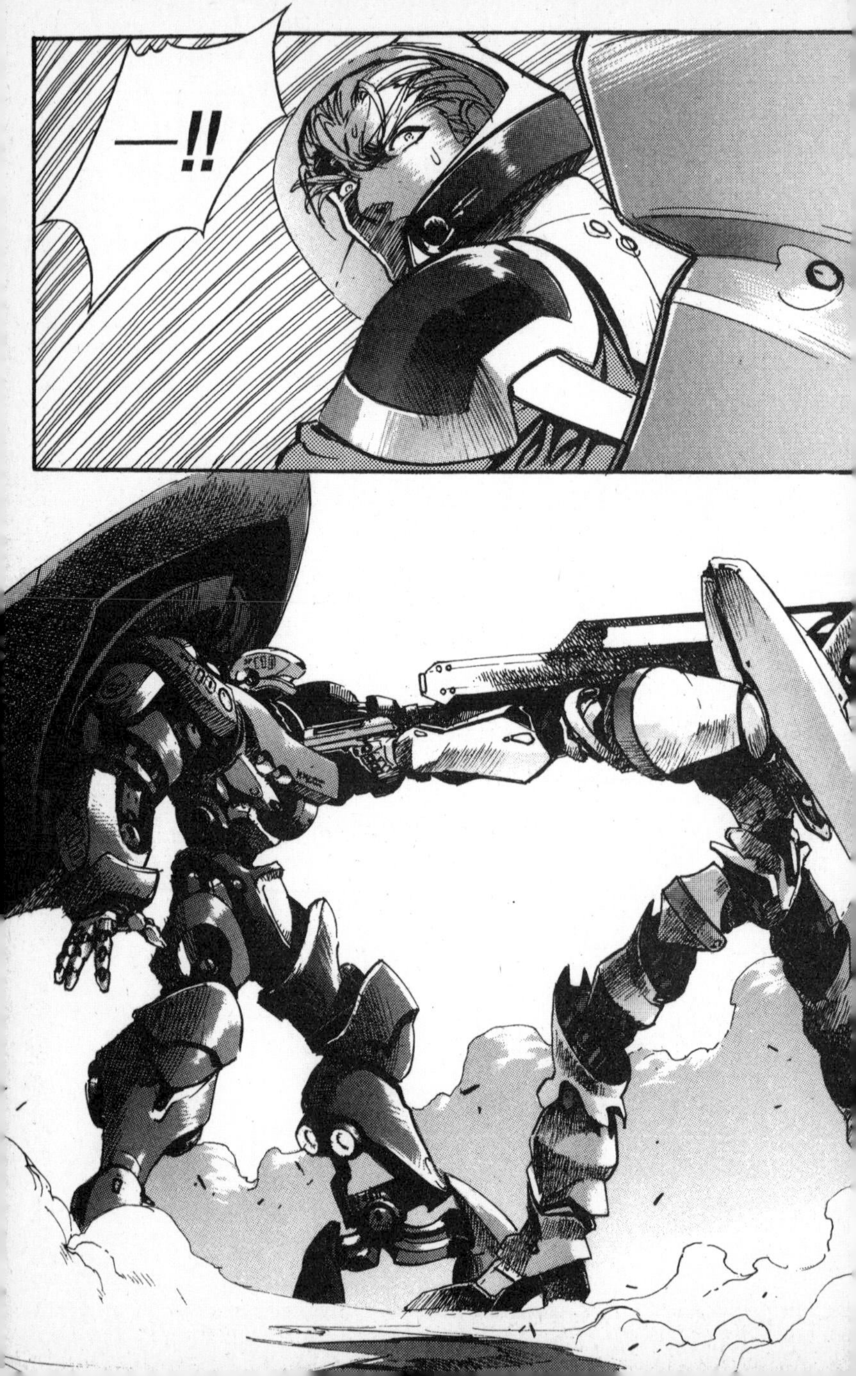
—!!

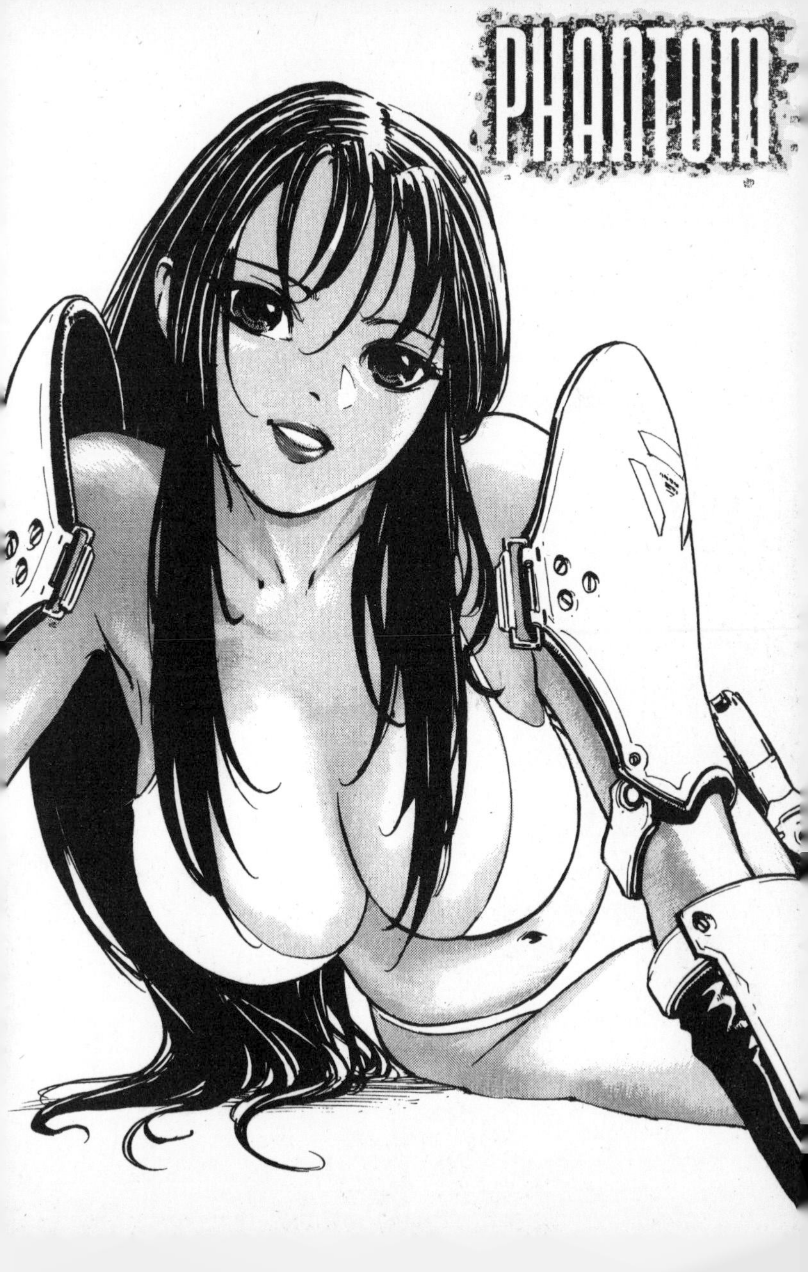
PHANTOM

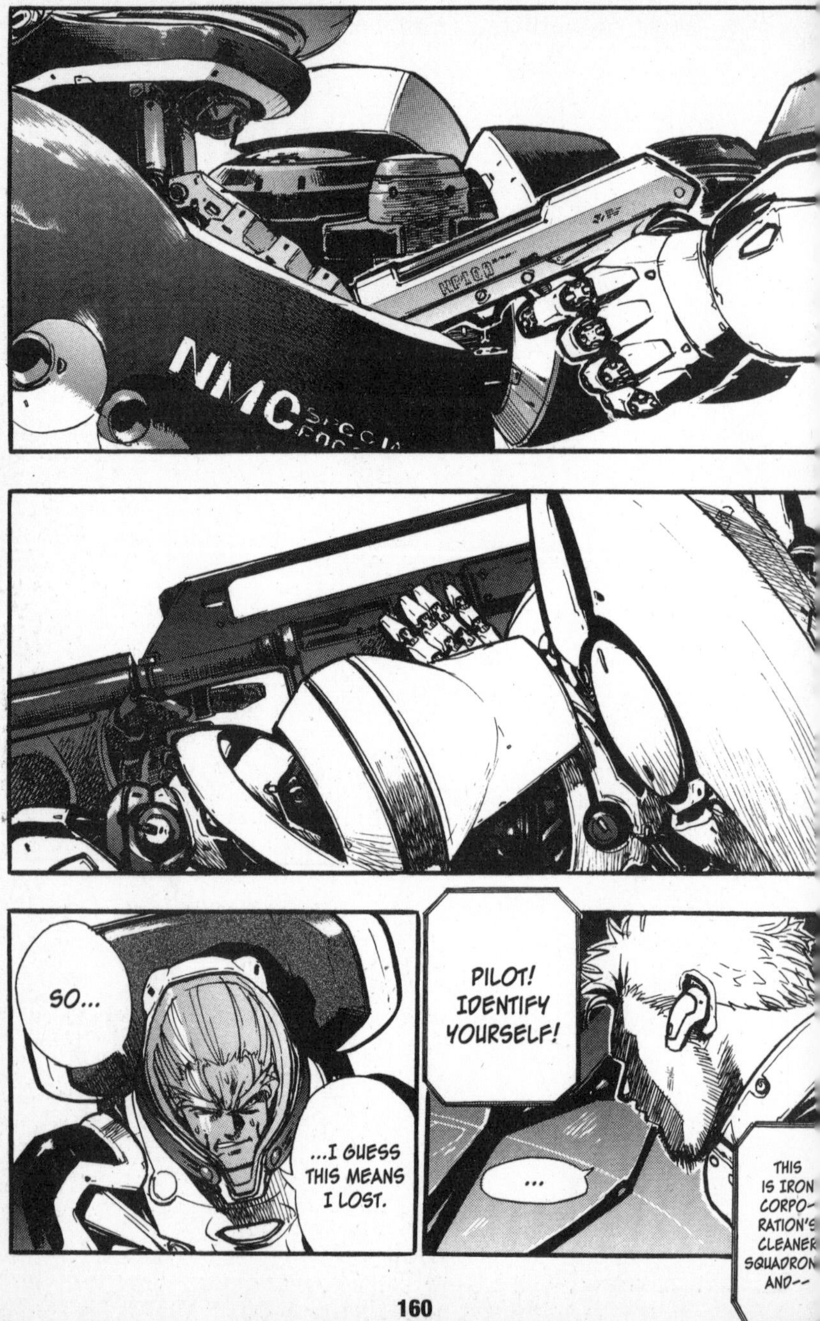
NMC
SO...
...I GUESS THIS MEANS I LOST.
PILOT! IDENTIFY YOURSELF!
...
THIS IS IRON CORPORATION'S CLEANER SQUADRON AND--

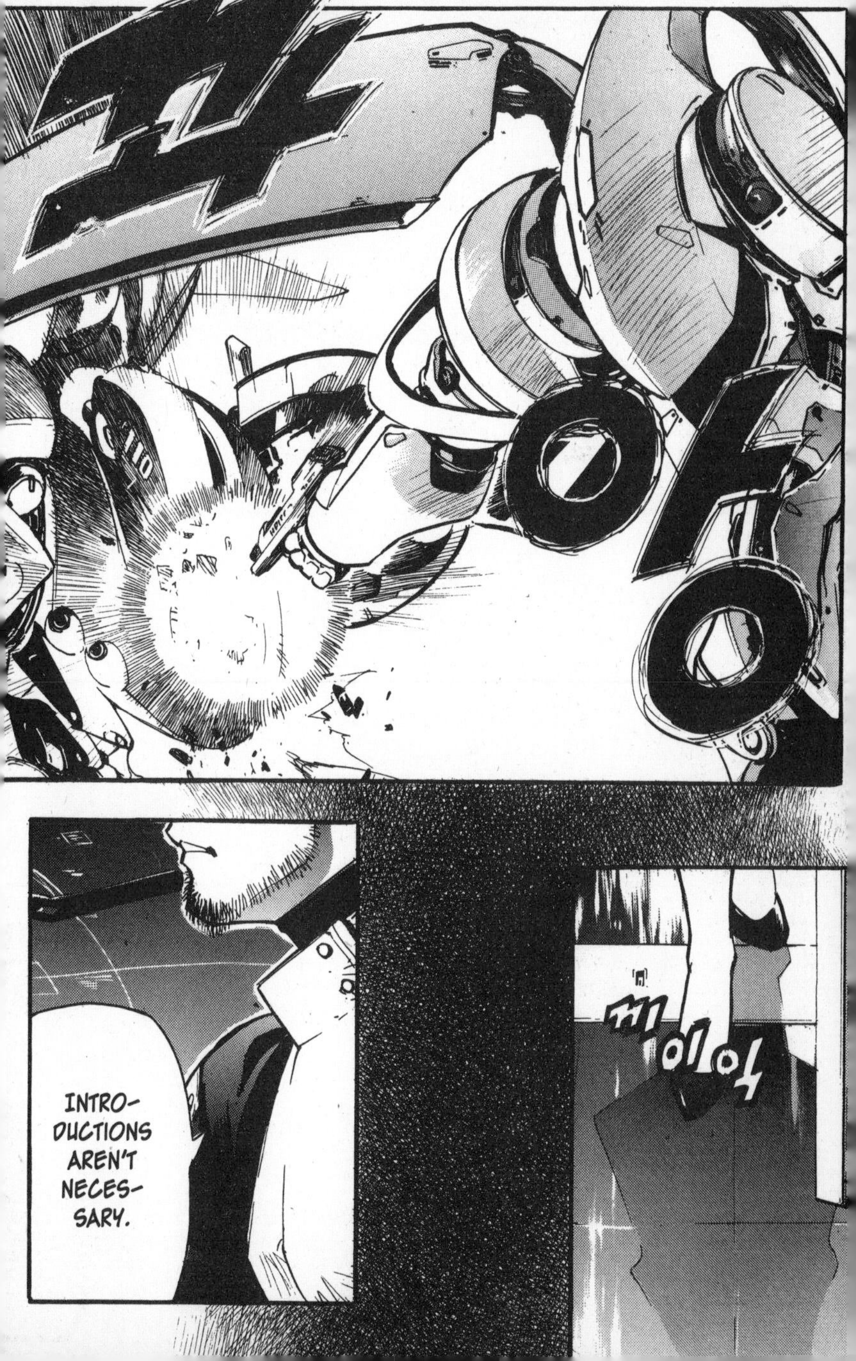
INTRO-
DUCTIONS
AREN'T
NECES-
SARY.

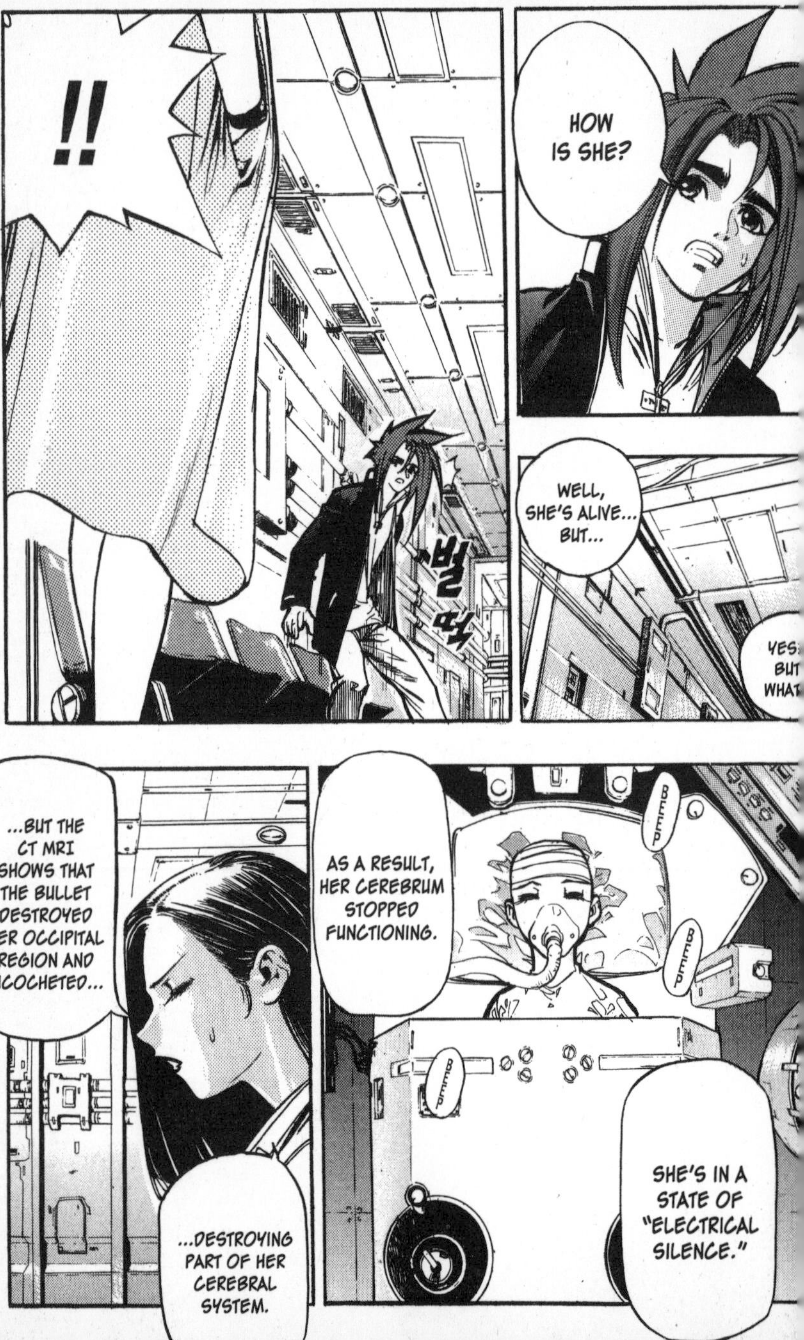
!!
벌떡
HOW IS SHE?
WELL, SHE'S ALIVE... BUT...
YES BUT WHAT
...BUT THE CT MRI SHOWS THAT THE BULLET DESTROYED HER OCCIPITAL REGION AND RICOCHETED...
...DESTROYING PART OF HER CEREBRAL SYSTEM.
AS A RESULT, HER CEREBRUM STOPPED FUNCTIONING.
BEEP
BEEP
BEEP
SHE'S IN A STATE OF "ELECTRICAL SILENCE."

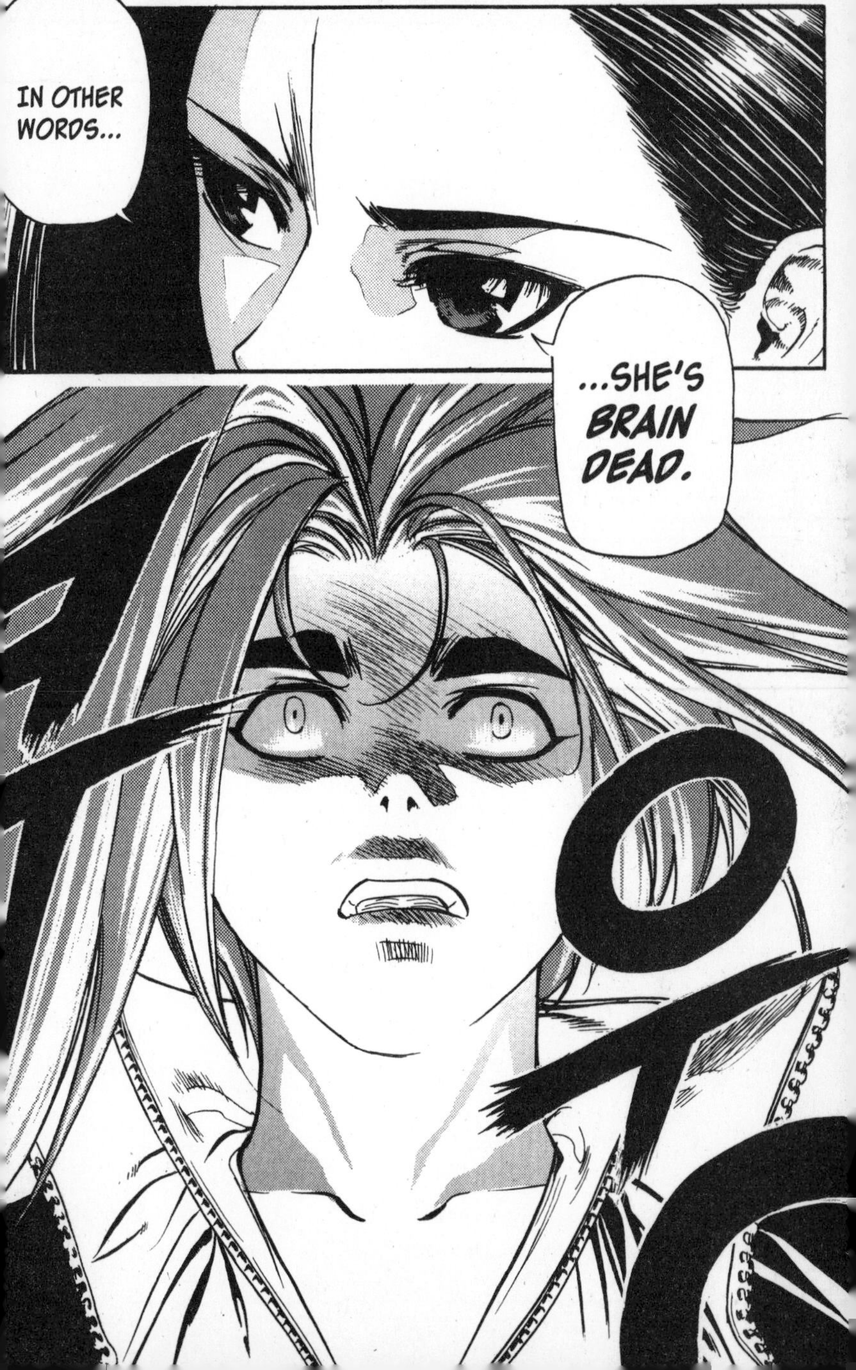
IN OTHER WORDS...
...SHE'S BRAIN DEAD.

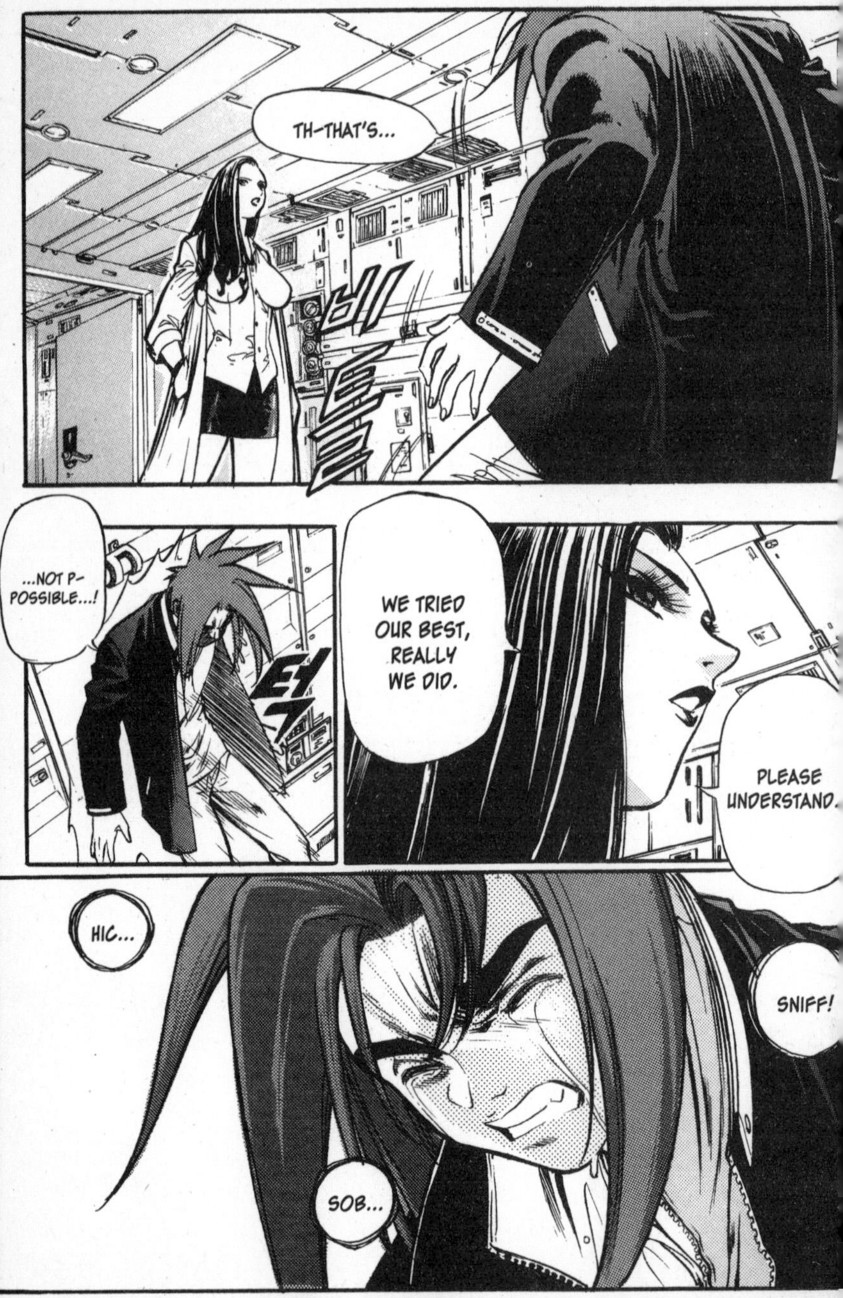
TH-THAT'S...
...NOT P-POSSIBLE...!
WE TRIED OUR BEST, REALLY WE DID.
PLEASE UNDERSTAND.
HIC...
SNIFF!
SOB...

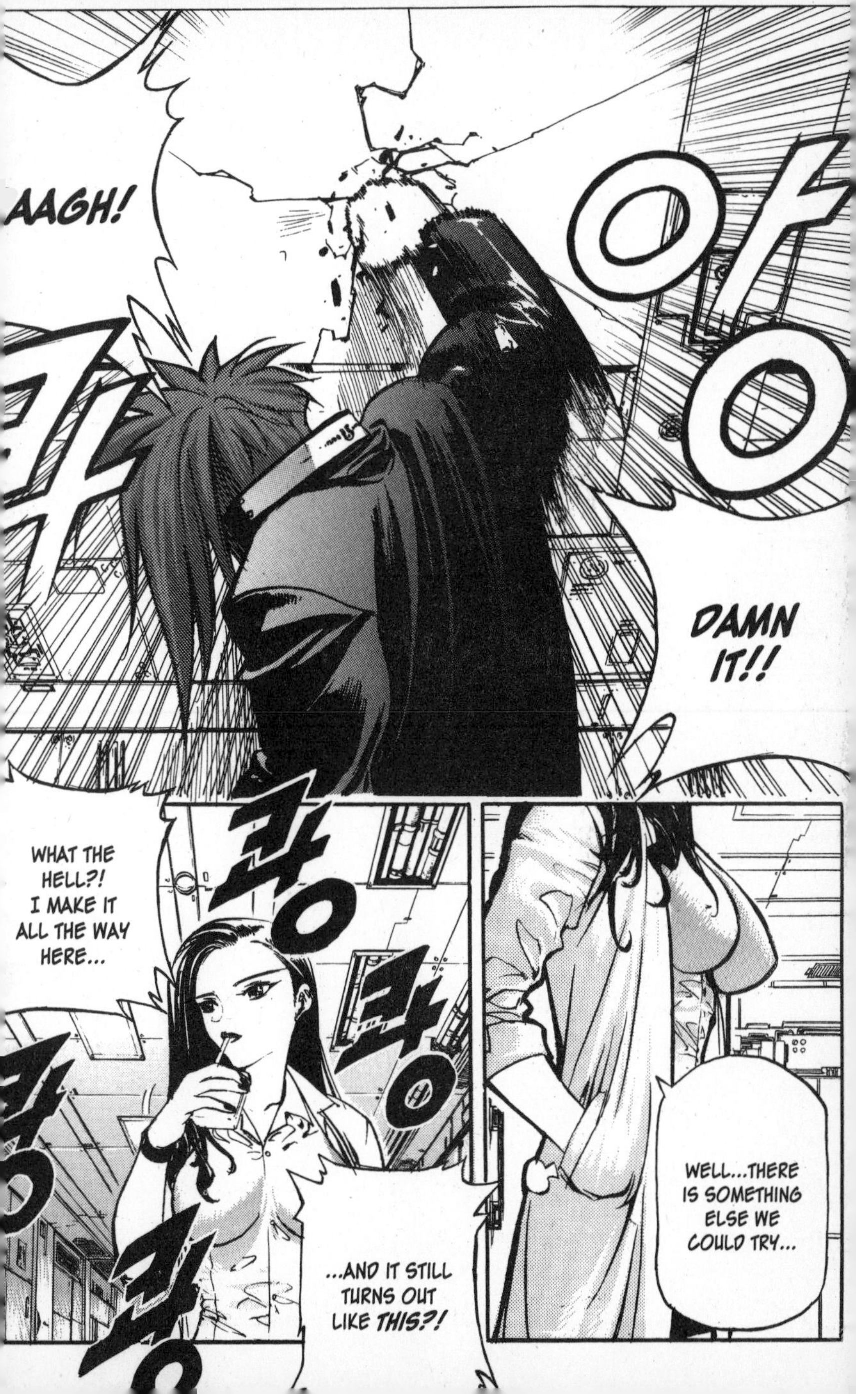
AAGH!
DAMN IT!!
WHAT THE HELL?! I MAKE IT ALL THE WAY HERE...
...AND IT STILL TURNS OUT LIKE THIS?!
WELL...THERE IS SOMETHING ELSE WE COULD TRY...

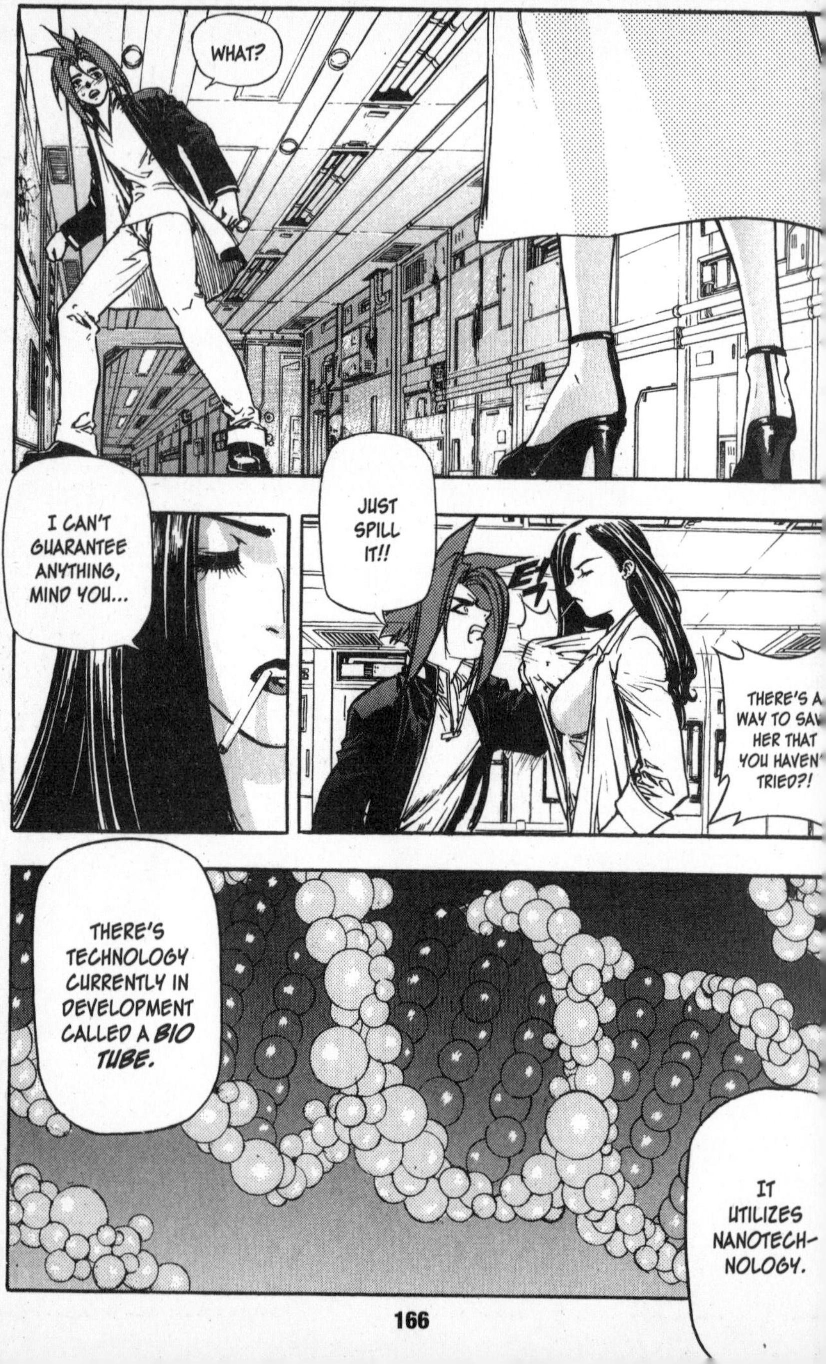
WHAT?
I CAN'T GUARANTEE ANYTHING, MIND YOU...
JUST SPILL IT!!
THERE'S A WAY TO SAV HER THAT YOU HAVEN' TRIED?!
THERE'S TECHNOLOGY CURRENTLY IN DEVELOPMENT CALLED A BIO TUBE.
IT UTILIZES NANOTECH-NOLOGY.

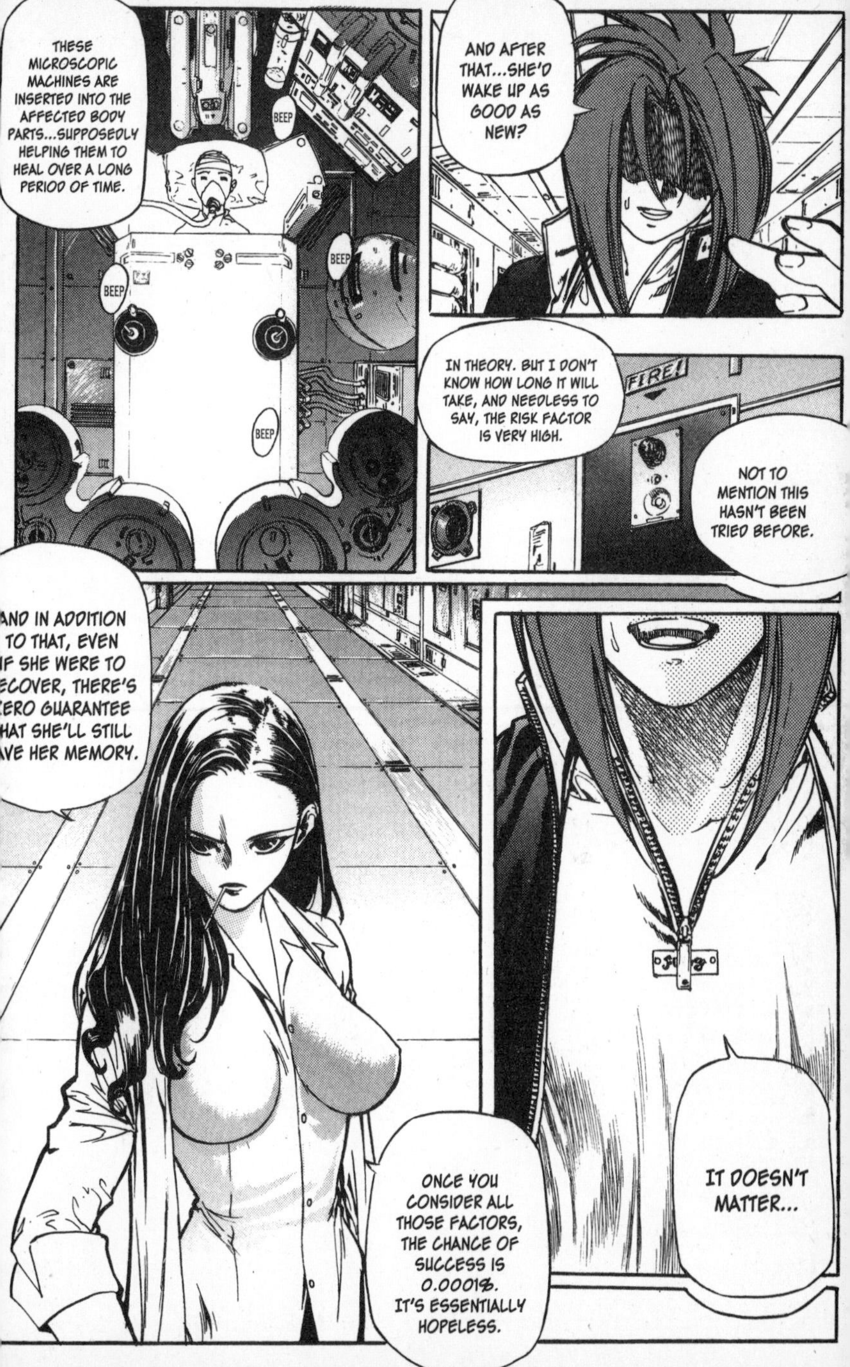
THESE MICROSCOPIC MACHINES ARE INSERTED INTO THE AFFECTED BODY PARTS...SUPPOSEDLY HELPING THEM TO HEAL OVER A LONG PERIOD OF TIME.
BEEP
BEEP
BEEP
BEEP
AND AFTER THAT...SHE'D WAKE UP AS GOOD AS NEW?
IN THEORY. BUT I DON'T KNOW HOW LONG IT WILL TAKE, AND NEEDLESS TO SAY, THE RISK FACTOR IS VERY HIGH.
FIRE!
NOT TO MENTION THIS HASN'T BEEN TRIED BEFORE.
AND IN ADDITION TO THAT, EVEN F SHE WERE TO ECOVER, THERE'S ERO GUARANTEE HAT SHE'LL STILL VE HER MEMORY.
ONCE YOU CONSIDER ALL THOSE FACTORS, THE CHANCE OF SUCCESS IS 0.0001%. IT'S ESSENTIALLY HOPELESS.
IT DOESN'T MATTER...

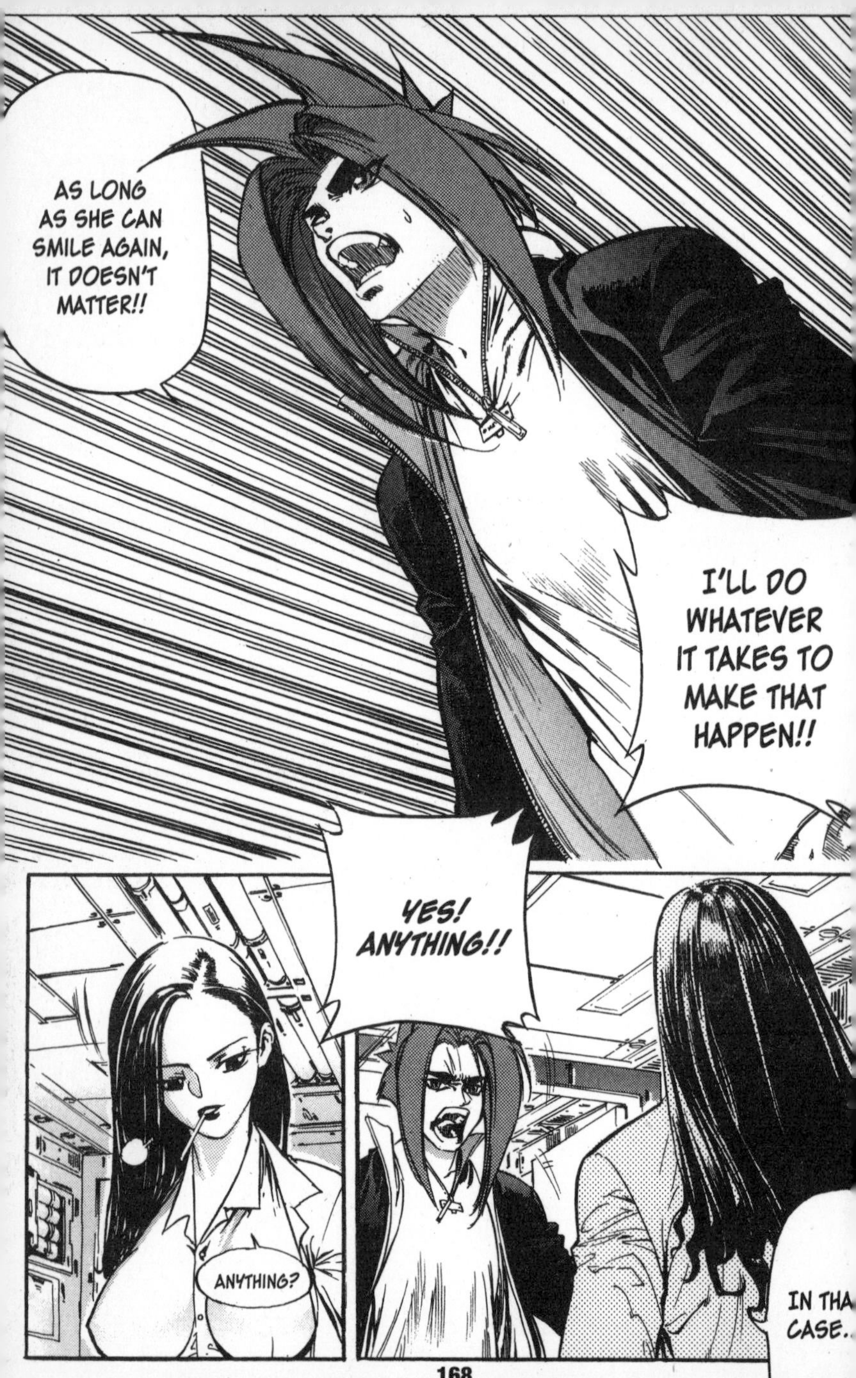
AS LONG AS SHE CAN SMILE AGAIN, IT DOESN'T MATTER!!
I'LL DO WHATEVER IT TAKES TO MAKE THAT HAPPEN!!
YES! ANYTHING!!
ANYTHING?
IN THA
CASE..

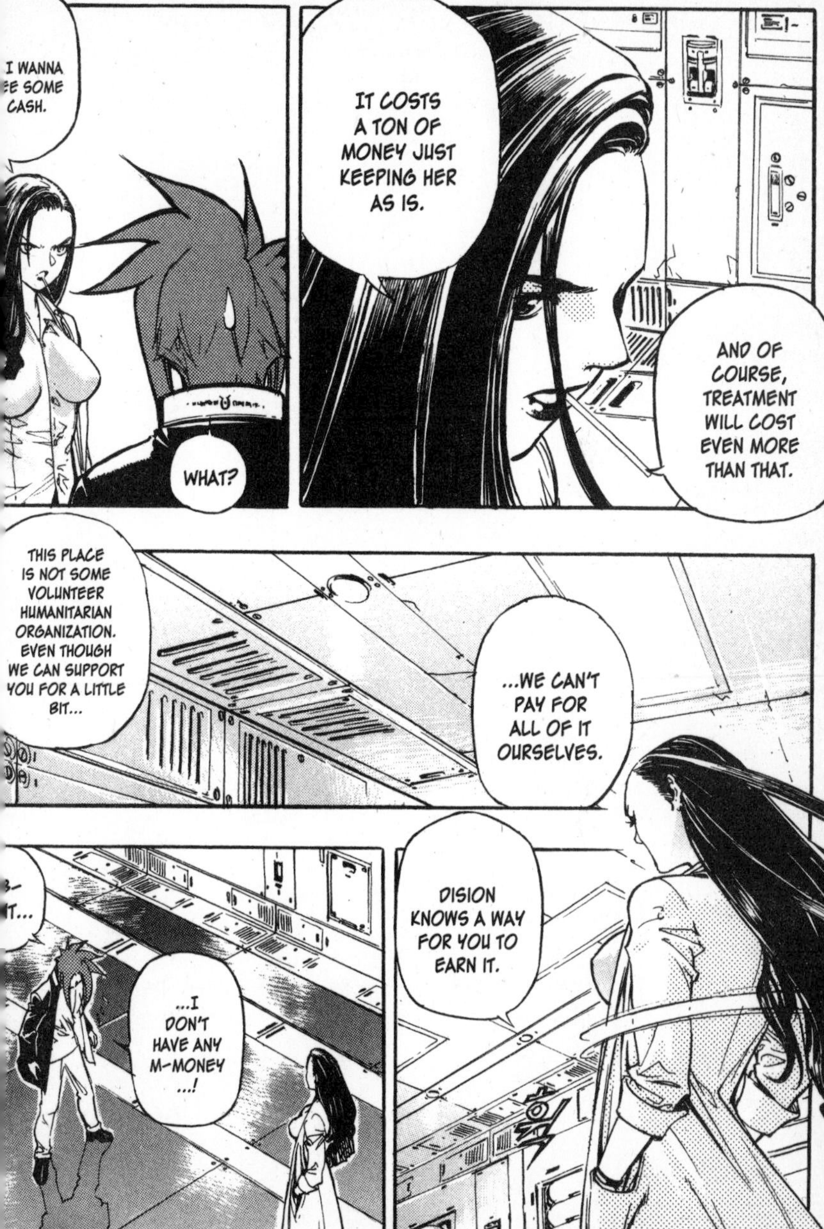
I WANNA EE SOME CASH.
WHAT?
IT COSTS A TON OF MONEY JUST KEEPING HER AS IS.
AND OF COURSE, TREATMENT WILL COST EVEN MORE THAN THAT.
THIS PLACE IS NOT SOME VOLUNTEER HUMANITARIAN ORGANIZATION. EVEN THOUGH WE CAN SUPPORT YOU FOR A LITTLE BIT...
...WE CAN'T PAY FOR ALL OF IT OURSELVES.
...I DON'T HAVE ANY M-MONEY ...!
DISION KNOWS A WAY FOR YOU TO EARN IT.

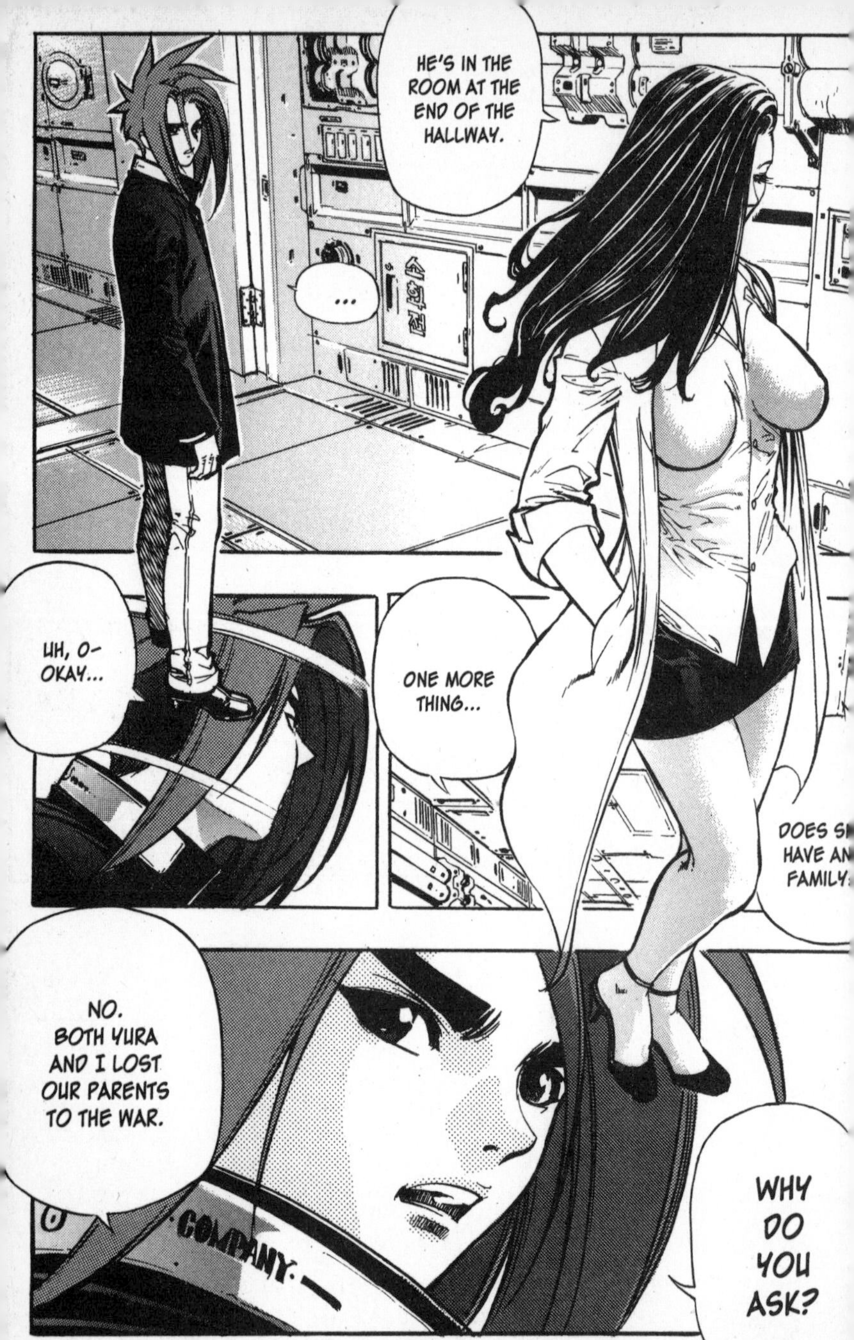
HE'S IN THE ROOM AT THE END OF THE HALLWAY.
...
UH, O-OKAY...
ONE MORE THING...
DOES S HAVE AN FAMILY
NO. BOTH YURA AND I LOST OUR PARENTS TO THE WAR.
COMPANY
WHY DO YOU ASK?

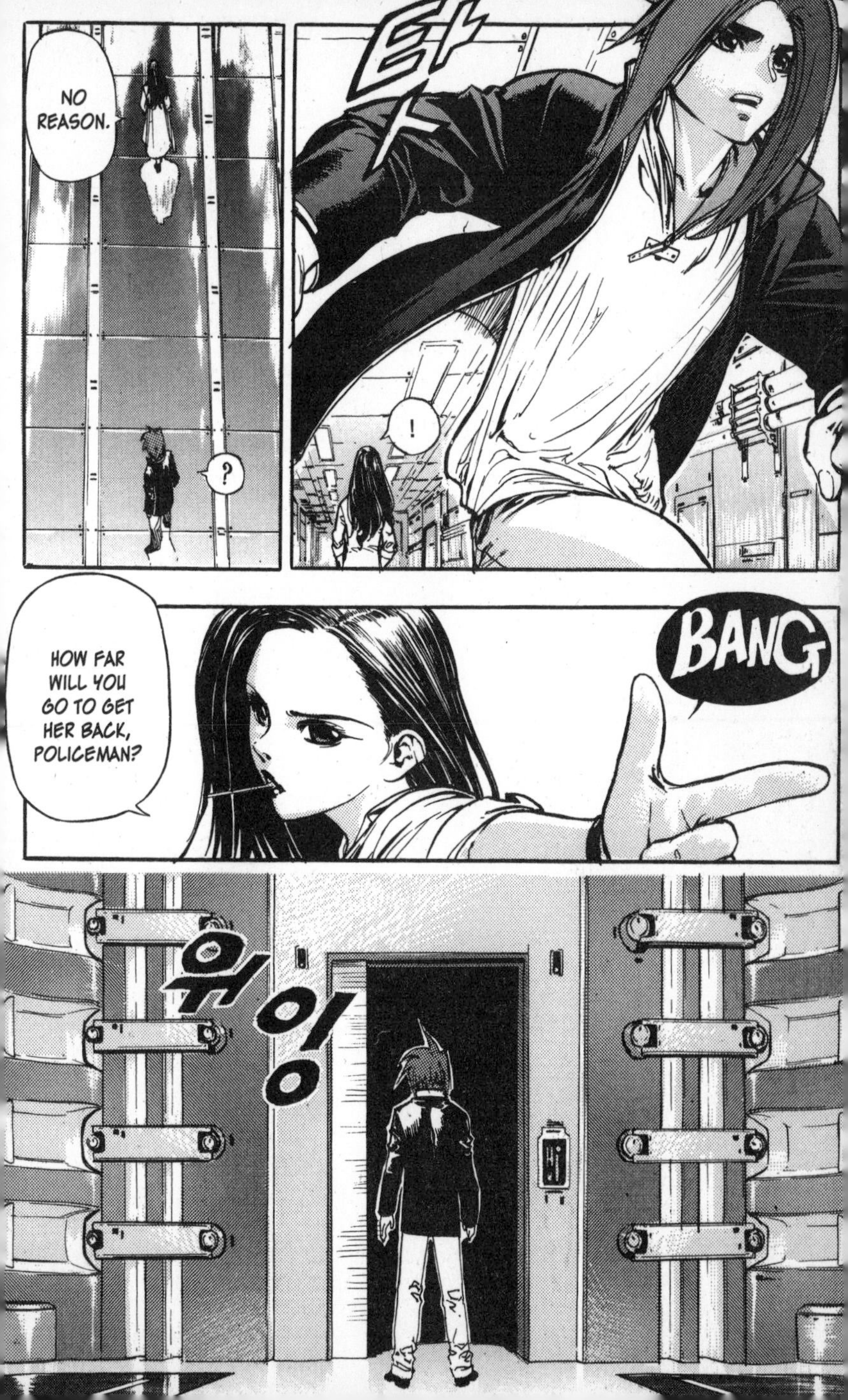
NO REASON.
?
탓
!
HOW FAR WILL YOU GO TO GET HER BACK, POLICEMAN?
BANG
와이이

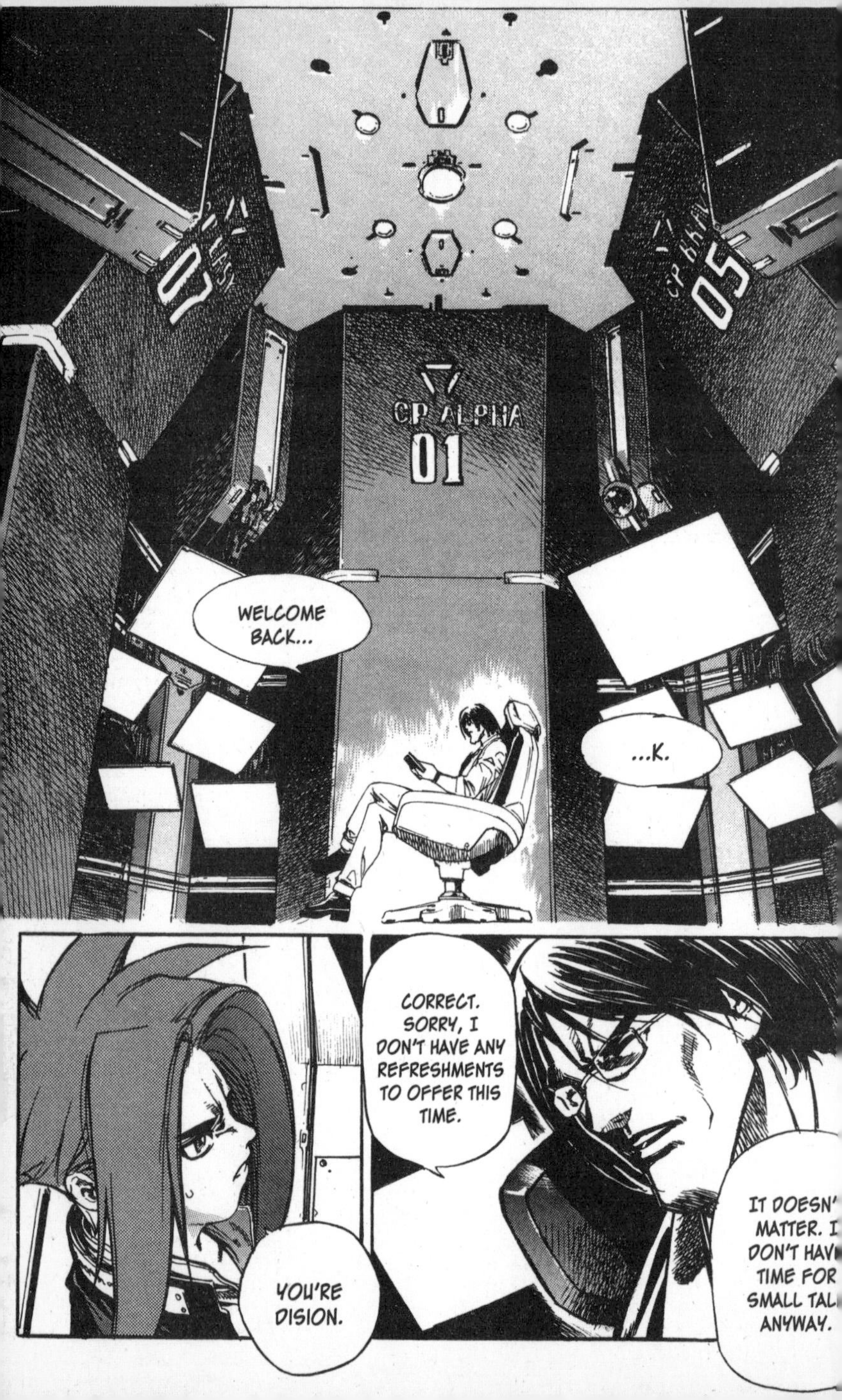
07
05
CP ALPHA
01
WELCOME BACK...
...K.
YOU'RE DISION.
CORRECT. SORRY, I DON'T HAVE ANY REFRESHMENTS TO OFFER THIS TIME.
IT DOESN' MATTER. I DON'T HAV TIME FOR SMALL TAL ANYWAY.

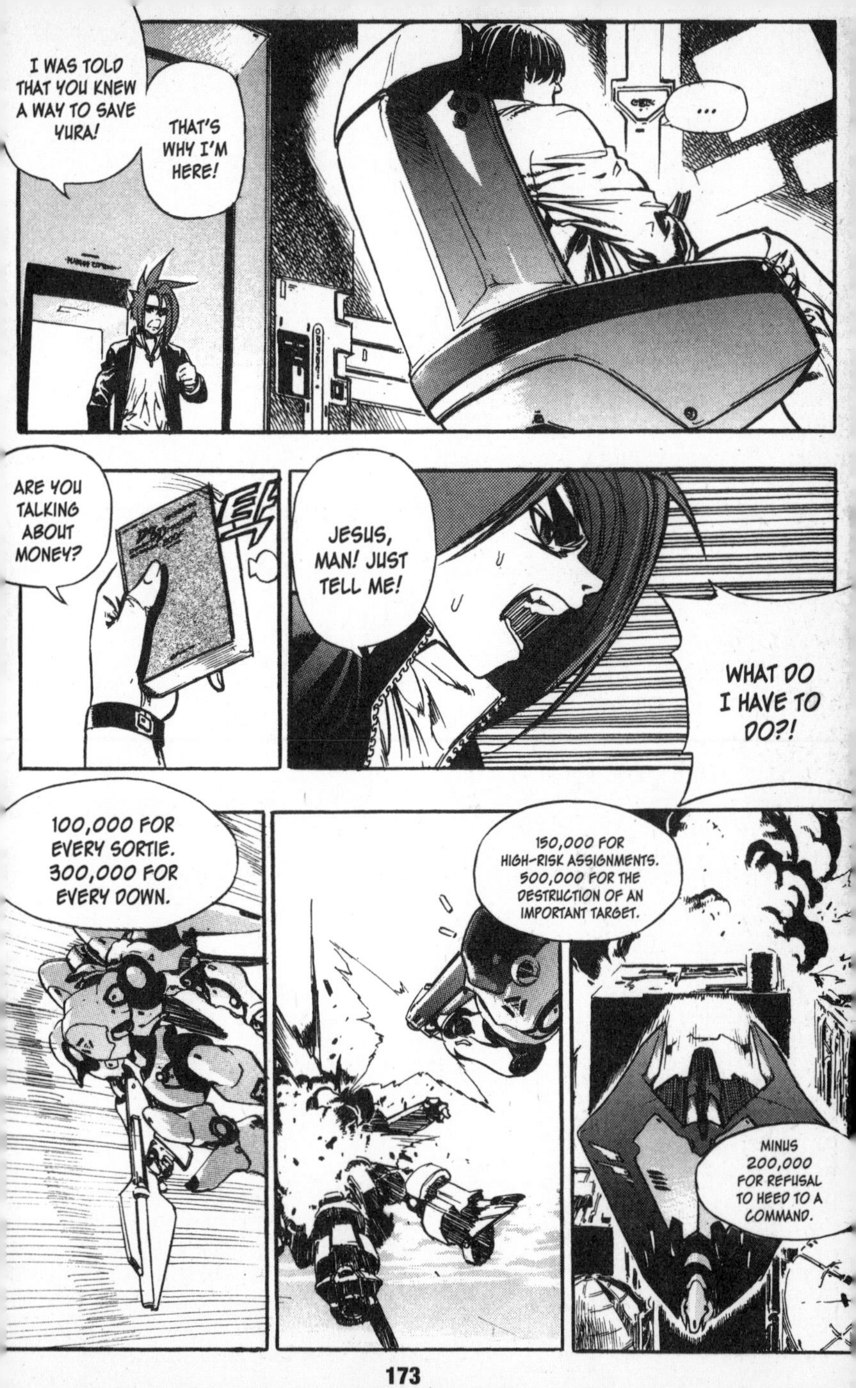
I WAS TOLD THAT YOU KNEW A WAY TO SAVE YURA!
THAT'S WHY I'M HERE!
...
ARE YOU TALKING ABOUT MONEY?
JESUS, MAN! JUST TELL ME!
WHAT DO I HAVE TO DO?!
100,000 FOR EVERY SORTIE. 300,000 FOR EVERY DOWN.
150,000 FOR HIGH-RISK ASSIGNMENTS. 500,000 FOR THE DESTRUCTION OF AN IMPORTANT TARGET.
MINUS 200,000 FOR REFUSAL TO HEED TO A COMMAND.

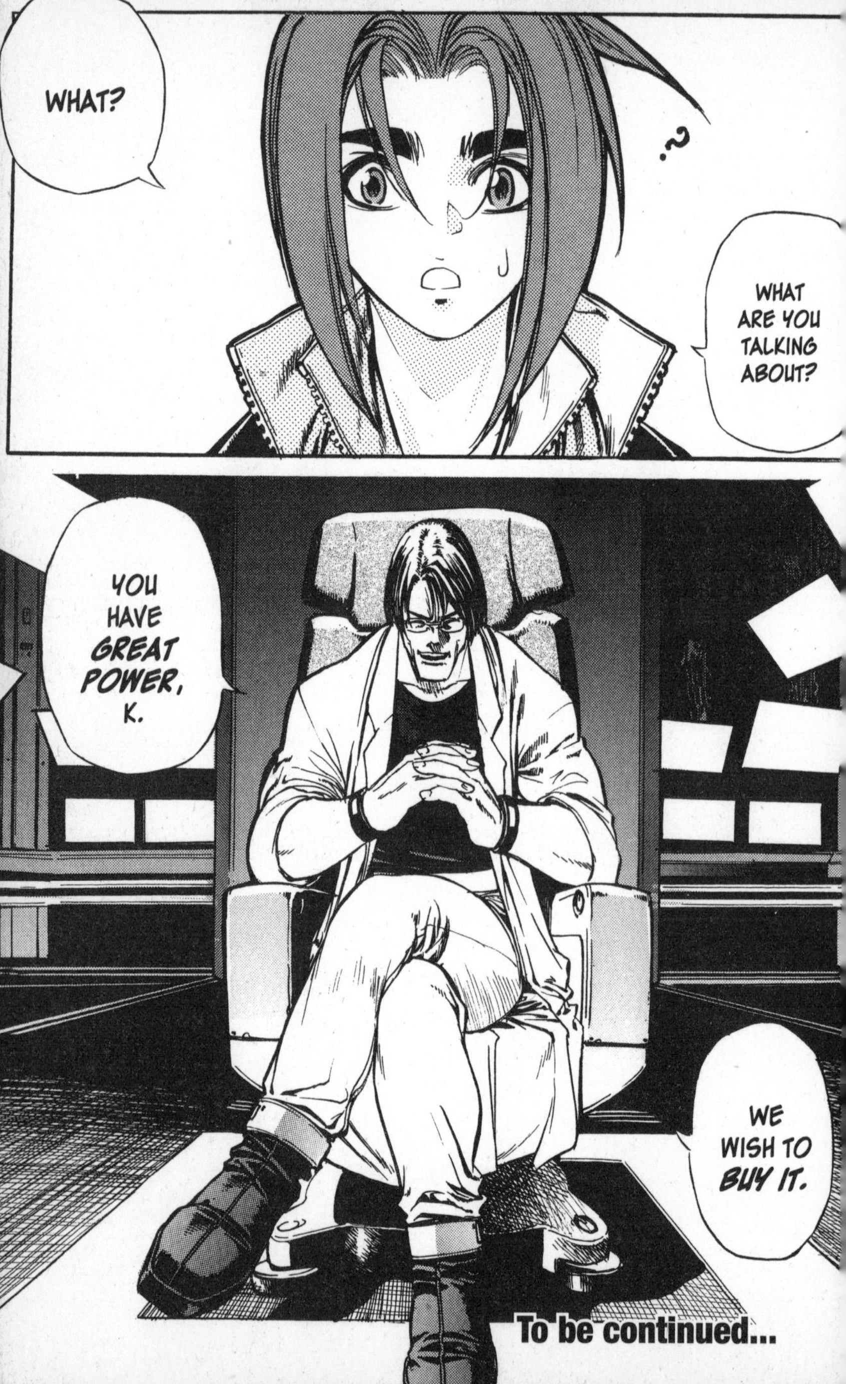
WHAT?
?
WHAT ARE YOU TALKING ABOUT?
YOU HAVE *GREAT POWER,* K.
WE WISH TO *BUY IT.*
To be continued...

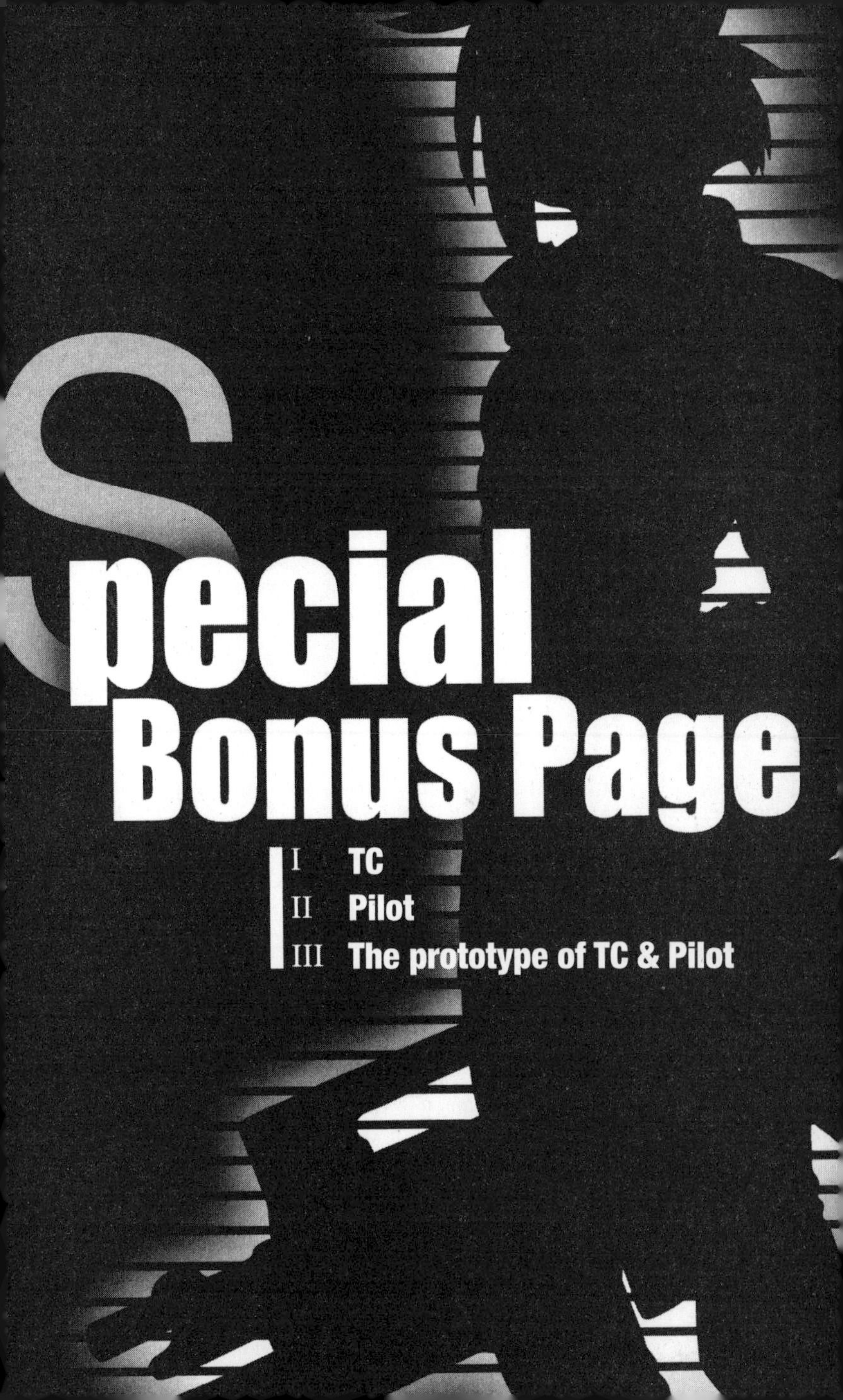

Special Bonus Page

I TC
II Pilot
III The prototype of TC & Pilot

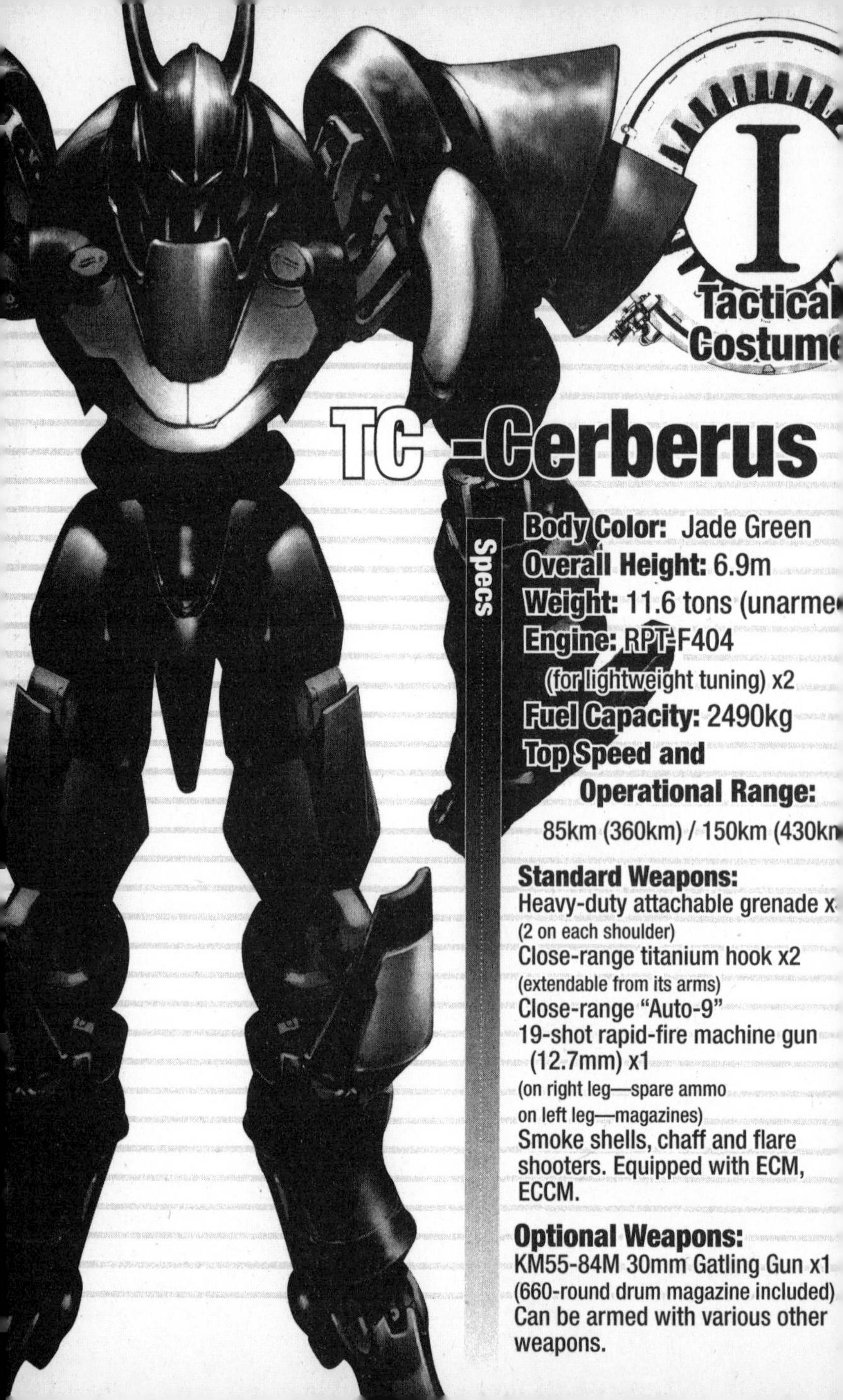

I
Tactical
Costume

TC -Cerberus

Specs

Body Color: Jade Green
Overall Height: 6.9m
Weight: 11.6 tons (unarme
Engine: RPT-F404
(for lightweight tuning) x2
Fuel Capacity: 2490kg
Top Speed and Operational Range:
85km (360km) / 150km (430kn

Standard Weapons:
Heavy-duty attachable grenade x
(2 on each shoulder)
Close-range titanium hook x2
(extendable from its arms)
Close-range "Auto-9"
19-shot rapid-fire machine gun (12.7mm) x1
(on right leg—spare ammo
on left leg—magazines)
Smoke shells, chaff and flare shooters. Equipped with ECM, ECCM.

Optional Weapons:
KM55-84M 30mm Gatling Gun x1
(660-round drum magazine included)
Can be armed with various other weapons.

The guard dog from hell, Cerberus.

> It roams the field in its blue-green armor. The cleaners will later give it the title "Blue Thunder" and coin the phrase "Stay away from Blue Thunder."

1. It was designed with speed in mind, hence it's light.

It used a Russian TC Fulcrum as its base. It has the highly touted new engine "Unigmo," which is light with a high-power output. It boasts 20% maneuverability increase over other high-speed TCs.

2. Reinforced to the limit— Advantageous during close combat.

This is a unit that was built with speed in mind, but it is also highly effective during close-range combat. Rynus Corporation has increased the overall durability of the armor, as well as reinforced specific "high-risk" parts.

3. The learning A.I. system, Aurora, is on board.

Aurora is Rynus Corporation's first real-world deployment of its A.I. system. It continues to evolve and learn as it goes through combat.

4. New Chassis

It includes the new chassis developed by Rynus called "MET," composed of a compound akin to human bones. This is a brand new prototype that's not on any other TCs, so it's unknown what type of effect it will have on its pilot and combat abilities.

ABILITY RANKS

Ground Combat	A
Air Combat	B (with Gripen)
Underwater Combat	C
Space Combat	?

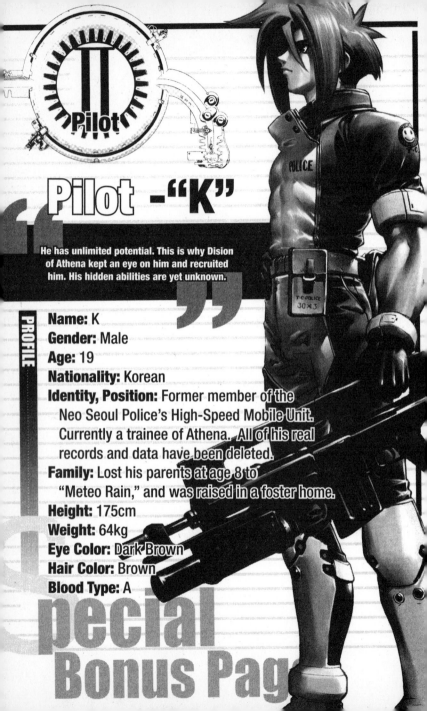

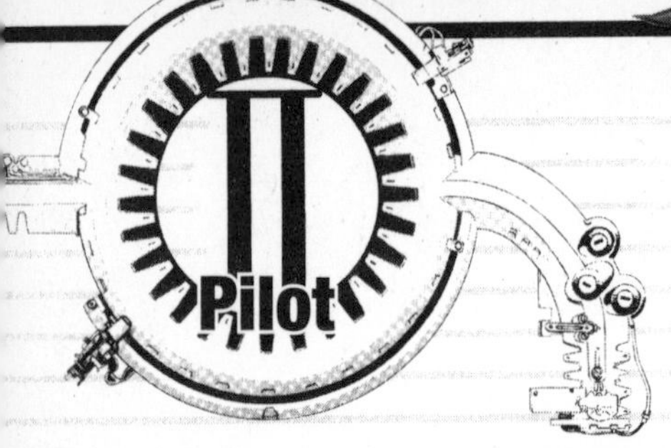
Pilot

Pilot -"K"

He has unlimited potential. This is why Dision of Athena kept an eye on him and recruited him. His hidden abilities are yet unknown.

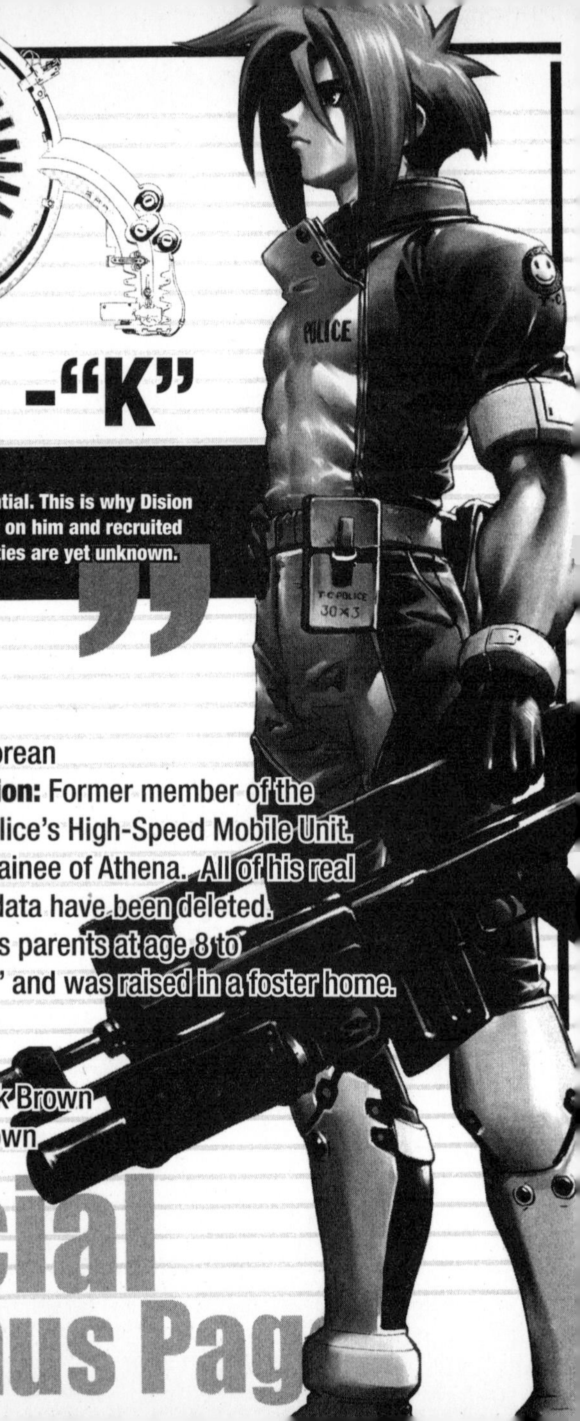
POLICE
T.C POLICE
30×3

PROFILE

Name: K
Gender: Male
Age: 19
Nationality: Korean
Identity, Position: Former member of the Neo Seoul Police's High-Speed Mobile Unit. Currently a trainee of Athena. All of his real records and data have been deleted.
Family: Lost his parents at age 8 to "Meteo Rain," and was raised in a foster home.
Height: 175cm
Weight: 64kg
Eye Color: Dark Brown
Hair Color: Brown
Blood Type: A

Special Bonus Pag

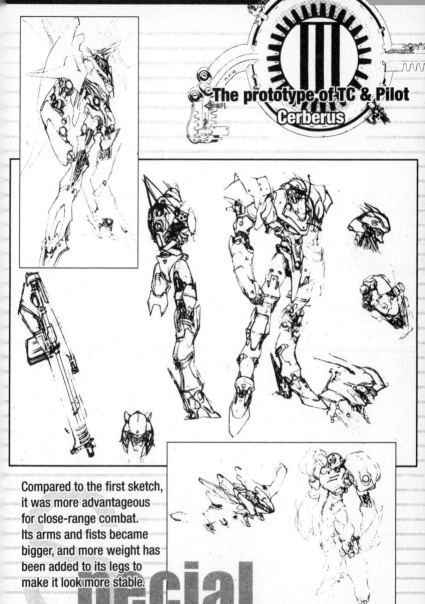

The prototype of TC & Pilot
Cerberus

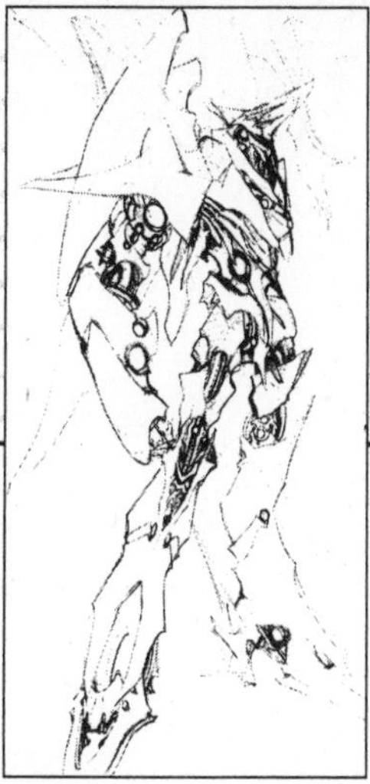

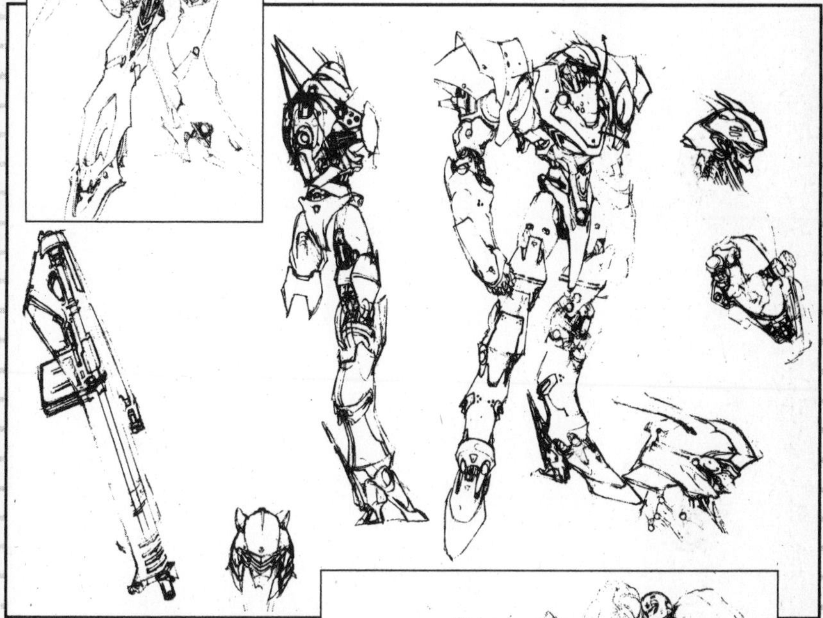

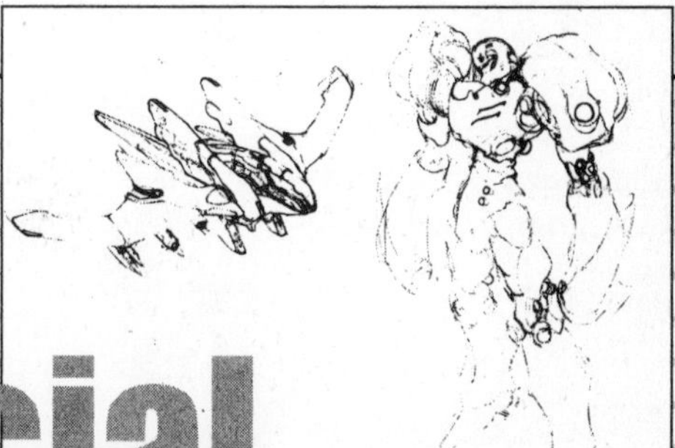

Compared to the first sketch, it was more advantageous for close-range combat. Its arms and fists became bigger, and more weight has been added to its legs to make it look more stable.

Special Bonus Page

The prototype of TC & Pilot

K

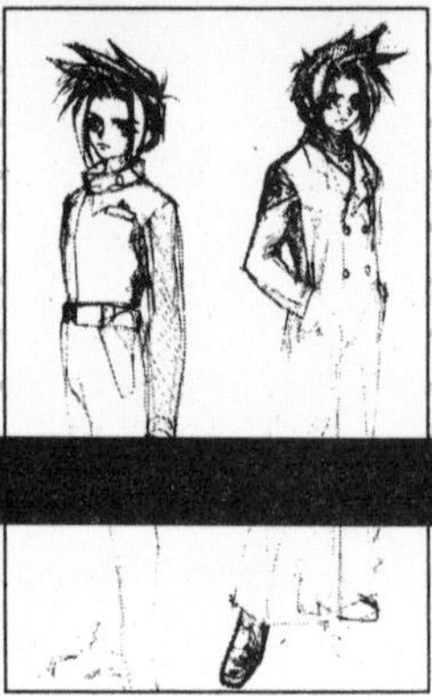

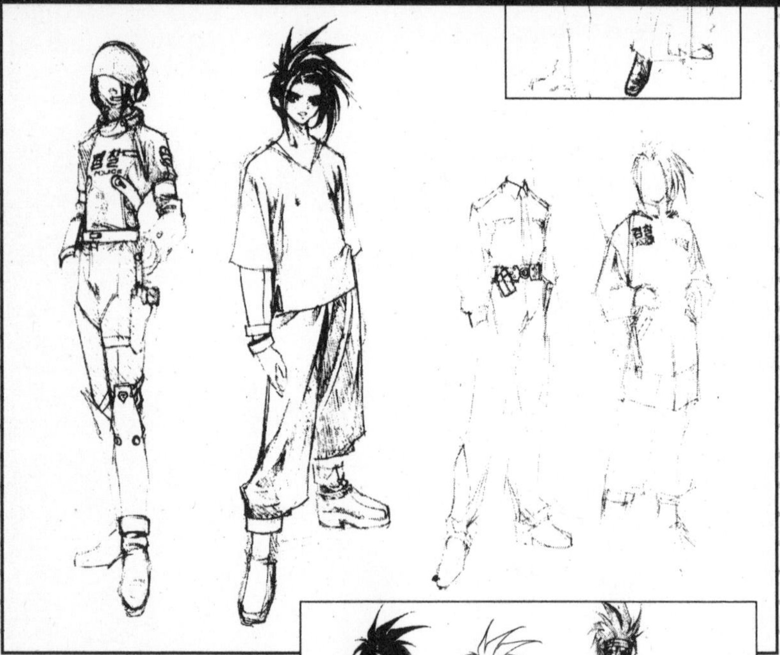

His hair changed to make it more suitable for wearing a helmet. There weren't many changes to his facial features, but as his torso became longer, so did his arms and legs.

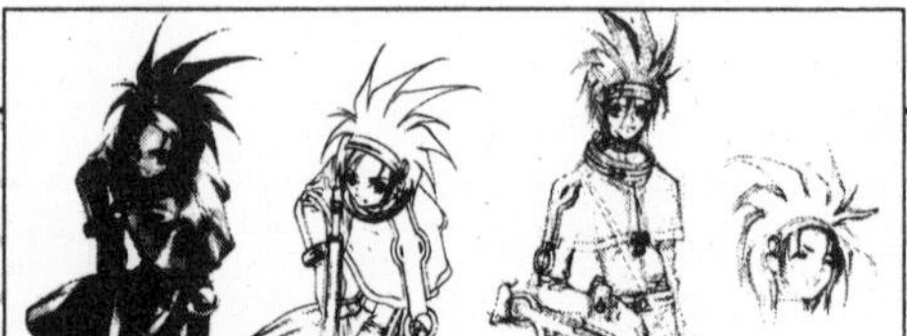

Special Bonus Page

Police Mech

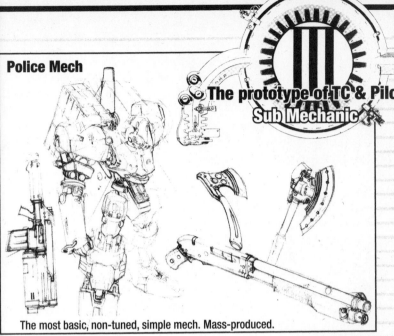

The prototype of TC & Pilot
Sub Mechanic

The most basic, non-tuned, simple mech. Mass-produced.

MNC Cleaner's Mech

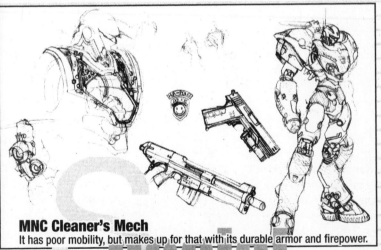

It has poor mobility, but makes up for that with its durable armor and firepower.

Special Bonus Page

F-4 PHANTOM.
PERSONALLY SPEAKING, IT'S MY FAVORITE
JET. IT'S DATED NOW, BUT I NEVER
GET TIRED OF ITS SENSUAL DESIGN. OF
COURSE, IT DOESN'T HAVE ANYTHING TO DO
WITH THIS WORK. OKAY, FINE. TO TELL YOU
THE TRUTH, IT'S WHERE I GOT THE TITLE.

Ki-Hoon Lee

I WANTED TO CREATE A COMIC THAT WOULD
BE FUN FOR EVERYONE TO READ, BUT...
IT'S NOT AS EASY AS I THOUGHT. OH WELL.
THANKS TO EVERYONE OUT THERE WHO
ENJOYED READING THIS.

Seung-Yup Cho

In the next

After agreeing to work for Athena, K is shipped off to a
TC combat training school to become an elite fighter.
There he encounters a tough-as-nails instructor with
impressive chops of her own. Meanwhile, Iron hires
a brilliant and unstable young tactician to eradicate
terrorist threats—specifically K!

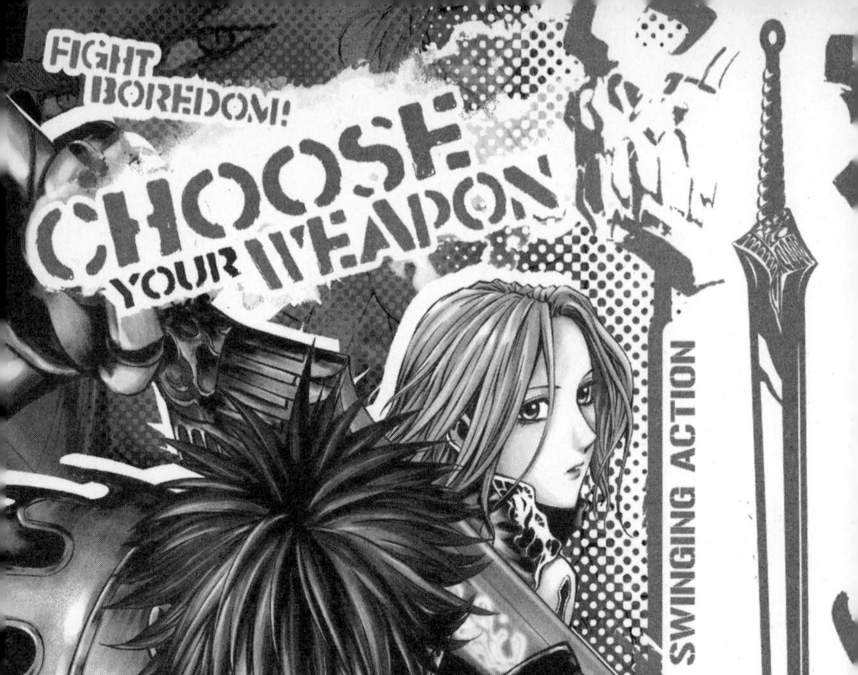
FIGHT BOREDOM!
CHOOSE YOUR WEAPON
SWORD SWINGING ACTION
READ THE MANGA THAT INSPIRED THE VIDEO GAME!
ARCHLORD™
ACTION
T
TEEN AGE 13+

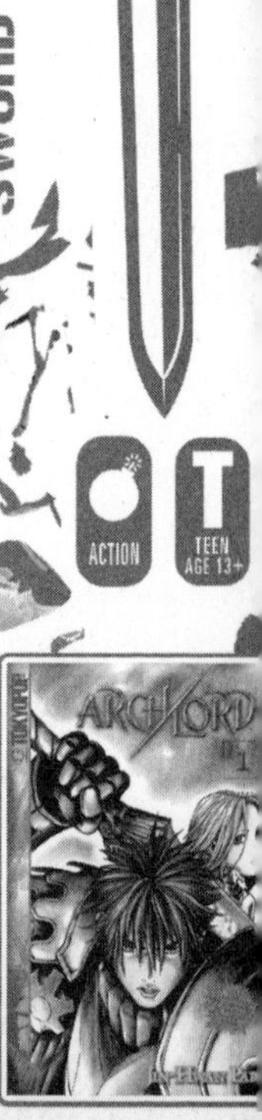
TOKYOPOP
ARCHLORD

Dulan, Year 517

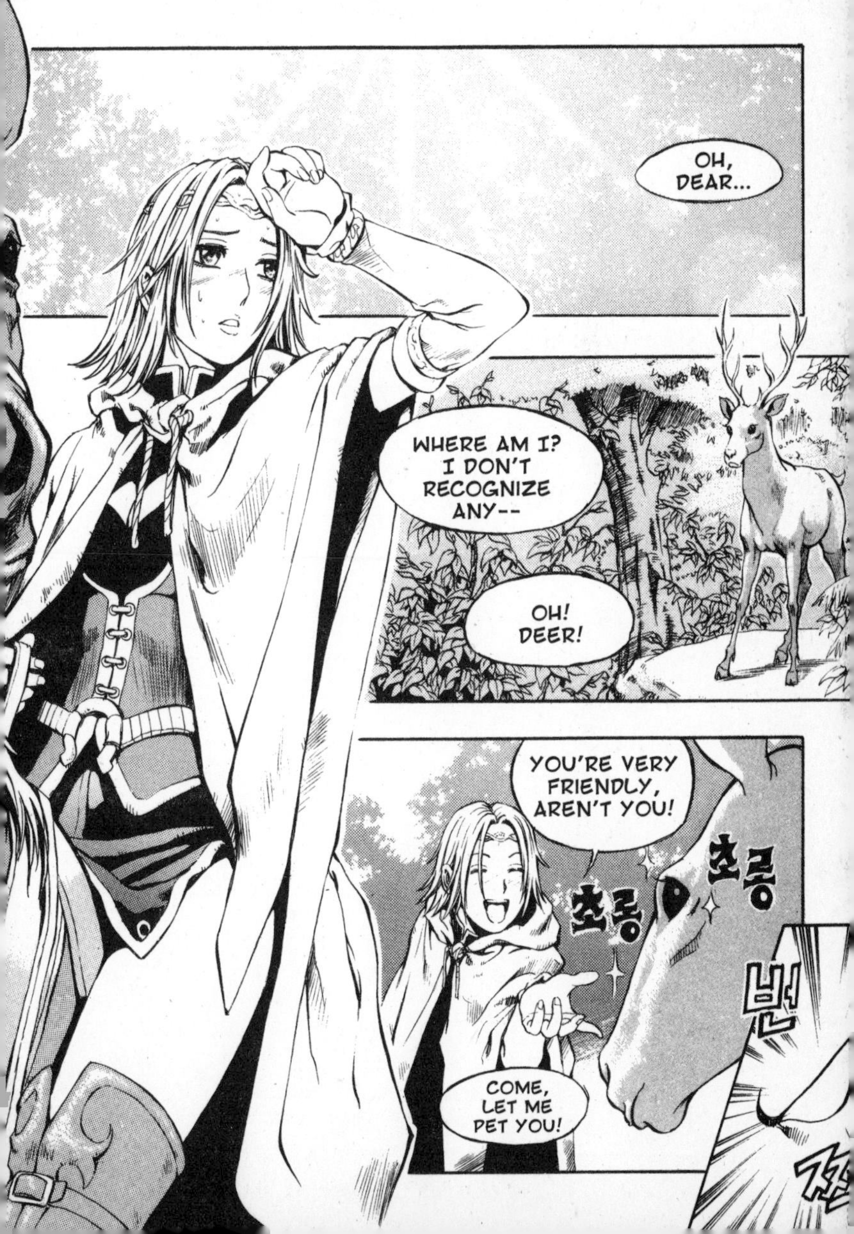
OH, DEAR...
WHERE AM I? I DON'T RECOGNIZE ANY--
OH! DEER!
YOU'RE VERY FRIENDLY, AREN'T YOU!
초롱
초롱
COME, LET ME PET YOU!
번

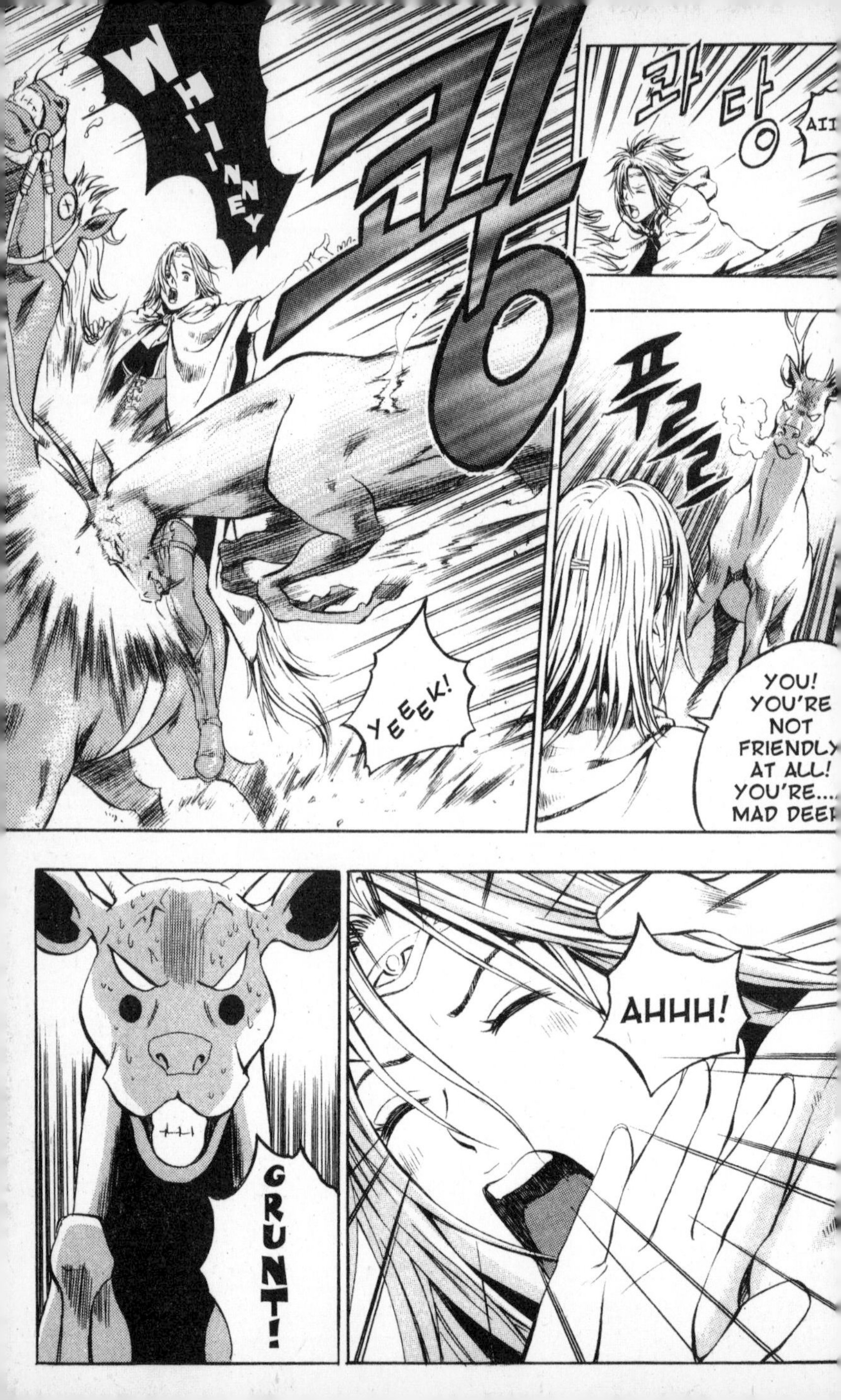
WHIINNEY
YEEEK!
콰당
AII
푸르르
YOU! YOU'RE NOT FRIENDLY AT ALL! YOU'RE.... MAD DEER
GRUNT!
AHHH!

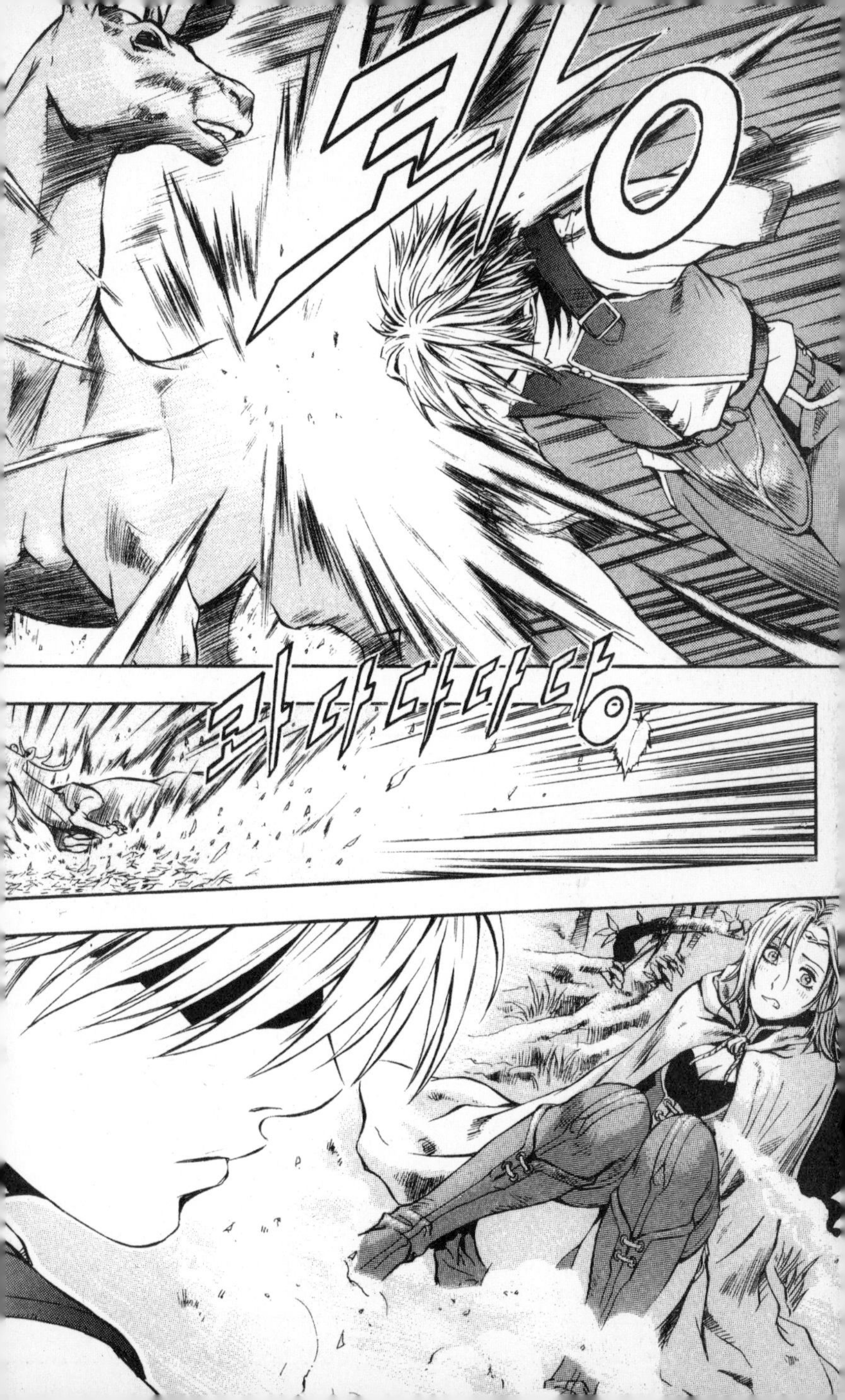
쾅
콰다다다당

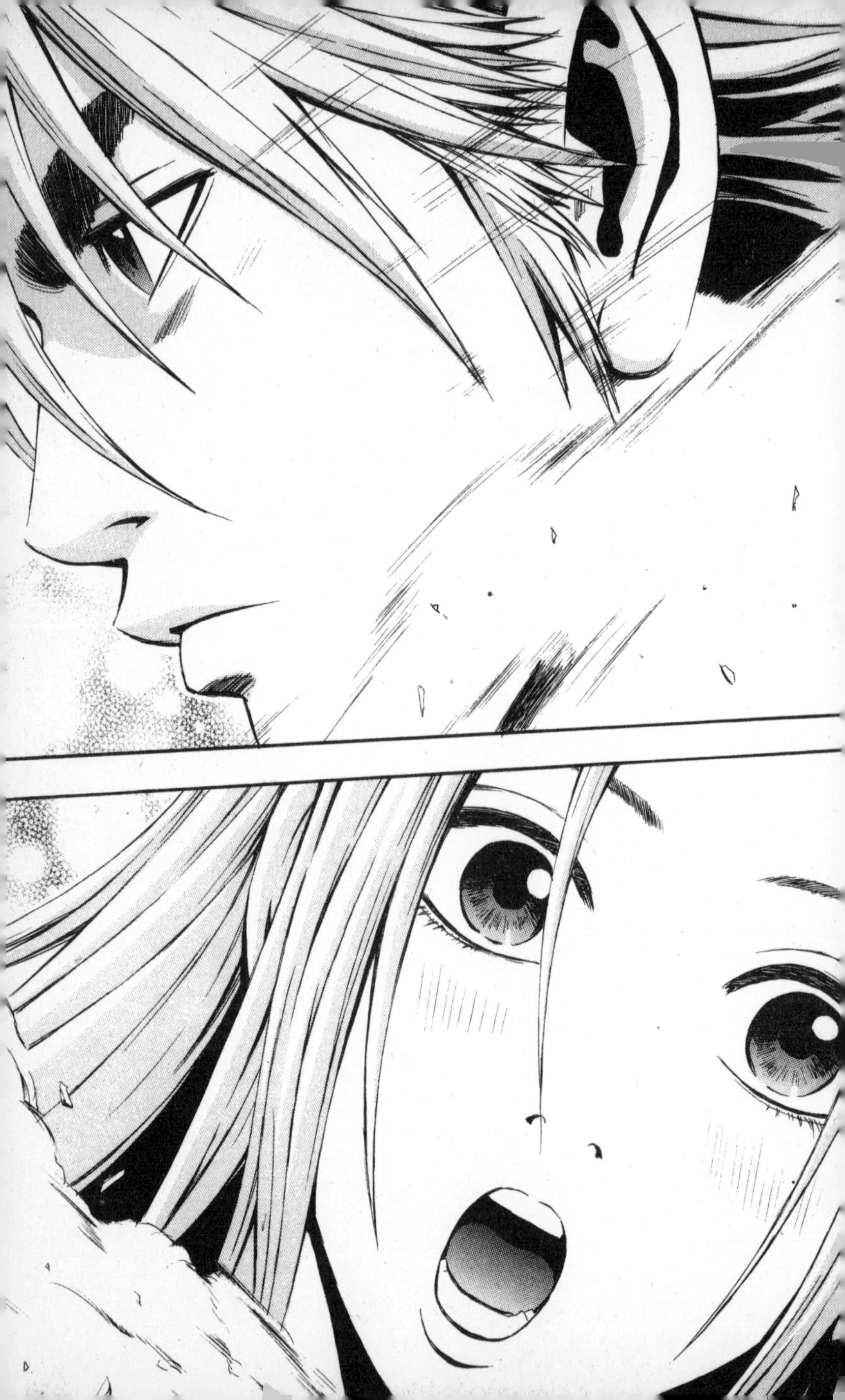

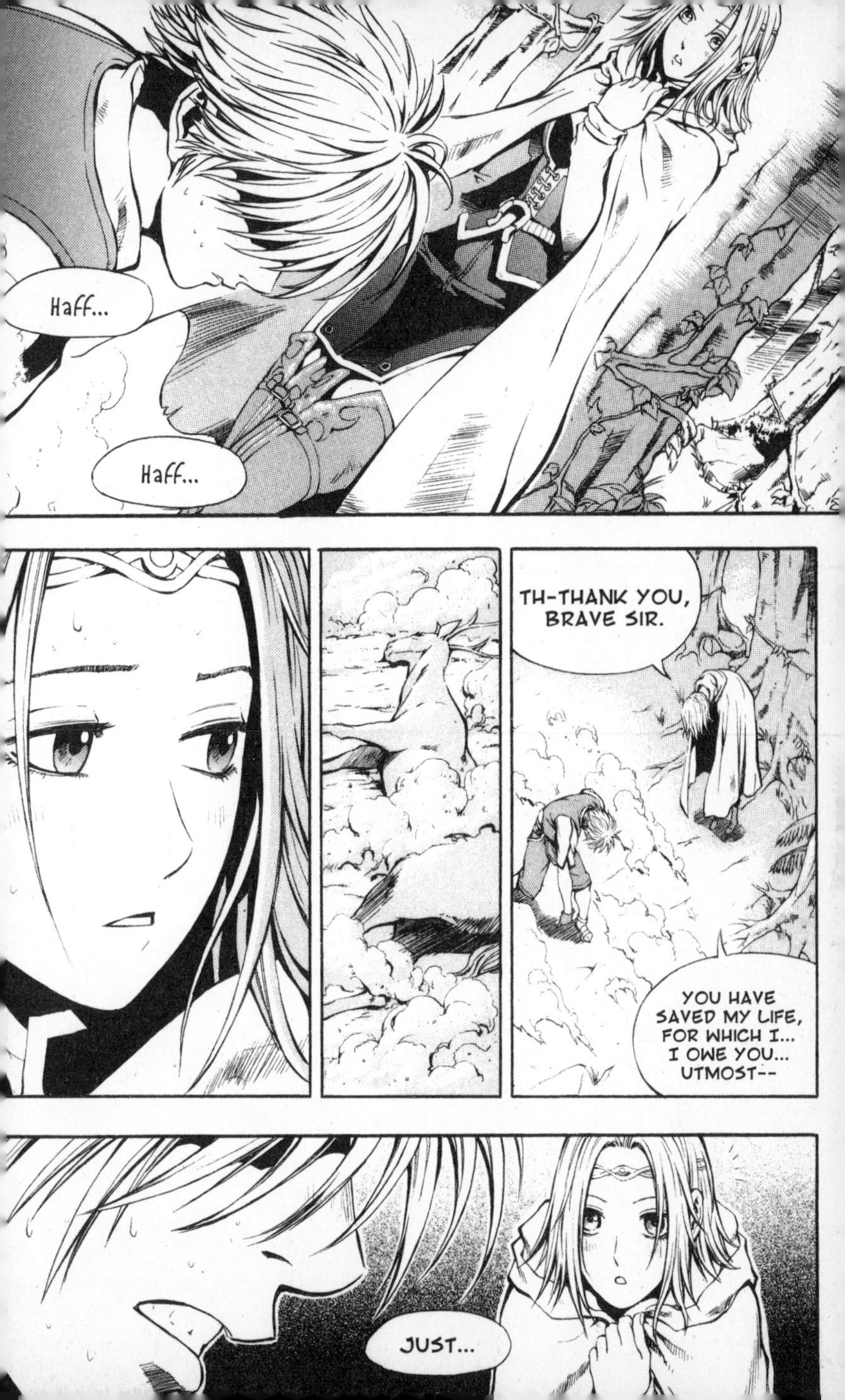
Haff...
Haff...
TH-THANK YOU, BRAVE SIR.
YOU HAVE SAVED MY LIFE, FOR WHICH I... I OWE YOU... UTMOST--
JUST...

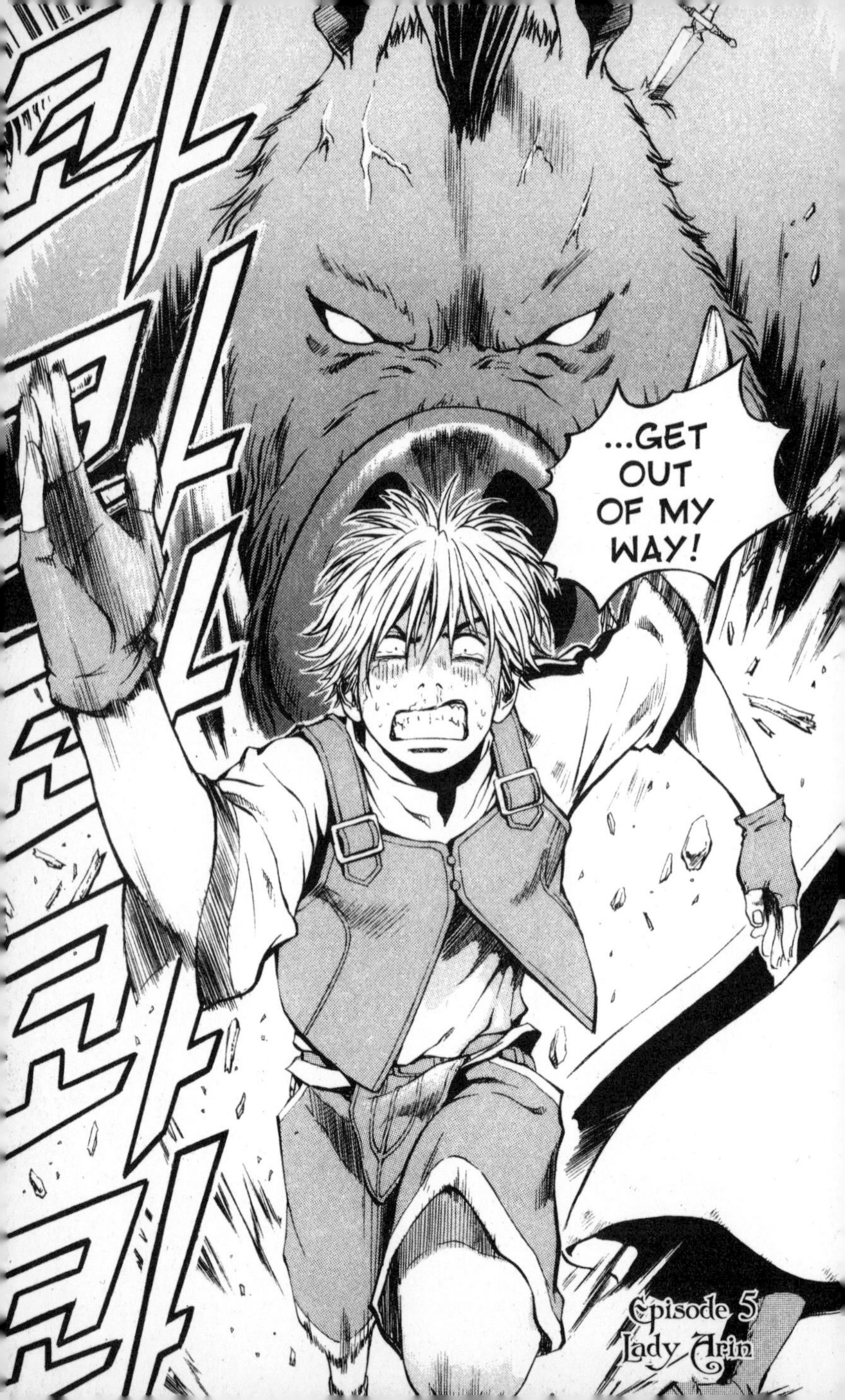
...GET OUT OF MY WAY!
Episode 5
Lady Arin

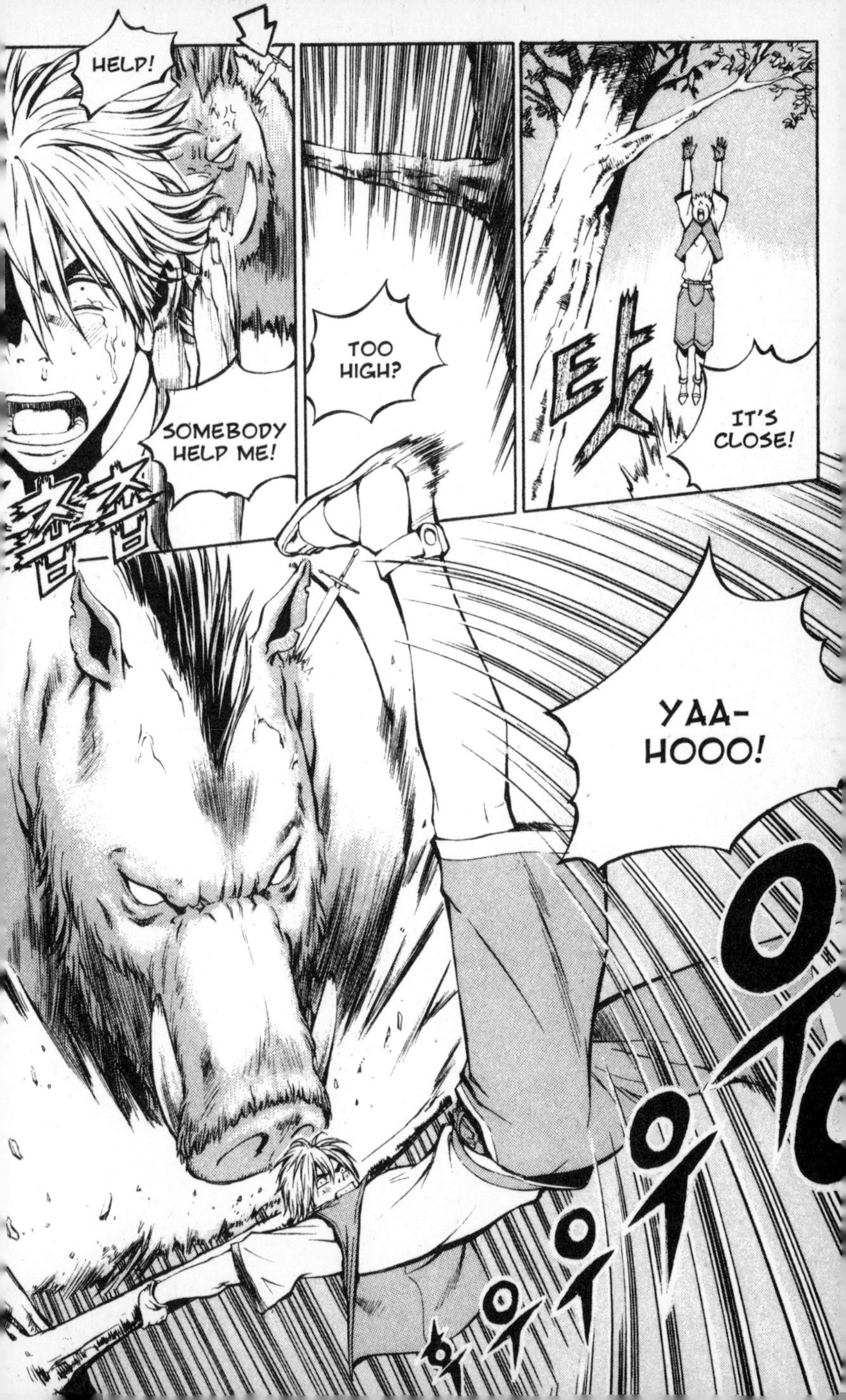
HELP!
SOMEBODY HELP ME!
TOO HIGH?
IT'S CLOSE!
YAA-HOOO!

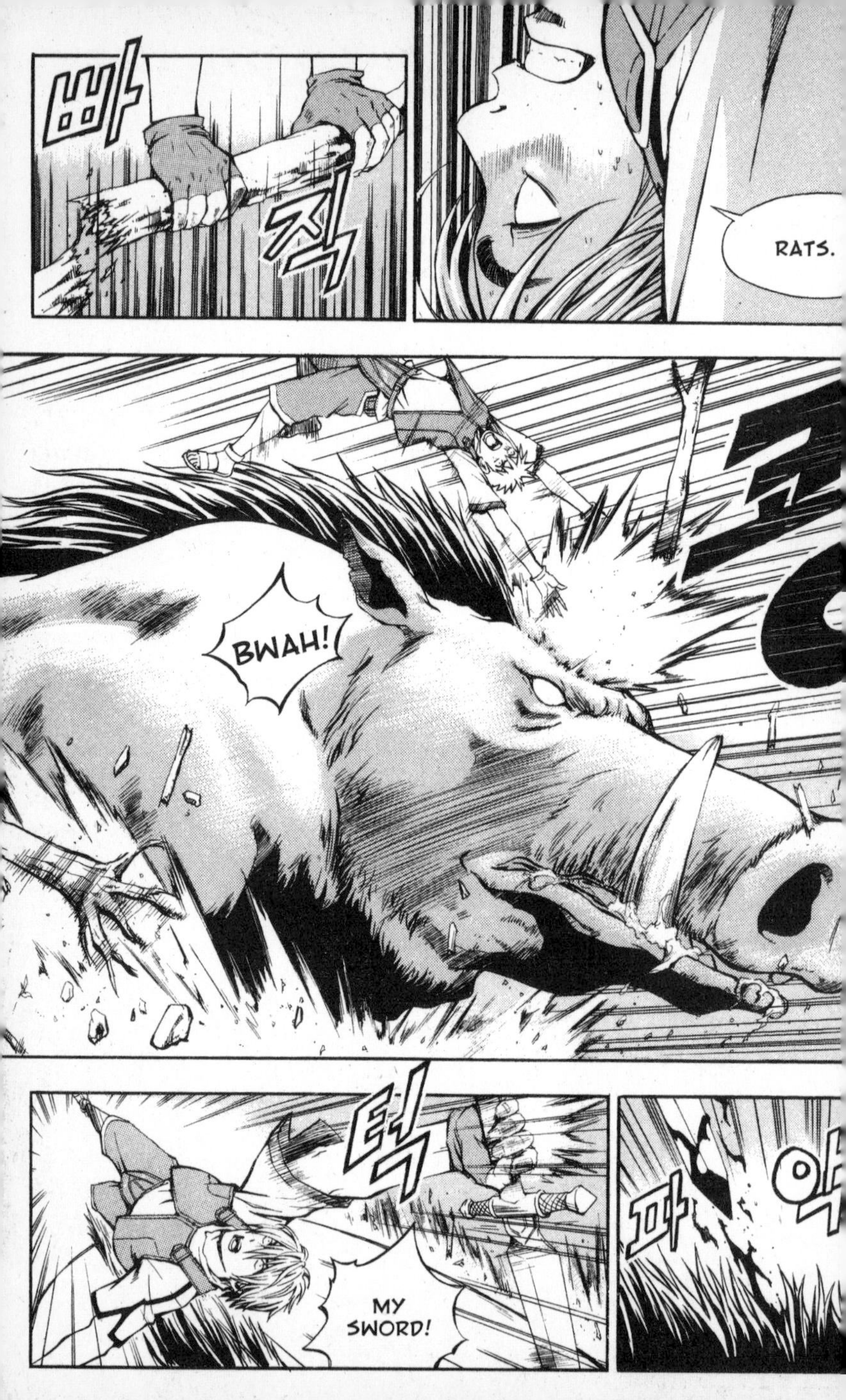
빠직
RATS.
BWAH!
턱
MY SWORD!

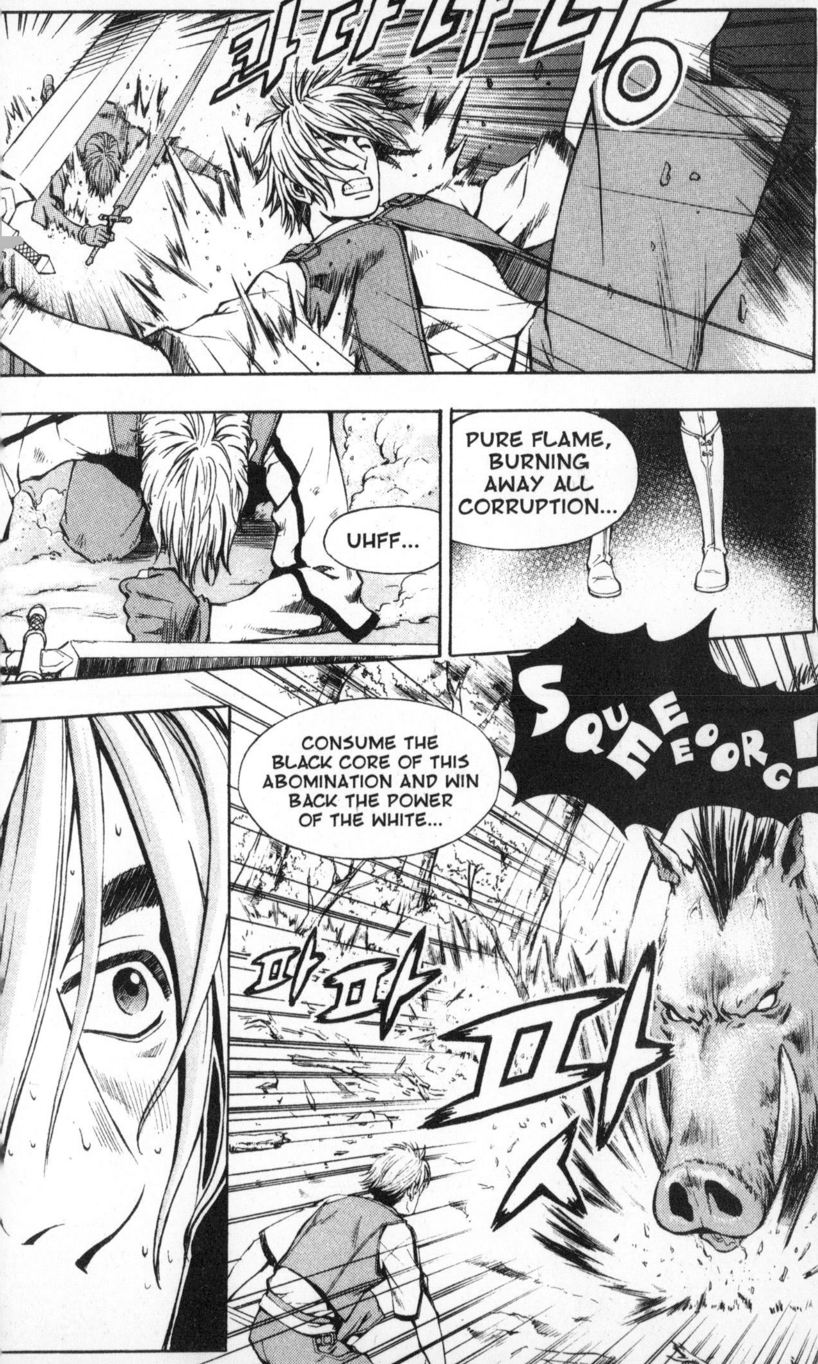
콰다다당
UHFF...
PURE FLAME, BURNING AWAY ALL CORRUPTION...
CONSUME THE BLACK CORE OF THIS ABOMINATION AND WIN BACK THE POWER OF THE WHITE...
SQUEEOORG!
파파팟

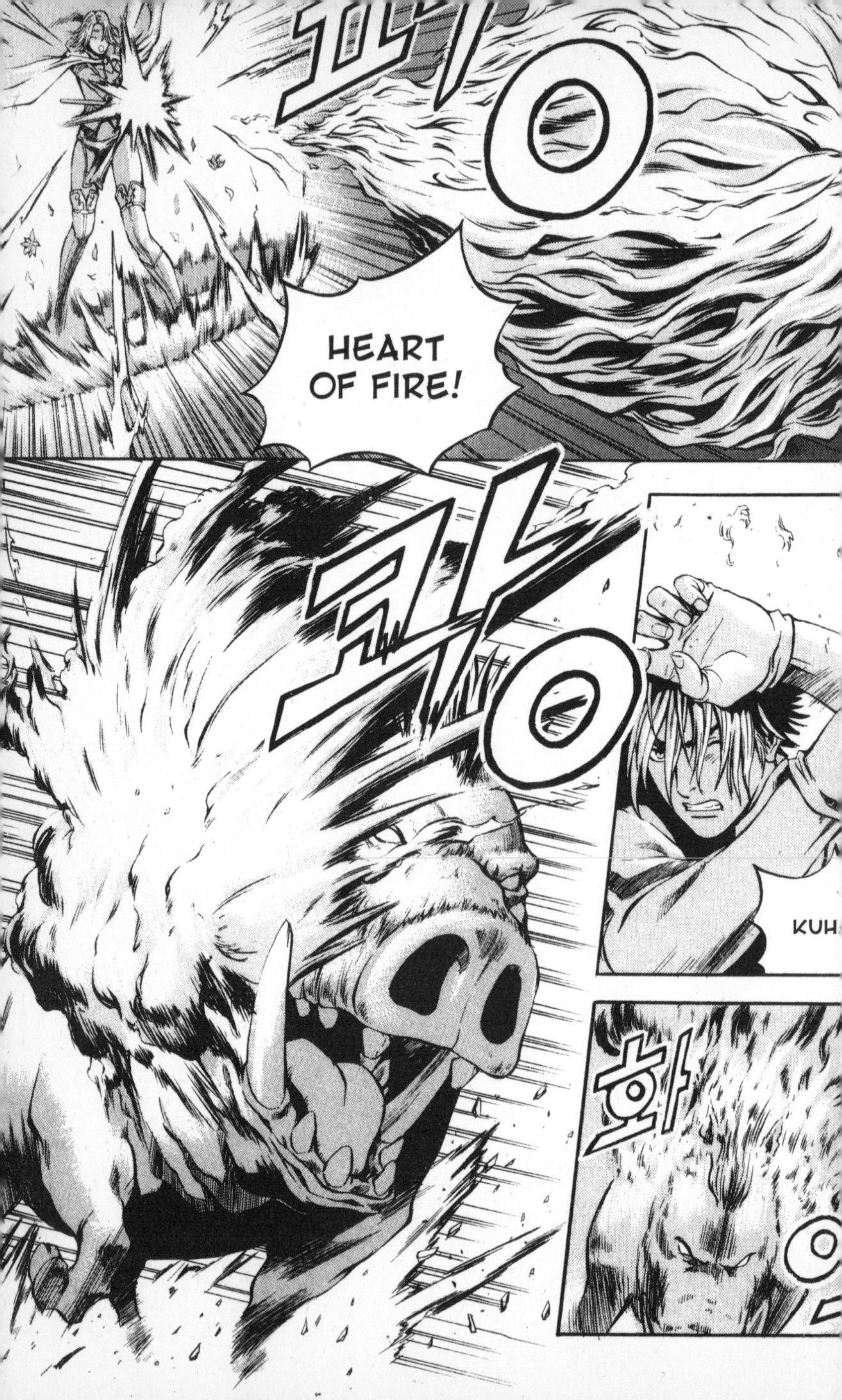
HEART
OF FIRE!
KUH

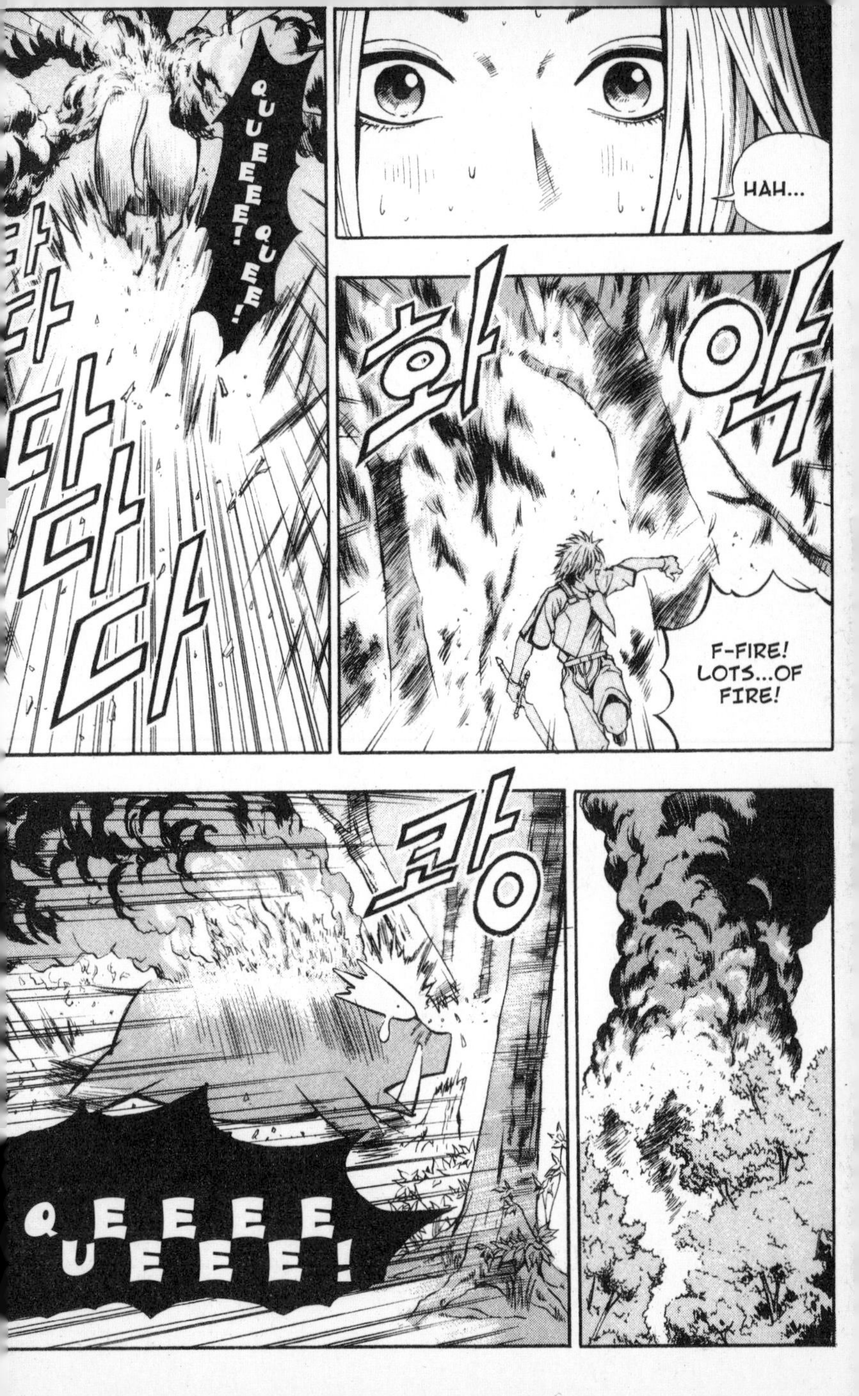
QUEEEEE! QUEEE!
다다다다
HAH...
화악
F-FIRE! LOTS...OF FIRE!
쾅
QEEEE
UEEEE!

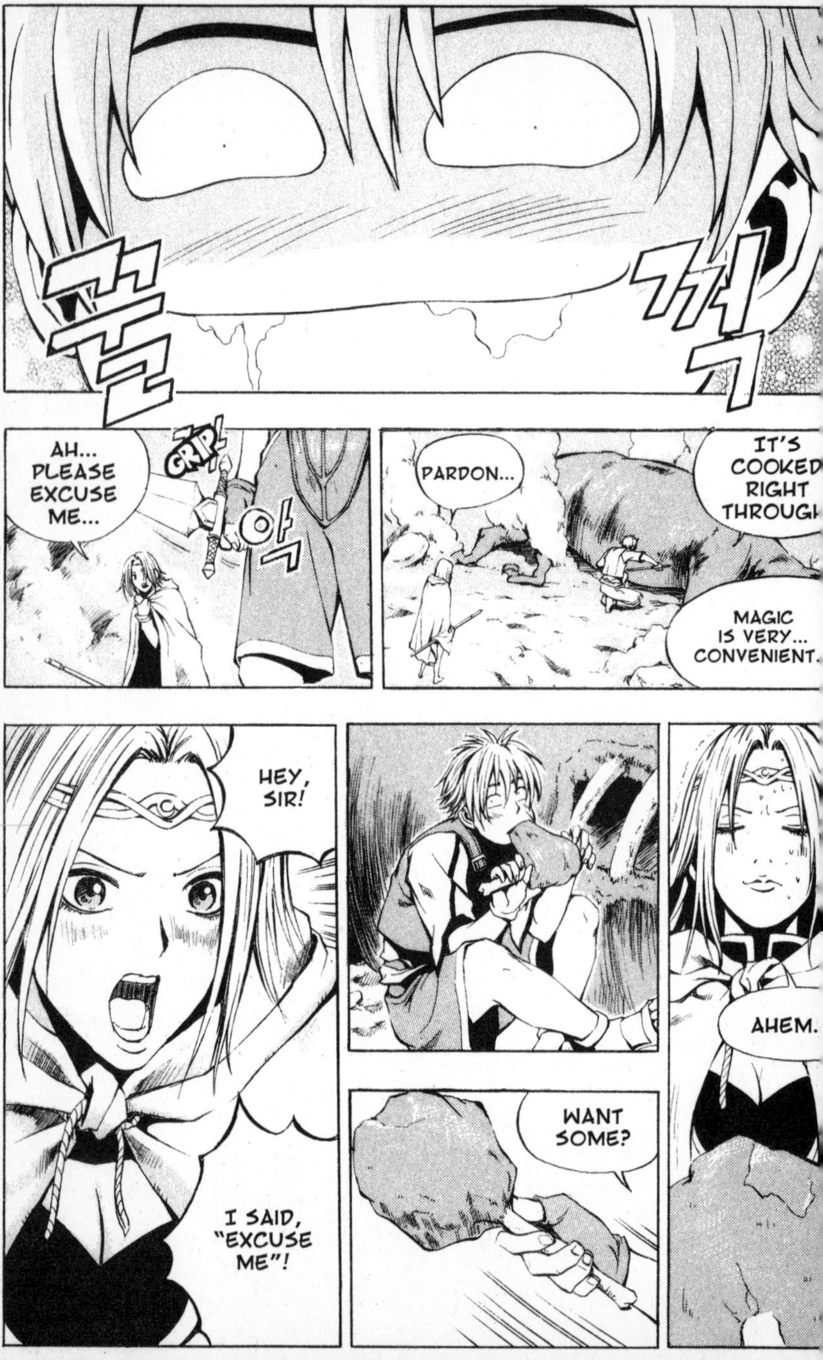
AH... PLEASE EXCUSE ME...
GRIP!
PARDON...
IT'S COOKED RIGHT THROUG
MAGIC IS VERY... CONVENIENT.
HEY, SIR!
I SAID, "EXCUSE ME"!
WANT SOME?
AHEM.

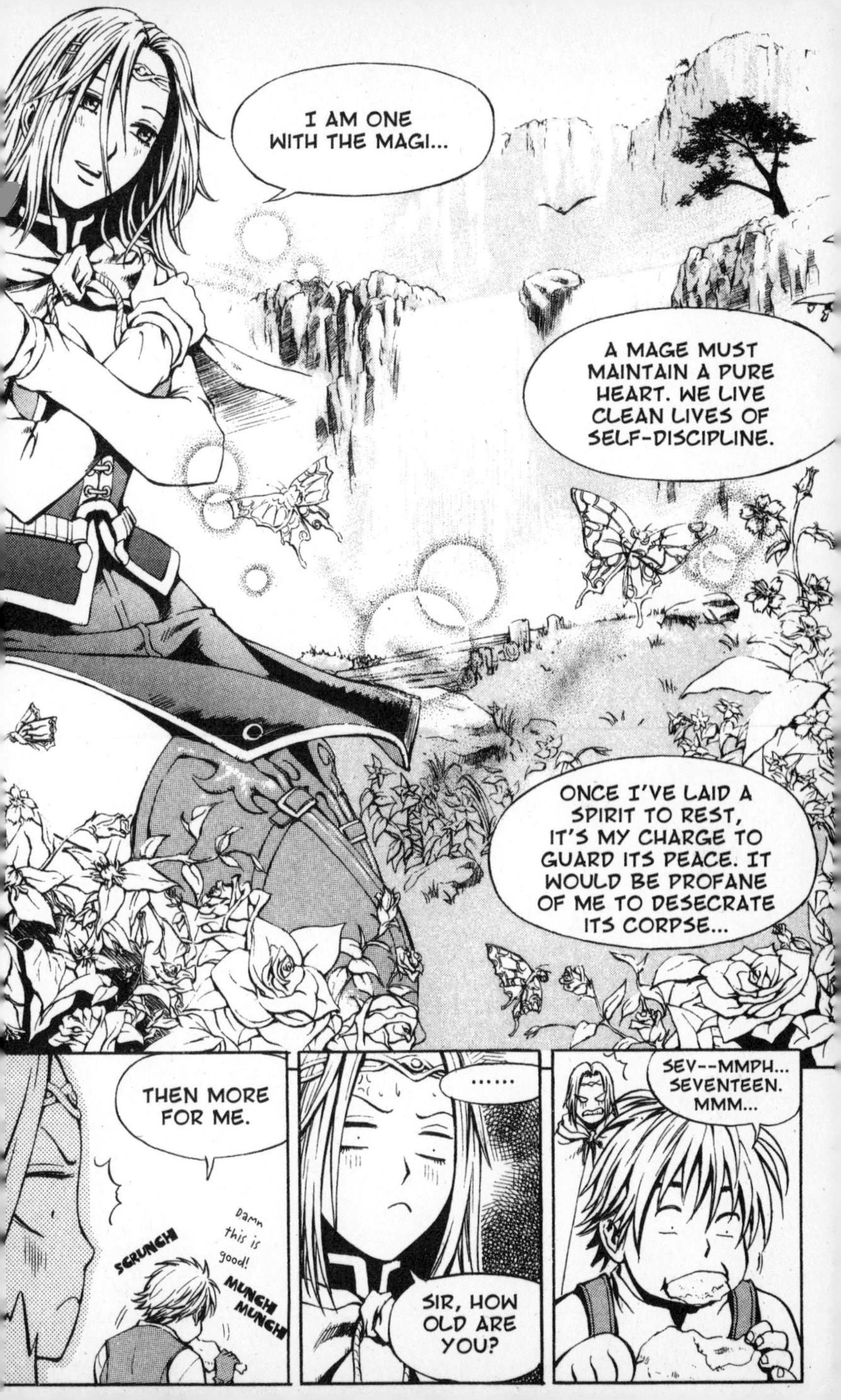

I AM ONE WITH THE MAGI...
A MAGE MUST MAINTAIN A PURE HEART. WE LIVE CLEAN LIVES OF SELF-DISCIPLINE.
ONCE I'VE LAID A SPIRIT TO REST, IT'S MY CHARGE TO GUARD ITS PEACE. IT WOULD BE PROFANE OF ME TO DESECRATE ITS CORPSE...
THEN MORE FOR ME.
Damn this is good!
SCRUNCH
MUNCH MUNCH
......
SIR, HOW OLD ARE YOU?
SEV--MMPH... SEVENTEEN. MMM...

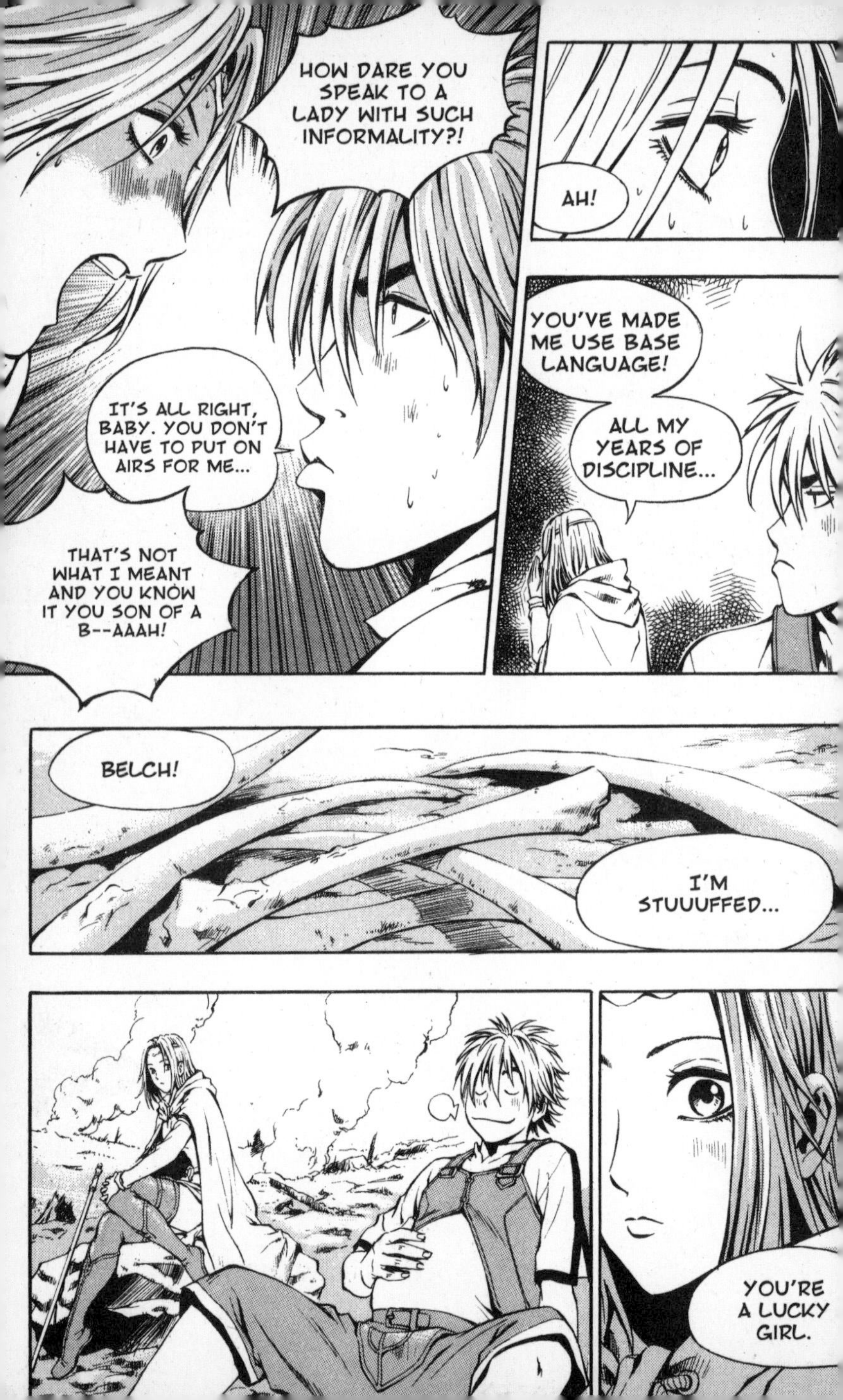
HOW DARE YOU SPEAK TO A LADY WITH SUCH INFORMALITY?!
IT'S ALL RIGHT, BABY. YOU DON'T HAVE TO PUT ON AIRS FOR ME...
THAT'S NOT WHAT I MEANT AND YOU KNOW IT YOU SON OF A B--AAAH!
AH!
YOU'VE MADE ME USE BASE LANGUAGE!
ALL MY YEARS OF DISCIPLINE...
BELCH!
I'M STUUUFFED...
YOU'RE A LUCKY GIRL.

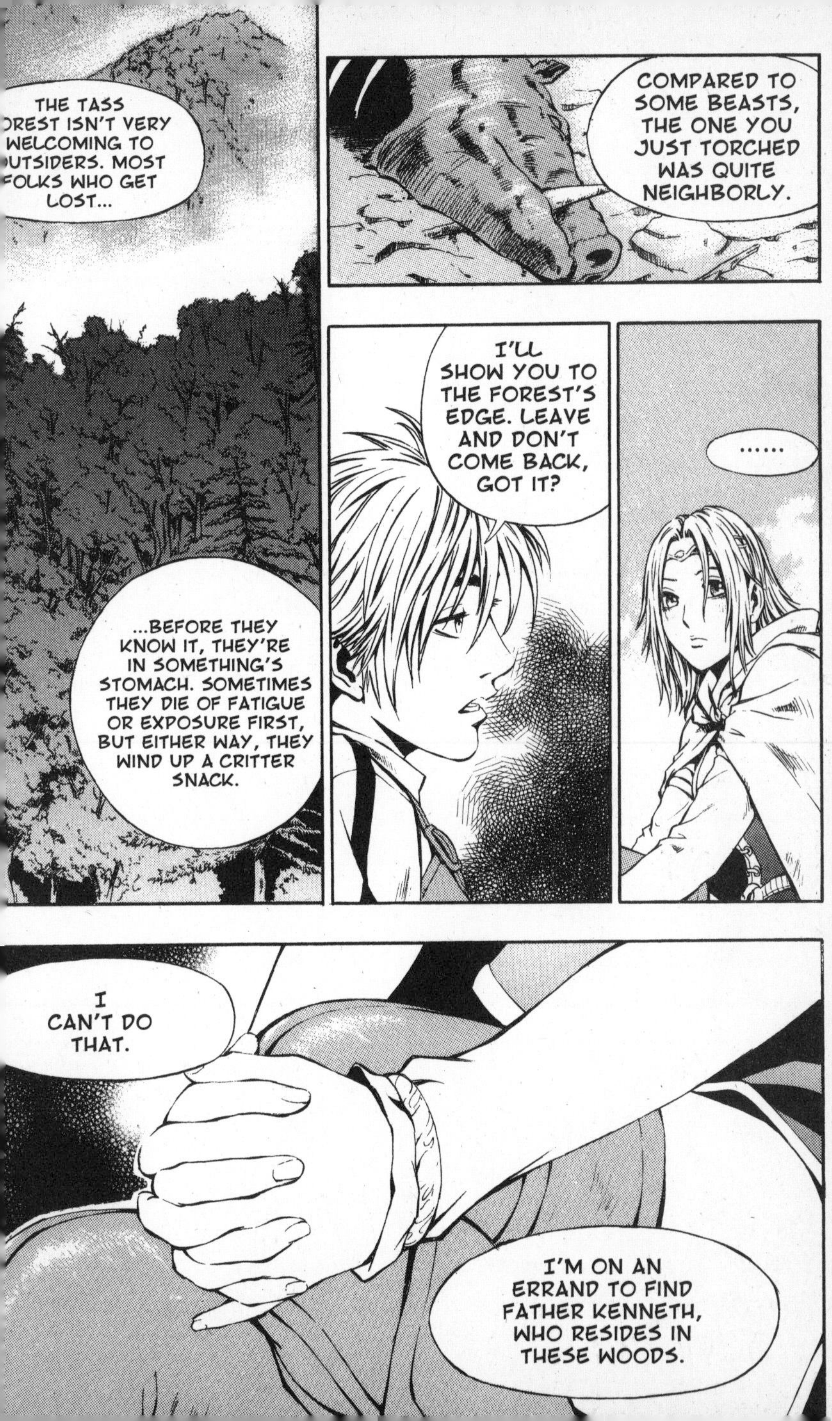
THE TASS OREST ISN'T VERY WELCOMING TO UTSIDERS. MOST FOLKS WHO GET LOST...
...BEFORE THEY KNOW IT, THEY'RE IN SOMETHING'S STOMACH. SOMETIMES THEY DIE OF FATIGUE OR EXPOSURE FIRST, BUT EITHER WAY, THEY WIND UP A CRITTER SNACK.
COMPARED TO SOME BEASTS, THE ONE YOU JUST TORCHED WAS QUITE NEIGHBORLY.
I'LL SHOW YOU TO THE FOREST'S EDGE. LEAVE AND DON'T COME BACK, GOT IT?
......
I CAN'T DO THAT.
I'M ON AN ERRAND TO FIND FATHER KENNETH, WHO RESIDES IN THESE WOODS.

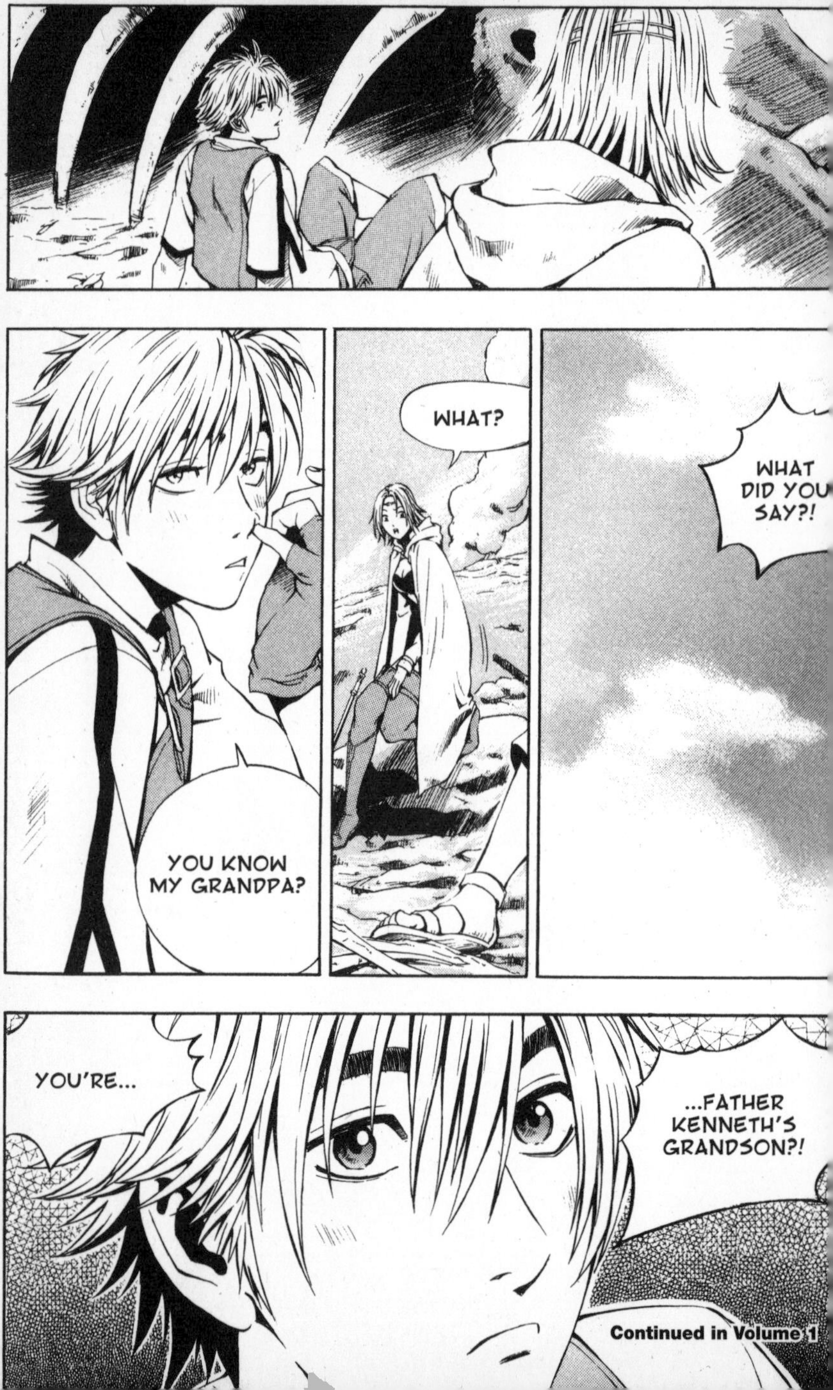
YOU KNOW MY GRANDPA?
WHAT?
WHAT DID YOU SAY?!
YOU'RE...
...FATHER KENNETH'S GRANDSON?!
Continued in Volume 1